jazz from detroit

jazz from detroit

Mark Stryker

University of Michigan Press
Ann Arbor

First paperback edition 2026

Published in the United States of America by the
University of Michigan Press
First published in paperback February 2026

A CIP catalog record for this book is available from the British Library.

Library of Congress Cataloging-in-Publication Data

Names: Stryker, Mark, author.
Title: Jazz from Detroit / Mark Stryker.
Description: Ann Arbor : University of Michigan Press, [2019] | Includes index. |
Identifiers: LCCN 2019001977 (print) | LCCN 2019002614 (ebook) |
ISBN 9780472125913 (E-book) | ISBN 9780472074266 (hardcover : alk. paper)
Subjects: LCSH: Jazz—Michigan—Detroit—History and criticism. | Jazz musicians—Michigan—Detroit.
Classification: LCC ML3508.8.D4 (ebook) | LCC ML3508.8.D4 S87 2019 (print) | DDC 781.6509774/34—dc23
LC record available at https://lccn.loc.gov/2019001977

ISBN: 978-0-472-05426-8 (paper)

Cover photo: Elvin Jones from McCoy Tyner's *The Real McCoy* session for Blue Note on Apr. 21, 1967, at Van Gelder Studio, Englewood Cliffs, N.J. Photo by Francis Wolff © Mosaic Images LLC.

The authorized representative in the EU for product safety and compliance is Easy Access System Europe, Mustamäe tee 50, 10621 Tallinn, Estonia, gpsr.requests@easproject.com

For Candace

CONTENTS

Preface ix
A Note on Sources and Recordings xv

PART ONE: SETTING THE STAGE

Jazz in Detroit, 1900–1950 3

PART TWO: THE GOLDEN AGE, 1940–60

Opening Chorus 11
Gerald Wilson: Head and Heart 17
Yusef Lateef: Gentle Giant 26
Milt Jackson: Bags' Groove 35
Sheila Jordan: Sheila's Blues 44
Barry Harris: Professor of Bebop 53
Tommy Flanagan: A Legendary Touch 63
Kenny Burrell: Community Builder 72
Donald Byrd: Renaissance Man 81
Roland Hanna: Magician 90
Curtis Fuller: Trombone on Top 100
Louis Hayes: The (Cymbal) Beat Goes On 109
Ron Carter: The Right Note at the Right Time 118
Joe Henderson: The Phantom 127
Charles McPherson: Reminiscing by Ear 136

PART THREE: THE JONES BROTHERS

Opening Chorus 147
Hank Jones: One Extra Ace 150
Thad Jones: Jonesisms 158
Elvin Jones: Philosopher King 167

PART FOUR: TAKING CONTROL—
SELF-DETERMINATION IN THE 1960S AND '70S

Opening Chorus 177
Detroit Artists Workshop, Detroit Creative Musicians Association, and Focus Novii 181
Contemporary Jazz Quintet and Strata Corporation 188
Tribe 197
Coda 203

PART FIVE: MARCUS BELGRAVE AND HIS CHILDREN

Marcus Belgrave: The Nurturer 207
Geri Allen: Back to the Future 217
Kenny Garrett: Sound and Spirit 226
Regina Carter: Searching for Roots 234
Gerald Cleaver: The Big Picture 242
Robert Hurst: Platonic Ideal 249
Rodney Whitaker: Family Man 256
James Carter: Volcano 264
Karriem Riggins: Dual Identity 272

PART SIX: TRADITION AND TRANSITION
IN THE 21ST CENTURY

Opening Chorus 281
Present and Future: Ralphe Armstrong, Marion Hayden, Michael Malis, Marcus Elliot 282
Coda 293

Appendix A: Jazz Musicians from Detroit 295
Appendix B: List of Interviews 303
Acknowledgments 307
Index 309

PREFACE

Whenever the Detroit-born pianist and composer Kenn Cox performed in clubs late in his life, audience members got not only a hefty dose of his impassioned musicianship but often an impromptu lecture, too. Cox, who died in 2008 at age 68, was a soft-spoken, sensitive man who clung stubbornly to his artistic ideals. He liked to ruminate between songs about his heroes or comment on the vagaries of the jazz life. Cox had earned his soapbox. He spent nearly all of his professional life in Detroit, where he cofounded the pioneering musicians cooperative Strata Corporation in the late '60s and played a leading role in the progressive Contemporary Jazz Quintet that recorded for Blue Note. Later he became a role model, mentor, and truth-teller for younger musicians and audiences. Like all Detroit-bred jazz musicians, Cox was a proud champion of the contributions his hometown made to the music.

One night in 2005, Cox led his trio through a vigorous set at Baker's Keyboard Lounge, a historic club on Detroit's north side that first started presenting jazz in 1934. Cox took the microphone at one point and began to wax poetically about fellow pianists produced by Detroit. He ticked off names like an honor role: Hank Jones, Willie Anderson, Tommy Flanagan, Barry Harris, Roland Hanna, Hugh Lawson, Terry Pollard, Kirk Lightsey, Harold McKinney, Johnny O'Neal, and Geri Allen. Cox then segued into a broader discussion about Detroit's impact on modern jazz.

He lamented that while the public knew about Motown and the city's pop music legacy, Detroit's contributions to jazz were still a secret to many. He mentioned some of the other leading figures from the city—vibraphonist Milt Jackson, guitarist Kenny Burrell, trumpeter Donald Byrd, tenor saxophonists Yusef Lateef and Joe Henderson, baritone saxophonist Pepper Adams, bassists Paul Chambers and Ron Carter, trombonists Curtis Fuller and Frank Rosolino, and Hank Jones' younger brothers, Elvin (a drummer) and Thad (a trumpeter, composer, and arranger). Cox ended his sermon with a benediction: "Jazz wouldn't be the same without Detroit."

He was right. Detroit has been indispensable to the history of modern and contemporary jazz. From the mid-20th century until the present day, the city has been one of the primary feeders of talent to the national scene, graduating scores of musicians to the front lines and a striking number of innovators into the pantheon. The explosion of Detroit talent reached a peak during the hard-bop era from about 1955 to 1965, when the city's influence arguably outpaced perennial hotbeds like Chicago and Philadelphia. It's almost impossible to pick up a recording made on the East Coast in those years and not encounter one, two, three, sometimes four or more musicians from the Motor City.

Even after 1970, as Detroit's population fell sharply and its economic might waned, the city continued to export significant talent to the major leagues. Many Midwestern and Rust Belt cities with large African American populations also experienced golden ages of jazz in the middle of the 20th century—Kansas City, St. Louis, Pittsburgh, Indianapolis, and Cleveland among them—but their musical impact eventually faded. Meanwhile, Detroit continued punching above its weight class.

Jazz from Detroit tells the story of the city's profound influence on jazz over the last eight decades. The bulk of the book focuses on more than two dozen of the most important musicians to emerge from the city since the 1940s. Expansive profiles detail their roots in Detroit, subsequent careers, personalities, styles, most important recordings, and impact on the wider course of jazz history. At the same time, the book connects the dots between musicians and eras. It explores how Detroit became a center for modern jazz and sustained its influence over decades, and it identifies stylistic traits and attitudes that define a distinctively Detroit approach to the music that transcends idioms and generations.

What happened in Detroit was not an accident. It was the result of specific historical, economic, social, and cultural conditions and the influence of particular people who played outsized roles in the development of jazz in the city. It is a multilayered story, starting with the Great Migration that brought hundreds of thousands of African Americans to Detroit from the South in the first half of the 20th century. The rise of the auto industry helped create a large black working and middle class in Detroit and the economic and social conditions that allowed jazz to grow. The combination of exceptional music education in the public schools, thriving nightlife, and influential mentors in the community, most notably Barry Harris, transformed the city into a jazz juggernaut in the 1940s and '50s. The embodiment of the oral tradition, Harris trained many of the musicians to emerge from Detroit during the '50s and early '60s, among them Yusef Lateef, Paul Chambers, Doug Watkins, Curtis Fuller, Donald Byrd, Pepper Adams, Charles McPherson, and Joe Henderson. With artistically satisfying work plentiful, Harris was able to stay in Detroit for longer than his talent might have otherwise demanded, amplifying his influence.

In the 1960s and '70s, Detroit's economic mojo stalled as the city coped with increasing racial strife, civil unrest, and depopulation. But jazz in the city soldiered on, bolstered by musician-led cooperatives and other self-determination efforts such as the Detroit Artists Workshop, Strata Corporation, and Tribe. Even as Detroit continued to shrink and a bloated automobile industry lost power to foreign competition through the 1980s and beyond, the culture of mentorship among Detroit jazz musicians and the enduring presence of engaged and informed audiences ensured that the city remained a national jazz power. There were many important teachers, but trumpeter Marcus Belgrave was the most critical. He taught for 40 years, shaping multiple generations, and his best-known protégés—including Geri Allen, Kenny Garrett, Robert Hurst, Regina Carter, and Gerald Cleaver—have helped define jazz in the late 20th and early 21st centuries. "The jazz community in Detroit raised us," said Carter, a violinist.

In the last 15 years, a new generation of teachers and mentors have picked up the baton. Meanwhile, nonprofits and major universities are planting musical seeds and helping fill gaps left by the widespread disappearance of music from Detroit's troubled schools. The city's finances reached their nadir with municipal bankruptcy in 2013–14, but the resilience of Detroit's jazz legacy provides a powerful symbol of the city's lasting cultural influence and a metaphor for Detroit's nascent renaissance.

Geography has always mattered in jazz. Unique regional styles pushed the music in new directions for 50-odd years. Think of the communal improvisation of New Orleans ensembles in the 1920s, the relaxed momentum of Kansas City swing in the 1930s, the rhythmic and harmonic advancements of bebop in New York in the 1940s, the gentler cool jazz that emerged on the West Coast in the 1950s. Epochal stylistic shifts associated with specific cities or regions largely dissipated after 1960. The world was now smaller, more interconnected via travel, recordings, and mass media. Perhaps the last major regional movement to add a new stylistic branch to the jazz tree was Chicago's Association for the Advancement of Creative Musicians in the 1960s. The Chicagoans created a free jazz more concerned with structure and composition than the so-called energy players associated with the New York avant-garde. Still, individual cities have retained jazz scenes with their own identities and customs. Detroit, Chicago, Philadelphia, Los Angeles, Boston, and others have had their own jazz microclimates shaped by specific musicians, tradition, repertoire, and the wider musical, social, and cultural history of each city.

Common lineage and shared musical values link Detroit musicians into an extended family. From the 1950s until the present day, partnerships initially forged in Detroit later flourished in recording studios and bandstands in New York and around the world. The city's integrated school system and musicians' union—until the 1950s, the only two American Federation of Musicians locals that were integrated were in Detroit and New York—helped cultivate productive relationships between black and white musicians, even as segregation remained in force elsewhere in Detroit. At the same time, Detroit musicians have always been nurtured by unusually knowledgeable jazz audiences—another manifestation of the familial bonds that strengthen and regenerate the scene.

Detroit musicians are almost all firmly rooted in the jazz tradition, especially bebop. You can hear it in their allegiance to the fundamentals of swing and blues, the balance of head and heart in their improvisations, and the marriage of fluid instrumental technique and soulful expression. Detroit players bring an eloquent intelligence to harmony and the construction of melodic lines. Much of this is a legacy of strong early music training coupled with Harris and Belgrave, who despite very different methods instilled in their students a disciplined respect for craft and tradition, along with the inspiration and desire to find their own voices.

Individuality and versatility are prized among Detroit musicians across the stylistic spectrum, and a wealth of Detroiters have become major influences on their instruments. Some helped changed the broader course of jazz—Elvin Jones, Thad Jones, Joe Henderson, Ron Carter, and Geri Allen among them. But the premium placed on training, fundamentals, and tradition also helps explain why avant-garde movements like free jazz never took hold in Detroit to the degree that they did in other cities. Many of the Detroit musicians who have made their mark in experimental circles, such as Allen, bassist Jaribu Shahid, guitarist A. Spencer Barefield, and drummers Tani Tabbal, Doug Hammond, and Gerald Cleaver, are conversant in many idioms—swinging post-bop, free jazz, fusion, odd meters, and funk.

This book is not meant to account for every significant jazz musician from Detroit. Nor does it chronicle all the notable bands and major clubs in the city as jazz developed. That ground was covered in the essential *Before Motown: A History of Jazz in Detroit, 1920–60* by Lars Bjorn with Jim Gallert (University of Michigan Press). *Jazz from Detroit* follows a different path. It carries the story of Detroit jazz from the 1940s into the 21st century, digging deeper into the lives of key musicians and the influence of the Detroit diaspora, while also keeping up with the action on the home front. Detroit's fertile jazz soil has long been a trope employed by critics and liner-note writers dating back to the 1950s, and many aficionados are aware in a general sense that the city has a special reputation when it comes to jazz. But this book demonstrates that the city's influence is broader and more significant than commonly understood and that the kinship among Detroit jazz musicians runs deeper than simply geography.

While most of Detroit's best-known jazz exports are included here, the city has been so prolific that there wasn't room for all who deserve the spotlight. Tough choices had to be made. If a full-length biography or substantial journalistic or scholarly accounts of a career already existed, I usually left that musician out. There are, for example, biographies of Paul Chambers, Betty Carter, and Pepper Adams. There are also deeply researched works about Frank Rosolino, drummer Roy Brooks, alto saxophonist Sonny Red, and tenor saxophonist Faruq Z. Bey.[1]

When I arrived at the *Detroit Free Press* in 1995 as an arts reporter and music critic, I knew that I was living on hallowed ground. I grew up as an alto saxophonist, and the Jones brothers, Joe Henderson, Barry Harris, Tommy Flanagan, and other Detroiters were among my heroes. But it wasn't until I began working for the *Free Press* that I came to fully understand the extent of the city's extraordinary jazz legacy. During more than two decades at the newspaper, I wrote extensively about Detroit jazz musicians—those who had left the city and become famous and the everyday heroes who populated the local scene. About half the profiles in this book started life as pieces for the *Free Press*, though they have been extensively revised and expanded.

Jazz from Detroit had its genesis in the informal lecture Kenn Cox gave at Baker's Keyboard Lounge all those years ago. Hearing him say that jazz wouldn't be the same without Detroit made me realize there was a larger story to tell about the city's impact. By collecting so many of Detroit's greatest musicians between its covers and exploring their contributions and influence and the connective tissue between them, I've tried to underscore the truism that Cox laid on his audience at Baker's: The history of jazz and the history of jazz from Detroit are indivisible. You can't tell one story without the other.

Note

1. William R. Bauer, *Open the Door: The Life and Music of Betty Carter* (University of Michigan Press, 2002); Rob Palmer, *Mr. P.C.: The Life and Music of Paul Chambers* (Equinox, 2012); Gene Lees, "The Joker: Frank Rosolino," in *Meet Me at Jim and Andy's: Jazz Musicians and Their World* (Oxford University Press, 1988); W. Kim Heron, "Musician Interrupted" (Faruq Z. Bey), in *Heaven Was Detroit: From Jazz to Hip-Hop and Beyond*, edited by M. L. Liebler (Wayne State University Press, 2016); Jim Dulzo, "Roy Brooks: Hard Bop Hard Time," *Jazz Times* (October 2002); Anders Svanoe, "Bluesville: The Journey of Sonny Red," *Annual Review of Jazz Studies* 13 (Rutgers University Press, 2003). Gary Carner, *Reflectory: The Life and Music of Pepper Adams* (lulu.com, 2021, Kindle edition).

A NOTE ON SOURCES AND RECORDINGS

Unless otherwise specified, all direct quotes are drawn from interviews with the author. (See appendix B for list.)

In biographical chapters, the first quotation by the subject is identified by year and all subsequent quotations by that musician date from the same year unless otherwise noted. Exceptions are chapters on Charles McPherson, Kenny Garrett, Regina Carter, and Robert Hurst. These musicians were interviewed multiple times, but to avoid awkward and confusing clutter in the text, not every quotation is identified by year.

In lieu of a single discography, recommended recordings are included at the end of most chapters. Every attempt has been made to select material currently available in a physical format (CDs, LPs), but most are also available through digital and streaming sources. Some issues will inevitably slip out of print, but readers should still be able to track down most titles without frustration or undue expense. Recordings mentioned in the text are found in the index sorted under two different headings for each major figure: "Recordings as Leader" and "Recordings with Others." Finally, in the text, the word "sides" is used literally to indicate the number of individual sides of a 78 rpm record: Two sides equals one 78 rpm record.

PART ONE
Setting the Stage

Jazz in Detroit, 1900–1950

Detroit and jazz grew up together in the first half of the 20th century. Both progressed swiftly. The music, rooted in African American culture and forged from a melting pot of American, European, and African influences, barreled through its boisterous early years fueled by one innovator after another—Buddy Bolden, Jelly Roll Morton, Louis Armstrong, Bix Beiderbecke, Earl Hines, Duke Ellington, Count Basie, Coleman Hawkins, Lester Young, Jo Jones, Billie Holiday, Art Tatum, and others. Meanwhile, Detroit spent the first decades of the 20th century sprinting toward its destiny as the Motor City, though no one could have predicted such a future in 1900. On the cusp of its bicentennial in 1901, Detroit was the 13th largest city in America with a population of 285,000. Growing but still insular, the city was just one of several centers of automobile experimentation. Ransom Olds opened Detroit's first car manufacturing plant in 1899, the same year Duke Ellington was born. A single Oldsmobile was the only car from Detroit exhibited the following year at a major auto show in Chicago.[1]

From here, however, things accelerated. Henry Ford's first two attempts at starting an auto company in 1899 and 1901 both stalled, but his third venture in 1903 changed the world. The Ford Motor Company introduced the Model T in 1908 and in 1913 created the first integrated, moving assembly line for auto production. A year later, Ford roughly doubled his worker's pay to five dollars a day, stabilizing his labor pool and jump-starting the creation of a blue-collar middle class in America. General Motors got started in 1908 as an umbrella company for Buick, Olds, Cadillac, and Oakland, which became Pontiac. Chevrolet joined GM in 1918. The Dodge Brothers opened for business in 1916, and Chrysler came along in 1925. By the time GM completed construction on its new Albert Kahn neoclassical building on West Grand Boulevard in 1923—the largest office building in the world at the time—Detroit automakers were producing 2.5 million cars annually.

Detroit's population had grown to nearly a million by 1920, making it the fourth largest city in the country. An increasing number of those residents were black. The Great Migration brought nearly three million African

Americans from the rural South to northern cities between 1900 and 1950 in search of better jobs and less overt racism. Hundreds of thousands landed in Detroit. They were attracted by an auto industry that offered some of the best wages in the country for African Americans. Blacks numbered about 5,700 in Detroit in 1910, about 1% of the population. By 1920, there were nearly 41,000 blacks in the city, and the number tripled to 120,000 in 1930. By 1950, with Detroit's population now at its peak of 1.85 million people, blacks accounted for more than 300,000—16% of the city's residents.

The auto industry led to a thriving black working class, which in turn fueled increasing opportunities for black business owners, entrepreneurs, and an emerging class of professionals including doctors, lawyers, and teachers. Still, Detroit remained segregated. Restrictive housing covenants kept blacks largely sequestered into just a few crowded areas, and substandard housing was rampant. The largest concentration of African Americans was in an area called Black Bottom, just east of downtown. (The neighborhood took its historic name not from its residents but from the rich, dark soil that French explorers first found there.)

As the number of African Americans in Detroit grew, so did a black entertainment district, Paradise Valley, which bordered Black Bottom on the north. With Hastings Street as its major north-south artery, the Valley was home to scores of theaters, hotels, nightclubs, bars, and restaurants. It was the center of black commercial and social life in Detroit from the late 1920s until about 1950, and most of the major hotspots for jazz were there. The area began to lose some prominence in the late '40s as the black population expanded into other parts of the city. Ultimately, Paradise Valley and Black Bottom fell victim to government-sponsored urban renewal in the second half of the 1950s and early '60s. The neighborhoods were gutted to make way for interstate highways I-75 and I-375.[2]

Detroit's black community boasted an active musical scene in the 1920s. There were blues pianists, appearances by visiting stars like Ma Rainey and Bessie Smith, and a network of black and white society bands playing syncopated music for dancing. The city's most notable impact on jazz in the '20s and early '30s came in the realm of big bands. McKinney's Cotton Pickers, a black band from Ohio, played five months at the Arcadia Ballroom in Detroit in 1926–27, before settling into a residency lasting several years at the Graystone Ballroom at 4235 Woodward in the heart of what today is known as Midtown. In March 1927, the influential arranger Don Redman (1900–1964), who also played saxophone, left Fletcher Henderson's pioneering New York band to take over leadership of the McKinney band.

Redman was a key figure in codifying big-band arranging conventions such as the antiphonal play of brass and reed sections, the elevated role of improvised solos, and written passages whose vocabulary flowed from leading jazz soloists. Redman, who remained based in Detroit until 1931, built the McKinney band into one of the country's best. The arrangements by Redman and trumpeter John Nesbitt were absorbed into the mainstream via the band's recordings, tours, and national radio broadcasts from the Graystone on WJR.

Jean Goldkette (1893–1962), a white bandleader, booking agent, and owner of the Graystone, was responsible for first bringing the McKinney band to Detroit. Goldkette—who was born in France and raised in Greece and Russia and arrived in Detroit via Chicago in 1922—led a polished dance band. Its importance to jazz rests primarily in its advanced arrangements by Bill Challis and star soloists like cornetist Bix Beiderbecke, C melody saxophonist Frankie Trumbauer, and violinist Joe Venuti. Tommy and Jimmy Dorsey also spent time in the band. Beiderbecke and Trumbauer were with Goldkette in Detroit in 1926–27.

The McKinney and Goldkette bands occasionally appeared together at the Graystone. Despite segregation throughout the city, bandstands and ballrooms were places where black and white musicians mingled, sharing information and, occasionally, bootlegged liquor. Beiderbecke and Nesbitt grew friendly. "Bix and Nesbitt were exchanging ideas and they both had a bottle," remembered Dave Wilborn, who played banjo in the McKinney band.[3] The warm relationship between the two trumpeters is among the earliest examples of the collegiality and collaboration between black and white musicians in Detroit that carry through to the present day.

Jazz in Detroit gained momentum during the Swing Era. A geographic crossroads, the city was a regular stop for the top big bands—Ellington, Basie, Lunceford, Calloway, Goodman, etc.—and Paradise Valley settled into a vibrant groove. Hundreds of local musicians performed in its hotels, ballrooms, and nightclubs. The Club Plantation, located in the African American–owned Norwood Hotel at 550 East Adams (between Beaubien and St. Antoine), was among the most important venues. Like several of the top clubs in the Valley, the Plantation was a black and tan, attracting a mixed-race audience. Earl Walton led the house band through much of the '30s, playing three floor shows a night, backing singers, a comedian, and dancers. The Cecil Lee Orchestra succeeded Walton's band in 1937. After the Club Plantation changed its name to the Club Congo in 1941, the newly christened Club Congo Orchestra became a training ground for emerging stars, among them tenor saxophonists Wardell Gray and Teddy Edwards, trumpeter Howard McGhee, bassist Al McKibbon, and pianist-arranger Johnny Allen. Along with vibraphonist Milt Jackson and tenor saxophonist Lucky Thompson, these were among the first wave of Detroiters to pick up on the emerging modern jazz—bebop—that was blowing in from New York in the mid-'40s.

Bebop took jazz improvisation to news levels of melodic, rhythmic, and harmonic invention. Spearheaded by Charlie Parker, Dizzy Gillespie, Bud Powell, and others, the music was cast in serpentine lines and lightning syncopation. Bebop aspired to new forms of artistic expression, while also mirroring the rapid changes in American society and culture—including early stirrings of black consciousness and a growing self-awareness among black musicians who, to paraphrase scholar Scott DeVeaux, sought greater professional autonomy within the marketplace.[4]

Beyond New York, Detroit was one of the first cities where bebop took root. A strong jazz infrastructure was already in place—plentiful clubs, relatively well-heeled and sophisticated black audiences, and elite African American musicians, many of them products of Detroit's superb public school music programs. Moreover, because bebop embodied both elevated artistic ambitions and progressive social attitudes among African Americans, the new music fit Detroit's established character as a locus of black advancement.

The arrival of bebop coincided with another growth spurt in Detroit. Auto plants transformed into manufacturing centers for vehicles and weapons during World War II, earning Detroit a prominent place in the Arsenal of Democracy. The city landed a remarkable $14 billion in war-related contracts in 1944, about 10% of all U.S. war spending. Converted auto plants were around-the-clock operations with three shifts a day. Detroit's economy remained bullish as postwar prosperity fueled a healthy demand for automobiles. Detroit's population peaked in the early '50s at nearly 2 million; it was the fifth largest city in the country, trailing only New York, Chicago, Philadelphia, and Los Angeles.

Race relations ebbed and flowed. Rising tensions over public housing discrimination exploded into three days of violent riots in 1943 that left 25 African Americans and nine others dead. A malevolent police force, redlining, and employment discrimination were facts of life for African Americans. Yet some restrictions were beginning to ease in select neighborhoods. Good wages in the auto industry led to increasing standards of living among black factory workers. A growing black middle class and an increasing number of black professional elites spread into the North End (east of Woodward Avenue and north of Grand Boulevard) and the west side (west of Woodward and north of Warren).[5] Jazz clubs followed the shifting black population.

With the city feeling its economic oats and the African American community on the rise, demand for entertainment, especially jazz, reached a new peak. Scores of new nightclubs, showrooms, theaters, bars, and restaurants opened across Detroit in the 1940s and '50s. Many of these have become legendary in Detroit's jazz mythology. The Paradise Theatre (previously Orchestra Hall), Flame Show Bar, Frolic Show Bar, Club El Sino, and Club Sudan (formerly Club Congo) all made their debut in or near Paradise Valley in the '40s. The Bizerte and Club Zombie opened in the North End and the Blue Bird Inn, Crystal, and Bowl-O-Drome opened on the west side.

By the '50s, the center of gravity for modern jazz in the city shifted to the west side. The Blue Bird morphed into the nerve center of the scene early in the decade, and Klein's Show Bar, Minor Key, Twenty Grand, and Hobby Bar all opened their doors. The West End Hotel, located among the industrial plants in the southwest corner of the city, became the favored spot for after-hours jamming. Nearby was another new spot, the Rouge Lounge, just outside Detroit in River Rouge, one of the city's first suburbs with a sizable black population. Later in the decade, venerable Baker's Keyboard Lounge, located on the northern border of the city on Livernois at Eight Mile Road, began booking modern jazz. "People had money in their pockets, and bebop was what they wanted to hear," pianist Tommy Flanagan said in 2001. "The music was everywhere in Detroit."

Notes

1. Information in this chapter about the history of Detroit and growth of the auto industry is drawn from *The Detroit Almanac: 300 Years of Life in the Motor City*, edited by Peter Gavrilovich and Bill McGraw and published by the *Detroit Free Press* (2000).

2. Information about early Detroit jazz history drawn from *Before Motown: A History of Jazz in Detroit, 1920–60*, by Lars Bjorn with Jim Gallert (University of Michigan Press, 2001).

3. Quoted in Bjorn and Gallert, *Before Motown*, 30.

4. Scott DeVeaux, *The Birth of Bebop* (University of California Press, 1997), 25–27.

5. Woodward Avenue, which runs north-south for the entire length of Detroit, divides the city into west and east sides.

PART TWO
The Golden Age, 1940–60

Pianist Hank Jones performs in an unidentified Detroit club in the early 1940s with bassist Paul Szglaggi, drummer Art Mardigan, and an unidentified trumpeter. Photo courtesy Jim Gallert Collection.

Opening Chorus

Detroit's role as a jazz incubator shifted into high gear during the formative years of bebop and ascended to fever pitch in the 1950s. A unique confluence of economic, cultural, social, educational, and artistic factors transformed the city into a bebop factory. The profound marriage of superb formal instruction in public schools with the informal academy that pianist Barry Harris ran in his home—plus a vibrant club scene operating at night—had a catalytic impact on jazz in Detroit. Musicians rolled off an assembly line, all part of a unified fleet, yet each a one-of-a-kind model with its own distinctive identity—a Milt Jackson, a Yusef Lateef, a Kenny Burrell, a Pepper Adams, a Roland Hanna, a Thad Jones, a Tommy Flanagan, and on down the line.

Music of all kinds was omnipresent in black communities in Detroit—in schools, bars, barbershops, dance halls, living rooms, backyards, basements, and community centers. Gospel, hymns, blues, jazz, classical, and early R & B were all part of the mix. Jazz seeped out of clubs, under doors, and through windows, coating the streets in black neighborhoods in a thick haze of blues and swing. Lateef, for example, lived above a theater on Hastings Street as a kid, and he soaked up the sound of bands playing stage shows from the front row.

Bebop demanded new levels of virtuosity in terms of speed, precision, and command of harmony. One often overlooked reason why Detroit musicians adapted to the style so swiftly is that the first-rate music education programs in schools produced a seemingly endless supply of instrumentalists with the skills suited to the new aesthetic. Detroit public school graduates also filled the ranks of major symphony orchestras all over the country during the second half of the 20th century. And these same schools trained many of the musicians who powered Motown as studio players, singers, songwriters, and producers. Public school music programs in Detroit had been recognized among the country's best by the mid-1920s. Elementary students had specialist-taught music classes three or four times a week, and it was common in the 1930s and '40s for students to start playing an instrument in the third grade. The most celebrated high school program was at Cass Technical High School, which operated as a magnet school for high-achieving students across many disciplines, among them science, engineering, art, and music. But there were also quality music teachers and bands at Miller, Northwestern, Northern, and Northeastern high schools.[1]

Schools in Detroit had been integrated by force of law since the 19th century. By the early 1930s, restrictive housing covenants, the evolving racial makeup of certain neighborhoods, and actions by the school board had begun to push in the opposite direction toward more segregation. Still, even schools that were overwhelmingly black, like Miller High School, and had to cope with inferior buildings and resources, remained centers of academic and musical excellence. The band director at Miller, Louis Cabrera, a Mexican American, played bass and taught Lateef, Jackson, Burrell, Frank Rosolino, and others. Burrell, for example, played guitar in the school's stage band and percussion in the concert band and studied bass with Cabrera. The teacher also introduced Burrell to conducting and challenged him to write arrangements—and then taught him the necessary skills. "Mr. Cabrera gave me theory lessons after school," Burrell said in 1996. "I was so well-prepared by the time I got to Wayne State University that I really didn't have to do homework for probably two years."

Cass Tech was the crown jewel of the system. Students spent half their day in music classes; the rigorous curriculum focused on the classical tradition. In addition to orchestras, concert bands, chamber groups, and choirs, there were sequential classes in theory, private lessons on a student's primary instrument, piano instruction, and instrumental techniques classes. String players, for example, were required to learn a wind instrument. Repertoire was ambitious—Beethoven, Brahms, Ravel, Stravinsky, and the like. Michael Bistritzky conducted the orchestras (1942–68). Harry Begian conducted bands (1947–64). They were charismatic leaders recognized today as legendary figures in music education. Many of the school's private teachers were members of the Detroit Symphony Orchestra.

At various times, Cass sponsored a dance band, but jazz was generally something students explored before or after school or snuck into their day during free periods. While there was prejudice among some faculty members, Begian famously treated his white and black students equally and was sympathetic to those with jazz proclivities. He allowed jam sessions in the band room, for example, but he was also a disciplinarian. "At the time, I thought he was the worst son of a bitch in the world," trumpeter Donald Byrd told the *Detroit Free Press* in 1999. "He wouldn't let you get away

Harry Begian, pictured here in 1959, conducted bands at Cass Technical High School in Detroit from 1947 to 1964. Photo: Harry Begian Papers, 1926–1997, Sousa Archives and Center for American Music, University of Illinois at Urbana-Champaign, and Michigan State University Archives and Historical Collections.

with a thing. But I love him." Begian, who died in 2010, remembered Byrd fondly. He told the newspaper that his student had a great sense of humor and such a love of music that it was hard to get him to put down his horn and go to class: "He was always over in the corner playing those jazz licks."

Cass Tech's reputation was such that big-name bandleaders would drop by in the 1930s and early '40s to scout talent. On one of those prospecting trips, Jimmie Lunceford first heard Gerald Wilson, who joined Lunceford's trumpet section in 1939. Beyond Byrd and Wilson, the list of jazz musicians who attended Cass Tech at midcentury is astounding—Wardell Gray, Howard McGhee, Lucky Thompson, Bobby Byrne, Al McKibbon, Major Holley, Billy Mitchell, Julius Watkins, Roland Hanna, Paul Chambers, Doug Watkins, Ron Carter, Hugh Lawson, Alice (McLeod) Coltrane, Kirk Lightsey, and Dorothy Ashby. In later decades, Kevin Toney, Ralphe Armstrong, Geri Allen, Regina Carter, Gerald Cleaver, Carla Cook, and Ali Jackson attended the school.

Pianist Barry Harris and saxophonist Yusef Lateef took on influential leadership roles in the city's jazz community in the 1950s. Young musicians flocked to Harris, who offered advanced training in music theory and improvisation in the bebop style. Lateef, who also studied with Harris despite being nine years older, led the most inventive band in Detroit from 1956 to 1959 and was exalted as a role model. Excellence was expected—at schools, at Harris' house, at the clubs. In a 1986 interview with Ben Sidran for National Public Radio, Pepper Adams described the overall high level of musicianship in Detroit in the '50s: "If you were a young musician and really aspired to work and make money playing your instrument, you had to get awful doggone good to be on a level to compete at all. I didn't realize how true this was until I left Detroit and went to the army. Got out in the rest of the world and found out the standards elsewhere were not nearly as high."

Detroit audiences were hip to modern jazz and could hear the difference between exceptional performances and those that were marginal or worse. "You had to have your stuff together," Joe Henderson said in 1996. "Detroit had the best listening audience. The audiences around Detroit were like musicians. I mean, they *knew*. No way to come up on the bandstand jiving. That could be injurious to one's ego."

Still, if big-city competitiveness and high expectations sharpened raw talent, small-town warmth also nurtured it. Many musicians describe a familial atmosphere when they talk about Detroit in the 1950s—a community of musicians and audiences bound together by shared passion for the music. One notable expression of this was the supportive relationship that developed between audiences and musicians at the jam sessions and concerts at the World Stage, a storefront theater at 13525 Woodward, two miles north of the Wayne State campus in Highland Park, starting in 1954. The New Music Society—Detroit's prescient first musician-run cooperative—hosted Tuesday night jam sessions in which young musicians shared the bandstand with seasoned pros in front of an appreciative audience. More formal concerts on alternating Sundays began in 1955. Elvin Jones once told fellow drummer Art Taylor that audiences treated musicians at the World Stage with a reverence akin to Carnegie Hall.

"I've never seen anything like it before or since: a whole community actively participating in the development of the form," Jones said in a 1971 interview. "It was a beautiful thing to see."[2]

You can hear the warm feedback loop between the audience and musicians on *Byrd Jazz* (Transition), Donald Byrd's first recording as a leader, taped at the World Stage in August 1955.[3] Fans whistle, clap, and shout encouragement. The sextet includes some of Detroit's top players, among them Byrd, Lateef, Harris, and Kiane Zawadi (then Bernard McKinney) on euphonium. Though bassist Alvin Jackson and drummer Frank Gant sound sluggish at times, the soloists' authority underscores the city's high standards.

At the time, Byrd was settling in New York, where he quickly joined a growing crowd of Detroiters making a splash. The scene was heating up. Gutsy hard bop, an alliance of bebop and bluesy roots influences, was brewing in the seminal bands of Art Blakey and Horace Silver. Meanwhile, the Miles Davis Quintet with John Coltrane and the Max Roach Quintet with Clifford Brown were codifying a large swath of the emerging mainstream. Jazz recording was booming in the wake of the newly introduced 12-inch long-playing record, and independent labels were thriving—Blue Note, Prestige, Riverside, Savoy, Atlantic, and others. With their hard-swinging styles, affinity for the blues, and polished craftsmanship, Detroit musicians were to the hard-bop manner born. As they migrated east, they populated the top bands, clubs, and record labels the way an earlier crop of Detroit exports—Milt Jackson, Lucky Thompson, Howard McGhee, and Gerald Wilson—contributed to the emergence of bebop.

Detroit musicians found an especially friendly welcome on Blue Note, the premier indie label of the era and the one most closely associated with hard bop. From 1954 to 1960, Julius Watkins, Frank Foster, Thad Jones, Kenny Burrell, Paul Chambers, Curtis Fuller, Donald Byrd, and Sonny Red all led sessions on Blue Note. Other Detroiters appearing on the label as a sideman included Tommy Flanagan, Louis Hayes, Pepper Adams, Roy Brooks, Elvin Jones, Roland Hanna, Barry Harris, Doug Watkins, Billy Mitchell, Milt Jackson, Gene Taylor, Al McKibbon, J. C. Heard, Hank Jones, and Tate Houston. The Detroit invasion was lauded contemporaneously on a gaggle of LPs named for the city and featuring lineups of all or mostly players from the city. Thad Jones' *Detroit–New York Junction* (Blue Note) and Pittsburgh-born Kenny Clarke's homage *Jazzmen: Detroit* (Savoy) were the first, recorded six weeks apart in early 1956. Lateef's initial recordings on multiple labels were part of the wave, and two records taped in 1959–60 by ad hoc bands of Detroiters even carry the same title: *Motor City Scene*—one led by Adams (Bethlehem) and one led by Thad Jones (United Artists). Record buyers couldn't help but get the message: Detroit was now a national jazz power.[4]

Notes

1. Historical information about Detroit Public Schools music education programs drawn from unpublished research shared with me by Lissa Fleming May, professor of music education and associate dean for instruction at the Indiana University Jacobs School of Music.

2. Arthur Taylor, *Notes and Tones: Musician-to-Musician Interviews*, expanded edition (Da Capo Press, 1993), 221.

3. Reissued as Byrd's *First Flight* and Yusef Lateef's *Yusef* (both Delmark).

4. Byrd and Adams are often credited as co-leaders of the Bethlehem LP, recorded in mid-November 1960, but Adams scholar Gary Carner told me it is the baritone saxophonist's date, falling in the gap between the end of Byrd's initial contract with Blue Note and before the trumpeter re-signed with the label. Moreover, two Adams originals appear on the record but none by Byrd.

Gerald Wilson

HEAD AND HEART

As Gerald Wilson sprinted toward his 90th birthday, his mind was so sharp, his curiosity so alive, and his big-band compositions and arrangements so timelessly modern that it was easy to forget that his big break came during Franklin Roosevelt's second term. His call of destiny arrived by wire.

It was June 1939. The 20-year-old Wilson, a hotshot trumpeter from Detroit and a graduate of Cass Tech, was on the road with Clarence "Chic" Carter. In New York, Jimmie Lunceford needed a trumpet player. Lunceford, who fronted the hippest band of the day after Ellington and Basie, had already met Wilson in Detroit. When he learned his quarry was in Dayton, Ohio, he sent a telegram to the black YMCA in town.

"They didn't know where I was staying, but you know how closely knit the black neighborhoods were," Wilson said in 2004. "They knew there was a guy named Gerald Wilson there playing with Chic Carter's band, and they found me and gave me that telegram. I could hardly believe it. I went down to the train station the next morning and they had a ticket and some money, and I got on the train to join Jimmie Lunceford's band."

Wilson, who died in 2014 at age 96, compiled a singular resume as a big-band composer, arranger, and leader. He wrote prescient charts for Lunceford and then innovative arrangements for his own proto-bebop orchestra in the mid-'40s and its successor in the '50s—bands that still haven't gotten their due. Starting in 1961, he led a superlative big band for more than half a century. In the 1960s and '70s, Wilson's band in Los Angeles was a West Coast counterpart to the Thad Jones–Mel Lewis Jazz Orchestra in New York. Both bands were built around visionary composer-arrangers—Wilson and Jones—whose shared roots in Detroit put an exclamation point on the city's landmark contributions to postwar big-band jazz. Wilson also wrote arrangements for Ellington, Basie, Dizzy Gillespie, Billie Holiday, Ray Charles, Nancy Wilson, Joe Williams, Ella Fitzgerald, Sarah Vaughan, Al Hibbler, and B. B. King. He wrote music for television, film, and the Los

Gerald Wilson leads his orchestra at the Detroit Jazz Festival in 2008. Photo by Clyde Stringer.

Angeles Philharmonic. He even earned a pop culture cameo in 1970, when a cover of his "Viva Tirado" by brown-eyed soul band El Chicano reached No. 28 on the Billboard Hot 100 chart.

Wilson's vast library ranges from thrilling swingers and romantic ballads to elegant essays in the blues and Spanish and Mexican-flavored works that capture the spirit of the bullfight and the heritage of his Mexican American wife, Josefina. His scores are rendered in a personal palette of thickly scored harmony, wailing melodies, and weighty ensembles that reach beyond fad and fashion to a direct expression of blues and swing. The gutsy "Moment of Truth" (1962), for example, is a slow blues with a stalking groove, outspoken melodies, and intense bursts of brass and reeds. Wilson delivers wise craftsmanship and emotional depth in Aristotelian balance—a textbook distillation of the Detroit aesthetic.

"Gerald would often say that the music has to be simple but not simple-minded," said veteran saxophonist Ernie Watts. "He wanted to have something accessible but that had substance. There are some bands where the music is so hard that you can't relax enough to play. With Gerald's music all the parts were like a song. It was comfortable to play. Even if it was hard you could feel it. Gerald knew a lot, but he didn't have to demonstrate how much he knew all the time."

Still, for all of Wilson's accomplishments, he remained underrated for most of his career. The jazz press has historically been East Coast–centric, and Wilson, who fell in love with California sunshine the moment he arrived in Los Angeles with Lunceford in the winter of 1940, spent his entire professional life based there. He didn't do himself any favors by shutting down his first acclaimed band after only three years in 1947. The forward-looking records he made in the '40s and early '50s were cut for small, poorly distributed labels and have never been reissued in a way that might spark reassessment.

Wilson's band in the 1960s was well-documented on the Pacific Jazz label but didn't tour outside the West Coast. Wilson, who had his fill of one-nighters back in the '40s, made his living in the studios, which allowed him time to compose on his own terms. Still, the lack of attention stung. "He knew others were receiving more recognition," said son Anthony Wilson, a guitarist. "He knew how strong a writer he was and how deep the band was. But he bore it with elegance. He knew that his path wasn't the same as others, and that the important thing was just to keep working."

During the last 25 years of his life, the breadth of Wilson's achievements began to dawn on the wider jazz world. The American Jazz Orchestra got the ball rolling with a retrospective concert in New York in 1988, and Wilson was named a Jazz Master in 1990 by the National Endowment for the Arts. The classy reissue label Mosaic boxed up his Pacific Jazz recordings in 2000, and five CDs on Detroit-based Mack Avenue Records in his final decade put him on the covers of the jazz magazines. His relationship with Mack Avenue also renewed his love affair with Detroit, and he became a regular at the city's annual Labor Day weekend jazz festival.

Wilson cut a dashing figure. He had a Cheshire cat smile, a bushy mustache, and a shock of white hair that put Einstein to shame. He spoke with contagious enthusiasm and never lost the drawl of his Mississippi birth. Though he appeared frail offstage, the decades fell away in the spotlight. At the 2007 jazz festival, the 89-year-old maestro commanded the lane in front of his saxophone section like a football coach prowling the sidelines. He clapped his hands, shouted encouragement, and choreographed phrases in sweeping arm gestures. His energy surged through the musicians and out to the audience. At the end of the opening number, Wilson stepped to the microphone and literally screamed over the last note. The audience screamed right back.

Gerald Stanley Wilson was born on September 4, 1918, in Shelby, Mississippi, a town of about 1,300 people located 100 miles southwest of Memphis, Tennessee. There were horses and wagons on the town streets when he was a boy. His father was a blacksmith. His mother, a graduate of what is now Jackson State University, a historically black college, taught at the only grammar school in town for blacks. She also gave music lessons and played piano in church. She taught her three children to play, and Wilson talked her into getting him a trumpet when he was 11 or 12. He heard records by Jelly Roll Morton and King Oliver and by the end of the '20s was staying up late to hear Duke Ellington radio broadcasts from Harlem's Cotton Club. Wilson made himself a baton out of a stick and waved it around, pretending to be a bandleader.

There was no school for blacks beyond eighth grade in Shelby, so Wilson's mother sent him to live with family in Memphis and start high school in 1932. He took trumpet lessons at Manassas High School, where Jimmie Lunceford had once been a teacher and athletic coach. A trip to the World's Fair in Chicago in 1934 left Wilson so exhilarated that he begged his mother to let him come north. She sent him that fall to live with friends in Detroit. Having spent his entire life in the segregated South, the city was a revelation. Wilson never forgot the elation of walking into Cass Tech on the first day of school and seeing white and black students together. "It felt like freedom," he said. "That was the way I always thought it should be."

Wilson studied trumpet at Cass Tech with Clarence Byrne, head of the music department. "Your whole day was practically music," Wilson said. "You had to take piano. You had to take harmony. You had to take percussion. I took trumpet and played in the concert band and in the jazz band. It was expert training. Had it not been for Cass Tech, I would not have become the musician I am."

Wilson first met Lunceford when the bandleader visited Cass Tech to look for talent. Wilson also became friendly with Lunceford trumpeter and arranger Sy Oliver during the band's Detroit residencies. Oliver—who spearheaded the bouncy, two-beat Lunceford style—let Wilson sit next to him during gigs. After graduating, Wilson leapt into the local scene, performing with, among others, the Cecil Lee Orchestra at the Club Plantation. Wilson took Oliver's place with Lunceford in 1939. The band was known for its mix of discipline, musicianship, and showmanship. The players had seven different uniforms, and Lunceford fined musicians for wearing the wrong color socks. Typical shtick found the trumpeters throwing their horns in the air and catching them in unison. But the music was no-nonsense. It was an arranger's band, with contributions from Oliver, Eddie Wilcox, Eddie Durham, and Willie Smith. Oliver's contagious swing, contrasting episodes, and integrated mix of brass, reeds, and rhythm left a lasting mark on Wilson's writing. At first, however, he just played trumpet. Wilson was an excellent section man and a competent soloist whose brassy sound can be heard on "Lunceford Special" (1939).

Wilson's fascination with harmony began at Cass Tech, and he wrote several rudimentary arrangements in Detroit. On the road with Lunceford he studied harmony and orchestration books, asked questions of every arranger he knew, and paid special attention to Ellington. Wilson's first pieces for Lunceford in 1941, "Hi Spook" and "Yard Dog Mazurka," marked him as a modernist. Both are fundamentally AABA forms but filled with quirky phrase lengths, advanced harmonies, savvy plotting, and visceral excitement. "Hi Spook" eschews typical 8-bar schematics in favor of an 11-bar bridge and a 13-bar final section. "Yard Dog Mazurka" makes hay out of a sly chromatic riff that arranger Ray Wetzel later appropriated for Stan Kenton's "Intermission Riff."

Wilson left Lunceford in early 1942 and settled in Los Angeles, where he had earlier crossed paths with Billy Strayhorn. "He really taught me to arrange," Wilson told Strayhorn's biographer, David Hajdu.[1] "Chord structure, how to get from one point to another—I couldn't figure out how he did all of those things. He sat me down and showed me: 'Here, Gerald, you can just do this.'"

Wilson was drafted into the Navy in 1943 and ended up playing and writing for service bands near Chicago. After a medical discharge, he returned to Los Angeles in 1944 and started his own band. He was 25. Bebop was picking up steam, and Wilson's Cass Tech training gave him a leg up. He had also met Dizzy Gillespie earlier in Detroit, where the two shared harmonic ideas at the piano. Wilson layered bebop harmony and rhythm on top of swing fundamentals and the pervasive influence of Ellington. "I feel like bebop was my time," Wilson said. "But I was lucky enough to come up just before. We don't throw anything away in our music. Everything is just another link."

Part of the allure of the great records Wilson made in the '40s for the Excelsior, Black & White, United Artist, and Aladdin labels is that the music morphs from swing to bop within the course of a single arrangement. "Et-Ta" (1946) is built around a two-beat mop-mop riff out of the Lunceford playbook, but when the band shifts into a walking 4/4, the music turns toward the future. The payoff comes in the third bar of the bridge when the ensemble lands on a tangy altered dominant chord wearing a flatted fifth like a bebop merit badge.[2]

Wilson's vibrant arrangement of "Groovin' High" (1945), the first big-band treatment of Gillespie's classic, was recorded only months after the composer introduced the song. Sultry ballads "Pensive Melody," "The Black Rose," and "The Moors" descend from Ellington and Strayhorn. The evocative masterpiece "Dissonance in Blues" (1947) opens with the mysterious haze of Red Callender's bass solo amid shadowy chords. Reeds and brass wake up, and hints of double-time bebop and pungent passing chords raise the heat and tease the emotions. "It's a very adventurous chart," said composer-arranger David Berger. "It's better than any of the other bebop writers of the time. He's incorporated all of the stuff that Tadd Dameron or Dizzy were doing, but it's richer."

The band was equal to the challenging book. The superb lead trumpeter, Snooky Young, was a charter member. Young beboppers like pianist Jimmy Bunn, trumpeter Hobart Dotson, alto saxophonist Buddy Collette and drummer Charles Thompson filled the ranks. Wilson was ahead of his time hiring women, notably 19-year-old trombonist and arranger Melba Liston and pianist Vivian Fears (sometimes known as Vivian Glasby). Wilson packed them in at the Apollo in New York, sold out shows on the road with Ella Fitzgerald, recorded with Dinah Washington, and signed a contract with Mercury Records. Yet in 1947 he disbanded, feeling the pressure of success. The road left little time to write, and he felt undernourished artistically. Wilson returned home to study, poring over scores by Bartok, Stravinsky, Debussy, Manuel de Falla, Prokofiev, Shostakovich, and Khachaturian. "People thought I was crazy, because we were so successful, but I wanted to broaden my horizons and see what I could learn that I could apply to jazz," Wilson said.

Wilson freelanced around Los Angeles and traveled with Basie in 1948–

49, contributing "The Royal Suite," a multi-movement work premiered at Carnegie Hall in 1948 but never recorded. He also played briefly with Dizzy Gillespie in 1949, who recorded Wilson's dramatic trumpet ballad "Dizzier and Dizzier" (also known as "Katy") and his screaming Afro-Cuban arrangement "Guarachi Guaro."

Ellington began calling when he got backed up against a deadline and needed arrangements fast. Wilson's first charts for Ellington were vocals in 1947, "You Gotta Crawl Before You Walk" and "You're Just an Old Antidisestablishmentarianismist." Wilson eventually wrote about a dozen charts for his idol—sometimes with credit, sometimes without—including "El Viti," "Imagine My Frustration" (outfitted with Strayhorn's lyrics for Ella Fitzgerald), and an explosive update of "Perdido" given its definitive recording on Ellington's *Great Paris Concert* in 1963 (Atlantic).[3]

Wilson moved to San Francisco for a couple of years around 1952 and organized a band. Saxophonist Jerry Dodgion, who was 19 when he played with Wilson in the Bay Area, said the group had a weekly Sunday afternoon gig at a well-known Oakland club called Slim Jenkins. The music Wilson recorded back in Los Angeles in 1954 and issued under the title of *Big Band Modern* (Audio Lab) shows the impact of his classical studies. He puts instruments in contrary motion, spreads chords across the ensemble in eight-part harmony, and employs exotic rhythms, percussion, and woodwind sonorities.

Three arrangements borrow classical themes: The brooding "Lotus Land" by Cyril Scott becomes a concerto for the full-bodied flute of Bill Green, one of the first black studio musicians in Los Angeles. "Romance," an up-tempo adaptation of the third movement of Khachaturian's *Masquerade Suite*, swings manically. "Bull Fighter" adapts a traditional fanfare melody, with Allen Smith the likely virtuoso trumpet soloist. Wilson's original "Algerian Fantasy" captures the sun and sand of North Africa, with Dodgion the flute soloist.[4]

Wilson wouldn't record again under his own name until 1961, when at age 42 he restarted his band in Los Angeles and inaugurated a nine-year association with Pacific Jazz that yielded 10 LPs. He now had a consistent presence in record stores for the first time, and *Downbeat* put Wilson on its cover in April 1964. "We play like no one else; no one else plays like us," Wilson told the magazine. "We keep studying, trying to find the new things."

Wilson's writing by then had assimilated hard bop and early modal pieces by Miles Davis. (Wilson's trumpet playing modernized in the '50s, but he played sparingly and gave up the horn in the '70s.) His strongest Pacific Jazz records are the first three—*You Better Believe It*, *Moment of*

Truth, *Portraits*—plus *The Golden Sword*. Many of Wilson's most familiar compositions are here, among them the moody waltz "Blues for Yna Yna," the Latin-based "Viva Torado," and "Nancy Jo," a blues with a fresh mix of 12-bar and 8-bar phrases and swanky saxophone passages. The A-list personnel combined veterans, newcomers, blacks, whites, Latinos, studio musicians, and diehard jazzers. A partial roll call: trumpeters Carmell Jones, Al Porcino, and Charles Tolliver; saxophonists Bud Shank, Buddy Collette, Anthony Ortega, Harold Land, Teddy Edwards, and Ernie Watts; vibraphonist Bobby Hutcherson; pianists Jack Wilson and George Duke; guitarist Joe Pass; bassist Jimmy Bond; and drummer Mel Lewis.

"Some big bands are systematic and all ensemble and precision oriented, but Gerald's band was the most *jazz*, because it was coming from the essence of jazz, which is improvisation and spontaneous creation," said Watts.

Wilson's primary living came as an arranger-for-hire. In the '70s, he also hosted a radio program in Los Angeles and taught at universities. In 1977–78 he was music director for Redd Foxx's variety show on ABC. "What I remember about my father working when I was a kid was that he didn't put on any airs," said Anthony Wilson. "He didn't have a studio like a lot of people. He wrote at the dining room table and shuttled back and forth to the piano, and he wrote extremely fast. He'd tinker on the piano a little while and sit down and score out a whole section of music: Boom. Boom. Boom. Then he'd go make a sandwich."

The Los Angeles Philharmonic and music director Zubin Mehta came knocking in 1972. Wilson was one of four black composers from the jazz world asked to contribute a movement to a large work celebrating Malcolm X. The others were Quincy Jones, Benny Carter, and J. J. Johnson. The idea was scrapped after black activists protested that the concert represented, as the *Los Angeles Times* reported, a "prostitution of Malcolm's ideals." Wilson was the only one of the original composers to remain involved, and his "Debut: 52172" was premiered at the Dorothy Chandler Pavilion on May 21, 1972. There's no recording. *Los Angeles Times* classical critic Martin Bernheimer was not enthusiastic, calling it "a sometimes brassy, sometimes melancholy, always facile manipulation of the big orchestra in the manner of an old-time jazz band." Wilson later wrote works for the Philharmonic and a gospel choir.

Of Wilson's autumnal recordings, the outstanding *Lomelin* in 1981 (Discovery) is the pick of the litter. The commissioned suites in later years vary in inspiration. *Theme for Monterey* (Mama) from 1997 opens with a ravishing melody but grows wearisome dressed in various rhythms and tempos for 45 minutes with little development; the distilled 15-minute version in 2003 on *New York New Sound* (Mack Avenue) is superior with Jesse Davis playing his heart out on alto sax. Overall, *In My Time* is the best of the Mack Avenue discs, but the most sentimental is *Detroit*, whose title suite premiered at the 2009 Detroit Jazz Festival and brought Wilson's career full circle as he celebrated his 91st birthday.

It was not easy in the end for Wilson, who suffered from macular degeneration so severe that to compose in his final years he had to dictate notes and rhythms one instrument at a time to an assistant. But he was still doing what he was trained to do in Detroit. "You're trying to swing," he said. "You're trying to show off your harmonic stuff and you're trying to make the people listen, to really catch their attention."

Recommended Recordings

Gerald Wilson, *Gerald Wilson and His Orchestra 1946–1954* (Chronological Classics)
Gerald Wilson, *Moment of Truth* (Pacific Jazz)
Gerald Wilson, *Portraits* (Pacific Jazz)

Notes

1. David Hajdu, *Lush Life: A Biography of Billy Strayhorn* (Farrar, Straus and Giroux, 1996), 94.

2. Finding Wilson's early recordings means entering a maze of European CDs that go in and out of print. Two Chronological Classics discs cover 1945–54, including *Big Band Modern*. *The Very Best of Gerald Wilson 1946–54* (Master Classics) presents the music with no dates or personnel. Jazz Factory paired *Big Band Modern* with a 1954 concert from Los Angeles, but the date and location are misidentified as 1950 and San Francisco; Jazz Moon issued the same material as a digital download.

3. Two lickety-split choruses for two tenor saxophones precede Wilson's arrangement. Ellington scholar David Berger reports that the first was written by Jimmy Hamilton and the second by Clark Terry.

4. Wilson's 1954 recordings were released on a 10-inch LP, *Progressive Sounds* (Federal), before Audio Lab issued the material with additional tracks as *Big Band Modern* in 1959. In a 2017 interview, Jerry Dodgion identified soloists and said, contrary to published discographies, that he played lead alto, Bill Green played second alto, Harold Wylie played baritone sax, and trumpeter Clark Terry was not present. Paul Gonsalves is the tenor sax soloist on "Romance" but was not a regular band member.

Yusef Lateef

GENTLE GIANT

Shortly before the 2007 Detroit Jazz Festival, local aficionados were consumed by a rumor that Yusef Lateef was going to play the blues when the 86-year-old legend returned home to perform. The "blues" was meant literally as the 12-bar musical form and as a metaphor for the fundamental modern jazz that the tenor saxophonist, flutist, and oboist used to play back in the day. It had been a long time since Detroiters—or anyone—had heard this kind of music from Lateef. For decades Lateef had been exploring a multiethnic idiom of earthy rhythm, exotic texture, and open form. He had also been writing notated classical music and veering off into poetry and visual art. Lateef, tall and thick across the chest, wore a purple dashiki at the festival. He fronted a traditional rhythm section of piano, bass, and drums, but the landscape for improvisation remained largely pan-African, Middle Eastern, and Asian. Halfway through the set, however, Lateef picked up his oboe and blew several spare 12-bar blues choruses at a walking tempo that were filled with bent pitch, quavering vibrato, and down-home soul. The audience took to it like ice cream.

Of all the jazz musicians produced by Detroit, Lateef, who died in 2013 at age 93, traveled farthest from his roots—from Hastings Street to the fields of Nigeria and the halls of academia. He played in groups led by Dizzy Gillespie, Charles Mingus, and Cannonball Adderley, fronted his own bands for 50-plus years and made roughly 80 recordings under his own name. He earned a doctorate in education and a Grammy Award in the New Age category. He developed individual identities on tenor sax, flute, and oboe and mastered myriad non-Western reeds and flutes. He recorded in practically every African American vernacular idiom: blues, swing, spirituals, bebop, hard bop, free jazz, funk, R & B, soul, and gospel. He wrote reams of formal concert music, including symphonies and string quartets. He wrote novellas, short stories, and poetry. He made exhibition-quality drawings of trees and plants in a vocabulary of geometric and biomorphic shapes.

Yusef Lateef Quintet at Klein's Show Bar, 1958, in Detroit, with Frank Morelli (baritone sax), Terry Pollard (piano), Will Austin (bass), Frank Gant (drums). Photo courtesy Frank Morelli Jr.

Most famously, Lateef was among the first jazz musicians to experiment with non-Western scales, drones, textures, rhythms, and instruments. He grafted these ideas onto the trunk of modern jazz in the '50s. Decades before the term "world music" came into vogue, Lateef drafted the template. You have to be careful about overstating direct influences, but a conceptual line connects Lateef's early recordings with John Coltrane's "India," the Codona trio with Don Cherry, and recent developments like Dave Douglas' Balkan-influenced Tiny Bell Trio, and Vijay Iyer and Rudresh Mahanthappa's hybrids of jazz and Indian music. Lateef did not change the course of jazz, but he pushed at its seams, cultivating a sage individualism and experimental streak that continued into his 90s. Yet his sound and ideas always resonated with an oracular understanding of the blues, and his forthright phrasing grabbed listeners by their collars and refused to let go.

Lateef was a seeker of truth. His Muslim faith, physical stature, shaved head, and serene countenance conjured a halo of mysticism. Everyone looked up to him. He was, to quote the title of his 2006 autobiography, a gentle giant. "Yusef Lateef was a presence," Sonny Rollins said. "He was an enormous spirit who everybody involved in our art loved. He was not only a great friend to me but also a role model." Most important to Lateef was the accumulation of wisdom. "To learn is a thrill," he said in 2001. "Whatever I do today is the whole continuum of my experience. Like John Dewey said in his book *Art as Experience*, you can't separate experience from the work of art. If I write for the symphony today, you're listening to everything that's happened to me since I was 18 years old."

Lateef was born on October 9, 1920, in Chattanooga, Tennessee. According to his autobiography, his name at birth was William Emmanuel Huddleston, though most references spell his middle name Emanuel. The family arrived in Detroit when Lateef was four, settling in Paradise Valley. Lateef's father was a laborer who did not make much money, and he adopted the surname Evans for unknown reasons. Lateef was known as Bill Evans until his conversion to Islam.

Lateef was drawn to the music that saturated Paradise Valley, but he also trained as a boxer as a teenager at the same Detroit gym where Joe Louis got his start. Lateef studied music under Louis Cabrera at Miller High School before taking up the alto saxophone in 1938 at age 17 or 18. He soon switched to tenor and must have been a quick study because he was playing gigs by 1940. He worked with trumpeter Mathew Rucker's Spirits of Swing, a big band started at Miller that was so good it turned pro. Pianist and organist Milt Buckner, who later wrote for Lionel Hampton, wrote snazzy arrangements for Rucker. Lateef took lessons at the Detroit Conservatory of Music, received tutoring from Ted Buckner (Milt's brother), and practiced with Lucky Thompson. Lateef also learned by sitting outside Wardell Gray's apartment and listening to him play.

Lateef married Sadie Harper in 1941 and the couple soon had two children he supported by working at a bedspring factory. He was hired by Lucky Millinder in 1946 on Thompson's recommendation but never joined the band because the saxophonist he was supposed to replace in New York decided to stay. Lateef instead worked on the East Coast with Hot Lips Page and Roy Eldridge and traveled the Midwest with Ernie Fields, whose band straddled swing and early R & B. Lateef landed in Chicago, where he played with Eugene Wright and his Dukes of Swing, a bluesy jump band that included pianist Sonny Blount—later known as Sun Ra, an avant-garde icon.[1] Lateef was assimilating his influences, especially Lester Young's tonal manipulations and Dexter Gordon's nascent bebop phrasing. Lateef's big break was joining Dizzy Gillespie's big band in early 1949 for nearly a year. He made his first recordings with Gillespie and solos exuberantly on "St. Louis Blues," "Hey Pete! Let's Eat Mo' Meat," and "Jump Did-Le Ba."

Lateef converted to Islam in Chicago in 1948. He had always been interested in spiritual matters and was intrigued when trumpeter Talib Dawud introduced him to the Ahmadiyya movement. The roots of the Ahmadiyya Muslim Community reach back to late 19th-century India. The Ahmadis emphasized interfaith tolerance, dialogue, and peace. They provided the first multiracial model for African American Islam, according to Richard Brent Turner.[2]

Many African Americans embraced the movement in the mid-20th century as it played to increasing racial consciousness and early stirrings of the civil rights movement. Turner writes that Ahmadi leaders argued that Christian churches were among the most segregated places in America and offered their version of Islam as a less prejudiced religion for blacks. The Ahmadiyya retained their primacy within African American Islam until overtaken by the separatist Nation of Islam in the mid-'50s. Lateef joined jazz musicians Ahmad Jamal, Art Blakey, Sahib Shihab, Kenny Clarke, and others in the faith. He changed his legal name, adopting Yusef after the prophet Joseph and Lateef meaning gentle, amiable, and incomprehensible. "It was clear to me that Islam, through prayer and doing good deeds, could direct one's life in a proper way," Lateef said in his autobiography. "Islam taught one the object of one's life and the means of obtaining perfection. Islam taught that you could realize paradise in this life as well as in the next."[3]

Lateef returned to Detroit in 1950 when his wife took ill. His autobiography avoids specifics, but she was incapacitated enough that Lateef became a de facto single father. His widow, Ayesha Lateef, said she believed Sadie suffered from mental illness. Lateef is silent on when his first marriage ended, but by the late '60s he was married to Saeeda Lateef. It's unclear when this marriage ended, but in 1973 Lateef married an artist, Tahira (Simpson) Lateef. Tahira died in 2009. Lateef married Ayesha, his fourth wife, in June 2012.

The 1950s took Lateef from age 30 to 40 and transformed him from regional journeyman into a national figure. Early in the decade he played blues and jazz gigs while working full time on a Chrysler assembly line. Kenny Burrell encouraged him to enroll at Wayne University (now Wayne State), where Lateef studied classical music. He took saxophone lessons from Larry Teal, a leading classical saxophonist, and he also studied flute and oboe. Meanwhile, Barry Harris taught him jazz scales and harmony. Lateef said in 2001 that he also had his first go at composing in a classical vein in the mid '50s. He wrote a string quartet, but lacking friends to play it, he left a copy—like a message in a bottle—in the mailbox of a Detroit Symphony musician. Lateef got no response. The episode offers a poignant metaphor for the obstacles facing black classical composers and foreshadows his difficulties 50 years later finding orchestras to play his pieces.

Studying Islam broadened his worldview. He researched other cultures, and a Syrian friend introduced him to an instrument the friend called a "rabat"—more accurately a form of either the Central Asian rubab or the Islamic rabab, particularly the plucked (rather than bowed) variety from Afghanistan.[4] The friend made one for Lateef, who described it as a one-string instrument made from goatskin and horsehair. Lateef used it to create pedal-point vamps on compositions like "Morning" and "Sounds of Nature." Lateef also discovered the Middle Eastern arghul, a double-pipe woodwind instrument with melody and drone pipes that produced an intensely buzzing tone.

A turning point came in April 1956, when Lateef embarked on a three-year tenure at Klein's Show Bar at 8540 12th Street on the west side. Klein's was a classy, spacious place, whose Jewish owner, George Klein, paid the musicians well. The club attracted integrated audiences and the kind of jazz fans who shushed people making too much noise. Quitting his job at Chrysler, Lateef led a quintet that worked six nights a week until Klein sold the bar in 1959. Lateef's first band included trombonist Curtis Fuller, pianist Hugh Lawson, bassist Ernie Farrow, and teenage drummer Louis Hayes. Others who cycled through the group included Wilbur Harden, Kiane Zawadi (Bernard McKinney), Frank Morelli, Terry Pollard, Will Austin, Frank Gant, and Oliver Jackson. "Yusef was respected as one of the top stars in Detroit," said Hayes. "The club was packed every night. He was older than we were and had a direction, so we all had to grow to keep up. He was unique—his music, the way he carried himself, his religion."

Though venerated by fans and musicians, Lateef was not immune from racial harassment and even violence. In his autobiography, he said that a white police detective was upset that a particular white woman kept returning to Klein's to hear the band. One night the cop accosted Lateef outside the club, forced him to the ground and accused him of drug dealing. The police hauled Lateef to the station and beat his hands with a blackjack. George Klein raced to the station and secured Lateef's release.

Lateef signed his first record contract with Savoy after an Associated Press reporter recommended him to Savoy producer Ozzie Cadena in New York. Starting in April 1957, Lateef's band piled into two cars at regular intervals and drove to New York to record. Lateef was 36, late to be making a debut as a leader. He caught up quickly, taping an astounding eleven and a half LPs in two and a half years for Savoy, Prestige, Verve, and Argo.

The initial Savoy LPs *Jazz for Thinkers* and *Jazz Mood* and Verve's *Before Dawn* feature Lateef's first band with Fuller, Lawson, Farrow, and Hayes. The material includes Lateef's exotic originals, hard-bop swingers, blues, experimental works, and meditative pieces. "Morning" suggests dawn breaking over the Arabian Desert. Farrow plucks an insinuating F pedal vamp on the rabab, accompanied by percussive scrapes and rattles. The 16-bar theme outlines an F minor pentatonic scale and the simple harmony evokes a prescient feeling of brooding modality. The most audacious compositions are sound collages recorded in October 1957. On "Sounds of Nature," flugelhorn smears, fluttering flute, and little percussion instruments anticipate the Art Ensemble of Chicago by a decade. On "Love and Humor," balloon squeals and a 7-Up pop bottle create a wacky, avant-jug band groove. More conventional, 1959's *The Dreamer* (Savoy) stands out for Lateef's brawny tenor solos, flute balladry, and debut on oboe, which he plays in a spare blues style with a snake-charmer tone. The record also showcases the electrifying and oft-forgotten Detroit bebop pianist Terry Pollard, whose fierce attack ignites the blues "Arjuna."

In January 1960, having accomplished everything he could in Detroit, Lateef moved to New York. He quickly found work with Charles Mingus and solos vigorously on the bassist's "Prayer for Passive Resistance." Later that year John Coltrane told *Downbeat* that Lateef's approach to Eastern music offered inspiration and ideas. Lateef recorded prolifically as a leader and sideman. His LPs for Riverside include the well-known quartet date *Eastern Sounds* and the overlooked *The Centaur and the Phoenix*, a nonet record with two ear-catching, fastidious scores by obscure classical composer Charles Mills.

Into Something (1961), with an all-Detroit rhythm section, is the most thrilling. Trio tracks like "Water Pistol" with bassist Herman Wright and drummer Elvin Jones sound like a stampede. (Barry Harris plays piano on half the songs.) Lateef's tone on tenor is now as massive as an orchestra, and his inflections encompass ringing overtones, false fingerings, split tones, and basement-register barking. The strength of his sound puts Lateef in a rare class with Sonny Rollins, with whom he sometimes practiced.

Lateef doesn't play chord changes with anywhere near Rollins' flair, but *Into Something* reminds you how much communicative power and personality rests solely within a jazz musician's tone.

Lateef's visibility skyrocketed in 1962–63 during a two-year stint with Cannonball Adderley's sextet. The alto saxophonist gave Lateef featured billing, and the gig reunited him with Louis Hayes. Lateef bunked on the road with Austrian pianist Joe Zawinul. "They were a funny team," Hayes said. "One day Joe didn't have a quarter for the soda machine, so he asked Yusef for some change. Yusef said, 'OK, but you have to sign this IOU.' He wasn't joking! Yusef was the kind of a guy who, when we checked into a hotel, might go to the YMCA because it was cheaper."

Lateef reformed his own band after leaving Adderley and started a three-year run with Impulse Records that included *Live at Pep's* (1964); the in-person electricity and intriguing material make for one of his best records. Still, Lateef grew restless. He enrolled at the Manhattan School of Music in 1966, majoring in flute and earning a master's degree in music education. He began teaching at Manhattan Community College in 1971 and finished a doctorate in education through the University of Massachusetts in 1975. (Dissertation: "An Overview of Western and Islamic Education.") Lateef spread his wings as a composer. "Symphonic Blues Suite" (1970), an 18-minute piece for orchestra and jazz quartet, has aged well. Issued on *Suite 16* (Atlantic), the music finds Lateef's tenor breaking through the orchestra's pointillistic textures and atonal harmony. The quartet swings robustly, before dabs of orchestral color splash across the canvas and Barry Harris improvises Messiaen-like fragments in the balcony of the piano—the closest this lifelong bebopper came to free jazz. Lateef performed the suite in 1970 with the Detroit Symphony at the Meadow Brook Music Festival north of Detroit.

This period saw Lateef organize his finest working band, with pianist Kenny Barron, bassist Bob Cunningham, and drummer Tootie Heath. Lasting from 1971 to 1975, it was a flexible quartet and close-knit family. On one trip to San Francisco, the group was scheduled to stay in a house run by the Black Panthers, but when Heath arrived with his white wife, she was refused lodging. "We can't stay here either," Lateef told the Panthers. "She's my sister."

Lateef addressed everyone as "Brother" or "Sister." He refused to shake hands with women, believing it improper to touch a woman who was not his wife. He radiated peace but took care of business. When a club owner once said he couldn't afford to pay the band, Lateef picked up the cash register and walked into the back office and refused to leave until he got paid.

"Physically, he was so big, and he was honest," said Barron. "When he said something, you could believe it. Musically, he was open and very freeing. He wasn't specific in instructions. Just be on time and no drugs."

Lateef's eclectic Atlantic recordings in the late '60s and '70s aim for a wider audience via cross-pollinations with R & B, soul, and more. Results are mixed, but *10 Years Hence* (1974) captures the straight-ahead excitement of Lateef's working quartet in a club, save two tracks blanketed by overdubbed brass, strings, and choir. The funky grooves and large ensemble on *Yusef Lateef's Detroit* (1969) get your body moving and the concept—all the pieces are named for city landmarks—reaffirms Lateef's connection to his hometown. By the late '70s, Lateef stopped using the word "jazz," citing dictionary definitions like "to copulate" and "nonsense," and after 1980 he stopped playing in venues that sold alcohol. Recorded in 1977, the signature piece on *Autophysiopsychic* (CTI) is the silly "Robot Man." Lateef's raspy vocal warns of dehumanizing technology backed by electric bass and a disco-funk beat. At 57, Lateef appears to have reached a dead end.

The final chapter of Lateef's creative life started with a fellowship in Nigeria from 1981 to 1985 studying African music and dance. He returned reinvigorated, settling into a tenured professorship at the University of Massachusetts and letting his muse take flight. Lateef's late output is difficult to get your arms around, because he covered so much territory and his self-released CDs on his own YAL label are hard to find. "He used to say, 'Brother Adam, we're evolutionists. When you get rid of one thing, you need to replace it with something else,'" said percussionist and longtime collaborator Adam Rudolph. "There's a courageousness that goes with that. His late work is so far from what people tend to call jazz that I look at it like a slow-motion version of what John Coltrane went through in the last two years of his life—opening up into this vast, experimental arena."

For a while Lateef explored meditative—sometimes somnambulant—music like *Yusef Lateef's Little Symphony* (Atlantic), which won a Grammy for New Age in 1988. At the opposite extreme, he made four raucous CDs on YAL with a traditional rhythm section and guest saxophonists—Archie Shepp, Von Freeman, Ricky Ford, and Rene McLean. After 1994, Lateef dispensed with jazz conventions. He explored world music, speech rhythms, open forms, and an intervallic composing system he compared to an endophyte—an organism living within another organism. Sometimes he and Rudolph split an ensemble in two, each composing for half without knowing what the other was writing. These ideas bear fruit on *The World at Peace* (YAL/Meta) for an improvising chamber ensemble.

Much of Lateef's formal concert music remains unpublished and unrecorded. Lacking classical-world connections, Lateef was disheartened that he couldn't find conductors or orchestras to take up his symphonies; three of the four have never been played. His chamber music has fared better. The lucid and deeply felt 14-minute String Quartet no. 3—premiered posthumously in 2015 by the Momenta Quartet in New York—unfolds in four concentrated movements that evoke the expressionism of Bartok and Berg. But Lateef's fanciful gestures and development are his own. Intervals of a fourth and fifth play recurring roles, and violin melodies sigh with Middle Eastern modality. A burst of tonal melody and harmony near the end stirs the heart. (Video of the premiere is on YouTube.)

Lateef's last performance in Detroit was his 2007 jazz festival appearance when he brought down the house with his oboe blues. Ritual was in the air, and Lateef also recited poetry. When his spirit welled up, his tenor sound splintered into expressive squawks. One composition married a swampy Bayou shuffle with a West African chant, and his plaintive tenor echoed like field hollers. It reminded you that Lateef never stopped playing the blues, even when venturing a long way from the 12-bar form. They were as much a part of his DNA as Detroit.

Recommended Recordings

Yusef Lateef, *Into Something* (New Jazz)
Yusef Lateef, *Live at Pep's* (Impulse)
Yusef Lateef and Adam Rudolph, *The World at Peace* (YAL/Meta)

Notes

1. Some discographies say Lateef recorded with Wright in December 1948, but by then Lateef had left the band.

2. Richard Brent Turner, *Islam in the African-American Experience* (Indiana University Press, 1997).

3. Yusef Lateef with Herb Boyd, *The Gentle Giant: The Autobiography of Yusef Lateef* (Morton, 2006), 57.

4. The rabab is one of a family of Islamic instruments with multiple strings played with a bow—an Arabic fiddle. The one-string instrument that Ernie Farrow plays with Lateef is plucked, and it's likely either a form of rabab from Afghanistan that's plucked or a lute-like instrument from Central Asia called the rubab. These instruments are related and there are many alternate spellings, but no sources I consulted used "rabat," which is used on Lateef's LP covers. *New Harvard Dictionary of Music*, edited by Don Michael Randel (Belknap Press of Harvard University Press, 1986).

Milt Jackson

BAGS' GROOVE

A critic once suggested that if the Detroit-born vibraphonist Milt Jackson ever played an unswinging phrase he must have done so in private. But odds are that not even the woodshed heard Jackson trip over an awkward rhythm or improvise a melody that didn't bloom with lyricism or leave the scent of the blues hanging in the air. Jackson, who died in 1999 at age 76, was perhaps the most naturally swinging and soulful musician in jazz for decades.

Timing is everything in jazz, and Jackson's control of rhythm was legendary. He created drama through relaxation and contrast. He'd strike notes behind the beat and then dart ahead, climbing over the top of the pulse, before retreating to the backside of the beat. He personalized each note with its own articulation. Serpentine lines merged with repeated-note triplet jabs that cut like a scalpel. The result was a charged forward momentum that still felt nonchalant. Jackson's improvisations at medium and fast tempos were ebullient outbursts of bebop melody, sly grace notes, witty triplets, and blues allusions that hung on his phrases like Christmas ornaments. His ballads shivered with eroticism. The sound he drew from the vibes captured the warm vibrations of human feeling.

Jackson wasn't just riffing on common forms when he played a 12-bar blues or a standard ballad. He was speaking from his heart, telling stories that reaffirmed the African American aesthetics of jazz. The late cultural critic Albert Murray might have said that Jackson transformed black experience into high style and elegance, offering heroic affirmation in the face of adversity. Vibraphonist Warren Wolf put it more colloquially: "When Milt played the blues, it not only sounded good, it felt good, and it made you feel good too."

Jackson remains celebrated as an innovator, but he's also easy to take for granted. He brought modern jazz to the vibes and revolutionized the sound of the instrument by creating a vocal-like expression, and his influence

Milt Jackson performs with the Jimmy Wilkins Big Band at the Lansdowne in Detroit on August 20, 1990. Photo by Patricia Beck / Detroit Free Press.

remains inescapable. Yet his art did not fundamentally change through the years, and his recordings after the early '70s blur into a generic wash of similar groups and repertoire. He's still most widely known for his decades of service to the influential Modern Jazz Quartet, yet pianist-composer John Lewis drove the conception of the band. But make no mistake: Jackson's best work marks him as one of the greatest pure bebop improvisers begotten by Charlie Parker. The startling freshness of the six cliché-free choruses he plays on "True Blues" (1952), or his 1955 version of "I Should Care," whose embellishments, accents, and dynamics rise and fall like the breath of a lover, display a storyteller arc few soloists in any era can match.

"It was Milt Jackson who showed us all how the vibes could be an expressive instrument," said Gary Burton, who along with Bobby Hutcherson was one of the two most original post-Jackson vibraphonists to emerge in the '60s. "He sounded very vocal and horn-like. He used softer mallets and played in such a flowing way. I've always considered Milt the most important vibes player in history."

The vibraphone is an odd contraption. It has tuned aluminum bars laid out like piano keys. Resonating tubes hang below each bar. Inside each tube is a motorized disk that twirls to produce a wavering tremolo analogous to vibrato on a wind or string instrument; there is also a sustain pedal.[1] Red Norvo and Lionel Hampton liberated the vibraphone from vaudeville and taught it to swing in the 1930s. Jackson was the first vibraphonist to adapt the sleek melodic lines, complex syncopations, and chromaticism of bebop in the '40s. To better imitate the human voice, Jackson slowed down the motor speed of the disk from Hampton's 10 revolutions per second to about 3.3 revolutions per second. The result was a warm, vibrato-like quality, a slow pulsation of sound without the nervous twitching of earlier players. Jackson made the vibes sing.

"This comes about from me having a desire one day to be a singer," Jackson told critic Ralph J. Gleason in a 1959 interview.[2] "In singing I found out the slower you have the vibrato, and this applies to singers and instrumentalists as well, that if you slow it down it has much more feeling to it than, say, the mechanical sound of the vibraharp or a trumpet player with one of those fast vibratos."

Jackson spent years experimenting with instruments, tremolo speeds, and mallets. His mellifluous sound and style reached maturity in 1951–54, after he acquired the prewar Deagan "Imperial" model that became his primary instrument. Not all the instruments Jackson had access to in his early days had variable-speed motors or were easily adjustable. Joe Locke, a leading vibraphonist on today's scene, was told by older musicians that Jackson used to shove objects such as Popsicle sticks into the motor to slow it down, sometimes breaking the instrument. "The sheer will of having that sound in his head come forth into the world puts him in the rare company of sound innovators in this music," said Locke.

Jackson was slightly built with a pencil-thin mustache and handsome face that grew craggy as he aged. He earned his nickname, Bags, in Detroit when a friend took note of the large pouches under his eyes that sprouted after too many celebratory late nights in a row. Despite the high spirits of his music, Jackson's face carried a stern look as he played. He sometimes punctuated a felicitous note or phrase by quickly looking up at the audience as if to say: *Did you get that?* "Jazz is an art, but it's in the form of an entertaining art," he told Whitney Balliett in *The New Yorker* in 1971. "I'm most relaxed in the blues or in ballads, which are my criterion. I get the most results for myself then, and I reach the audience quicker."

Those who knew Jackson say he was a man of few words—smart but streetwise. He liked to play pool and cards. He liked to cook and bake cobblers. He liked to listen to other soulful musicians play the blues. One day in the 1990s, Jackson's quartet was relaxing at the Pittsburgh home of drummer Joe Harris, whose living room was crammed with percussion instruments. Jackson was in the kitchen when a good-time blues by pianist Ray Bryant came on the radio. "What's that!?" yelled Jackson. He sprinted from the kitchen, picked up mallets and started playing along on the vibes. "He had to get a taste of that groove," said Mike LeDonne, Jackson's pianist at the time. "I never knew anyone who loved swinging as much as that guy."

Jackson could be gruff with people he didn't know, and he could hold a grudge if he felt disrespected. In Gary Burton's first national interview in *Downbeat* in 1964 he was quoted saying that he didn't think any vibes player, including Jackson, was in the same class as Miles Davis, John Coltrane, Sonny Rollins, Bill Evans, or Stan Getz. "If Milt played any other instrument at the same level, he wouldn't be a name musician," Burton told the magazine.

Jackson was livid. Burton writes in his 2013 autobiography, *Learning to Listen*, that a few months later he and Jackson found themselves playing the same festival in Chicago. Jackson's tour manager asked if he could use Burton's vibes. Jackson played first, and as he came off stage he turned to Burton and said, "Let's see what you can do, motherfucker!" Burton writes that Jackson hated him for decades and that the tension only dissipated when both men were booked on the same jazz cruise and pianist Cedar Walton pushed Jackson to make peace.[3] Burton and Jackson eventually became friendly enough that they played some gigs together.

Milton Jackson was born in Detroit on January 1, 1923. He was the second of six boys born to parents who had come north from Georgia and North Carolina. He grew up in Black Bottom and attended the Church of God in Christ, a sanctified church that featured exultant gospel music. Jackson always credited church music as the source of his affinity for the blues. His father worked in auto plants and played several instruments, and all the children sang and played something. The family sang blessings before meals in harmony. Jackson took up guitar at age 7, and he took two years of piano lessons starting at 11. He had perfect pitch and knew immediately he wanted a life in music.

Jackson absorbed jazz from the radio. At Miller High School he played five instruments—drums in the marching band, timpani and violin in the symphony, guitar and xylophone in the dance band. He also sang in the choir and learned to play bass. Jackson's classmates in the dance band included older brother Alvin, a bassist, as well as trombonist Frank Rosolino and drummer Art Mardigan. It's a measure of how seriously music was regarded in Detroit schools that Miller acquired a set of vibes, a rarity for any high school in the 1930s, much less a predominately black school. One day in 1938 the band director, Louis Cabrera, asked his versatile pupil if he wanted to try the new instrument. "I got hung up on it immediately," Jackson told Balliett. "I gave up the drums and concentrated on the vibes."

Jackson kept singing a little longer. In 1939 he performed briefly with a gospel quartet that broadcast every Sunday on CKLW in Windsor, Ontario, just across the Detroit River. He also sang around town on gigs. Jackson's father bought his son a set of vibes in 1939. It was made by Jenco and was small enough to fold up in a case that looked like an ironing board. The set had a variable speed control, which allowed Jackson to experiment. He was inspired by hearing Lionel Hampton at the Michigan State Fair around 1940 but wasn't influenced by his style.

Jackson played gigs in the area with bandleader George E. Lee and led his own group as early as 1942. Drafted, he spent two years stateside in the Air Force, returning to Detroit in 1944. He organized one of the city's most progressive early modern jazz groups, the Four Sharps, with guitarist Emmett Slay, bassist Millard Glover, and pianist Willie Anderson. With Mardigan joining on drums, the quintet backed tenor saxophone titan Coleman Hawkins at the Detroit Institute of Arts in February 1945 and a month later accompanied Dizzy Gillespie. Jackson told interviewers that a turning point was Gillespie hearing him at a jam session at the Bizerte, though it's unclear when this occurred. But with Gillespie's encouragement, Jackson moved to New York in October 1945 and joined the trumpeter's band.

By the end of year, Jackson was on tour in Los Angeles with Gillespie's sextet including Charlie Parker. Jackson called sharing the bandstand with Parker among his greatest experiences. One night in the middle of "Round Midnight," Jackson burst into tears. "I was just so deeply moved listening to this man play that there was no other reaction I could get," Jackson told Gleason.

Jackson was ubiquitous during the first wave of bebop. He toured and recorded with Gillespie's big bands and small groups for three years, worked with Parker on 52nd Street and recorded with Thelonious Monk,

Howard McGhee, Fats Navarro, Sonny Stitt, Tadd Dameron, Ray Brown, and Hawkins. Jackson made his recording debut in December 1945 with singer Dinah Washington and an octet led by his friend from Detroit, Lucky Thompson. Jackson's records with Gillespie in the mid-'40s show a command of bebop melody, but his rhythmic gait is herky-jerky. His beat-up vibes and hard mallets produced a crackling tone that Gillespie likened to the sound of milk bottles. Jackson had made significant progress by the time he recorded for Dial in December 1947 with a sextet led by the Detroit-raised trumpeter McGhee and featuring two additional Motor City musicians—Hank Jones and J. C. Heard. On "Night Music," a thinly veiled version of "Body and Soul," Jackson's phrases are legato and relaxed, and he improvises a magnificent eight-bar bridge. Still, his tone is brittle, his tremolo fidgety. Jackson's first four sides as a leader, cut in Detroit in April 1948 for Sensation, show increasing confidence but similar tonal qualities.

More crucial are the records he made in 1948 and 1951 as a sideman with Monk on Blue Note. Jackson's sound is rounder, and the bracing marriage of his sturdy lyricism and Monk's jabbing piano has a stark beauty that still packs an avant-garde punch 70 years later—especially on Monk's seminal songs "Misterioso," "Evidence," "I Mean You," and "Epistrophy." Jackson and Monk would also appear together on the 1954 Miles Davis session on Prestige that includes the definitive recording of Jackson's anthemic blues "Bags' Groove."

After working about year with Woody Herman, Jackson rejoined Gillespie's small group in 1950, playing vibes and piano. Jackson even sang with Gillespie on "Time on My Hands" (1951), though his voice is thin and off-pitch. He sounds only marginally better on two later vocal LPs, *Milt Jackson Sings* (1964) and *Soul Believer* (1978). Caveat emptor.

The Modern Jazz Quartet began taking shape in 1951 when Jackson led two sessions for Dee Gee, the label Gillespie started in Detroit with his friend Dave Usher, who worked in his family's oil reclamation business.[4] Jackson was joined on one session by John Lewis, Ray Brown, and Kenny Clarke—the rhythm section from the 1946 Gillespie orchestra. The chemistry was strong, but Brown was too busy to commit, so bassist Percy Heath was recruited. The quartet legally incorporated as a cooperative in early 1952. When Clarke left for Europe in 1955, he was replaced by Connie Kay—the last personnel change until Kay's death in 1994. The MJQ stayed together 22 straight years, until Jackson's desire to strike out on his own split up the group in 1974. The quartet reunited periodically from the early 1980s through 1997.

With Lewis as music director and primary composer, the MJQ was a chamber ensemble whose disciplined marriage of composition and improvisation posited an alternative to the theme-solos-theme structure of most small-group jazz. Lewis' meticulously plotted scores like the alluring "Django" and Bach-inspired "Vendome" relied on multi-sectioned construction, counterpoint, and dynamics. The heart of the ensemble was the creative tension between Lewis' Apollonian elegance and order and Jackson's Dionysian fire and spontaneity.

Jackson spent the rest of his career in two worlds. In the Lewis-dominated MJQ, he was an actor playing a role. Meanwhile, he recorded prolifically under his own name and led bands that favored unbridled swinging and unfussy blues, bebop, and ballads. No group lasts more than four decades if the players don't fundamentally get along or respect each other. But Jackson had mixed emotions about the MJQ that intensified over time. He felt constrained by Lewis' aesthetic, and in the 1990s would refer to MJQ tours as "going back to prison." These are complicated issues. To hear Jackson cut loose, turn to his own records. The MJQ can sound stuffy and precious if you're not in the mood; Lewis' insistent accompaniment can overcrowd the vibes. But no one should dismiss the unified artistry of the MJQ's best work, or Lewis' innovations with form and his skills as a melodist and spare bluesman. Sometimes Jackson's electrifying solos are all the more effective for emerging from within Lewis' scaffolding. Examples include "Delaunay's Dilemma," an "I Got Rhythm" swinger (1953); "The Comedy," an ambitious suite inspired by commedia dell'arte (1962); and "Jazz Ostinato," a Third Stream mélange of classical music and jazz with orchestra (1973). The most rewarding MJQ surveys are two live albums for Atlantic, *European Concert* (1960) and *The Last Concert* (1974).

The MJQ's dignified aura, from custom tuxedoes to the scrim of classical music, broke down racial stereotypes. It was the first modern American jazz group to play many of the leading European concert halls, and it commanded fees and mainstream acceptance denied other modern black jazz musicians. The MJQ afforded Jackson an enviable income and stability rare in jazz. He had a house built in the early '70s in a well-to-do, integrated section of Scarsdale, New York, where he lived with his wife and daughter. The MJQ was among the best-paid groups in jazz. In 1973, for example, the quartet received $2,700 for a concert at the University of Michigan in Ann Arbor—plus another $300 for a lecture-demonstration, according to university records. That's about $17,500 in 2018 dollars. Even with 25% likely taken off the top for management and booking, that's an impressive payday.

Still, Jackson thought the MJQ should have made more. He announced his departure in September 1974. "We should have had a least a million dollars in assets," he complained to Len Lyons in *Downbeat* in 1975. Jackson said he didn't necessarily think he could do better on his own, but if he wasn't going to make what he deserved, he'd rather play music he truly wanted to play. At 52, Jackson resented the lack of radio and record industry promotion accorded jazz musicians, particularly black players. Lewis told the *Los Angeles Times* that the MJQ had made a good living and it was unrealistic to compare the income of jazz artists with the millions flowing to popular entertainers. When the MJQ resumed performing part time in 1981, its fees rose to reflect its legendary status. Records kept by the Chamber Music Society of Detroit show that the quartet received $20,000 to perform at Orchestra Hall in 1996. The society paid the Tokyo String Quartet $9,500 that same season.

Most of the essentials of Jackson's mammoth discography as a leader are concentrated in the 1950s and '60s. *Milt Jackson Quartet* (Prestige) from 1955 remains imperative, particularly for the aforementioned "I Should Care." Jackson's Savoy recordings yielded sublime music, especially *The Jazz Skyline* and *Jackson's-Ville* (1956) with Lucky Thompson's sumptuous tenor and the divine trio of Hank Jones, Wendell Marshall, and Kenny Clarke. Of Jackson's diverse LPs for Atlantic, the tête-à-tête with Coleman Hawkins (1958) trumps more celebrated meetings with John Coltrane and Ray Charles. *The Ballad Artistry of Milt Jackson* (1959) delivers poetry with strings smartly arranged by Quincy Jones and Jimmy Jones. On Riverside, *Bags Meets Wes* (1961) pairs him with guitarist Wes Montgomery, whose blues feeling and swing are closely related to Jackson's own. *Invitation* (1962) and *Live at the Village Gate* (1963) are also a cut above.

In the early '70s, Jackson signed with producer Creed Taylor's CTI, the most commercially savvy jazz label of the era. CTI made hay with high production values, slick packaging, and shrewd concepts that gave established stars crossover appeal without mortgaging their integrity. The approach wasn't always successful, but *Sunflower* (1972) is among the finest CTI dates—a well-paced concept LP exploring a dusky moodiness. Don Sebesky's atmospheric strings and winds enhance committed work by Jackson and a fashionable group of young stars—Freddie Hubbard, Herbie Hancock, Ron Carter, Billy Cobham.

Jackson jumped to Pablo in 1975, where owner-producer Norman Granz favored studio blowing dates, live jam sessions, and a small circle of mainstream label mates. If Taylor's weakness was overproduction, Granz's flaw was underproduction. But *Soul Fusion* (1977) with the Monty Alexander Trio emits sparks. Of Jackson's late recordings on the Qwest label, *Sa Va Bella* (1997) captures the familial spirit of his working quartet with Mike LeDonne, Bob Cranshaw, and Mickey Roker, plus guest vocalist Etta Jones. *Explosion* (1998) with the Clayton-Hamilton Jazz Orchestra features spirited soloing over roaring charts by John Clayton.

Jackson's playing never slipped with age. Colleagues say he could be jetlagged and sleeping backstage but wake up on a moment's notice and sound like a million bucks. Just 11 months before his death from liver cancer in 1999, Jackson recorded a heroic a cappella version of "Nature Boy" issued on *The Very Tall Band* (Telarc). His final appearance in Detroit was the 1996 MJQ concert at Orchestra Hall. Jackson played passionate solos that gave off the heat of red-hot embers, and the hometown audience cheered. After a bravura solo on "Bags' Groove," Jackson looked up to greet the wild applause, and his steely expression broke into a wide grin.

Recommended Recordings

Milt Jackson, *Milt Jackson Quartet* (Prestige)
Milt Jackson, *Milt Jackson Quintet & Sextet with Lucky Thompson: Complete Savoy and Atlantic Sessions* (Fresh Sounds)
Milt Jackson, *Sunflower* (CTI)

Notes

1. Patrick Edward Roilet, "Milt Jackson: The Creative Genius Behind Bags' Groove," PhD diss., University of Washington, 2002, 23–24. Roilet also summarizes the history: Two companies introduced mallet instruments with motors in the 1920s. Leedy Manufacturing was first with its steel-bar "vibraphone," followed by J.C. Deagan Inc.'s "vibraharp" with aluminum bars and other refinements. "Vibraphone" and "vibes" assumed common currency, though Jackson often said "vibraharp" in deference to his Deagan instrument.

2. Ralph J. Gleason, *Conversations in Jazz: The Ralph J. Gleason Interviews* (Yale University Press, 2016).

3. Gary Burton: *Learning to Listen: The Jazz Journey of Gary Burton* (Berklee Press, 2013).

4. Dee Gee folded in 1953. By early 1958, Usher was producing jazz records in Chicago for Argo, a subsidiary of Chess Records. He returned to Detroit in 1960 and subsequently transformed his father's oil reclamation business into Marine Pollution Control, a leading oil and hazardous waste clean-up company that made its name in the industry by cleaning up the Exxon Valdez spill in Alaska in 1989.

Sheila Jordan

SHEILA'S BLUES

If it wasn't for jazz music I wouldn't be alive today
—SHEILA JORDAN, LYRIC TO "SHEILA'S BLUES"

Sheila Jordan reached a crossroads in 1987. The Detroit-born singer was 58 and known to a small cadre of musicians and insiders as a treasure of unconventional expression and magical spontaneity. She was also only recently sober, after decades of alcohol abuse and a short but intense battle with cocaine. A single mother, Jordan had worked for more than 20 years as a typist at Doyle Dane Bernbach, a Manhattan advertising agency. She used her vacation time for sporadic touring and recording. But now the agency was merging with another company, and she had a choice: She could stay on as a roving secretary or she could retire with a year's severance pay.

"I started to cry," Jordan said in 2011. "I was so upset. I thought, 'Oh my God, I'm losing my job. I don't think I want to float around from office to office.' Then a voice said to me real clear, 'You've been praying that you'd sing more, so shut up and take the money and run!'"

For nearly all of the next 40 years, Jordan, who died in 2025 at age 96, traveled the world performing, recording, and teaching. Once a cult figure, she entered the pantheon. In 2012, at 83, she was named a Jazz Master by the National Endowment for the Arts. The nation's highest honor in jazz, the $25,000 prize put an exclamation point on the autumnal flowering of her career. It was a warm hug from the establishment after a lifetime in the shadows, where she overcame an impoverished childhood, bigotry, drink and drugs, abusive men, and hardships of the jazz life. She willed herself into greatness.

There was no sound in jazz quite like Jordan in her prime. She transformed an unlikely featherweight soprano into a gossamer instrument, dancing unpredictably through time and pitch like a butterfly riding a gust of wind. She phrased like a horn. Her primary influences were instrumentalists, especially alto saxophonist Charlie Parker, the Prometheus of be-

Sheila Jordan in a New York club in 1953 with fellow Detroit musicians Doug Watkins, *left*, and Barry Harris, *right*. Photo courtesy Sheila Jordan.

bop, who dubbed her the kid with the million-dollar ears when she was a teenager in Detroit in the 1940s. Jordan improvised on many levels, slyly bending the familiar lyrics of a standard into fresh melodic shapes. Sometimes she made up new lyrics on the spot, turning an ad-lib blues into a charmingly discursive ramble. She was an irrepressible swinger and an elite scat singer. Her taste for adventurous improvisation made her a kind of white twin to Betty Carter (1929–98), an African American and the other influential postwar jazz vocalist from Detroit.

Unlike some jazz singers who get so hung up trying to improvise that they make a mess of a song's meaning, Jordan's variations almost always deepen the intent of a lyric rather than obscure it. Even at 90, with age having taken a toll on the once-pristine purity of her voice and intonation, she could bring listeners to tears with a ballad. Exactly how she did this was a mystery, though the answer had something to do with the beguiling alchemy of her plainspoken honesty, narrative instincts, and the authority of her time and phrasing.

Bassist Steve Swallow remembered a moment with Jordan around 1960 at the Page Three, a dimly lit gay bar on Seventh Avenue in Greenwich Village. The tune was "I'm a Fool to Want You," an essay in the dangers of desperate love. "I was just playing the roots of the chords on the downbeats, and all of a sudden, I just burst into uncontrolled sobs," said Swallow. "That had never happened before, and it completely blindsided me. To this day that's a very important and profound experience for me but one I don't really understand. I've choked up more than once playing with her. Sheila tells the story of a song with such poignancy that I find myself listening and becoming involved with the words. She draws you into the narrative. She takes extraordinary chances and liberties, but she never distorts the meaning of the tune or the musical line. It has the integrity of a Roman arch; from point A to point B the tension is perfectly sustained. It's a high-wire act, and she never does fall."

At times I wonder where my life would be if I'd never heard the music of Bird back when I was just a kid.

—SHEILA JORDAN, LYRIC TO "QUASIMODO"

Jordan talked about her life and music one afternoon in 2011 while sitting at the dining room table in the same rent-controlled, one-bedroom apartment on 18th Street in the Chelsea neighborhood of Manhattan where she lived since 1964. An upright piano backed against the wall, and there was an assortment of moody oil paintings and photographs, including one of Parker and several of her daughter, Tracey Jordan, a marketing consultant and publicist. Tracey is the product of a brief marriage in the '50s to Parker's onetime pianist Duke Jordan, an African American. Since 1981, Jordan also owned a modest farmhouse upstate about 40 miles from Albany, where she recharged her batteries. Jordan stood just a little over 5 feet tall, her round face framed by dark hair in a 1950s pageboy cut. She wore black pants and a green sweater with red ladybugs on it, and there was an amusing dissonance between her grandmotherly countenance, girlish speaking voice, and hipster vocabulary: "You know that song 'Chasin' the Bird'? That really was our scene, man!"

Sheila Jeanette Dawson was born to a 17-year-old mother at home on a Murphy bed in Detroit on November 18, 1928. She shared her birthday with Mickey Mouse, who made his official debut in *Steamboat Willie*, released the same day. Jordan's father was not in the picture. Her mother was unable to care for her, so she was sent to live with her grandparents in Summerhill, Pennsylvania, a coal-mining hamlet in the Allegheny Mountains. The family was large, dirt poor, and riddled with alcoholism. The electricity was forever being turned off for unpaid bills. There was an outhouse and no running water inside the house. Jordan, who always spoke with a bit of an Appalachian twang, sang from the age of 3, mostly to chase the blues away. She returned to Detroit at 14, but life was precarious with an alcoholic mother and abusive stepfather who beat up her mom. When he began eyeing Jordan, fondling her, she moved out at 17 into a home for young women and finished school while working part time. Jordan started high school at Cass Tech, but transferred after a year to the High School of Commerce, a sister school next door, where she studied secretarial skills.

Jordan had already been singing hit parade tunes in talent shows and on the radio when one day in 1946 she dropped a nickel in the jukebox at a burger joint. She saw a song that looked interesting by a band listed as Charlie Parker and his Reboppers. It was the newly minted "Now's The Time," an urtext of bebop. Parker plays an electric solo, filled with swooping blues ideas and crystalline double time. "I heard four notes, man, and I gotta tell you my heart was about to jump out of my throat, and the hair rose up on my arms and I felt faint," said Jordan. "That was *it*. That was the music I was destined to sing."

Jordan devoured Parker's records as if they were chocolate. She started singing along with the melodies and improvisations, and it wasn't long before she was able to correlate bebop tunes with the standards upon which their harmonies were based—she recognized that "Ornithology" had the same structure as "How High the Moon," that "Donna Lee" was based on "Back Home Again in Indiana," and that "Anthropology" was based on "I Got Rhythm."

She became friends with Barry Harris, Tommy Flanagan, and Kenny Burrell, and she hung out at the Club Sudan, a Paradise Valley spot friendly to minors because it didn't sell booze. She met young black singers Skeeter Spight and Leroy Mitchell, who were already putting words to bebop melodies and scat singing in the style. Soon they were a trio: Skeeter, Mitch, and Jean (from Jordan's middle name). Jordan's repertoire still includes songs from those days like "Little Willie Leaps" and "Confirmation," with lyrics by Spight and Mitchell.

When Parker came to town, Jordan would doll herself up in red lipstick, grab her mother's birth certificate and some unfiltered Lucky Strikes, and try to sneak past the doorman. One night the owner of El Sino told her, "You better go home little white girl and do your homework or I'm going to get in trouble." Undeterred, Jordan and her buddies snuck around back to the alley, where Parker opened the stage door so they could hear the music. The first time Jordan sat in with Parker, she crooned one of his songs right into his ear. He responded by telling her that she had "million-dollar ears."

Parker was a genius but also a junkie who burned out like a comet at age 34. Like many who knew him well, Jordan remembered a gentlemanly, fiercely intelligent man, well-versed in all the arts and always dressed in a suit and tie. It was Parker who introduced her to modern painters and dropped off records by Bartok and Stravinsky at her loft. It was Parker who sent a car to take a pregnant Jordan back and forth from his gigs. "He'd announce a tune and he'd use words this long," Jordan said, opening her arms wide. "They have such stories about him, that he turned everybody on to drugs, but that is so wrong. I remember after I was with Duke in New York and Bird came up to the loft one time. Duke was nodding out on the couch and Bird said, 'Man, didn't you learn anything from me?'"

From an early age Jordan identified more with African Americans than her white peers. In Summerhill she was teased mercilessly by white kids about her family's poverty; the sting raised her awareness of discrimination. Falling in love with jazz deepened her cultural identity as black. She was accepted by black musicians from the outset but hassled constantly by racist cops and others who couldn't stomach a white woman singing or socializing with black men. Jordan and Barry Harris were once chased by thugs bent on violence and narrowly escaped by hopping on a streetcar. There were scores of incidents with the police, and she lost count of the number of times she was dragged in for questioning.

Racial tension was particularly high in Detroit in those days. Thousands of Southern blacks and whites had migrated to the city for war jobs, precipitating a housing crisis. Yet city fathers refused to integrate public housing. White workers struck the Packard Motor war plants in early June 1943 because blacks were hired to work next to them. By the end of the month, three days of race riots would result in 34 deaths. In a report on the violence, the army general in charge of restoring order lambasted the Detroit police for their "harsh and brutal" treatment of blacks. In the wake of all this, Jordan began a romantic relationship with black saxophonist Frank Foster in 1950. Jordan and Foster were soon living together in his apartment. One day Foster and Jordan and another interracial couple were driving to a picnic when two detectives stopped the car.

"I had a cigarette and I threw it out the window and this cop crawled under the car to get that cigarette to smell it, because he thought I was smoking dope," Jordan said. "They took us down to the station, separated us from the men, and started giving us the third degree. I was really angry, but I tried to be cool. My friend Jenny didn't say much of anything, but I was mouthy. The cop said to me, 'I want your number. What is your mother's number?' I said, 'I don't live with my mother.' And I'll never forget what he said as long as I live. He said, 'You see this gun in my holster? I have a nine-year-old daughter at home, and if I thought I was gonna find her the way I found you two tonight, I would take this gun home and blow her brains out.'"

In later years, when Jordan saw an interracial couple with a stroller, she always approached them and said, "What a beautiful family!" She smiled, and they smiled back.

"You are my sunshine, my only sunshine."
—OLD-TIME COUNTRY BALLAD

Jordan moved to New York near the start of 1952. She worked as a typist to put food on the table, and she married Duke Jordan in 1953. His addiction to heroin and womanizing doomed the marriage, and he abandoned her after their daughter was born in 1955. Meanwhile, she studied music with pianist Lennie Tristano, and in 1958 she landed a weekly gig at the Page Three. Soon the job expanded to two nights a week. Jordan would sing until 4:00 a.m. and pocket six dollars, half of which went to the babysitter. She'd get two or three hours of sleep before taking Tracey to nursery school and going to work. "Sheila was magic," pianist Dave Frishberg wrote in his online memoirs about the Page Three. "The customers would stop gabbing and all the entertainers would turn their attention to Sheila and the whole place would be under her spell."

One night the progressive composer-pianist George Russell heard Jordan and was smitten with her musically and personally. They started dating, and he financed a demo recording and brought her to the attention of Blue Note. That led to her first LP in 1962, the classic *Portrait of Sheila*, with guitarist Barry Galbraith, bassist Steve Swallow, and drummer Denzil Best.[1] The astonishing performances are as concentrated as espresso.

Rodgers and Hart's "Falling in Love with Love" lasts just two and a half minutes. Jordan swings through three uninterrupted choruses, her rhythms bouncing off Swallow's bass line as if it were a trampoline. Her improvised variations stray farther and farther from the original melody with each 32-bar frame. By the third chorus she's leaping octaves, leaning hard into the blues and recomposing the song on the spot. She italicizes the knowing cynicism of the lyric—"falling in love with love is playing the fool"—recognizing that the heart operates independently of the mind. Tadd Dameron's "If You Could See Me Now" is another miracle. Jordan adopts a daringly slow tempo and delivers the gorgeous melody and anguished lyrics (by Carl Sigman) in a confessional whisper. The rainbowlike substitute harmonies the band plays were devised by pianist Bill Evans. He wrote them out for Jordan on a cocktail napkin at a club.

Russell and Jordan traveled to Pennsylvania to see her family. One night they went to a beer garden where a coal miner asked her to sing a song from her childhood, "You Are My Sunshine." Russell was so taken with Jordan's approach that he devised a surreal, concerto-like setting for the song on *The Outer View* (Riverside) in 1962. It's full of ghostly dissonance, shifting tempos, and elusive flashes of melody and improvisation that suggest recovered memories. Halfway through the 12-minute performance, the band stops. Jordan enters alone, soft as cotton, stretching the tune almost to its breaking point. She builds with the band, cresting with chilly long notes sung without vibrato. Her vulnerability destroys. "Every time I sing a song that I might have sung a million times, I always feel like it's the first time," she said. "I don't know what does it. I think it's just trusting the rhythm section or other instrumentalists. I never force improvisation. If I don't feel it in my gut or heart, I'd rather sing what's there."

Jordan's first recordings attracted laudatory critical attention, including a feature in *Downbeat* in May 1963. For a couple years she was able to work a little more in New York clubs. But attention faded, and Jordan wouldn't make a second record under her own name until 1975—a 13-year gap that took her from age 34 to 47. It's a tragedy that such a large chunk of her prime vocal years went undocumented. One blessed exception is a 25-minute program recorded in 1971 for Norwegian television in which Jordan leads a quintet with Jan Garbarek, Bobo Stenson, Arild Andersen, and Jon Christensen. Jordan is in fantastic form, singing a suite-like program of songs related to children. Her expressive freedom moves well beyond her bebop roots.

In many ways, however, Jordan remained too sophisticated for the room. But slowly the winds changed in her favor. Her flexibility landed her in post-bop and avant-garde circles with pianist-composer Carla Bley, trombonist Roswell Rudd, and the George Gruntz Concert Big Band. *Sheila*, a 1977 duet record with bassist Arild Andersen (SteepleChase), marks a breakthrough. It's a risky format, leaving no place to hide. Singing standards and contemporary originals, Jordan reaches for the stars. At 48, she is in complete control over her pitch and vibrato. The duet setting with bass became her trademark and led to later performances and recordings with either Harvie Swartz or Detroit-born Cameron Brown. By the end of the '70s, Jordan was singing arty contemporary material with pianist Steve Kuhn's quartet and reuniting on record with Swallow, with whom she sang intriguing settings of poetry by Robert Creeley. The records Jordan made for ECM with Kuhn (especially *Last Year's Waltz*) and Swallow (*Home*) are landmarks for adding to the small amount of vocal jazz that treats the singer like another horn rather than the focal point. "She always insisted that she wanted to be just part of the group," Kuhn said.

If you search beyond the madness, there is peace of mind to gain
—SHEILA JORDAN, LYRIC TO "THE CROSSING"

The 1970s were also when Jordan began to deal with the demons of addiction and low self-esteem that fueled problems, including a penchant for ending up in mentally or physically abusive relationships—the gentlemanly Foster and Russell being notable exceptions. Jordan believed she inherited her drinking problem from her mother. Jordan was never an everyday drinker, but binges on the weekend led to blackouts. She stopped drinking around 1975 and, after a relapse, quit again in 1977. But she soon filled the gap with cocaine. "I thought you couldn't get hooked on it," Jordan said. "Yeah, right! I just changed seats on the *Titanic*." With the help of Alcoholics Anonymous, she finally sobered up completely in the mid-'80s, shortly before taking her company's severance package.

Jordan worked constantly after turning 60. Where she was once shy on stage, standing like a statue, she began to joke easily with audiences. Her singing became more rococo in recent decades, especially when she scatted. The most potent of her later recordings date to the 1980s and early '90s, including *Old Time Feeling* (Palo Alto) and *The Crossing* (Black Hawk).

Despite various maladies, Jordan remained a road warrior into her mid-90s. She spent her 90th birthday performing overseas in London, the climax of a 25-day European tour that took her to 11 cities in seven countries. She celebrated her 96th birthday by singing at Birdland in New York, and she released a new album in early 2025, *Portrait Now* (Dot Time), her 26th as a leader. Jordan never became a big star, but she made a steady living singing jazz and influenced multiple generations of singers. "I don't do this music to be known," she said. "I do this music to keep it alive. I don't want to do this music out of anger or resentment. My calling is that Bird gave me this message as a young kid in Detroit, and I said I'm going to dedicate my life to this music."

Recommended Recordings

Sheila Jordan, *Portrait of Sheila* (Blue Note)
Sheila Jordan, *Sheila* (SteepleChase)
Steve Kuhn, *Last Year's Waltz* (ECM)

Note

1. In 2021, Capri Records issued *Comes Love: Lost Session 1960*, a previously unissued recording Jordan made on June 10, 1960, during her tenure at the Page Three. An astounding discovery, the music captures a 31-year-old Jordan more than two years before her Blue Note debut and in the throes of discovering her maturity. Accompanied by an unidentified rhythm section, Jordan's improvisatory phrasing turns ballads such as "These Foolish Things" and "Glad to Be Unhappy" into devasting and layered essays of lost love. The swingers enrapture. Her opening phrase on "They Can't Take That Away From Me" floats abstractly over the beat in the manner of Sonny Rollins—a frisson of emotion. Jordan soars, and so does a listener's spirit.

Barry Harris

PROFESSOR OF BEBOP

On the Upper West Side of Manhattan, just beyond the shadow of the bejeweled Juilliard School, sits the Lincoln Square Community Center. For many years this scruffy neighborhood gathering place was the home of the longest-running master class in jazz. Barry Harris, the Detroit-born pianist and professor of bebop, taught in some fashion or another since he was a precocious sage in Detroit in the 1950s. When I visited his class on a Tuesday night in 2000, he had been in residence at the community center for more than a decade.

Harris was the foremost bebop muse on the planet for decades before his death at age 91 in 2021. He spent his career channeling the spirit of Charlie Parker, Dizzy Gillespie, Thelonious Monk, and Bud Powell through his own foxy wit, vivid harmonic imagination, distinctive rhythmic rumble, and individual phrasing. He worked or recorded with everyone from Lester Young and Coleman Hawkins to Sonny Stitt, Cannonball Adderley, Dexter Gordon, and Lee Morgan. Less well-known, however, is his role as a legendary teacher. Harris codified the modern jazz language into an integrated system and, like a swinging Socrates, has guided students for more than 60 years in a quest for truth, beauty, and the hippest chords to play on "Embraceable You." Harris' influence in Detroit at midcentury was definitive. His teaching was a critical component in the city becoming a world-class factory for modern jazz musicians. Baritone saxophonist Pepper Adams spoke for all the young talent in Detroit when he told *Downbeat* in 1957, "I couldn't begin to tell you how much I've learned from him. I call him Uncle Barry."

Harris taught thousands of students in New York and workshops all over the world. To watch him in action was to witness the oral tradition at its most profound. Students drawn to Harris were freshly minted graduates from overly starched music schools, young musicians getting it together, midcareer pros searching for new avenues of expression, and middle-age

Barry Harris teaches at his weekly class at the Lincoln Square Community Center in New York in August 2000. The student pianist is Itay Goren. Photo by Susan Tusa / Detroit Free Press.

amateurs with a passion for jazz and the camaraderie of the class. They came because of Harris' charisma and because his system arrived with Talmudic authority. In an age in which the traditional apprentice system in jazz collapsed, Harris remained a direct link to the masters. In 2000, students showed up at the community center in waves: pianists at 6:30 p.m., singers at 8:30, and horn players at 10:30. They paid $8 for the night, plus a one-time registration fee of $30. (Classes today cost $10, plus an annual registration fee of $45.) The space was large and hollow like a gymnasium with dingy light, a concrete floor, and two baby grand pianos pushed to one side like orphaned twins.

As the clock ticked past 6:40, Yoko Kawaguchi, a recent graduate of Indiana University, moved to a piano and began to play "Over the Rainbow." Harris cocked his ear, shuffled over to the piano bench, and took a seat next to her. A dozen other pianists huddled around them, some standing on chairs. Tape recorders were turned on. Manuscript paper was readied. Class was in session, though even Harris didn't yet know the agenda. Kawaguchi worked carefully through the song, measuring each phrase like a cook wedded to a recipe. When Harris heard a missed opportunity to add a new spice—to improvise—his hands darted to the keyboard. He played a clever descending sequence of diminished and dominant arpeggios that excited a transition with flavor and texture.

Kawaguchi smiled. She copied the notes, tripping at first. Harris repeated the idea slower. Back and forth they went, Harris making up variations, exploring the problem from several angles. "OK, get up," he said. The other students took turns playing the sequence. An hour passed. "Each class takes on its own shape," said pianist Michael Weiss, a longtime Harris friend. "Barry puts something on the table and says, 'Let's solve this together.'"

Harris had an analytical mind. He was a whiz at crossword puzzles and Scrabble, and he once said if he hadn't pursued music he might have become a math teacher. He was fascinated with the nuts and bolts of harmony—the bittersweet lyricism of chords layered on top of each other, voice-leading, and finding new harmonic colors to apply to songs the way a painter like Bonnard might use six shades of red in a landscape. The relationship between chords and scales was another favorite topic. "A scale gives you movement," he told the class, repeating a lesson learned from Coleman Hawkins. "Don't play chords, play movements."

Soon the class turned into a game of stump the teacher. Weiss, who had stopped by to say hello, found himself drafted into the colloquium. "Have you thought of this?" Weiss asked. He fingered a series of complex chords derived from a minor scale. Harris looked puzzled. "Don't say nothing!" he said, cutting Weiss off before he could explain. Harris played the sequence, savoring each odd consonance like sips of an exotic wine.

Around 9:00 p.m. the following day, Harris downed sushi at a Japanese restaurant on Eighth Avenue while outlining the broad strokes of his life. He broke into a gap-toothed grin. "I must be the dumbest kid in the class because I've been in it the longest," he said in a gentle baritone. "I'm the biggest thief in the class because I steal from everybody."

Harris had hunched shoulders, a high forehead, a drooping bottom lip, and puppy eyes that peer above glasses. His hair, full on the sides, thin on top, was ivory white like his mustache and beard. He had a humble presence, and his passion for teaching was the flip side of a lifelong quest for self-improvement. He started taking classical piano lessons again in the 1970s and kept at it for decades; his notable teachers included Vladimir Padwa, Joseph Prostakoff, and Sophia Rosoff. "The more I learn, the more

I can see where Bird, Bud, Diz, and those cats didn't do it all," he said. "You need to learn the rules, so you can bend the rules and extend the rules and come up with new answers."

Harris was barely into his 20s when he began to mentor slightly younger players like Paul Chambers, Doug Watkins, Donald Byrd, Curtis Fuller, and Pepper Adams. His second wave of students included Charles McPherson, Lonnie Hillyer, Roy Brooks, and Joe Henderson. Yusef Lateef studied with Harris. So did future Motown bassist James Jamerson and countless others in Detroit. As Harris' reputation grew, musicians traveling through town stopped by to see what he was up to. McPherson recalls seeing Sonny Rollins and John Coltrane at Harris' home on separate occasions in the mid-'50s. Coltrane pulled a chair up to the piano one afternoon and asked Harris, "What is it you're doing these days?"

"Barry basically said that he'd been thinking about the dominant seventh chord—the V chord," said McPherson. "And that when you solo over a ii–V progression, you can just think of playing over the V chord and not think about the minor ii chord that comes before it."

After Fuller learned J. J. Johnson's trombone solo on Miles Davis' 1954 recording of "Walkin'," he began playing it note-for-note on the bandstand. Fuller remembered: "Barry called me aside and said, 'You can't do that. That's another man's solo. You have to formulate your own ideas.' I started going over to Barry's house when I was in high school. One musician would be leaving as another one was arriving. Sometimes everybody would be there; sometimes just a few of us. He insisted we learn 'A Night in Tunisia' and things like that. He was teaching ii–V–I, turnarounds, scales, thirds and sevenths, the lead tones. It opened that academic door to chord structures, the connections with scales, and how to bring it all together—seventh scales, diminished scales, major, minor, augmented, flat-fives, the whole bit."

The fundamentals Harris devised in the '50s remained the backbone of his teaching. He put the virtuoso improvisations of Parker, Powell, and others under a microscope and discovered the musical syntax and grammar that make bebop work. Harris then organized rules that help musicians play like natives. His method relied on diminished chords as building blocks for related scales. Those scales have specific chromatic tones added to create smooth melodic lines and possibilities for harmonic movement. "Barry's theory is derived directly from the practice," said Weiss. "More often than not in universities they have it backward." Various aspects of Harris' method seeped into the mainstream of jazz education. Still, he never held a formal position in any academy beyond temporary residencies and master classes. He was a lone wolf, an uncompromising idealist, whose allegiance to bebop had a Gandhi-like glow of inner purpose.

Barry Doyle Harris was born December 15, 1929. Formal piano instruction began at age four with his mother, a church pianist. He took classical lessons from several teachers, and for a time both he and Tommy Flanagan studied with the same woman, Gladys Wade Dillard. Like all musicians of his generation, Harris learned jazz on the bandstand, at jam sessions, and by copying solos by ear from recordings. At Northeastern High School he played boogie-woogie piano, as did classmate and Motown Records founder Berry Gordy.

Harris began playing dances when he was in high school but found his calling when he heard modern jazz at age 17. He discovered one of the seminal bebop records, "Webb City," featuring Bud Powell, Sonny Stitt, and Fats Navarro. Harris used a variable-speed record player to slow down the side and learn the melody and Powell's piano solo. Harris would steal chords from Flanagan by standing behind him when he played and watch his hands. Harris also paid attention to Chicago-born pianist Will Davis, who spent a decade in Detroit starting in the late '40s. Saxophonist and composer Frank Foster, who later wrote for Count Basie, was also a mentor. A Cincinnati native, Foster relocated to Detroit in 1949 and stayed until drafted into the army in 1951. Foster gave Harris a cheat sheet crammed with orchestration tips that he still has.

Harris' first recording in 1950 at age 20 reveals an impressive command of bebop. Issued under Harris' name on the Toledo-based New Song label, these two sides have never been reissued. The band includes Foster, guitarist John Evans, bassist Ray McKinney, and drummer Ralph Clark. "Hopper Topper," a swift workout over the harmony to "Cherokee" with no written theme, opens with two fluid choruses by Foster. Harris feeds him chords and then romps through a confident solo chorus with an even right-hand attack, precise beat, and jabbing left hand; he sounds a bit like early Horace Silver. Two years later Harris recorded an imposing Powell-like solo at a racehorse tempo on "Take Me Out to the Ballgame" as a sideman with Detroit trombone virtuoso Frank Rosolino for the homegrown Dee Gee label.

Harris remained anchored in Detroit throughout the 1950s. He succeeded Flanagan in the house band at the Blue Bird Inn in May 1954, joining Pepper Adams, Beans Richardson, and Elvin Jones. Harris later worked regularly at the Rouge Lounge, where he led his own group and backed traveling performers Roy Eldridge, Ben Webster, Flip Phillips, Lee Konitz, and Lester Young. Harris also sat in with Charlie Parker along the way, most memorably at a dance at the Forest Club where the saxophonist was performing with his string ensemble. "When Bird played a chill just went through your body," Harris said. "I always wanted to make people feel that way, the way Charlie Parker made us feel."

Harris' most extensive national exposure came when he toured for several months with Max Roach in summer 1956. At the same time, Harris made recordings in New York with Thad Jones, Donald Byrd, and Hank Mobley. But it wasn't until Cannonball Adderley convinced him to go on the road in early 1960 that Harris finally left Detroit. He stayed with the alto saxophonist six months, before settling in New York. At 30, he was more than ready. There is stunning film of Harris with Adderley's quintet at the Newport Jazz Festival in July 1960. Paced by Detroiter Louis Hayes on drums, Harris cuts everyone on "Del Sasser" with a dazzling attack and inspired flow of melody cast in dramatically long phrases. In New York, Harris cemented his reputation as a musicians' musician, known for his allegiance to classic bebop and unwillingness to compromise. In introducing a Harris master class at New York University in 2004, critic Gary Giddins recalled hearing him in the early '70s at a noisy 52nd Street bar called Jimmy's. One night a table of fat cats pooled a wad of cash and presented Harris with a proposal: "Would you please not play, because we're having a conversation?" Harris picked up the money and threw it back: "I will *not* stop playing!"

In the '60s Harris grew close to pianist-composer Thelonious Monk, the idiosyncratic genius of modern jazz, and Coleman Hawkins, the first king of the tenor saxophone. Hawkins was a pre-bop player but an inveterate progressive whose sophisticated style resisted reductive clichés and expanded Harris' horizons. "He showed me there was more to the music than what Bird played," Harris said. Hawkins had previously worked with Hank Jones, Roland Hanna, and Tommy Flanagan, so he had a taste for the quick ears and stimulating accompaniment offered by Detroit pianists. The first time Harris played with him, Hawkins called a tune Harris didn't know. He figured out the harmony on the fly, and when they finished Hawkins said: "Another goddamn Detroit piano player!"

Harris also became a close friend of Pannonica de Konigswarter. Known as the "Jazz Baroness," she was a Rothschild scion who became the guardian angel of many jazz musicians, most notably Monk. She lived in a hard-edged contemporary home in Weehawken, New Jersey, that sits on a cliff with a panoramic view of Manhattan. This was the famous "Cathouse"—named for the musicians who hung out there and her 100 adopted felines.

Harris moved into the house in the mid-'60s and still lives there; Nica died in 1988 but made arrangements allowing him to stay as long as he wants. Monk also moved into the house in 1972, spending his last decade there, much of it clouded by mental illness.

"Everything about Monk was unique," said Harris. "How he talked, how he played, how he lived, how he practiced. Most people practice practicing, but Monk practiced *playing*. He would take one tune and play it in tempo for an hour or 90 minutes straight." Monk rarely touched the piano in his final years, but one day around 1980 he walked out of his room and joined Harris at the piano. He started to play "My Ideal." The pair traded choruses for what Harris said was more than an hour. "I really wish that had been recorded," he said.

Harris' mature voice is first documented on the five records he made for Riverside from 1960 to 1962. His first LP as a leader, *Breakin' It Up* (Argo), had been recorded in 1958 in Chicago with Detroiters Will Austin and Frank Gant; it's a polished debut but lacks the depth that lay around the corner. *At the Jazz Workshop* (1960), with Sam Jones and Louis Hayes, is the true coming-out party. Harris' articulation and inflection are in constant flux on tracks like "Lolita" and "Is You Is or Is You Ain't My Baby." He's really *talking* on the piano.

This is the essence of Harris' individuality—the storyteller expression that makes a beeline from his heart and mind directly into yours. The magic lies in the eloquent flow of spontaneous melody and harmony, the intensity of his swing, and the variety of his rhythm, phrasing, and articulation. As much as Harris' teaching emphasized scales, he doesn't play "theory." He plays endless melody, rhythm, beauty, and drama. You can't swing any harder than Harris does on "Stay Right with It," a blues on *Chasin' the Bird* (1962). Harris slaps the syncopated beat around for a dozen serpentine choruses, conversing with Clifford Jarvis' animated drums. Harris reminds you here that he's a grittier pianist, more deeply connected to the drums, than fellow Detroiters Hank Jones, Tommy Flanagan, and Roland Hanna.

Harris began a long association with producer Don Schlitten in 1967 that would carry through the early '80s and encompass records on the Prestige, MPS, and Xanadu labels. The sextet LPs *Luminescence!* (1967) and *Bull's Eye* (1968) are Harris' best records with horns. *Magnificent!* (1969) and *Vicissitudes* (1972) are rarefied trio records, the latter filled with some of Harris' most creative compositions. Xanadu was a haven for middle-aged beboppers in the '70s. Harris made five LPs as a leader for the label and appeared on about 20 as a sideman. His own dates document the distilled lyricism that blossomed in his playing during the decade. The solo piano recording *The Bird of Red and Gold* (1979) sings with the sublime radiance of a Shelley ode: "Pourest thy full heart / In profuse strains of unpremeditated art." A similar spirit illuminates *Solo* (1990) on the German-based September label. A stroke in 1993 robbed Harris of some dexterity and speed in his left hand, but he continued to play and record at a high level. More recently, advancing frailty has taken a more noticeable toll on his technique, but the wisdom and allure of his expression transcend.

The celestial ballad that gives *The Bird of Red and Gold* its title defines Harris' cosmology. He even sings his own poetry with casual grace:

Within the confines of one's soul
There sits a bird of red and gold.
Its wings at all times set to fly,
For if it does not, it will die.
If set free, it will soar to
Heights unknown to other men,
Lands unseen by other eyes;
And as the beauty of the universe
Unfolds, what joy the pleasure then
Of truth revealed, limitations
Then unsealed
This is the Almighty's gift to you.

Back at the community center on the Upper West Side, the clock swept past 10:30 p.m. Harris now faced 20 horn players and, like a swinging drill sergeant, put his squadron through calisthenics designed to train the fingers, ears, and mind to work as one. He sang phrases and the class played them back in unison. The instructions came quickly, given in musical shorthand: "Start on the tonic of A-flat and come down the scale, put a half step between the 6 and 5 and stop at the third of F."

Harris' workshops were a fixture in New York since about 1974. In 1982 he moved operations to the Jazz Cultural Theatre, a beloved performance space that he cofounded on Eighth Avenue between 28th and 29th Streets (and which the Baroness supported financially). When the rent skyrocketed in 1987, the theater closed, and Harris resumed his itinerant wandering. He explained his loyalty to the class with a story dating back to the '70s: "One day I forgot about the class. At seven o'clock—I was supposed to be there at four—I realized I forgot, and I jumped in a cab up to 58th Street.

Everybody was still there waiting for me! That's when I said, 'We're going to have the class from now on.'"

He remained indefatigable. Even after a debilitating fall in Europe in late 2017 put him in the hospital and a rehabilitation facility for about 10 weeks, Harris soon resumed teaching and headed to Italy for a residency. He taught his final class from his home via Zoom less than three weeks before his death. His commitment to students was matched by their devotion to him. On the night I attended class, a young pianist from Japan brought Harris special cookies from her homeland. Harris thanked her with a grandfatherly peck on the cheek. Students knew that no other musician of Harris' stature practically gave away his secrets. They knew they could skip the entry fee if short on cash. They knew Harris funneled most of the revenue from the class into covering expenses. Like many teachers placed on a pedestal, Harris found the adulation intoxicating. Yet nothing gave him more pleasure than the twinkling smile of a student graced by the shock of discovery. "Everything's worth that smile," he said.

Not everything about Harris was unassailable. As a bebop fundamentalist, he distrusted subsequent styles that altered or rejected the melodic, harmonic, and rhythmic language of Charlie Parker and contemporaries. In a 1985 NBC News piece about Harris, the pianist dresses down young musicians at the Jazz Cultural Theatre who have just finished playing McCoy Tyner's modal "Passion Dance." Something Harris heard upset him, and he launches into them like an old-school basketball coach: "I don't like what I hear! . . . There are a lot of places for you to go and play that kind of music. You go to those places. This is going to be a jazz house: Bebop! 'Cause I starve here and have to pay the rent here, and I'm not going to tolerate one thing in here that I don't dig!"

Still, Harris ventured occasionally outside the confines of classic bebop. He gets down with his funky self on Lee Morgan's "The Sidewinder" (1963) and even ventures into the avant-garde on Yusef Lateef's "Symphonic Blues Suite" (1970). But these were rare exceptions. Given Harris' pedigree, however, he earned his prejudices, and savvy students grasped that his fundamentals represented eternal truths that transcend style.

As the clock reached 11:30 p.m., Harris barked instructions. "You have to play more than eighth notes," he said. "Triplets rule the world!" Harris began to dictate ideas and link them together like cars of a train. One phrase led to another and before long Harris found himself orchestrating an arrangement based on a 55-year-old Dizzy Gillespie introduction to "I Can't Get Started." Harris assembled the pieces like a puzzle. First the saxophones crooned supple chords. Then the trumpets played a nimble melody carved from curlicue rhythms and snazzy harmony. Then a lone tenor sax added a countermelody. It was after midnight by the time Harris completed the eight-bar construction, and when the professor finally heard it played in a single take, he beamed: "Oh man, that's fun!"

Recommended Recordings

Barry Harris, *At the Jazz Workshop* (Riverside)
Barry Harris, *Bull's Eye* (Prestige)
Barry Harris, *Vicissitudes* (MPS)

Tommy Flanagan

A LEGENDARY TOUCH

Tommy Flanagan descended the steep staircase leading from Seventh Avenue to the Village Vanguard in Manhattan and briefly surveyed the empty club before shuffling to the piano. His hands fell on the keys as if shaking hands with an old friend. Flanagan first played the Vanguard as a sideman with J. J. Johnson in the late 1950s. For the last two decades of his life, the Detroit-born pianist's blissful trios spent many weeks in residence at this hallowed Greenwich Village temple, and he recorded two exemplary albums here. But now, in the afternoon stillness of a summer day three months before his death in November 2001 at age 71, Flanagan played for himself and the ghosts of Thelonious Monk, John Coltrane, and other departed heroes whose photos line the smoke-stained walls of the world's most famous basement. One soft-spoken chord meandered into another until a melody emerged from the mist—"Gone with the Wind," a 1937 gem with music by Allie Wrubel. Flanagan glided into a walk-in-the-park tempo, improvising fluid ideas ripe with insouciant swing and fine-spun melodies that weaved through the chords with the relaxed mastery of an artist with a lot to say and nothing to prove. Flanagan's lyrical touch was legendary. Each note sounded like a pearl wrapped in silk. This was the first topic he addressed when the song ended.

"My touch comes from listening and trying to get a sound that I had in my head," Flanagan said in a gentle voice that rarely rose above a stage whisper. "I never did get much out of playing too hard. When I thought I was playing too loud, I'd use the soft pedal. I liked that; you play harder but get a softer sound. I had an old, harsh-sounding piano at home, anyway."

Flanagan seduced listeners through a sublime marriage of swing, poetry, wit, and warmth. His elegant brand of modernism was so universally admired during the 1980s and '90s that it's sobering to remember that until launching the second act of his career, he was a secret to almost everyone but fellow musicians. Most observers regarded him as a career accompa-

Pianist Tommy Flanagan at his home in New York on August 3, 2001, three months before his death at age 71. Photo by Susan Tusa / Detroit Free Press.

nist. Flanagan's self-effacing personality worked against him. He spent 13 years as Ella Fitzgerald's pianist, from 1963 to 1965 and from 1968 to 1978; in between was a brief stint with Tony Bennett. Flanagan recorded sparingly as a leader, releasing two records under his own name in 1957 and 1960 and then nothing until 1975. Still, he appeared on hundreds of LPs as a sideman, among them such classics as Miles Davis' *Collectors' Items*, Sonny Rollins' *Saxophone Colossus*, Coltrane's *Giant Steps*, Gene Ammons' *Boss Tenor*, *At Ease with Coleman Hawkins*, and *The Incredible Jazz Guitar of Wes Montgomery*.

The turning point came in 1978, when a heart attack put him in the hospital. Flanagan quit smoking, cut down on drinking, and gave his notice to Fitzgerald. He formed the first in a series of trios specializing in nattily tailored interpretations of superior standards and underplayed jazz originals by Thad Jones, Monk, Tadd Dameron, Billy Strayhorn, and others. Flanagan became a fixture in New York clubs and overseas festivals and recorded a string of thrilling albums, mostly for smaller labels in Europe and Japan. By the 1990s, his brilliance was received wisdom, and he was named a Jazz Master in 1996 by the National Endowment for the Arts.

Flanagan's style is deceptive. He's known for his satin touch, but he can play with a cunningly sharp attack and swings as deeply as anyone. He's a child of bebop and a master of its hornlike piano style pioneered by Bud Powell. But Flanagan's roots also reach back to pre-bop pianists like Teddy Wilson, Art Tatum, and Fats Waller, transitional figures like Nat Cole and little-known Detroiter Willie Anderson, and the versatile early modernist from Pontiac, Hank Jones—all pianists with active left hands and refined élan. "I was first influenced by Teddy Wilson," said Flanagan. "He was a firm player, but he also had a beautiful touch. If that's your first inspiration, you really want to improve on it. In the last 20 years or so my volume has increased. In fact, I had a drummer once who left the group because he said the piano was too loud. Imagine that—a drummer telling the piano player he was too loud."

Pianist Michael Weiss pointed out that a large part of Flanagan's identity is his pianistic approach to dynamics, attack, pedaling, and orchestration. "Each note or chord has a carefully considered sonority, as opposed to a generic kind of voicing," said Weiss. "He might start a melody in single-note lines then play something in thirds, octaves, or full chords. That carries over to his improvising. If he's soloing and ascends to a climax, he'll orchestrate that moment—put a chord under the melody note to color or accent what he's doing."

Flanagan manipulates the keyboard pedals like a virtuoso, employing the sustain pedal to connect his ideas in a smooth legato without allowing his notes to bleed into a puddle. "Sometimes guys just come and watch my feet," he said. "You know, there's a way of breathing when you use the pedals. It's like phrasing."

Flanagan's orchestral conception and pearly touch are clear on a song like Dameron's "A Blue Time," a harmonically enriched blues with an openhearted melody and leisurely gait. Flanagan recorded it in 1977 on one of his finest LPs, *Eclypso* (Enja) with bassist George Mraz and drummer Elvin Jones. Flanagan carries the melody in sumptuous chords suggesting a brass chorale. He begins several choruses with soulful triplets played behind the beat. This elicits skipping rhythmic responses from Mraz that, in turn, put an extra spring in Flanagan's step. The temperature rises in the third chorus with Flanagan's lithe double-timing and a clever rhyme leading to swooning tremolos. He slides from single notes into chords with such finesse entering his fourth chorus that you don't *hear* the music shift into a higher gear, but you *feel* it.

As good as the records are, however, you had to hear Flanagan in person to grasp how strongly his focused creativity and cultured intensity shaped a trio in his own image. The music sounded polished yet casual. In comfortable surroundings with a quality piano, he was mesmerizing. I heard Flanagan, Mraz, and drummer Kenny Washington two nights at Sweet Basil in New York in 1988. The club was packed, and among the fans one night was pianist Cecil Taylor, an avatar of the avant-garde. Flanagan spotted Taylor on a break and broke into a wide grin: "Hey C. T.!" he half-shouted from across the room. The trio played a frisky "Raincheck" (Strayhorn), a lustrous "Lament" (J. J. Johnson), and an alacritous "Verdandi" (Flanagan)—the latter sometimes known as "Mean Streets." Even the peerless *Jazz Poet* (Timeless), recorded with the same players in similar repertoire six months later, doesn't quite match the glowing halo of perfection at the club those nights.

Flanagan lived on the Upper West Side of Manhattan on 82nd Street with his wife, Diana, a former singer and vivacious woman whom he married in 1976. Married once previously, he had three children from his first marriage and six grandchildren. When I visited in August 2001, the apartment was tastefully decorated and cluttered with books. A Steinway grand piano stood in one corner of the living room. Photos of Charlie Parker and Ellington were scattered about, along with paintings, including a small landscape by Nancy Balliett, wife of jazz critic Whitney Balliett. A caricature of Flanagan by cartoonist Al Hirschfeld watched over the piano.

Flanagan was a distinguished-looking man, but he had grown frail, and his clothes now hung loosely on his small frame. He had a long face, tender eyes, a sweet smile, and wore round glasses. He lost his hair early, and only a wisp of white remained above and behind his ears. A bushy gray mustache almost hid his dimples. Flanagan did nothing in a hurry, least of all talk. He answered questions in stages, leaving long gaps of silence. Still, when the mood struck, he was an agile conversationalist with a martini-dry wit.

Pianist Jimmy Rowles once told Whitney Balliett that whenever he'd ask Flanagan how he was getting along, the response was always, "Doing the best I can with the tools I have." Detroit pianist Bess Bonnier remembered sharing a New York cab with the Flanagans as they headed to a gig. Traffic was a nightmare, and they were running late. Diana became increasingly agitated. Flanagan said nothing for a long time. Then he checked his watch. "We're gaining on it," he said.

On this August afternoon, the couple nuzzled on the sofa while paging through *Before Motown: A History of Jazz in Detroit, 1920–60*. Flanagan reminisced and smiled at photos of lifelong friends Barry Harris, Kenny Burrell, Elvin Jones, and Pepper Adams. Diana squealed at the pictures of her husband. "Oh, sweetheart! What a darling you were! I would have loved you!"

"Stand in line," Flanagan deadpanned. He stopped joking and continued in a sincere voice: "I couldn't have gotten far without those days in Detroit. We had good role models. They didn't use that term then, but we had some people we respected who played as well as those people who came into town that we'd go see. We had people like Milt Jackson, Yusef Lateef, Lucky Thompson, Wardell Gray."

Thomas Lee Flanagan was born March 16, 1930, and grew up in northeast Detroit in Conant Gardens. He was the last of six children. His father was a postman, and both parents loved music. Flanagan started on the clarinet at 6, but by then he was already climbing up on the piano bench and imitating the lessons he heard his brother practice. Flanagan started piano lessons at 10 with Gladys Wade Dillard, who also taught Barry Harris, Kirk Lightsey, and Alice (McLeod) Coltrane. Flanagan retained a lifelong fondness for Chopin and Ravel.

He got interested in jazz when his brother started bringing home the latest Billie Holiday records with Teddy Wilson on piano. Flanagan heard Art Tatum and Nat Cole and was especially impressed by Detroit pianist Willie Anderson, a local hero perched between the two. Anderson (1924–1971) assimilated Tatum's rapid-fire attack and Cole's poised swing. He bridged swing to bop styles and inspired all the young modernists in Detroit. He had opportunities to go on the road with Benny Goodman, Coleman Hawkins, and Billy Eckstine but turned them down. The six sides Anderson recorded in 1947–48 for the Detroit-based Fortune and New York–based Jamboree labels have never been reissued. Flanagan loved Anderson's version of "The Man I Love" (Jamboree). He opens rhapsodically, before launching into a buoyant tempo and unfurling a fast, crystalline right hand. His left hand is a full participant, even joining his right hand in double octaves. There's a lot going on, but the performance has clarity, swing, and ebullience. "Willie had technique and taste and was just a beautiful musician," Flanagan said.

Flanagan attended Northern High School, where he and his friends absorbed the new music of Parker, Gillespie, and Powell. In 1948, Flanagan played with a little big band led by Lucky Thompson that also included Kenny Burrell and Pepper Adams. In 1949, after Flanagan backed Harry Belafonte at the Flame Show Bar, the singer offered him a gig in New York. But Flanagan's mother decided her baby was too young to leave town.

A private tape made in April 1950 at the Blue Bird Inn—six years before Flanagan began recording in New York—reveals how mature he was by age 20. The quartet includes tenor saxophonist Frank Foster, drummer Art Mardigan, and either Alvin Jackson or Beans Richardson on bass. On Powell's "Bouncing with Bud," recorded for the first time just eight months earlier, the young Detroiters reflect the latest sounds from New York in real time. Foster starts his solo by quoting Sonny Rollins on the record. Mardigan, the top bebop jazz drummer in Detroit, who had already recorded in New York with Dexter Gordon, drops bombs on the bass drum. Flanagan's vocabulary comes out of Powell, yet he already has a personal way of finishing his ideas and he improvises in complete sentences. There's a smooth quality to his tone and technique. On Jerome Kern's ballad "Yesterdays," fluent runs suggest Willie Anderson, and dissonance winks at Thelonious Monk. Flanagan sounds as capable as any of the second-wave bebop pianists in New York.

Flanagan was drafted into the Army in 1951. When orders came to ship out to Korea, he stuffed several Monk records into his suitcase so he'd have the latest music with him overseas. Returning to Detroit, Flanagan joined the house band at the Blue Bird in August 1953 with leader Billy Mitchell, Thad Jones, Beans Richardson, and Elvin Jones. Flanagan first played with Miles Davis at the Blue Bird, and he sometimes backed visiting stars like Carmen McRae at the Rouge Lounge. Flanagan also played with Charlie Parker at the Broadway Capitol Theater. In a 1994 interview with WKCR-FM in New York, Flanagan told Ted Panken that he was working a regular Saturday concert series when Parker was announced as a surprise guest: "We all looked at each other dumbfounded. 'What, Bird? This cat's got to be kidding!' Sure enough, Bird comes out of the wings, walks by the piano, says, 'Give me eight bars of "Moon," G,' and I fumbled through an introduction of 'How High the Moon' in G! It was my first time to play with Bird. . . . After that we felt at ease, like we had come of age. We'd played with Bird!"

Flanagan's memories of Detroit are not all pleasant. "I always wished I'd left earlier," he told me. "Detroit started to grind on me. There wasn't much freedom to move around. The police were horrible then. They'd hassle you in your own neighborhood. One night when I was about 12, I was walking by a printing shop where they'd found some subversive material and they stopped me, guns drawn. I said, 'What are you going to do? I'm just a kid.'"

Flanagan and Burrell moved to New York together in early 1956. Within six months, the pianist had recorded with Miles Davis, Sonny Rollins, Thad Jones, Burrell, Kenny Clarke, Oscar Pettiford, and Phil Woods. Flanagan also played a month that summer with Ella Fitzgerald. He was nervous his first night with the singer in Cleveland, and she didn't help matters by sidling up to him while he was playing and saying. "If it's going to be like this, I'm getting out of the business." Mortified, he hung on the best he could.

At the March 1956 session that produced Davis' *Collectors' Items* (Prestige), the trumpeter pulled a scrap of paper from his pocket containing a barely legible sketch of Dave Brubeck's "In Your Own Sweet Way." Davis supplied the chord voicings for the levitating introduction that Flanagan plays, but the pianist devised the rhythm. Flanagan's lyrical touch on this track captivated a young Kenny Barron, a student in junior high school in Philadelphia who would grew into a major pianist. "That's what got me," said Barron.

In 1959, Flanagan appeared on John Coltrane's influential *Giant Steps*. The daunting harmony of the title song races through several key centers with chords moving rapidly in unusual patterns. Coltrane knew it wouldn't be easy, so he dropped by Flanagan's apartment before the session to show him the tune. But Coltrane didn't tell him the supersonic tempo he planned. Flanagan assumed a moderate speed, perhaps even a ballad tempo. As the first pianist called upon to play "Giant Steps," Flanagan drew one of the short straws in the history of jazz recording, and he scuffles badly. More than two decades later, however, he recorded a redemptive version with his own trio in 1982.

Flanagan's accompaniment—"comping" in jazz parlance—is celebrated for the way he provides stimulating harmonic, rhythmic, and melodic support to a soloist or singer without getting in the way. "He knows just what to do and when to do it," Sonny Rollins said. *Ella in Hamburg '65* (Verve) is a textbook in how to play with a singer. Flanagan's spellbinding rapport with tenor saxophonist Coleman Hawkins in the early '60s is documented on a dozen LPs. Particularly glorious are the Moodsville LPs *At Ease with Coleman Hawkins*, *Good Old Broadway*, and *Make Someone Happy*—the latter two featuring the suave all-Detroit rhythm section of Flanagan, Major Holley, and Eddie Locke.

Flanagan's recordings as a leader are so consistent that it's hard to go wrong. Taped in Sweden in 1957, *Overseas* (Prestige), with Wilbur Little and Elvin Jones, is one of the strongest debut LPs of the era. *The Tommy Flanagan Trio* (Moodsville) from 1960, with Tommy Potter and Roy Haynes, is a winsome sequel. Of the later trio dates, the aforementioned *Eclypso* and *Jazz Poet* are the best of the best, but also excellent are *Super-Session* (Enja), the Monk tribute *Thelonica* (Enja), *Nights at the Vanguard* (Uptown), the Thad Jones retrospective *Let's* (Enja) and two valedictory CDs from 1996 and '97, *Sea Changes* (Evidence) and *Sunset and the Mockingbird* (Blue Note). Kenny Burrell joins the pianist's trio on *Beyond the Blue Bird* (Timeless), a sweet tribute to their shared roots. Flanagan made just two solo piano recordings. *Alone Too Long* (Denon) from 1977 is often eloquent but also unsettled in spots. The rare *Solo Piano* (Storyville), recorded in 1974 but not released until 2005, is nearly impossible to find. When the label discovered that half the 20 tracks are from another session by an unidentified pianist—not Flanagan—it withdrew the disc.

Finally, 1957's *The Cats* (Prestige) presents another mystery. No leader is identified, and it appears on the surface to be a cooperative blowing session with a large contingent of Detroiters—Flanagan, Burrell, Doug Watkins, Louis Hayes—plus Coltrane and Idrees Sulieman. But it's a Flanagan record in all but name: He wrote the four originals and plays a gorgeous "How Long Has This Been Going On?" as a trio feature. Flanagan told colleagues in later years that it was his date, but there's no explanation why it wasn't released as such.

Back at Flanagan's apartment, the pianist continued telling stories about the old days: There was the time the J. J. Johnson Quintet alternated sets at the Village Vanguard with Jack Kerouac, who read from his books or extemporized. Flanagan, Elvin Jones, and Kerouac ended up at the pianist's apartment one night. "Before the morning was over, Elvin threatened to kill him," Flanagan said. "Kerouac said something outrageous—I don't remember what—and Elvin took offense. I think I did too, but Elvin was more menacing."

Talked out, Flanagan stood up and moved to the piano. He played a few enigmatic arpeggios before slipping into the Jimmy McHugh ballad "Where Are You?" with a fanciful twist of harmony that unlocked a back door to the song. He played a chorus sotto voce and then a second with more volume, movement, and emotion. The results were so affecting that I quickly requested Harold Arlen's "Last Night When We Were Young" to keep Flanagan at the keyboard. It's a theatrical song—Alec Wilder called it "a concert song without a trace of trying to be." Flanagan hadn't played it in ages, and he watched his hands with a perplexed look on his face, as if his fingers belonged to another pianist. When he got stuck for a note, his wife softly sang Yip Harburg's lyric from the sofa. "*To think that spring had depended / On merely this: a look, a kiss*." The music shuddered with feeling. When it was over, Diana had a tear in her eye and Flanagan a faraway look in his.

Recommended Recordings

Tommy Flanagan, *Overseas* (Prestige)
Tommy Flanagan *Jazz Poet* (Timeless)
Coleman Hawkins, *At Ease with Coleman Hawkins* (Moodsville)

Kenny Burrell

COMMUNITY BUILDER

Kenny Burrell had been mulling a concept record focused on the blues for about a year before entering engineer Rudy Van Gelder's studio in Englewood Cliffs, New Jersey, on January 8, 1963. At 31, the Detroit-born guitarist envisioned an LP that would sustain a moody, after-hours expression with relaxed tempos and an intensity that simmered rather than boiled. Burrell wrote all the music, save the Don Redman chestnut "Gee Baby Ain't I Good to You." The guitarist channels the spirit of the Black Bottom neighborhood of his youth, where the blues encompassed not just one idiom but many, each with a different avatar—Basie, Ellington, Charlie Parker, John Lee Hooker, T-Bone Walker. Burrell even sketched a potential cover design. It featured the title *Midnight Blue* rendered in block letters with the word "Blue" colored blue and taking up most of the cover. Blue Note owner-producer Alfred Lion liked it enough to give to his ace graphic designer Reid Miles to complete the final cover based on Burrell's idea.

Midnight Blue, a nexus of soul-jazz and hard bop, ranks as one of Burrell's greatest masterpieces. The music offers solace and rejuvenation. The sympathetic cast includes tenor saxophonist Stanley Turrentine, Detroit bassist Major Holley, drummer Bill English, and percussionist Ray Barretto. The 12-bar blues "Chitlins Con Carne" slithers out of the box with an insinuating bass vamp and a Latin beat adorned with conga drums; Burrell and Turrentine play the theme in unison, but the guitarist drops in a repeated chordal riff between phrases that deepens the groove. Burrell structures his solo with similar call-and-response phrasing, assuming the role of both preacher and congregation. "Soul Lament," a beguiling solo guitar piece in E minor without improvisation, unfolds as a wistful elegy; Burrell conjured the piece on the spot in the studio.

Like all master jazz musicians, Burrell's personality starts with his tone. Instantly recognizable, it's a singing sound, a seductive purr, with a faint halo of reverb and a refined attack that's crisp upfront but finishes as warm

Kenny Burrell performing in Detroit on September 2, 1980. Photo by William Archie / Detroit Free Press.

and mellow as cognac. Many guitarists boast flashier technique and fierier personalities. Burrell plays a different game. On *Midnight Blue* he forges a group sound defined by his soulful lyricism, which spreads among his bandmates and reaches out to listeners, inviting them inside the tent. Making music is an act of social engagement for Burrell. “Kenny always seemed to invoke community to me,” said guitarist Pat Metheny. “It was less about being *the soloist* and more about being *in* the music, *in* the band, *in* the pocket.”

Burrell, who turned 94, in 2025, has been a major figure since first arriving in New York in 1956. His articulate playing, which connected the dots between bebop and the down-home sensibility of the earliest blues guitarists, quickly became a signature of East Coast hard bop. Burrell embodied all the Detroit-bred qualities that made Motown musicians so valuable in the era—a sophisticated approach to harmony and melodic construction, a robust way of swinging, the ability to fit into any context without sacrificing an individual identity, and a deep feeling for the blues. In the late ’50s, Burrell became the de facto house guitarist at Blue Note and Prestige, two of the period’s defining labels. He appeared on hundreds of LPs within his first decade in New York. Eventually, he released roughly 100 recordings as a leader and appeared on some 500 more as a sideman—and that doesn’t include countless anonymous pop and R & B studio sessions. Though a bebop baby, Burrell forged productive relationships with swing-era heroes Billie Holiday and Coleman Hawkins, and by the 1970s was recording ambitious tributes to Duke Ellington. Burrell took to the blowing-session aesthetic of the late ’50s like a duck to water, but he later made structured recordings that showed a knack for careful planning and fruitful collaborations with arrangers and producers.

Few musicians in jazz boast a résumé as diverse or as loaded with innovators. Burrell’s credits include Louis Armstrong, Hawkins, Holiday, Dizzy Gillespie, Charlie Parker (with whom Burrell played in Detroit), Milt Jackson, Jimmy Smith, Sonny Rollins, John Coltrane, James Brown, and Aretha Franklin. Burrell also worked regularly for several years in Broadway pit orchestras. “Kenny made it sound easy to sit there as a guitarist and hang with John Coltrane or Stanley Turrentine and a long list of his contemporaries,” Metheny said. “But as a listener you don’t especially notice how hard it is to do that, which is a real testament to how evolved he was as a player.”

The empathetic accompaniment Burrell offers Coltrane on their duet “Why Was I Born” (1958) proves Metheny’s point. So does Burrell’s exceptional solo ballad performances like “But Not for Me” (1956). The deft marriage of single-note lines, lush chords, and savvy voice-leading reveal a romantic expression, patience, and taste uncommon for a musician still in his mid-'20s. "The most important things to me in music are depth of feeling, honesty, individuality, and a spiritual connection," Burrell said in 1996.

Burrell was among a wave of major guitarists who emerged between 1955 and 1961. Jim Hall, six months older than Burrell, developed an understated, melodic voice, while Grant Green, four years younger than Burrell, favored linear, single-note lines steeped in the blues. Wes Montgomery, eight years older than Burrell, would not break out of Indianapolis until 1960—after which he quickly grew into the most widely imitated jazz guitarist of all since Charlie Christian essentially invented the electric guitar solo in the late '30s. But Burrell got out of the blocks first, and his ubiquity on records magnified his influence. He's left marks on multiple generations and guitarists as different as Green, George Benson, Metheny, John Abercrombie, Bobby Broom, Russell Malone, Dave Stryker, and Lionel Loueke. Burrell's circle of fans extends beyond jazz to B. B. King and Jimi Hendrix, both of whom sang his praises.

Burrell, who has lived in Los Angeles since the early '70s, is a tall, elegant man with a handsome face, tan skin, and full head of now-white hair. Flip through the covers of his recordings and you see a dapper dresser, stylish rather than flamboyant—an apt metaphor for the savoir faire with which he plays and conducts his life. He remains closely associated with UCLA, where he started teaching in 1978 with a single course on Ellington and was the founding director of jazz studies from 1996 to 2016. Those who have worked closely with Burrell say that his even-keel personality has a calming effect on those around him, but no one should mistake his easygoing nature as license for anything less than professionalism at the highest level.

Burrell can be a shrewd judge of how to get what he wants. Guitarist Bobby Broom recalled one of the first rehearsals with the three-guitar band Burrell formed in the mid-'80s that included young colleagues Broom and Rodney Jones. Burrell said he wanted solo guitar numbers by each of them to be part of the band's repertoire and made Broom and Jones play one on the spot. Unaccompanied playing is a stiff challenge for even experienced guitarists, let alone a 25-year-old like Broom taken by surprise. It didn't go well. "It was the worst day of my life," Broom recalled. "No one said a word. I've got egg on my face. That was a wake-up call. Kenny knew exactly what he was doing. He didn't have to say, 'You need to get that together.'"

Burrell got his own act together quickly in Detroit, where he was known as the best guitarist in the city as a teenager. "Detroit was a school without walls," Burrell said. "It was that kind of free access that we had based on mutual respect and a love for the music. We all were striving to be excellent in this thing that we love called jazz, and most of us had our sights set on making it in New York. The preparation for that happened in that very fertile workshop called Detroit."

Kenneth Earl Burrell was born July 31, 1931, the youngest of the family's six children. The three eldest siblings, all sisters, died young of childhood diseases. Burrell's parents both came to Detroit from Virginia in the Great Migration. His father, an auto mechanic, died when Kenny was six, and his mother supported the family by working multiple jobs, mostly cleaning office buildings. Burrell grew up with music in church and in the house; his mother sang and noodled on the piano. He started piano lessons at eight, but they didn't stick. He was more intrigued by the guitar that his older brother Billy played and the records by Basie, Ellington, Goodman, and others his brother brought home.

Burrell heard guitarists play and sing the blues everywhere, from street corners to neighborhood parks. He wanted to play the saxophone, but his family couldn't afford one, Instead, he bought his first guitar at age 12 for $10 from a pawnshop in Black Bottom and taught himself to play. When Billy—11 years older—returned from the Army, he gave his brother his first lessons. When the gifted youngster caught up and passed his brother, Billy switched to the Fender electric bass and the brothers and drummer Hindal Butts formed a trio that played in Paradise Valley.

Three guitarists made the biggest impact on Burrell—Charlie Christian, Oscar Moore, and Django Reinhardt. "Charlie began to play the electric guitar in a way the horns were playing," Burrell said. "With an amplifier he could function just like a trumpet or a saxophone. That said to me the guitar is not so bad after all. Then I heard the great Oscar Moore, who was with Nat King Cole, and I said, 'Wow, all those beautiful chords he's playing.' That was a piano-like approach because Nat didn't play a lot of piano when he was singing, and it left a lot of space for the guitar to fill." Reinhardt's influence was less a matter of copying specific techniques than extrapolating from the Gypsy guitarist's one-of-a-kind approach the lesson that it was the responsibility of jazz musicians to develop their own sound and identity. Burrell took the lesson to heart.

He started gigging at about age 15, and by 1948 was playing with peer Tommy Flanagan at the Club Sudan. At Miller High School, Burrell studied under band director Louis Cabrera, who not only taught him advanced classical music theory but also showed him how it related to jazz and made him assistant conductor of the concert band. This training gave Burrell a leg up when he entered Wayne University (Wayne State) as a composition major in 1951. (Burrell had graduated from high school at 16 and then took a few years off to work full time as a musician.) At Wayne he studied classical guitar with Joe Fava, a noted player and teacher and later the author of guitar instructional books.

For a while, Burrell led a trio with Flanagan and bassist Alvin Jackson modeled on Nat King Cole's trio. In 1953, the guitarist began billing his group as Kenny Burrell and the Four Sharps with original members Harold McKinney on piano, Paul Chambers on bass, and Hindal Butts on drums. On ballads they'd sing in four-part harmony. Burrell sang in a mellifluous, Cole-inspired voice that was promising enough that in 1960 he recorded an urbane vocal album for Columbia, *Weaver of Dreams*. It's a great blindfold test record, but sales were disappointing, and Burrell packed away his vocal cords. Still, he'd occasionally sing a tune on club gigs for the next 20 years if the spirit moved him.

Burrell made his first recordings in Detroit in the early '50s. Gillespie hired the 19-year-old guitarist for a 10-day gig at the Club Juana on Woodward Avenue, just west of Paradise Valley, in early 1951 with a band that included Coltrane and Milt Jackson. While in Detroit, the group recorded four sides for Dee Gee, among them the minor blues "Birks' Works," which includes a brief guitar solo. Gillespie offered Burrell a chance to go on the road, but encouraged by his mother—"If they want you now, they'll want you later"—he went to college instead. The Gillespie session is usually considered Burrell's recording debut, and these sides were first in the marketplace. But the guitarist said in *Before Motown* that he thinks his first recording session with pianist Otis "Bu Bu" Turner came earlier. Released in 1953 or 1954, these sides have never been reissued. Burrell makes a stronger impression here than with Gillespie. On "I Goofed," his tangy-sweet chording recalls Oscar Moore, while his solo lines reveal supple swing-to-bop phrasing.

Burrell's first recording as a leader was made for Joe Van Battle's J-V-B label in Detroit circa 1954–55. Van Battle owned Joe's Record Shop, a landmark in the black community located just north of Paradise Valley at 3530 Hastings Street at Mack. Van Battle recorded gospel, blues (including John Lee Hooker), rhythm and blues, and jazz in the back of his shop. He also recorded sermons by Rev. C. L. Franklin at New Bethel Baptist Church and was the first to record Franklin's gifted teenage daughter, Aretha, singing at the church in 1956. Burrell's alluring tone and nimble lines are in place on "Kenny Sound"—a 32-bar "I Got Rhythm" tune in C with a "Honeysuckle Rose" bridge and an A-section melody pilfered from Dexter Gordon's "Dexter Digs In." Yusef Lateef's burly tenor saxophone complements the limber melodicism of Burrell's solo. Laying down the beat are Billy Burrell on electric bass and probably Elvin Jones on drums.[1] The identity of the vibraphonist is unclear but possibly Abe Woodley (later Nasir Hafiz). On the other side, Burrell confidently sings "My Funny Valentine" over a mysterious bed of flute and vibes, and the band contributes backup vocals.

A natural leader and organizer, Burrell also spearheaded the formation of the New Music Society in 1953–54, becoming its founding president and inaugurating the jam sessions and concerts at the World Stage theater as a way for young musicians to learn from more experienced pros. The society, which grew to several hundred members, was the first musicians' cooperative in Detroit and provided inspiration for later efforts in the 1960s and '70s like the Detroit Artists Workshop, Strata Corporation, and Tribe. After graduating in 1955, Burrell toured for about six months with pianist Oscar Peterson's trio as a substitute for Herb Ellis, who was fighting a drinking problem. At the start of 1956, he and Tommy Flanagan drove east together in Burrell's Chrysler.

Of the first rush of Burrell recordings, the most vital include his Blue Note debut, *Introducing Kenny Burrell* (1956), with former Four Sharp members Flanagan and Chambers, plus drummer Kenny Clarke and percussionist Candido; *Kenny Burrell / John Coltrane* (New Jazz) from 1958; and *A Night at the Vanguard* (Argo), with bassist Richard Davis and drummer Roy Haynes from 1959. The latter retains iconic status among guitarists for how Burrell fills out the texture in the guitar-bass-drum trio format.

By 1960, Burrell, who made a point of developing sight-reading skills in Detroit, had become so busy doing studio sessions for pop and R & B records that he felt he wasn't practicing enough and growing as a musician. When he got a call from conductor Elliot Lawrence with an offer of regular work on Broadway in the pit for *Bye Bye Birdie*, he leapt at the opportunity. That led directly into *How to Succeed in Business Without Really Trying*. The steady income over these four years allowed Burrell time to practice and compose, and it was during this period that he conceived two of his most notable recordings, the aforementioned *Midnight Blue* and *Guitar Forms* (Verve), a collaboration with arranger Gil Evans recorded in 1964–65. The nine tracks each investigate a different style, mood, genre, or instrumentation, among them country blues, classical, bossa nova, small and large ensembles, and solo guitar. It's a one-stop shop for all the things Burrell can do on the instrument.

The commercial and artistic success of *Midnight Blue* and *Guitar Forms* allowed Burrell to tour with his own band for the first time. His public recognition rose significantly in the '60s. His records sold well, particularly in black communities, and 45-rpm singles drawn from *Midnight Blue* and two superb Prestige LPs, *Bluesy Burrell* and *Soul Call*, were jukebox staples. Some of his LPs made it into Billboard's Top 200 pop album chart, including *Blue Bash!*, co-led with Jimmy Smith (Verve) and *The Tender Gender* (Cadet). Meanwhile, Burrell's groovy *Have Yourself a Soulful Little Christmas* (Cadet) was a hit in the Christmas genre in 1966. Two more of Burrell's large-ensemble recordings in the late '60s and early '70s, both arranged by Don Sebesky, delivered that elusive combination of artistic and commercial appeal—*Blues: The Common Ground* (Verve) with a big band, and *God Bless the Child* (CTI) with a starry small band including Freddie Hubbard and Ron Carter and just the right amount of sweetening from four cellos. Two underrated LPs recorded in 1974 on Fantasy, *Up the Street, 'Round the Corner, Down the Block* and *Sky Street*, walk a similar tightrope, even as they funnel fusion into the mix.

Burrell accrued enough currency among urban black audiences in the late '60s and early '70s that he even did a radio commercial for Schlitz Malt Liquor that ran on soul and R & B programs in markets like Philadelphia, New York, and Detroit. A few bars of a bluesy waltz from Burrell's guitar sets up the spot: "Kenny Burrell here," his suave voice intones. "You know, the guitar's a pretty popular instrument right now. People play it all kinds of ways. People make malt liquor all kinds of ways too. But Schlitz Malt Liquor has the premium quality and big-boss taste. That's why it's Burrell's brew."

In later decades Burrell balanced recording, touring, and teaching. Ironically, it was his most negative experience at Wayne State that inspired his move into academia. Jazz was frowned upon at Wayne in the early '50s. Burrell even failed one class because he kept trying to raise the subject of jazz as a topic of discussion and the professor considered the music unworthy. Burrell vowed that someday he would give jazz its due in the classroom. When he developed his first course at UCLA in the late '70s, he focused on Duke Ellington, because Burrell thought Ellington's genius offered the most potential impact of anything he could present in a humanities class. Ellington's spiritual connection to music and his profound individuality remain central to Burrell's philosophy inside and outside the classroom.

"Don't be afraid to be yourself, 'cause that's where your real strength is, and you can't be anybody else anyway," Burrell said in a 2010 interview with the Smithsonian Jazz Oral History Project. "But most of us can't even be ourselves. We can't be who we are. But the ones we love, the ones we adore, the ones who are our heroes, they're the ones who dare to be who they are and courageous enough to say, 'Here I am.'"

Burrell became a hero in jazz because he took the dare. His music says a lot of things in a lot of ways, but mostly it says: Here I am.

Recommended Recordings

Kenny Burrell, *A Night at the Vanguard* (Argo)
Kenny Burrell, *Midnight Blue* (Blue Note)
Kenny Burrell, *Guitar Forms* (Verve)

Editor's Note

As this book was going to press in May 2019, news broke that Kenny Burrell was in dire financial straits due to medical expenses following an accident and other circumstances that included identity theft and related legal and credit bills. Burrell's wife, Katherine, outlined these issues in a GoFundMe crowdfunding announcement. The Jazz Foundation of America, which supplies emergency assistance to musicians, confirmed the veracity of Burrell's plight, although specific details were not reported publicly. The GoFundMe campaign sprinted past its $100,000 goal to more than $160,000 raised from over 3,000 contributors in less than a week. This response underscored just how beloved a man and musician Burrell remained more than 60 years after first making his mark in jazz. The guitarist issued a statement on the GoFundMe page that said, in part, "Thank you, everyone, for helping us get through this crisis. We will always be grateful to you for your love and caring."

Note

1. The identity of the drummer is not 100% clear. Both Hindal Butts and Elvin Jones worked with Burrell in this period. I previously cited Butts as the drummer in the original edition of this book, but deeper listening has convinced me that the aggressive snap of the brushwork and the notably wide beat make Jones the likely drummer.

Donald Byrd

RENAISSANCE MAN

A good place to start when trying to wrap your arms around Donald Byrd's polyglot life as a trumpeter, composer, hard bopper, fusion star, pioneering educator, black music scholar, perpetual student, wealthy businessman, and art collector is with his full name: Donaldson Toussaint L'Ouverture Byrd II. Byrd's namesake, Toussaint L'Ouverture, was the brilliant, self-educated former slave who led the Haitian revolution in the late 18th century. He became a potent symbol of black empowerment for African Americans in the first half of the 20th century. Byrd believed that it was his responsibility to live up to the ideals embodied by the name his father chose for him.

Rev. Elijah Thomas Byrd was what his son Donald called a "negrophile"—a man passionate about black history and culture. Reverend Byrd held degrees from Alcorn State University in Mississippi and the Gammon Theological Seminary in Atlanta and did graduate work at Morgan State in Baltimore. He ministered at a United Methodist church in Detroit, but the family income came from his job in the city sanitation department. Donald grew up on the east side, comfortably middle class. Good grades, reading, and lofty ambition were expected.

"My father taught me about the history of my family, about who I was, where I came from, and with him being a United Methodist minister, it was expected of me to act a certain way," Byrd told James Graves in a 1987 interview broadcast on Pacifica Radio.

The result was that Byrd, who died in 2013 at age 80, lived a life of Whitmanesque multitudes. He made his initial splash as a ubiquitous hard-bop stylist. Arriving in New York in 1955 at age 22, he appeared on over 100 LPs in the next five years with Art Blakey, John Coltrane, Thelonious Monk, Jackie McLean, Sonny Rollins, Horace Silver, and others. Byrd's warm and burnished tone, fluent technique, and aggressive-yet-graceful swing were rooted in Clifford Brown and Fats Navarro. But the pristine clarity of his sound, gangly looseness of his beat, and dazzling length of his phrases

Donald Byrd, *left*, and Pepper Adams recording Byrd's *Royal Flush* (Blue Note) on September 21, 1961, at Van Gelder Studio, Englewood Cliffs, N.J. Photo by Francis Wolff © Mosaic Images LLC.

were markers of an individual voice. As Byrd matured, he tempered his hummingbird fluttering with more space in ways that recalled Miles Davis, though as Byrd's technique diminished during the '60s his playing lost its lustrous veneer.

Byrd's field of vision was wide. He recorded spiritual-like material with choirs in the '60s, and his interest in black popular music and sharp commercial instincts made him rich in the '70s. As his soul–R & B album *Black*

Byrd and its sequels soared up the charts, Byrd parlayed his windfall into his own production company and a lucrative spinoff band of his former students, the Blackbyrds. He later saw his royalties mount as records he led or produced were sampled hundreds of times. Byrd earned multiple degrees from the Manhattan School of Music and a doctorate in music education and teaching from Columbia University's Teachers College. He studied composition with pedagogue Nadia Boulanger in France. He took law school classes to better understand contracts and copyrights. He was among the first African Americans to teach jazz in universities. He wrote articles about black-music aesthetics and the business of music and lectured on the relationship between math and music. He obtained a pilot's license, amassed a library of 3,000 books on black history, and built a large collection of African American art.

"Donald talked about education all the time," said trumpeter Jimmy Owens, who studied with Byrd in 1959. "When I was getting ready to graduate from high school, he would always talk to me about getting advanced degrees and improving myself, because that's what he was doing."

Musically, Byrd was a savvy consolidator who put his stamp on ideas already in circulation. He chose collaborators to help manifest his concepts: Pianist-composer Duke Pearson arranged his choral albums. Producers Larry and Alphonso (Fonce) Mizell shaped Byrd's crossover albums. Byrd also borrowed ideas from Miles Davis. Not everything Byrd did was of equal quality or originality. Sometimes his early work is undone by a facile verbosity, and his later music remains contentious for its unabashed commercialism. But there's a larger point to be made.

Byrd's most creative invention was himself. At a time when African American musicians fought institutionalized racism and stereotypes that limited opportunities and defined black culture in narrow terms, Byrd lived a life without borders. He was as comfortable on the bandstand as he was in the boardroom or the classroom. "You'd be around him one day and he'd talk like he was from the streets, and the next time you saw him he was talking about the bottom line and business," said trumpeter and music publisher Don Sickler. "He always had certain things he was trying to find out. Donald was always looking for an angle. He was a complex man."

Byrd's education, wealth, and success bred an ego as large as his discography. But his braggadocio also reflected his agile mind and independent spirit. He refused to believe that jazz demanded a vow of poverty or bohemian clichés. He set up his own publishing company in the '50s, when musicians routinely surrendered publishing rights to record companies.

Byrd made the system work for himself. "No one is going to take you by the hand," he told *Downbeat* in 1966. "A lot of talented guys behave like a young girl at a dance. You can't wait to be asked. You have to take the future in your hands."

Byrd was born in Detroit on December 9, 1932. His mother, whose family had been in the hotel business in Baltimore, took him to hear all the top bands. He got his first trumpet at age 10. His teachers included James Tamburini, principal trumpet of the Detroit Symphony Orchestra, and Leonard B. Smith, former DSO principal trumpet and founder of the Detroit Concert Band. Saxophonist Sonny Red introduced Byrd to bebop in eighth grade at Hutchins Intermediate School, where Byrd played in the jazz band. In high school at Cass Tech he played in the top orchestra and top concert band. After school Byrd would walk up Woodward Avenue to the public library and listen to classical and jazz records. Sometimes he'd cross the street and wander the galleries at the Detroit Institute of Arts. He also attended the workshops and jam sessions at Barry Harris' house.

At 16, Byrd sat in with Lionel Hampton and made his recording debut with tenor saxophonist Robert Barnes on Detroit's Fortune Records. These four sides from 1949 have never been reissued. Identified as Sahib Byrd on the label, he plays a precocious 16-bar solo on "Bobbin' at Barbee's," an "I Got Rhythm" tune with a jumping beat. Byrd opens with a rousing break, riding 12 repeated high Cs and reaching up to graze an E-flat. He solos in a fledgling bebop vocabulary.

Byrd fell one English course shy of graduating from high school. He told Ursula Broschke Davis in her book *Paris without Regret* that all he wanted to do was play the trumpet, so he dropped out in 1950.[1] (Byrd does not mention his father's reaction, but he could not have been pleased.) Davis' book, a study of four black artists who spent part of their careers in Europe, offers the most detailed account of Byrd's early life and personal relationships. He was elusive in interviews, and many reference books and obituaries are filled with mistakes. Contrary to some sources, Byrd never obtained a bachelor's degree from Wayne State University nor completed a law degree.

While there were many women in his life, he was married only once, to Lorraine Glover from 1955 to 1963, according to their son, Donaldson Toussaint L'Ouverture Byrd III. The couple also had a daughter, Donna. Byrd's companion later in life was Yourna DeSilva, whom he had known since the '50s and with whom he had a daughter, Jenai DeSilva. Yourna is the impeccably dressed and coiffed beauty in a famous 1960 photograph by

William Claxton in which she holds Byrd's trumpet while standing on 48th Street in New York. (Captions identifying her as Byrd's wife are incorrect.)

Byrd joined the Air Force in 1951, playing in military bands while stationed in upstate New York. A warrant officer pushed him to enter a college program for servicemen. "This old guy was probably one of the most formative people in my life because he told me to get my shit together and go back to school," Byrd told Davis. He attended Manhattan School of Music, played required military shows, and flocked to clubs in off hours. After his discharge in 1954 he enrolled at Wayne State for what school records say was a single semester. He returned to New York in summer 1955. The next six years were a blur. Byrd played and recorded with *everybody.* In the space of a year he worked with three heavyweight bandleaders: Art Blakey, Max Roach, and Horace Silver. His Detroit-bred professionalism, flexibility, and consistency were valuable commodities. So was his reliability at a time when drugs were a scourge. Club owners often relied on Byrd to get band members to gigs on time and in condition to play.

Sorting out Byrd's massive early discography is daunting. He appeared on dozens of casual blowing sessions, but he sounds more substantive in structured settings like Blakey's *The Jazz Messengers* (Columbia), Silver's *Six Pieces of Silver* (Blue Note) and Paul Chambers' *Whims of Chambers* (Blue Note). On the latter, Byrd opens and closes his composition "Omicron" with thrilling high notes that soar over Latin rhythms; he plays two exhilarating solos, each a chorus in length, snaking through the harmony with the swagger of a ladies' man. He was 23. No wonder his phone rang off the hook. Byrd's first records as a leader for Transition and Savoy were blowing sessions, but in 1957 he teamed with alto saxophonist-composer Gigi Gryce to co-lead the Jazz Lab Quintet, which specialized in detailed arrangements of jazz originals. Though the records lack a certain spark, Byrd learned much from Gryce, who was ahead of his time in fighting for publishing rights.

Byrd signed with Blue Note in 1958, inaugurating his most rewarding period as an improviser, composer, and bandleader. For the next three years he co-led a captivating quintet with a pal from Detroit, fire-breathing baritone saxophonist Pepper Adams. Byrd's maturity coincided with the pinnacle of his trumpet command in 1958–60, a result of studies with two classical trumpet greats, William Vacchiano and the elder Joseph Alessi at the Manhattan School. Byrd's tone took on a sculptural strength and beauty akin to marble. His tender virility and endurance are marvels on "When Your Love Has Gone" from *Off to the Races.* In bars 5 and 6, the trumpet ascends a C minor seventh chord to an airborne B-flat, before sighing down the scale to an F. The clarion authority and resplendent vibrato Byrd brings to this passage touches the heart, and his patient improvisation deepens the bittersweet feeling. *Byrd in Hand*, *Byrd in Flight*, *At the Half Note Café* (vols. 1 and 2) and *The Catwalk* all impress with infectious material, bold solos, and high spirits. Byrd's sideman appearances on Blue Note in this period with Jackie McLean (*New Soil*), Walter Davis (*Davis Cup*), and Sonny Clark (*My Conception*) are also exceptional.

Trouble, however, lurked on the horizon. Byrd's tone began to lose some muscle mass in 1961, and issues with his embouchure deepened in the second half of the decade. Byrd told saxophonist Bob Belden that the problems stemmed from overwork and failure to warm up properly when he was spending all day in school and all night in clubs. Byrd's son was told by some of his father's friends that he began to suffer from Bell's palsy, a partial paralysis of facial muscles, in the mid-'60s. In the short run, however, Byrd still had a few imposing records left in him. Taped three months apart in late 1961, *Royal Flush* and *Free Form* are Byrd's strongest statements as a composer; they also introduce a startling 21-year-old newcomer named Herbie Hancock whom Byrd discovered in Chicago. Byrd's diverse originals range from the stop-time blues "Hush" to forward-leaning structures like "Shangri-La" and "French Spice." With jazz turning a corner in the early '60s and trumpeters Freddie Hubbard, Booker Little, and Don Cherry defining the cutting edge, it can be easy to overlook Byrd as old-fashioned before his time. But the sound world he created on his early Blue Notes reveals a deep-seated individuality and integrity.

Byrd earned a bachelor's degree and a master's degree in music education at the Manhattan School of Music in 1962–63. By the time of *A New Perspective* (Blue Note) in 1963 his tone is noticeably thinner. But he summons everything he's got on "Cristo Redentor," Duke Pearson's prayerful lament scored for choir and jazz group. The song became an anthem in black communities, and the record was Byrd's best-selling LP until the '70s. Meanwhile, Byrd showed Hancock the ropes on and off the bandstand. He helped him land a contract with Blue Note and made sure he retained his own publishing rights. In his 2014 memoir, *Possibilities*, Hancock fondly recalls Byrd as a mentor and free spirit, who introduced the pianist to marijuana and would hightail it out the fire escape when an IRS investigator showed up at his apartment to inquire about unpaid taxes.[2]

Byrd's complicated personal life expanded his horizons. Davis writes in *Paris without Regret* that at the same time Byrd married Lorraine Glover, he met

Marilyn Grayson, a Jewish woman and an intellectual, whose appreciation for art sparked his interest in collecting. They remained close until her death in 1975. Byrd left for Europe in 1963 with French-born Denise Genillon, whom he had met years before in Paris. They spent the summer in Montreux, Switzerland, before settling in Paris. "Denise taught me the European thing, and Marilyn taught me the American Jewish thing," Byrd told Davis. "Marilyn made me more conscious of the American culture and Denise of the European."

Byrd spent more than three years in Paris, returning occasionally to New York to record. He studied with Boulanger, played European festivals and club gigs, and wrote for radio orchestras. He moved home for good in 1967, having reached a crossroads at age 34. Byrd dove into jazz education, continuing to record but performing less frequently. He joined the faculty at Howard University in Washington, D.C., in 1968, where he founded the black music department in 1970. He had a rocky tenure, fighting conservative leaders over curriculum, resources, standards, and respect for jazz at a school where Western classical music still ruled. Byrd left Howard in 1975 for another historically black school, North Carolina Central University, and later taught at the University of North Texas (then North Texas State), Oberlin, and Delaware State.

The jazz-rock movement caught Byrd's ear in the late '60s, and he monitored Miles Davis' move into fusion. Like Davis, Byrd wanted to reach a younger black audience and sell more records. Byrd explored boogaloo, soul, funk, electric instruments, thicker textures, and percussion. Still, improvisation retained primacy. Byrd's trumpet could still be effective in a Davis-like language of short, rhythmic jabs, but he was not the player he once was. Involved in so many projects, he was unable or unwilling to devote the time and energy that rebuilding his technique demanded. The lingering effects of Bell's palsy may have been an issue too.

The decisive break came in 1972 when Byrd teamed with his former students Fonce and Larry Mizell. Fonce, a trumpeter, had been part of the Corporation, the Motown team that created hits for the Jackson 5. Larry, a keyboardist, graduated from Howard with an engineering degree and worked at NASA, before he and his brother formed their own production company. Byrd asked the Mizells in Los Angeles if they had any tunes he might like. The brothers played him "Flight Time" and "Mr. Thomas." Byrd recorded both. With Larry Mizell producing, Byrd recorded five more of the brothers' songs six months later to complete *Black Byrd* (Blue Note). "Byrd was the catalyst, but he gave us free rein," Larry Mizell said. "We kept in mind that we weren't writing for Marvin Gaye or anybody like that, but we kept it in that genre. We were looking for instrumental music that had a groove to it."

Released in 1973, *Black Byrd* is a highly polished blend of R & B and soul with breezy hooks, occasional vocals, and minimal improvisation. Byrd plays airy trumpet and contributes vocals. Black radio embraced the record. It sold hundreds of thousands of copies, peaking at No. 36 on the Billboard 200 chart, No. 2 on the R & B chart and No. 1 on the jazz chart. Byrd and the Mizells followed with *Street Lady*, *Stepping into Tomorrow*, *Places and Spaces*, and *Caricatures*. Byrd's new sound succeeded on its own terms. The Mizells made well-crafted, commercial music that got people moving on the dance floor. Yet I lose interest—too many string and synth sweeteners and mushy vocals. Byrd's live performances at the time packed a stiffer punch than the records, but if I want to boogie, I prefer Hancock's Head Hunters or Earth, Wind & Fire.

Jazz critics pounced. So did some of Byrd's peers. "Donald's sellout was very obvious, and there was nothing musically valid in what he did," Thad Jones told Leonard Feather in the *Los Angeles Times* in 1978. Yet alto saxophonist Phil Woods offered his blessing. "I'm for any musician able to keep his smarts and his ass together," Woods said in 2012. "Do I think he sold out? No way. No more than I thought Quincy Jones did. Words like 'sellout'—those are for journalists, not artists."

Byrd said he was "selling up," not "selling out," grabbing a piece of the capitalist pie usually denied black jazz musicians. Less defensibly, he often said, "That which sells the best is the best"—an untenable position he may have adopted as a shield against the purist trope that anything popular must be artistically inferior. Byrd formed a backup band comprised of his Howard students, but sensing greater business potential, he cut them loose as the Blackbyrds and launched a company to produce, manage, and market them. The band—including Detroiters Kevin Toney and Allen Barnes—struck gold. More than a dozen of its singles charted, including the Top 10 hit "Walking in Rhythm." Byrd told *Downbeat* in 1977 that Blackbyrd Productions had generated more than $10 million in four years. Byrd enjoyed his wealth. He bought fine art and sharp clothes, and once decided on the spur of the moment to rent a plane in Santa Monica and fly to Las Vegas, where he and the Mizells spent two days at a glittery hotel playing tennis and planning the next record.

Unfortunately, Byrd's relationship with the Blackbyrds ended in court. Keyboardist Kevin Toney said that an audit conducted of Blackbyrd Productions on behalf of the band showed the players were owed significant amounts of additional money. When Byrd failed to address the issues, the band sued Byrd's company for breach of contract in 1979, seeking to void its publishing deal and assume ownership rights to the name of the group. A federal judge ruled that the band should be released from Blackbyrd Productions but had to pay a licensing fee to call itself the Blackbyrds. The judge also ruled the publishing deal would remain in place for its final two years. The band received no settlement money but was able to move ahead on its own. Byrd's students were exercising rights they had learned in his classes.

"Byrd's heart was in the right place," said Toney. "However, there was greed and a mind-set that would not allow us to grow and be properly rewarded on the business side. But I can say with much adoration that he gave me the tools to develop my musical voice. He was always about the pursuit of excellence."

Byrd's trumpet playing was in shambles by the early '80s. Whether Bell's palsy was still a root cause of this condition isn't clear. Byrd eventually regained enough technique to attempt a comeback, but his return to straight-ahead jazz on Landmark Records (1987–91) yielded disappointing results. Byrd stayed connected to black popular culture through hip-hop; producers sampled funky beats from his '70s LPs, and he appeared in the video for Guru's "Loungin'" (1993).

The tributes after his death in 2013 spoke to the diversity of his fan base and accomplishments. Jazz aficionados hailed his early work. Black audiences who came of age in the '70s celebrated his popular hits. The hip-hop community remembered him as a godfather. The educational establishment honored his legacy. All claimed Byrd as one of their own, which would have pleased the trumpeter—and his father too.

Recommended Recordings

Donald Byrd, *Byrd in Hand* (Blue Note)
Donald Byrd, *Royal Flush* (Blue Note)
Art Blakey, *The Jazz Messengers* (Columbia)

Notes

1. Ursula Broschke Davis, *Paris without Regret* (University of Iowa Press, 1986).
2. Herbie Hancock with Lisa Dickey, *Possibilities* (Penguin, 2014).

Roland Hanna

MAGICIAN

During the early days of the Thad Jones–Mel Lewis Jazz Orchestra, one of the rituals of the band's Monday night gigs at the Village Vanguard was the moment when Jones turned the bandstand over to pianist Roland Hanna for a solo number. One night a puzzled Jerry Dodgion turned to fellow saxophonist Jerome Richardson and asked if he knew what song Hanna was playing. Richardson couldn't figure it out, so he leaned forward and asked Jones, who shrugged his shoulders. When Hanna finished, the audience erupted. As the room settled, Jones turned to the pianist: "Say, Roland, would you mind telling us what song you were playing?"

A disgusted look came over Hanna's face. "For Christ's sake!" he said indignantly. "'Body and Soul!'"

That was Hanna—a magician who could improvise spontaneous variations so abstract that even seasoned pros might not recognize source material as familiar as "Body and Soul." He synthesized Lisztian bravura, aristocratic grace, and sportin' life blues into a freewheeling but tasteful style that swelled with orchestral dynamics, expressive harmony, polyphonic detail, and sly wit. Hanna, who died in 2002 at age 70, remains the most elusive and underrated of the great jazz pianists to emerge from Detroit at midcentury. Like Hank Jones, Barry Harris, and Tommy Flanagan, Hanna built a career of major-league associations, from Benny Goodman and Coleman Hawkins to Charles Mingus, Sarah Vaughan, and fellow Detroiters Thad Jones and Ron Carter.

At the same time, however, Hanna stood askew to the postwar pianistic mainstream. He studied at the Juilliard School, and his assimilation of classical music (especially Chopin, Rachmaninoff, and Debussy) set him apart. Hanna favored a fulsome approach with an active left hand. Almost everyone else of his generation emulated Bud Powell—the defining bebop pianist whose nimble right hand carried the show. Hanna's orchestral conception flowered most brilliantly when he played alone; he was among the

Pianist Roland Hanna, *right*, and Thad Jones perform with the Thad Jones–Mel Lewis Jazz Orchestra c. early 1970s. Photo: © K.Abe / CTSIMAGES / Institute of Jazz Studies.

best solo pianists in jazz. Conventional hard-bop groups were not his natural habitat, and he appeared on few canonical LPs. He was also a more ambitious composer than most, writing 400 pieces in myriad idioms—jazz, classical, solo piano, chamber music, ballet, and orchestra.

Hanna recorded prolifically as a leader during the last 30 years of his life but mostly for hard-to-find European and Japanese labels. His three favorite pianists were Tommy Flanagan, Art Tatum, and Arthur Rubinstein, and

Hanna's touch and rhythmic pulse owed much to Erroll Garner (1921–77), another pianist who, like Hanna, comprised a category of one. Hanna spent all his practice time on classical literature, and the grandeur of 19th- and early 20th-century Romanticism and the shimmer of French Impressionism were rarely far from the surface in his playing. Yet these elements never detracted from the core African American values of jazz—swing, blues, improvisation. Hanna was asked in a 1970 interview in *Downbeat* whether he considered his playing conservative, modern, avant-garde, or something else. "First of all, *musical*," Hanna answered. "I'm quite a musical person. . . . I don't believe any of these categories that you mention could, in a sense, contain me."

At the peak of his powers in the 1970s and '80s, Hanna's originality came at you with gale force. On 1979's *Swing Me No Waltzes* (Storyville), the title song explodes out of the gate in a startling rush of triplets—dominant seventh sharp 9 chords moving by minor thirds. Hanna's hummable melody calms the waters, before the swinging dynamism of his improvisation and interplay of left and right hands seem to lift the piano off the ground. The ruminative "Free Spirit—Free Style" finds Hanna channeling Rachmaninoff and Chopin. A sweet, rubato melody filled with childlike wonder grows into an elaborate fantasia. "Roland had an incredible beat, just a rock-solid groove," said pianist Jeb Patton, who studied with Hanna in the 1990s. "That's one of the things that separates him from others, including the more purely classical guys in a jazz vein. He has this forward momentum, mixed with the left thumb doing counterpoint against the melody. It's a multi-lined approach. He's great at following through on his inner lines, combined with a strong, funky, Erroll Garner beat."

Bassist Ron Carter said that what was most fun about playing with Hanna was the way the pianist developed his ideas. "I liked to hear him take an idea in the first eight bars of his solo and expand that idea for the next four or five choruses. I was so appreciative of a guy who could take a figure and make it last for an entire song."

Hanna's lifelong focus on classical music forged a prodigious piano technique and an expansive palette. In Shanaphy and Knowlton's *Do It Yourself Handbook for Keyboard Playing*, Hanna said: "Take a look at Rachmaninoff's Piano Concerto No. 3. There are all kinds of elements here that are similar to jazz. He begins with a melody. Then he develops it the way a jazz artist develops a tune. He improvises on the chords while the melody appears in the orchestra. It is similar to what I do all the time: cadenza passages, changes in voices, reworkings of rhythmic ideas, Chopin is another good model for jazz pianists. He will play a certain melodic idea over and over, but with a slight change in the harmonies each time. Scriabin uses 7th and 9ths and 11ths in his harmonies, and these sounds form the basis for contemporary piano styles. . . . But when I study and analyze his music, it doesn't become a part of me until I'm playing jazz. In performing, I can begin to see what each of these composers meant. That's why I use this music. I don't want to copy what someone else has done. But it is important to be able to grab the elements from each musical tradition so I can use them in my own way."[1]

Hanna's physical appearance and personality were as singular as his playing. He was a compact man, five feet, five inches tall, round in the middle, with a high forehead and goatee. One of his albums was called *Sir Elf*, and it represented an affectionate mashup of his appearance and the formal knighthood bestowed upon him by the president of Liberia in 1970, after Hanna performed benefit concerts in the country to raise money for education. Thereafter, he was often referred to as Sir Roland Hanna. He was well-read, funny, politically aware, and a sports fan especially fond of football. Friends say he loved to argue, relished playing the contrarian and tended to see the world and people in stubborn absolutes.

Conductor, composer, and arranger David Berger worked with Hanna in the late '80s and early '90s with the Jazz at Lincoln Center Orchestra. Berger recalled that on one tour the bus became a source of controversy. The windows didn't roll down, the air-conditioning was broken, and swivel seats made it impossible for guys to stretch out. Older musicians in the band bitched constantly about the bus—except for Hanna. "I don't know what you guys are talking about," he'd say. "I love the bus." This went on for days: "I love the bus. What's wrong with it? I *love* the bus." Finally, Berger told Hanna that Rob Gibson, a recent addition to the Jazz at Lincoln Center staff, whom Hanna disliked, also loved the bus. "I *hate* the motherfucking bus!" were the next words out of Hanna's mouth.

Roland Pembroke Hanna was born on February 10, 1932, in Detroit. Raised in the North End, he was one of eight children. His father was a carpenter and mason by profession but also ministered in church and played saxophone. Hanna told interviewers that when he was four or five he found a music book in the street and taught himself to play piano. By age eight he could play pieces by Bach and Chopin. Hanna started lessons at age 11 with Josephine Love (1914–2003), an important musical and cultural figure in Detroit's black community. She had earned a diploma in piano at Juilliard, an English degree from Spelman College, and a master's degree in musicology from Radcliffe College.

Records in Hanna's Juilliard file say that he studied with two leading classical teachers in Detroit, Edward Bredshall (from 1947 to 1949) and Mischa Kottler (from 1953 to 1955)—both of whom also taught Ruth Laredo (née Meckler), five years younger than Hanna and destined for classical stardom. Bredshall had studied with Nadia Boulanger in France and punctuated lessons with lectures about art, history, and literature with a cigarette dangling from his lips. Born in the Ukraine, Kottler was a virtuoso with a Russian soul, though his teachers included Alfred Cortot and Emil von Sauer. As a teenager, Hanna also took two years of cello lessons and played alto saxophone in high school.

Hanna didn't like jazz until he was 13 or 14 and met Tommy Flanagan at Northern High School. Hanna would skip academic classes and practice on a grand piano in the auditorium. "I was on one side of the auditorium playing Rachmaninoff Preludes, Tommy was on the other side playing Bud Powell," Hanna told the *Los Angeles Times* in 1988. "I got up and went over to him to find out what he was doing and how he was doing it. He sort-of made it seem like I could do it too, so I jumped in."

Hanna continued classical lessons but also attended jam sessions. Just as Barry Harris had stood behind Flanagan to steal chords, Hanna learned by standing behind Flanagan and watching him practice. Hanna listened to jazz records and frequented a summer recreation center where bassist Major Holley was a counselor and taught kids to play the blues. Hanna also heard Art Tatum many times at an after-hours club run by Freddie Guinyard, an associate of heavyweight champ Joe Louis. Tatum, whose lightning speed and creativity inspired awe and fear in other pianists, hung out at Guinyard's house when in town. Tatum would sometimes play all night, and Hanna would be right there.

By the late '40s, Hanna was part of cooperative group with saxophonist Joe Alexander, bassist Ali Jackson, and drummer Oliver Jackson. Though Hanna started at Northern High School, he spent his final two years at Cass Tech, graduating in 1950. He joined the army and spent two years assigned duties as a musician and cook. Eager to continue his classical studies, he entered the Eastman School of Music in Rochester, New York, in 1953 but lasted only about a month. The faculty still held troglodyte views about jazz. After teachers spotted Hanna playing in clubs to support himself, he was told Eastman students weren't allowed to play jazz in public or private.

Hanna rejoined the roaring jazz scene in Detroit and started piano lessons with Kottler. He led a trio at Chic's Show Bar on the west side with Ray McKinney and Benny Benjamin, and he became friendly with trumpeter Thad Jones. Hanna also married Detroiter Ramona Woodard in 1953. They had a son by the time Hanna entered the Juilliard School in 1956; three more children would follow. Hanna worked a day job as a medical attendant at Detroit Receiving Hospital to support his growing family. As a student in New York, he played for dance classes and worked at a home for Jewish seniors.

His major teacher at Juilliard was Gordon Stanley, an English pianist and pedagogue. Hanna also studied with Beveridge Webster, celebrated for his performances of Ravel and Debussy, and Hanna sang in the Juilliard Chorus. One of a handful of blacks at Juilliard, his career aspirations at the time are difficult to discern. In a 2000 interview for the Fillius Jazz Archive at Hamilton College in upstate New York, Hanna said that when he was 16, he promised himself that he would become a concert pianist—but at Juilliard realized it was incumbent upon him to ultimately play "the music of my people," meaning jazz. "You are born into a certain situation, and you have to learn to accept that and to do something with that," he said.

Hanna never directly addressed in interviews the discrimination—overt or subtle—that was reality for black musicians pursuing classical music in those days. His son, Michael Hanna, doesn't remember his father talking about thwarted ambitions. However, in a posthumous tribute in the journal *Belles Lettres*, Detroit-born drummer Eddie Locke said: "Roland really wanted to be a classical musician. That's the sad part of being a black man. It's hard enough to be a classical musician if you're any color. To be a classical musician when he was growing up, for him there was no chance." Locke noted Hanna was also castigated by some fellow jazz musicians for bringing his classical influences to bear so directly on his jazz playing.

Hanna's Fillius Jazz Archive interview has the ring of a man denied his first choice of a career but determined to retake control of his own narrative by embracing—and transcending—cultural norms. His ultimate triumph was that he forged an artistic identity that expressed the full breadth of his humanity by leaping over the racial stereotypes and cultural redlining coursing through mid-20th-century America.

While at Juilliard, Hanna played jazz gigs around town, made his recording debut with saxophonist Seldon Powell in 1956, and landed a high-profile job with Benny Goodman in 1958. At 26, Hanna was so nervous when he went to audition at Goodman's home that he mistakenly told the doorman he was there to see Tommy Dorsey. Hanna traveled overseas with Goodman and recorded with the clarinetist's big band and small group. Goodman even called the dean at Juilliard to work out an extension for Hanna when extra days added to the tour meant he would miss exams. Hanna backed tenor saxophonist Coleman Hawkins on *Art Ford's Jazz Party*, a local television program in New York in 1958. By summer 1959, Hanna was working with volatile modernist Charles Mingus and remained in the bassist's circle nearly a year, appearing on *Mingus Dynasty* (Columbia) and *Pre-Bird* (Mercury). Hanna made his first LPs as a leader for Atco in 1959. His burgeoning jazz career forced him to withdraw from Juilliard in March 1960 without receiving a degree.

Hanna's early recordings are striking for how different he sounds than his contemporaries. With Goodman, he nods to pre-bop pianists like Teddy Wilson. With Mingus, he channels Ellington and earthy blues. On Art Ford's television show, his right hand speeds through "Lover Come Back to Me" like a supercharged Garner but with bebop triplets in the mix. Hanna's Atco debut, *Destry Rides Again*, is undercut by uninspired material from Harold Rome's musical, but the spritely follow-up trio LP, *Easy to Love*, should be better known. Hanna worked with singers Sarah Vaughan, Carmen McRae, and Al Hibbler in the early '60s and was asked to write the score for the Japanese film *Asphalt Girl* (1964) and bring a quartet to Tokyo. Hanna never completed a full score, but there's a wild scene in the film in which Hanna, Thad Jones, Ernie Farrow, and Albert "Tootie" Heath are seen playing a driving blues in the middle of a swarm of finger-popping Japanese listeners and dancers.

Hanna played often with Coleman Hawkins during the 1960s. They bonded over their shared love for classical music and spent countless hours exploring Hawkins' record collection—Bach, Mozart, Schumann, Mahler, Strauss, Ravel, Debussy, Bartok, Ives. Hawkins helped Hanna understand how he could funnel more of his classical training into his jazz playing. There are no recordings of them together other than a few pieces of video in 1958. Producer Bill Sorin—a onetime Hanna student, who eventually started the IPO label—financed a doomed studio session in an attempt to document the partnership. Sorin said the session likely took place in 1968, Hawkins' last stand in a studio before his death in 1969. The saxophonist thought so highly of Hanna that he agreed to record on the condition that the group only play the pianist's compositions.

Unfortunately, Hawkins' playing had deteriorated, and he was drinking heavily. Visitors to his apartment might encounter empty Hennessy bottles stacked outside the door like milk bottles. The session started at 10:00 a.m. Hawkins, hungover, couldn't function. Hanna and drummer Eddie Locke positioned him in front of a music stand that held "After Paris," an impressionistic ballad in F-sharp minor and notated with a maze of accidentals. "I still can't imagine what the double sharps looked like to Hawkins under those circumstances," Sorin said. The quartet, including bassist Buddy Catlett, tried two numbers, both unsalvageable; Hanna recorded a half dozen solo pieces that remain unissued.

Hanna joined the Thad Jones–Mel Lewis band in 1966 shortly after its founding and stayed until 1974. His off-the-cuff personality found a mirror image in Jones. Jerry Dodgion remembered the pair playing Cole Porter's "I Love You" as a duet, starting with the verse: "They would play it free—not just rubato, but *free*—and they would literally communicate. Those guys played music together so beautifully and in ways you can't imagine. It was on such a high level of embellishment, feeling and respect for melody."

An intriguing twist to their relationship is that Hanna almost certainly composed "A Child Is Born," the gentle waltz credited to Jones and his most-covered song. (Alec Wilder even wrote lyrics to it.) The precious melody unfolds in simple quarter notes and dotted half notes and sounds nothing like Jones—there's no syncopation—and everything like Hanna's Romanticism. David Berger, who was at the Village Vanguard for most of the band's gigs in the early years, remembers Hanna developing the song over many weeks during his improvised solo features; Jones showed up one night with a full-band arrangement of what Hanna had been playing. Hanna confirms this story in his Fillius Jazz Archive interview. He doesn't mention the song by name, but it could only be "A Child Is Born."

"I said, 'Thad, isn't that my tune?' He said, 'No, it's mine.'" Hanna chuckled as he recounted the story. If there were ever any hard feelings, he appears to have let them go. He excuses Jones' pilfering as akin to Ellington appropriating melodies improvised by his sidemen. "I never faulted [Thad] for that because he was just doing what bandleaders did," Hanna said. "If you throw an idea out there, he'd take it and write it down."

Hanna never contested Jones' authorship publicly, but he told friends privately that he wrote the song. "I gifted it to Thad" is how he put it to pianist Michael Weiss. The title was likely conjured by Jones, and the child in question may be the song itself. "A Child Is Born" was among the solo pieces Hanna recorded at the aborted Coleman Hawkins session, which took place as much as two years before the Jones-Lewis band recorded it in 1970. The pianist also recorded it in 1969 on Richard Davis' *Muses for Richard Davis* (MPS)—though an interesting wrinkle is that Hanna seemingly credits Jones for the piece at the start of the track when he says into the microphone: "'A Child Is Born'—Thad Jones."

No records were issued under Hanna's name in the '60s. *Child of Gemini* (MPS), taped in Germany in 1971, broke the dry spell. Hanna wrote all the music, including a suite marrying classical and jazz ideas; the trio with Dave Holland and Daniel Humair sounds game but a bit unsettled. Once the logjam was broken, more than 50 recordings as a leader appeared over the next three decades—plus six with the suave New York Jazz Quartet, whose various iterations included Frank Wess, Ron Carter, George Mraz, Ben Riley, Grady Tate, or Richard Pratt. Hanna's 16 solo piano recordings are a stunning achievement. In addition to the aforementioned *Swing Me No Waltzes*, the most magical include *Perugia* (Arista), *Plays the Music of Alec Wilder* (Trio / Inner City), *Sir Elf* (Choice), *Bird Tracks* (Progressive), *A Gift from the Magi* (West 54), and *Tributaries: Reflections on Tommy Flanagan* (IPO). Hanna's most frequent bass partner was George Mraz, whose fluency and taste made him a simpatico mate. *Sir Elf Plus One* (Choice) is half solo piano, half duets with Mraz, and all great. Drummer Ben Riley makes it an inspired trio on *This Must Be Love* (Progressive).

Of Hanna's more formal compositions, the seductive 24 Preludes, Book 1 and 2 on the King label deserve wider currency. These miniatures breathe with fresh melody and harmony, alternating through-composed "classical" pieces for solo piano with "jazz" duets (with bass) that include improvisation. In the '90s, Hanna's charming Sonata for Chamber Trio and Jazz Piano was recorded on Angel, and BalletMet in Columbus, Ohio, commissioned a jazz ballet premiered in 1992. Hanna performed his "Oasis" for piano and orchestra, a tone poem of languid repose, with the Detroit Symphony in 1993. He also performed Gershwin's *Rhapsody in Blue* with the National Symphony Orchestra and music director Leonard Slatkin in 1997—though Hanna would almost surely have rather played Ravel's Piano Concerto in G Major.

Hanna began teaching in the late '60s to make ends meet, and later was a professor at Queens College in New York. He died in 2002 of cardiac arrest in the wake of treatment for lung cancer. He never broke through to a wider jazz audience in America, but fellow musicians and insiders knew he was a unique force. "The essence of jazz is the expression of ideas that are reworked in one's mind, heart and soul," Hanna told the *Detroit Free Press* in 1991. "It truly expresses the depth of one's being. I play it with all my heart."

Recommended Recordings

Roland Hanna, *Perugia* (Arista)
Roland Hanna, *Swing Me No Waltzes* (Storyville)
Roland Hanna, *Plays the Music of Alec Wilder* (Trio / Inner City)

Note

1. Edward J. Shanaphy and Joseph L. Knowlton, *Do It Yourself Handbook for Keyboard Playing* (Astor Books, 1990).

Curtis Fuller

TROMBONE ON TOP

Talk about fast out of the blocks. Detroit-born trombonist Curtis Fuller arrived in New York in April 1957 at age 24. After nine months he had recorded eight LPs as a leader or co-leader for Prestige, Blue Note, and Savoy and appeared on 15 other sessions as a sideman with John Coltrane, Bud Powell, Jackie McLean, Yusef Lateef, Sonny Clark, Jimmy Smith, and others. Fuller hadn't had time to learn the subway, but he was already the hottest new man on his instrument in jazz. Like other young Detroiters flocking to New York, Fuller's combination of swing, intellect, soul, melodic imagination, and quicksilver technique was catnip to the scene.

"The thing that's most distinctive is his sound and swing and the groove in his playing," said trombonist Steve Davis. "Nobody swings harder than Curtis. It's very melodic, soulful, direct, and clear, but there's also an adventurous side to his playing too. Technically and phrasing-wise, he liberates the trombone."

The best early example of what Davis is getting at is Fuller's solo on the title track of Coltrane's iconic *Blue Train* (Blue Note). Recorded in September 1957, the LP documents the flowering maturity of the leader's tenor saxophone playing and composing. The band—which also includes Lee Morgan, Kenny Drew, Paul Chambers, and Philly Joe Jones—is in peak form on this wailing blues. Fuller's five-chorus solo is one for the ages. He starts casually, riding the groove. His sound is large and sonorous, athletic but lithesome. The rhythm section shifts into double time at the end of the second chorus, but Fuller holds back, picking off a high C and sticking to his tempo. Two bars later he shifts into high gear and the notes speed by, perfectly enunciated, swooping through the full range of the horn. Who says the trombone is a bulky instrument? Strutting riffs start the fourth chorus. Syncopated flourishes carry him to the top of the fifth. The rhythm section slows to the original tempo as tenor and trumpet throw extra coal on the fire. Fuller lays out for a bar and then calls the congregation home,

Trombonist Curtis Fuller prepares music at Van Gelder Studio in Hackensack, N.J. on January 22, 1958, during *Two Bones* session for Blue Note. Photo by Francis Wolff © Mosaic Images LLC.

swaggering down a blues scale, turning somersaults behind the beat. He goes out with soul, grace, and a taste of the bouncing articulation that would become a trademark. The excitement, authority, and construction of Fuller's solo explain why he became a major influence.

Fuller, who died at age 88 in 2021, spent an afternoon in 2012 speaking about his life and career. At the time, he was living in Massachusetts, about 45 miles west of Boston, but by 2016 he had relocated to Detroit to deal with health issues and be closer to family. Fuller is of medium build with an expressive moon face, deep-set eyes, and a warm laugh. He is so loquacious that it made sense to present his interview in a question-and-answer format. Here is our conversation, condensed for clarity, with interludes added to mark turning points in his biography.

Detroit Beginnings

Fuller was born on December 15, 1932.[1] His parents died when he was young, and he grew up in an orphanage in Detroit. Reference books and liner notes give conflicting accounts of how and when he took up the trombone, but Fuller is adamant that he started on the instrument at 12 or 13, shortly after hearing J. J. Johnson—the first to translate bebop to the trombone.

STRYKER: *How old were you when your parents died?*

FULLER: About six or seven. I remember hearing Roosevelt on the radio at the orphanage in 1941. My father died of tuberculosis and my mother died of a weird condition; I don't know what it's called. I had a brother and sister, and I was the baby. My father was from Jamaica and my mother was from Atlanta. There was a mix of all kinds of people where I grew up on the east side around Delmar and Cardoni—blacks, Italians, everybody.

STRYKER: *What orphanage did you enter?*

FULLER: The Children's Aid Society near Wayne State. It was difficult. There were not a lot of black kids. I was 13 or 14 when I went to live in a home for boys in Inkster just west of Detroit. That's where I went to high school. People would also come and get you to do some work for them—hoeing fields, planting potatoes and corn. I worked on some farms in upstate Michigan.

STRYKER: *How did you get interested in music?*

FULLER: My sister was a classical pianist. She was a prodigy and played Liszt and Beethoven and won competitions. Later they had instruments for the orphan kids. The young white students got the cream of the crop. I grabbed the violin, but I was told my people didn't play the violin. I was 10 or 11. I had heard Tommy Dorsey on the radio and that sounded good to me, but I hadn't played trombone at all until I heard J. J. Johnson when I was around 12 or 13. After that I saw Frank Rosolino, who was from Detroit, and I thought, "This guy is fantastic." By then the trombone was the only thing left at the orphanage. Later I played some baritone horn in high school.

STRYKER: *Did you have formal training?*

FULLER: There were some people around the neighborhood who showed me things. I remember a Mr. Trent who showed me some things about the instrument. Pianist Claude Black also played trombone, and he showed me things. The teachers in school usually didn't play brass instruments, so you were primarily on your own. Frank Rosolino helped me. Cannonball Adderley led the Army band when I was in the service for two years after being drafted in 1953. After I got out, I studied for a short time with the bass trombonist in the Detroit Symphony, Elmer Janes. Barry Harris showed me chords, scales, and theory. I took a few classes at Wayne (State) University and roomed with Joe Henderson there for a short time.

STRYKER: *When did you first hear J. J. Johnson?*

FULLER: It was with Illinois Jacquet at the Paradise Theatre around 1947. One of the women from the orphanage took me. Illinois Jacquet was an act—honking and screaming, biting the reed, squealing, and that stuff. The crowd would go wild. But J. J. just stood there and played, and he looked like *the guy*, the person who really knew what he was doing.

STRYKER: *What kind of sound attracted you?*

FULLER: I liked a majestic sound; I've always been a French horn guy. I was really attracted to that warm, lyrical, hornlike sound like Frank Rosolino had when he wasn't doing all that embellishing. Frank and I were close for a long time.

STRYKER: *How did you learn to play so fast and clean?*

FULLER: I practiced hours a day. I'd take the horn to bed—and I was sleeping on a cot! Listening to Rosolino and J. J. Johnson was a big influence. We didn't have all these books and videos that people have now. If you can't learn today you have to be genuinely backward! We'd go by the Blue Bird and stand outside the door, because we were too young to go in. They'd open the door during the summer with the screen and you'd stand right there and hear Billy Mitchell and Thad Jones. I remember one night at some place: I had just learned the changes to "Just You,

Just Me" from Barry, and I could get around "Cherokee" and "Rhythm" changes a little. I asked if I could sit in. It was Frank Foster and Wardell Gray—two saxophone players going after each other—and I got all up in that mess. They looked at me like I was crazy. I sounded terrible, but they let me play. They said, "We hear you, kid."

STRYKER: *Was there any tension between the black and white players at that time?*

FULLER: Relationships were very good. It was all mixed. I admired Pepper Adams so much that I thought he was the greatest who ever played the baritone saxophone, and he was white. Playing with Pepper was pivotal. If you stand next to a guy long enough, it's going to rub off. Pepper would write out Thad Jones songs so I could see the notes. These weren't simple even by today's standards, but because Pepper played them I did too. I can't impress upon you how much I respected and admired him. If I hadn't met Pepper, it never would have happened for me.

On to New York

Fuller made his first recording at age 21 in Cambridge, Massachusetts, on April 20, 1956, at a session organized by Tom Wilson—a pioneering African American producer who later worked with Bob Dylan, Simon and Garfunkel, and the Velvet Underground—for his new Transition label. Pepper Adams, John Coltrane, and Paul Chambers were among those on the date. Some discographies incorrectly list the album under Chambers' name, but Adams scholar Gary Carner has dug up a letter from Wilson to Adams in which it's clear that the baritone saxophonist was originally intended to be the leader. Carner said Adams never wrote any material for the session and at the last minute Fuller became a co-leader. Fuller sounds fluent but overly indebted to J. J. Johnson.

Fuller came to New York with Yusef Lateef to record in April 1957. When the band returned to Detroit, Fuller stayed behind. Among the best of the early LPs under his own name are *The Opener* (Blue Note) and *Imagination* (Savoy). Fuller's rapport with tenor saxophonist and composer Benny Golson is documented on a dozen LPs between 1958 and 1960, including the superb *Groovin' with Golson* (New Jazz) and *The Curtis Fuller Jazztet with Benny Golson* (Savoy). The Jazztet moniker lived on as the name of a new band organized by Golson and Art Farmer with Fuller a charter member. Fuller stayed just long enough to appear on *Meet the Jazztet* (Argo) in 1960, best known for introducing Golson's "Killer Joe," though Fuller's high-speed romp on "It's All Right with Me" remains a touchstone for trombonists.

STRYKER: *Describe your early days in New York.*

FULLER: Oh, boy, that was fasten-your-seat-belt time! When I got to New York, I sat in with Miles at the Café Bohemia—I had met him back in Detroit—and he asked me to join his band, so I started working at the Bohemia right away. Alfred Lion from Blue Note had heard about me, and he came to hear me with Miles. Alfred took to me immediately. But I was also something that I shouldn't have been: I was still a clone of J. J. Johnson. I was playing one Monday at Birdland with Coltrane and Lee Morgan and J. J. came in. I could hear J. J.'s voice over everybody else saying, "He's playing all my stuff!"

STRYKER: *When did you begin to transcend Johnson's influence?*

FULLER: I started that moment when I heard J. J. say that in the club. I felt that I had infringed upon him. I studied everybody, not just trombone players—Stan Getz, Clifford Brown, Miles. The solos that made sense to me were well-developed. There was a sense of order, melodic construction, and lyricism. If you're just playing arpeggios or scales, that's not improvising. I found that the guys who played interesting stuff were like Charlie Parker. Those are melodic and lyrical lines. (Fuller sang "April in Paris" like Parker might play it, with curtains of double-time melody embellishing the song.)

STRYKER: *What was it like recording* Blue Train?

FULLER: That was unique, so much so that Trane left the material alone after he recorded it. There was something sacred about that record. People will say, "Let's play 'Moment's Notice,' and I'll say, "Oh, after you had 50 years to learn it? We had all of two hours to learn it." Do you have any idea what it was like to have a two-hour rehearsal one day and then go into the studio for Blue Note the next day to record *Blue Train* in three hours? You had to be accountable for everything you played for eternity.

I do get credit for naming one of the songs. I told John, "How are you going to pull a song out on us like this on a moment's notice?" The lines and the chords don't move like on standard tunes. But he thought that was funny and that's how "Moment's Notice" got its name. I spent a lot of time with Trane. I would go by his house every day. Saxophone players like Wayne Shorter would go over there and sit there just like me. He would look over at them and say, "Take out your horn. Can you play this?" He'd always ask me at some point during the day if I could play on the trombone what he just played on the tenor—lots of diminished patterns. (Fuller sang examples.) I tried to play to them.

STRYKER: *How did you come up with the bouncing articulation in your lines, using dotted 8th and 16th notes in a long-short pattern rather than more even 8th notes?*

FULLER: All of us got some of that from Lee Morgan. He got a lot of it from Kenny Dorham. Lee would really get into it, and one night I remember Miles admonished him: "You're playing that Howdy-Doody shit!"

STRYKER: *What makes a successful solo?*

FULLER: Humor and dialogue. Billie Holiday used to say, "When you play, you're talking to people." Music is English composition. Each song should have a subject, and phrases should have a noun, a verb, and like that. It should be expressive. Exclamation points: Bap! When you put a group of sentences together, it makes a paragraph. You're telling a story.

The Jazz Messengers

Fuller played with drummer Art Blakey and the Jazz Messengers from summer 1961 to the end of 1964. For most of those years, Fuller's bandmates were trumpeter Freddie Hubbard, tenor saxophonist Wayne Shorter, pianist Cedar Walton, and bassist Reggie Workman. The music turned a corner from bluesy hard bop into a more progressive post-bop with new layers of harmonic complexity, modes, and vamps. Fuller's playing became more rhythmically concentrated with Blakey. The Messengers' records from this period are revered, especially the ultra-intense *Free for All*, though Fuller is probably heard to better effect on *Mosaic*, *Indestructible* (both on Blue Note), and *Caravan* (Riverside).

STRYKER: *Art's music changed at this point. It became more modern.*

FULLER: The writing changed. Art asked me to write something right away, so I came up with "A La Mode." Wayne became musical director. The band wanted to get away from the Bobby Timmons and Benny Golson things like "Moanin'" and "Blues March." We were all moving forward in the same direction. We tried to stay out of the regular keys to push ourselves away from regular patterns. I wrote "Three Blind Mice" in B and Wayne would write in A. I wrote "Buhaina's Delight" so Art would have something special to play with those solo breaks. That band was as tight as a band can get.

STRYKER: *What did it feel like to play with Art Blakey behind you?*

FULLER: The most creative playing you ever were going to do in your life would be with Art Blakey. A lot of people were great, but Art was an institution when it came to laying down the carpet of rhythm and swinging. He didn't care too much about perfection per se. He wanted us to be ourselves. He would say, "I want you to reach for the stars every night."

STRYKER: *What other guidance did Blakey give you?*

FULLER: Art would say, "Don't practice on my gig." He didn't like for one song to go too long. He'd say, "You don't play everything you know on one song. Play your good stuff and then get out of the way." Another thing he'd say was, "I don't want any music on the bandstand. You learn it. Charlie Parker never had any music on the stand."

Paying Dues, Earning Dividends

The late '60s and early '70s were fallow years for Fuller. Work slowed. Nine years elapsed between recordings as a leader. At one point around 1968, he worked for about a year at a desk job for Chrysler near Wall Street. Fuller toured with the Count Basie Orchestra for three years in the mid-'70s. By the 1980s he was working more steadily with his peers in the Timeless All-Stars and a Jazztet reunion. Fuller's finest post-1970 albums were made in 1978—*Four on the Outside* (Timeless) and *Fire and Filigree* (Bee Hive). His chops are in sterling shape, and the former, a reunion with Pepper Adams, features five compelling Fuller compositions, including the enchanting "Suite Kathy." Issues with his lungs and teeth slowed Fuller down in the 1990s and the accuracy and strength of his playing diminished considerably. Still, a judiciously paced appearance at the Detroit Jazz Festival in 2011 showed that he could still be effective at 76. As of December 2018, he had not performed in several years due to various health problems.

STRYKER: *It looks you were scuffling after you left Blakey?*

FULLER: I was. And I was out there looking for something, dating the wrong people, living the wrong life. I began to drink, which is something I didn't do earlier. I was angry and bitter for a while. I floated around with a lot of bands. Then eventually order was restored. I had met my late wife when I was with Count Basie and we got married in 1980. Basie was a good job, I wanted that development, and I really wanted to play with singers—Frank Sinatra, Tony Bennett, Ella Fitzgerald. I recorded "In the Wee Small Hours of the Morning" after hearing Sinatra sing it.

STRYKER: *Did you know Sinatra?*

FULLER: Yeah. He let the musicians use his dining room at the Sands in Las Vegas. He would always leave me a bottle of champagne. He called me Bone-ski. I remember once we played a command performance in London for the Queen, and they pulled the bus on me. I thought, "Oh, man, I'm gonna be out here all night trying to get a cab." But Frank and Shecky Greene were back there with Queen Elizabeth. Frank had a limo and he said, "Hey Bone-ski, get in the car. We're going to the White Hall." I was staying in another hotel, but I thought, "OK, we're going to the White Hall."

STRYKER: *You had a serious health issue in 1994. What happened?*

FULLER: God took a lobe of my right lung. I had the beginning of what would have become cancer. A small growth had developed. They told me if they took it out I'd live and play. I never had to have chemotherapy or radiation, but it was more than a year before I could really play. There was a time guys were just doing me a favor to get me on a gig, but where I am now is not too bad for a guy my age. I've lost a step, but I got the chance to play a lot of music with some of the greatest musicians, and all the guys I recorded with and everything else. I mean, I didn't miss a whole lot.

Recommended Recordings

Curtis Fuller, *The Opener* (Blue Note)
Art Blakey, *Mosaic* (Blue Note)
Curtis Fuller, *Four on the Outside* (Timeless)

Note

1. Standard references list Fuller's birthdate as December 15, 1934, which he confirmed to me in a 2012 interview. However, after his death, *Washington Post* obituary writer Matt Schudel learned from the trombonist's daughter, who cited government documents including his passport, that her father was two years older than commonly believed. His birthday is December 15, 1932.

Louis Hayes

THE (CYMBAL) BEAT GOES ON

It's almost impossible to look hip behind the wheel of a rented minivan, but nobody makes the scene like drummer Louis Hayes, who arrived in New York in the summer of 1956 as a 19-year-old Detroiter with quick hands, sharp ears, and a swinging cymbal beat. Forty-six years later, on a sweltering July 4 in 2002, Hayes wore a stylish muscle shirt, linen pants, and oversized designer glasses and projected such unstudied cool driving down the West Side Highway that he might as well have been piloting a Ferrari rather than a Ford Windstar. Riding shotgun was his wife, Nisha, a real estate agent with her own distinctive style and dress. Hayes was scheduled to perform in Atlantic City in nine hours. The trip is only two hours from Manhattan, but Hayes insisted on an early start. He follows a strict pre-performance regimen of practice, rest, and concentration. "He's always on a schedule," said Nisha. "I went to Paris with him, and he's been 50 times and had never seen the Eiffel Tower. I had to drag him there."

Hayes headed for the Lincoln Tunnel. When it was time to merge, Hayes, who is not as attentive a driver as he is a drummer, came within feet of ramming a bus. Nisha looked horrified. "Louis, he doesn't care that you play the drums!" Hayes barely raised an eyebrow.

Hayes, who turned 88 in 2025, continues to lead his own bands and record, and he was named an NEA Jazz Master in 2023. Hayes was a teenage phenom. He anchored two of the defining hard-bop bands in jazz during his first decade in New York, spending three years with the Horace Silver Quintet and six more with the Cannonball Adderley Quintet and Sextet. He toured with the Oscar Peterson Trio for two years in 1965–67 (and another year in 1971–72), and in the late '60s briefly co-led the Jazz Communicators with Freddie Hubbard and Joe Henderson. In the '70s and early '80s, Hayes freelanced and led a series of artistically vital if financially challenged bands, including a group co-led at different points with Woody Shaw or Junior Cook.

With a daughter entering college, Hayes returned to a steady sideman

Drummer Louis Hayes, right, with Horace Silver at the 19-year-old Hayes' first recording session, which yielded Silver's *Six Pieces of Silver* (Blue Note). Van Gelder Studio in Hackensack, N.J. on November 10, 1956. Photo by Francis Wolff © Mosaic Images LLC.

role with pianist McCoy Tyner in the mid-'80s, but by the end of the decade he was again balancing freelance work and leading his own band. Hayes has appeared on roughly 250 recordings with everyone from John Coltrane to Johnny Hodges. He's also made 22 as a leader or co-leader, the most recent being *Serenade for Horace* (Blue Note), a tribute to his former boss, issued in 2017. Hayes still fronts his Cannonball Adderley Legacy Band and a wider-ranging ensemble under the Jazz Communicators moniker.

"I was so fortunate," Hayes said. "I came to New York with a job and worked straight through with a major group all the way up until 1968. I wasn't written about all that much, and I had some tricky times in the '70s. But the major thing is being creative and making history. That's still the way I look at things."

Hayes came of age in an era saturated with great drummers but quickly took his place near the top of the pecking order. He corralled his influences into a recognizable identity that married fiery swing with a graceful touch and crackling precision. His quick reflexes turned heads—the clever way he accented written melodies and responded to soloists, and the vivid snap of his drum solos. He brought remarkable control to fast tempos, and he mastered the art of "tippin'"—swinging with fierce intensity but soft-shoe elegance. The heart of Hayes' identity is the unique way he phrases the ride cymbal beat—the ding-dinga-ding rhythm at the core of modern jazz drumming. The cymbal beat is a drummer's DNA; no two will sound exactly alike. Hayes burst onto the scene with a crisp and driving attack, favoring consistent patterns on the cymbal and placing his beat just ahead of the basic pulse without rushing. From the late '60s through the '80s, his cymbal beat grew splashier as it opened to a wider range of styles and rhythms. There was a trade-off—the loss of some of his formerly immaculate definition—but he always swung heroically.

"Louis is the kind of a guy, even to this day, if you were to handcuff his left hand to the drum stool and just have him play time on the cymbal, it would swing just as much," said drummer Kenny Washington.

Though not an innovator, Hayes has influenced drummers of several generations. He was, for example, an important mentor to Tony Williams (1945–97). Before Williams helped reshape jazz drumming in the '60s as a teenager, he would take the train from Boston to New York to hang out with Hayes on weekends. The swifter the tempo, the more you can hear the connection between them. Hayes was the first drummer to smooth out ultrafast tempos into a continuous wave of rhythm, Washington said. An early example is a breakneck "Lover" with John Coltrane (1958), where the 20-year-old drummer gallops confidently at roughly 360 quarter notes per minute. The band isn't always together, and Hayes isn't always steady, but there's a cohesive flow to his beat at this tempo that already equals if not surpasses his elders Max Roach and Philly Joe Jones.

Drummer Peter Erskine called Hayes "the missing link" who connected pacemakers of the '50s like Roach, Jones, and Art Blakey with Williams' post-bop style. Erskine said that Hayes provided a model for contemporary drummers who wanted to sound up-to-date without necessarily copying Williams or Elvin Jones. The ever-modern Roy Haynes might be the ultimate example of what Erskine means, but Hayes qualifies too. "Louis brought all of the previous developments in jazz drumming language to the mid-'60s and provided a road map for all non-Elvin as well as non-Tony players to follow," said Erskine. "Regarding him in that way makes his influence seem more universal."

The night before his Atlantic City gig, the 65-year-old Hayes talked about his life and career at his home in Riverdale, a leafy neighborhood in the northwest corner of the Bronx. He and Nisha own a 10th-floor co-op with a spectacular view of the Hudson River and the George Washington Bridge. The apartment was decorated with African masks and sculptures, vaguely Afrocentric paintings, and photos of family and friends. Hayes is a compact man, in good shape to this day, save a slight paunch, and looks younger than he is. He walks with a streetwise gait and shoulder hunch that suggests a coiled spring. To beat the heat on a sultry New York night, he wore shorts with no shirt, accentuating toned forearms as steely as those of a boxer. In conversation, Hayes stares at you intensely with his eyes wide open and a blank expression on his face. He responds in discursive fragments, and if he agrees with you, he'll nod his head and exclaim, "You're right on it!" or "That's Mellow D!" quoting a Horace Silver title that puns on the word "melody."

"Louis deals with everyone the same way," said pianist Rick Germanson. "He doesn't put on an act around younger or older musicians or critics or record producers." Trombonist Curtis Fuller warned not to be fooled by his old friend's laid-back demeanor: "He's very knowledgeable, even if he doesn't seem like it," Fuller said. "He'll stand back in reserve and appraise the situation, and then make his comment."

Louis Sedell Hayes was born May 31, 1937, in Detroit and grew up on Philadelphia Street on the west side. Both parents were avocational musicians. His father, an autoworker, played drums, while his mother, who waited tables and eventually owned her own diner, played piano. Hayes started on the piano at age 5 and took up drums at 10. The key influence in his early development was his cousin Clarence Stamps, an accomplished drummer who grounded Hayes in technical fundamentals and lessons that stuck for life. Hayes remembered: "He'd say, 'If anything in the band goes wrong, it's your fault.' And 'When you're playing, and you look out into the audience and you don't see anyone pattin' their feet, then you're not playing shit.' And 'You can't just play the drums and not know where you are in the tune. You have to be in control of the band, and you have to make music out of the drums.'"

By the time Hayes was 15, he was spending all day in the basement practicing the drums, memorizing Charlie Parker solos, and dabbling on piano and vibes. Bassist Ernie Farrow introduced Hayes to the records of Kenny Clarke, the bebop pioneer who was the first to move the basic beat to the ride cymbal from the bass drum, snare, and hi-hat. Hayes would spend hours listening to Clarke's pristine cymbal beat and hours more practicing his own version. Along the way he also assimilated the hot-oil sizzle of Philly Joe Jones.

He began playing with friends like saxophonists Eli Fountaine and Eddie Chambliss at spots around town, including a teenage club called the Club Tropicano in Paradise Valley. Hayes also played at the World Stage jam sessions, testing his mettle with big-league musicians like Kenny Burrell and Barry Harris in front of a jazz-savvy audience. "I was very nervous about playing there," Hayes said in *Before Motown*. "But after I played there a few times, these guys who I felt were my heroes really accepted me. That put me in another environment than with my friends."

Hayes took another leap forward in April 1956 when, at age 18, he joined the Yusef Lateef Quintet at Klein's Show Bar. The job was six nights a week, and Hayes had his hands full trying to come up with rhythms and textures to accompany Lateef's exotic compositions. A few months later in New York, Horace Silver, one of the most important pianists, composers, and bandleaders in jazz, needed a drummer. Silver's bassist, Detroiter Doug Watkins, had a recommendation: "Get the baby boy out of Detroit."

Silver's formally sophisticated compositions were girded by a finger-snapping beat. He didn't provide explicit instructions about how to play, leaving it to Hayes to come up with his own parts. The money wasn't great—$125 a week (about $1,140 in 2018 dollars) when the band was working, out of which Hayes had to pay his expenses on the road. But he was young, with no responsibilities other than music. Watkins provided entrée into the scene, introducing Hayes to all the musicians. Hayes first lived at the Alvin Hotel on 52nd Street, and from his window he could see Birdland and take note of who was going in and out of the club. Before long he and Watkins were sharing a studio apartment on the Upper West Side.

Hayes made friends with Papa Jo Jones, whose fluid swing and dynamics with Count Basie in the 1930s and '40s made him one of the most influential drummers in jazz history. Dapper, well-read, and opinionated, Jones liked to school younger musicians in African American musical and social history. He took Hayes under his wing, instructing him in life and music, keeping him on the straight and narrow. Hayes would put on a coat and tie at night and hit the town with Jones. "Jo was extremely intelligent," said Hayes. "He liked me. I paid attention. You know, if you listen, you can learn."

Hayes made five classic studio albums with Silver on Blue Note between 1956 and 1959: *Six Pieces of Silver*, *The Stylings of Silver*, *Further Explorations*, *Finger Poppin'*, and *Blowin' the Blues Away*. (The last two included another Detroiter in the band, bassist Gene Taylor.) On complex material like "The Outlaw," "Pyramid," and "Moon Rays," Hayes underscores the shifting Latin and swing rhythms, suspensions, vamps, and breaks by deftly choosing just the right color, texture, and accent to orchestrate each moment. On the rhumba sections during the solos on "The Outlaw" (1958), he plays quarter notes on the hi-hat on all four beats—perhaps the first recorded example of a technique Tony Williams would later elevate into a signature innovation.

Hayes left Silver in 1959 to join Cannonball Adderley. The alto saxophonist's eclectic, blues-braised book mixed soul-jazz hits like "This Here" and "Work Song" with hard-bop originals, bebop, standards, ballads, and, a couple years later, modal-inflected pieces. With Adderley's charismatic personality out front, the music was as audience friendly as a backyard barbecue. Adderley's frontline partner was his brother Nat on cornet, but the entire quintet was like family, particularly after pianist Joe Zawinul joined in 1961. Hayes and bassist Sam Jones formed a dynamic duo, creating a big beat with lots of snap. The pair showed up on dozens of record dates together, including sessions led by Wes Montgomery, Grant Green, Kenny Drew, J. J. Johnson, Barry Harris, and Phineas Newborn. "Sam and I had this great rapport on and off stage," said Hayes. "We were so similar in the way we thought about time and the way we felt the beat. He was Mr. Dependable. The sound of Sam and I playing together just laid out this red carpet for anyone who played with us."

The Riverside label recorded Adderley frequently in clubs and concerts to capitalize on the exuberance the band generated in front of an audience. *Cannonball in Europe* (1962) is particularly rewarding for capturing a hot night by the sextet—Lateef had joined by then on tenor sax, flute, and oboe—and because the drums are up front in the mix. Recorded in Tokyo in 1963, *Nippon Soul* includes a euphoric "Easy to Love" with the tempo way upstairs. Adderley and Hayes enunciate the time with pinpoint diction and the controlled abandon of cheetahs running down prey.

Hayes left the band in 1965 when Adderley added more commercial material into the mix like songs from "Fiddler on the Roof." In retrospect, he wished that he and Jones started their own band. Instead, both joined Oscar Peterson's trio. Hayes liked Peterson personally, and the pianist's celebrity meant that Hayes' salary nearly doubled. But Peterson's scripted concept was like a train that ran on a single track. Hayes chafed under the restrictions, and Peterson often had to lecture him for going off script during performances. Sometimes Hayes would have a couple of drinks at a post-gig party and lecture Peterson, who would fire him—but then hire him back the next day.

Hayes' style began to shift in the late '60s and early '70s. His cymbal beat patterns became more varied, less predictable, and he interacted more aggressively with soloists. The result was a more ringing swirl of sound and texture compared to the single-lane groove of his earlier work. You can hear Hayes adapting on tracks from 1967 like "Tetragon" with tenor saxophonist Joe Henderson and the meter-shifting "For B.P." with trumpeter Freddie Hubbard. Hayes even ventures into free-form playing on Hubbard's epic "Spacetrack" (1969).

The 1970s were tough years for acoustic jazz, but Hayes forged ahead, a reminder that many of the hard boppers who came up in the '50s and early '60s continued to evolve, flanked by fusion on one side and free jazz on the other. The outstanding live 1973 recordings by pianist Cedar Walton's quartet offer a sweeping expression and collective depth that the players—tenor saxophonist Clifford Jordan, Walton, Jones, and Hayes—could not have mustered a decade earlier. Hayes' *Breath of Life* (Muse), a three-horn septet session from 1974, is a bit ragged around the edges but offers a spirited snapshot of how the mainstream idiom absorbed '60s modalism and Afro-Cuban influences. Hayes' debut recording as a leader, *Louis Hayes* (Vee-Jay), had been taped back in 1960—an invigorating LP with the drummer fronting Adderley's quintet but with Lateef in place of the leader and interesting material by Detroiters Sonny Red, Barry Harris and Lateef. The Louis Hayes–Woody Shaw Quintet of 1976–77 was a mainstream beacon of the era. Hayes and tenor saxophonist Junior Cook started the band, and Shaw got featured billing. When Cook departed, the trumpeter became co-leader, and alto saxophonist Rene McLean joined pianist Ronnie Matthews and bassist Stafford James in the group. Shaw's expansive, Coltrane-inspired approach and evocative compositions like "The Moontrane" and "In Case You Haven't Heard" gave the band a wide berth. Its studio LPs for Muse, *Ichi-Ban* and *The Real Thing*, are hard-hitting musically but poorly engineered. Better are the live European broadcast recordings on High Note and TCB that capture the band stretching out in clear fidelity.

Variety Is the Spice (Gryphon) from 1979 is Hayes' best record and one of the decade's unsung glories. His working quartet comprises the core ensemble—the criminally neglected alto saxophonist and flutist Frank Strozier, pianist Harold Mabern, and bassist Cecil McBee. Two percussionists and idiosyncratic vocalist Leon Thomas add contrast. The music is at once ecstatic and concentrated, and the range of material justifies the title. The only misfire is the thumpa-thumpa disco cover of "Dance with Me." Otherwise, magic: Marvin Gaye's "What's Goin' On" is reinvented as a fast, fervent waltz. Strozier's beguiling alto dominates a commanding "Invitation" and a stunning "Stardust" reharmonized à la Coltrane. Hayes sounds relentless, fearless, magisterial, and completely up-to-date.

Back on Independence Day in 2002, Hayes navigated his rented Windstar into Atlantic City around 2:00 p.m. He headed down Atlantic Avenue to the Trump Taj Mahal, a hotel the size of Rhode Island with a kitschy Ali Baba decor. A few hours later, he was deep into his preconcert routine. He sat in an overstuffed purple chair with a practice pad propped up in front of him. His right hand was a blur of motion, and it took a moment to realize that he was playing his cymbal beat at a racehorse tempo. The TV was tuned to CNN, and Hayes watched the news while continuing his calisthenics. He played nonstop for 20 minutes, took a 30-second break for water, and then went back to work. Hayes was practicing far more in his 60s than when he was on the road 40 years earlier. "The older you get, the harder things get," he said. "I could do things when I was younger that now I really have to practice to even attempt to be able to do. My peak was when I was about 40—I was liable to do anything."

Hayes changed clothes and headed for the amphitheater at the south end of the boardwalk near Chicken Bone Beach, a once-segregated playground frequented by the African American elite in the decades before the 1964 Civil Rights Act. Hayes wore loose-fitting, pale-yellow pants, matching shirt, and a necklace setting of a large earth-colored stone. A middle-aged woman watched him set up his drums. "Wow, he sure looks good," she said. "How old is he?"

"Sixty-five," I said.

"Mmm, mmm," she responded.

The group was Hayes' Cannonball Adderley Legacy Band. The sole survivor of Adderley's original quintet, Hayes enjoys playing the old tunes. Band members were 27 to 40 years younger than the leader and included the rousing alto saxophonist Vincent Herring and trumpeter Jeremy Pelt. The quintet tore through its set, playing tight grooves befitting hard-bop convention. Hayes' right hand swarmed over the cymbal, and his snare drum popped like pistol shots. He is not flamboyant. His limbs stay close to his body, and he appears to be staring down his ride cymbal like a sharp-shooter in the Old West. Hayes soloed sparingly, but there was never any question that he was in charge.

Afterward he fielded congratulations, shook hands, posed for pictures, and chatted with older fans, most of them African Americans eager to relay stories about the time they heard Hayes back in the day with Adderley or Horace Silver. "You cats were burning back then," said one gentleman of a certain age. "You still sound damn fine."

Hayes smiled: "You're right on it!"

Recommended Recordings

Horace Silver, *Further Explorations* (Blue Note)
Cannonball Adderley, *Cannonball in Europe* (Riverside)
Louis Hayes, *Variety Is the Spice* (Gryphon)

Ron Carter

THE RIGHT NOTE AT THE RIGHT TIME

About the most complicated thing you can do with a double bass, other than build one from scratch, is play modern jazz on it. You must delineate the harmony of a song. You must anchor the rhythmic pulse and time in the band. You must play melodic walking lines. You must form a death-grip bond with the drummer but also negotiate, on the fly, individual relationships with the pianist and horn soloists. And you must play with a resonant tone, expert intonation, and dogged stamina—no matter how many choruses the long-winded tenor saxophonist takes. On the most elemental level your job boils down to playing the right note at the right time. That's why the Detroit-bred Ron Carter is one of the greatest bassists in jazz history: Since 1960, no one has played the right note at the right time more often than he has.

Carter's sound and style entered the DNA of jazz during his tenure with the groundbreaking Miles Davis Quintet from 1963 to 1968. As part of a magic-triangle rhythm section with pianist Herbie Hancock and drummer Tony Williams, Carter built a bridge from the big-beat swing of bebop to the advanced harmonies, complex rhythms, and elastic structures of the 1960s. The trio pioneered a hide-and-seek approach to time and space, evolving a multilayered dialogue that erased distinctions between foreground and background. He was among a group of bassists—Scott LaFaro, Jimmy Garrison, Charlie Haden, Richard Davis were others—pushing the bass beyond its traditional timekeeping role. Carter revealed how much a bass player, working outside of the spotlight, could influence the shape and direction of the music. His full-bodied tone, harmonic imagination, rhythmic freedom, rock-ribbed groove, impeccable taste, lightning reflexes, imperturbable profile, and uncanny ability to bring out the best in others proved so compelling that everybody wanted to work with him.

Carter, who turned 88 in 2025, has been certified by Guinness World Records as the most recorded bassist in jazz history, with 2,221 credits to his name as of September 2015. (The number continues to grow.) It's hard to find

Ron Carter performs at the Dirty Dog Jazz Café in Grosse Pointe Farms just outside of Detroit in June 2016. Photo by John Osler.

a major jazz musician of his time with whom Carter has not worked. He's appeared on scores of iconic recordings by Davis, Hancock, Wayne Shorter, Bobby Hutcherson, Joe Henderson, Eric Dolphy, Eddie Harris, Sam Rivers, McCoy Tyner, and countless others. "Playing with Ron feels like being cradled in your mother's arms it's so comfortable," Hancock said. "But at the same time, it's so provocative that it inspires you to create new ideas."

This is the paradox that has made Carter such a vital force: He is a peerless accompanist because he is the ultimate team player. But he deliberately introduces enough creative tension to push players out of their comfort zones, lifting the bandstand to a higher plane of improvisation. Carter relishes controlling the flow of the music, but his musicianship is so profound that the conflict between selflessness and ego disappears the way sugar dissolves in hot coffee. It's like the way Michael Jordan elevated the play of his teammates while always making sure the Chicago Bulls' offense ran through him. Potent early examples of the Carter Effect can be heard on "My Funny Valentine" and "Stella by Starlight" performed in concert by the Davis quintet in February 1964. Issued on *My Funny Valentine* (Columbia), these performances unfold like collectively improvised symphonies. Carter's surprising note choices shake up the harmony, and his repeating patterns, pedal points, tempo modulations, and rhythmic shifts create an environment in which anything can happen at any time.

"He is the center that all things revolve around," said bassist Scott Colley, speaking of the Davis quintet performance of "My Funny Valentine." "Ron is the one who establishes the initial tempo, outlines the form and harmony, responds to the soloists moving between the initial pulse and the double-time feel and back again, negotiating transitions in an organic way. His approach allows the dialogue of each soloist and propels the creative exploration to occur with power and grace."

More recently, Carter played a thrilling set of duets with guitarist Pat Metheny at the 2015 Detroit Jazz Festival. Addressing jazz classics and standards, the bassist's distilled rhythms and imaginative note choices opened a window on the infinite. Metheny ran with the possibilities Carter left hanging in the air. The bass playing was not flashy, and it was easy to overlook the offhanded brilliance if you weren't paying attention; Carter has been so consistent and ubiquitous for so long that he has sometimes been taken for granted.

One issue for some critics is the amplified volume and sonority of Carter's tone in the 1970s and '80s, an era favoring hot bass pick-ups and amps and the direct-input method of recording the instrument. Carter's tone sometimes acquired a rubbery quality on records in these years, though in recent decades his overall volume has decreased and more "wood" has returned to his sound. Another issue is that Carter's bands have concentrated on refinements of mainstream principles rather than experimentation—though as Hancock noted, Carter played five years with one of the most innovative bands in jazz history and has the right to explore other avenues of expression. Where Carter has moved into new territory with his own groups, it's been on two fronts. First, he pioneered the use of the piccolo bass, pitched higher than the regular double bass and used by Carter as a "horn" in front of a traditional rhythm section. Second, he's explored fusions of classical music and jazz, improvising on themes by Bach and others. These projects have not always been successful, but the best have expanded the language of the bass.

The larger point is that the subtleties of great bass playing can be elusive, even to musicians. Carter recalled a record date at which his decision to not play solos prompted consternation in the studio: "I said, 'Did you hear the last three tunes? Did you hear what I played? That's enough for me. I don't have to play a solo. I want people to hear how a bass player can manipulate the music.' Hopefully, people will get past the need to hear me stand out to appreciate what I do. Listen to what kind of colors I draw from the guys I'm accompanying. If I can leave a record date feeling that I've made these four or five players a better group, or made them more dedicated to music, or trust my judgment, or play better on some tune, or play differently than they usually do, then I don't need to solo. That's the fun for me."

Playing the right note at the right time. It sounds simple. It's anything but.

Carter spoke at his Upper West Side home in Manhattan on a sweltering summer day in 2003. The co-op apartment, which he bought in 1973, is an interior designer's dream: The elevator opens into the 10th-floor apartment, a sprawling layout with hardwood floors, neutral colors, modern furniture, and abstract and figurative paintings and sculpture by African American artists. Carter's first wife, Janet, who passed away in 2000, was responsible for the art and decor. The couple married in 1958, when he was a senior-to-be at the Eastman School of Music in Rochester, New York, and they raised two boys. Janet was a founding board member of the Studio Museum in Harlem and briefly owned a New York gallery specializing in African American and African art. (In 2012 Carter married Quintell Williams, a fashion designer and former model.) "It's very calming to come home after playing a nightclub and just hear the art," Carter said. "I don't need music, I don't need conversation, I don't need food. But to walk in here at two o'clock in the morning and walk through the rooms listening to the art—it's fabulous."

He sat at his dining room table, a colorful spiral collage by Detroit native Al Loving behind him. Carter is six feet four and lanky, with a long face, large hands, and a neatly trimmed salt-and-pepper beard. In deference to the heat, Carter wore shorts, a short-sleeve shirt, and sneakers. On stage he favors tailored dark suits, and his bands wear similar uniforms with matching ties that Carter provides. He speaks quietly, and something about his soft eyes and reserved countenance hints at a vulnerable soul beneath a taciturn shell. He is well-read, cultured, famously punctual, and business savvy. "Professionalism" is a sacred word to him; pity the sideman who shows up late on Carter's gig. He knows his proper place in the hierarchy of jazz. Some musicians find him arrogant, but those who know him well say he's a sensitive soul who refuses to suffer any sign of disrespect and warms quickly once you get past a crusty exterior. Carter is not bitter, but his own experiences have taught him the score when it comes to racism in America.

Ronald Levin Carter was born on May 4, 1937, in Ferndale, a bedroom community bordering the north side of Detroit. He was the fifth of eight children. His father, Lutheran, worked multiple jobs as a handyman, factory janitor, and the like to make ends meet. Carter's mother, Willie, worked as a domestic. Dan Ouellette's 2013 biography of Carter recounts an early episode that left a racial scar. When a sister graduated from junior high, the principal gave two speeches, one for white students in which they were encouraged to continue to high school and college, and one for blacks in which he seemed unable to conceive of their future in terms of anything other than ditch diggers. Carter never forgot the sting of the principal's racism.[1]

Carter took up the cello in school at age 10. He progressed swiftly, taking a paper route to pay for lessons. He was 14 when his father got a job as a bus driver in Detroit, and the family moved to the city's northwest side. Carter started at Cass Tech in 1952, playing cello in the orchestra led by Michael Bistritzky; senior Paul Chambers was in the bass section. String players at Cass were also required to study a wind instrument for a year, so Carter took up the clarinet and later played alto clarinet in the top band led by Harry Begian. Carter was a straight-A student in his academic classes.

He switched to bass when he realized only the white cellists were getting calls for gigs, even though Carter played better than they did. With a dearth of bass players at Cass, he reasoned that his talent would be impossible to ignore. He dipped his toe into jazz as a senior, playing casual gigs with a friend's band, but he remained focused on classical music. He earned a full scholarship to Eastman, where he studied with bassist Oscar Zimmerman, a legendary player and teacher. Carter graduated in 1959 and received a master's degree from the Manhattan School of Music in 1961. Near the end of his time at Eastman he became disillusioned with the classical world. When Carter was 21, Leopold Stokowski, conductor of the Houston Symphony, came to lead the Rochester Philharmonic. Carter was the first black musician to play in the orchestra. Stokowski pulled him aside after rehearsal: "Mr. Carter, I like the way you play, and I'd love to have you in my orchestra in Houston, but they're not ready for colored people who play classical music."

"What?!" Carter said to himself. "You mean I spent all this lifetime practicing and you're telling me I can't be a part of this because I'm black? OK, if that's the name of this tune, what kind of music can I play and have a good time doing it?"

Carter, who had been working off-campus in jazz groups to earn money, set his sights on a jazz career. He moved to New York in August 1959 and found work with Chico Hamilton. Jobs followed with Eric Dolphy, Jaki Byard, Bobby Timmons, Randy Weston, Art Farmer, and, in early 1963, Miles Davis. Carter's first record session was in February 1960 with Don Ellis on the Enrica label, but the album remains unissued. His next sessions were in March and April with Ernie Wilkins (*The Big New Band of the '60s*) and Charli Persip (*The Jazz Statesmen*). By the time Carter entered the studio with Miles Davis in April 1963, he had appeared on more than 50 records. His debut as a leader came in 1961 at age 24. *Where?* (New Jazz) features Carter on cello and bass, and the appearance of vanguard multireedman Eric Dolphy positioned Carter as a progressive.

While Carter was never integral to the local scene in Detroit, his musical intelligence, command of harmony, studied technique, versatility, individuality, and irrepressible swing all mark him as a product of the city. He is the spiritual heir to Paul Chambers (and underrated Detroiter Doug Watkins), though Carter seems to have swallowed the entire bass tradition whole. Queried about influences, he mentioned two interesting figures—trombonist J. J. Johnson, whose deliberate, enunciated style finds an echo in Carter's meticulous approach, and baritone saxophonist Cecil Payne, who developed a nimble voice in the basement register.

Carter is easy to identify by the depth of his tone, legato strut of his walking lines, skip-a-dee-do triplet embellishments, and marriage of harmonic adventure and clarified melody. Two imitated trademarks are his pregnant long notes and the elongated portamento—a deep-knee-bend slide—that causes the music to hover as if Carter turned off gravity. As bass pickups became standard in the late '60s and early '70s, Carter's sound grew plumper with amplification, and this sonority became part of his brand recognition too.

Harmonic motion in music is all about constructing pathways between point A and point B. Creative jazz musicians not only know multiple routes but invent them in the moment. For Carter the options appear infinite. "I don't think anyone has significantly added to the innovations that Ron made on his instrument harmonically as far as creating bass lines," said bassist Christian McBride. "Ron was one of the first to be able to reharmonize a song on the spot. As the new era came in, chords got more complex, bigger, and more impressionistic, and if you don't know much about harmony, you'll stay close to home. But Ron knows what notes work with any chord and can break it all down because he's so well-trained. A lot of bassists do it with a wing and prayer and hope they land in the right spot. Ron thought in terms of theory, but you only think about that when the record is off—when you're listening to Ron, it's all about groove and sound."

Carter developed a melodic style of soloing ornamented by his calling-card triplets, tremolos, and trills. He is not a speed demon, but the surface simplicity is deceptive, and he never mortgaged the idiomatic glories of the bass. "You need a lot of technique to play what he does," said bassist Kelly Sill. "He's shifting all over the place and using very clever fingerings. Ron doesn't really play like a horn player, but he does play melodically. Some guys play like horn players, but the music doesn't come out as melody because it doesn't sound like a bass."

Often overlooked, Carter's distinctive voice as a composer also reflects similar melodicism. Pieces like "Third Plane," "12+12," "Rufus," "Einbahnstrasse," and "Tinderbox" are witty, singsong constructions and irresistible. "Little Waltz," a tranquil ballad, the Spanish-flavored "El Noche Sol," and the Latin rhythms of "Parade" explore other sides of his personality.

Carter's most influential work remains his five years with Miles Davis. After tenor saxophonist and composer Wayne Shorter joined in 1964, the band's balance of form and freedom rewrote jazz history. The group turned familiar standards and penetrating originals into cubist abstractions. Herbie Hancock called the approach "controlled freedom." In slow motion it works like this: Carter chooses a surprising bass note that forces Hancock into new harmonic territory. The combination of Carter's note and Hancock's chord pushes Shorter to slide out of key and twist his next phrase into a pretzel. Tony Williams reacts with hopscotch rhythms on the drums that imply a related meter. Carter responds to the new sound world, and the feedback loop shifts into another gear. The quintet stretched form and broke rules—but with all-encompassing knowledge and purpose. They went out on a limb as an *ensemble*. "It was really about all five of us interacting," Carter said. "We didn't know it would evolve to the level that it reached. We enjoyed each other's company, which is important."

The records form a cornerstone of the canon. In addition to the studio albums on Columbia—*ESP*, *Miles Smiles*, *Sorcerer*, *Nefertiti*, *Miles in the Sky*, *Filles de Kilimanjaro*—there are essential live recordings from the Plugged Nickel in Chicago (1965) and concert performances issued as *Live in Europe 1967: The Bootleg Series Vol. 1*. For an example of the Carter Effect, try "No Blues," recorded November 2, 1967, in Copenhagen. "After the melody, a very simple 12-bar blues in the key of F, Ron starts Miles' solo in the key of D-flat, a very dissonant choice," said Detroit-born bassist Robert Hurst. "You can hear that his fellow musicians are trying to figure out what the hell he's doing. Ron continues this harmonic suspension for several choruses and eventually resolves in the key of F, which creates an astonishing moment of satisfaction."

Sorting through Carter's massive discography is a challenge. Beyond classics with Davis, a few key sideman appearances in the 1960s and '70s include Dolphy's *Far Cry*, Hancock's *Empyrean Isles* and *Maiden Voyage*, Eddie Harris' *The In Sound*, Shorter's *Speak No Evil*, Bobby Hutcherson's *Components*, Sam Rivers' *Contours*, McCoy Tyner's *The Real McCoy* and *Trident*, Joe Henderson's *Power to the People*, Freddie Hubbard's *Red Clay*, and Antonio Carlos Jobim's *Stone Flower*. More recently, the rock-ribbed grooves Carter lays down on Joey Baron's *Down Home* (Intuition) in 2007 are a marvel.

Carter has made more than 50 recordings as a leader. *Uptown Conversation* (Embryo) from 1969 remains dazzling in its period eclecticism, and trio tracks with Hancock and Billy Cobham sparkle. Of Carter's records for CTI and Milestone in the 1970s and early '80s, *All Blues*, *Third Plane*, and *Piccolo* are a cut above. 1982's *Etudes* (Elektra Musician) features strong material and an inviting quartet with flugelhornist Art Farmer, saxophonist Bill Evans, and Tony Williams. The lovely *Orfeu* (Blue Note) from 1999 explores Brazilian-flavored music with an unlikely front line pairing old-school tenor saxophonist Houston Person and contemporary guitarist Bill Frisell. *The Golden Striker Trio* (Blue Note) captures a potent 2002 edition of a signature Carter group with guitarist Russell Malone and pianist Mulgrew Miller. The 1988 solo-bass recording *All Alone* (Emarcy) is a stunning achievement, wringing maximum expression from seemingly limited means. Finally, Carter has been an exemplary duet partner, most notably with guitarist Jim Hall (start with *Live at the Village West* on Concord) and Person, with whom he's made six duo recordings since 1989. All are gems. Since this book was originally published in 2019, Carter has appeared on roughly 20 additional recordings (and more are likely awaiting release). He showed few signs of slowing down as he passed his 88th birthday celebrating this latest milestone by leading his quartet for a week at the Blue Note in New York. He still tours widely throughout the United States and overseas. In recent years, he has also become a social media maven, posting almost daily on X (formerly Twitter) and Facebook. On his website, RonCarterJazz.com, he is often referred to as "Maestro," a moniker he has more than earned.

The straight-ahead idiom and transparency of most of his music in recent decades are a long way from the abstraction of the Miles Davis Quintet 60 years earlier. Some nights the music with Davis became so dense with shifting meters and oblique harmony that the players lost their way—except Carter, who earned the nickname Checkpoint Charlie because he could sense when the music was about to fall apart and would unify the band with a precisely placed downbeat or tonic note. "I was the kind of person who would just throw myself out there, and I'd get really lost sometimes," Herbie Hancock remembered. "I'd look around, you know, to say, 'Help.' And Ron in a fraction of a second would throw me a life preserver. He always seemed to know where he was. If he didn't, he fooled me."

Carter threw his head back and laughed when Hancock's words were read back to him. "I never got lost," he confirmed. "I may not have played the best note for that moment—that's one of the risks of playing music—but it was the right place in the music to take that chance."

Recommended Recordings

Miles Davis, *My Funny Valentine* (Columbia)
Sam Rivers, *Contours* (Blue Note)
Ron Carter, *Uptown Conversation* (Embryo)

Note

1. Dan Ouellette, *Ron Carter: Finding the Right Notes* (Retrac, 2013), 40.

Joe Henderson
THE PHANTOM

Perhaps one day a jazz-savvy historian will catalog the most unlikely global events of the 1990s and the list will look like this: Soviet Union collapses. Nelson Mandela elected president of South Africa. Joe Henderson becomes a star.

For most of his career, Henderson, one of the most original and quietly influential tenor saxophonists of the modern era, had the unfortunate distinction of being the most underrated jazz musician on the planet. Having honed his craft in the crucible of Detroit in the late 1950s, Henderson was revered as an innovator by his peers. Students memorized his licks like scripture and his compositions entered the standard repertoire. Yet for 30 years the wider jazz audience shrugged. Most critics, too. Henderson, who died from emphysema-related heart failure in 2001 at age 64, was too widely known to be a cult figure, but he was more likely to be damned with faint praise than recognized as one of the defining saxophonists of his time.

Then fate did a somersault. By the early '90s, the Wynton Marsalis–inspired young lion craze had begun to splinter, and major labels took a second look at mainstream veterans. Henderson released a series of canny songbook CDs on Verve starting in 1992 including friendly tributes to Billy Strayhorn, Miles Davis, and Antonio Carlos Jobim. With the promotional muscle of corporate giant Polygram now in his corner, Henderson found an audience. Verve marketing staff told me in 1996 that his first three albums for the label sold 650,000 combined copies worldwide—at a time a when a typical independent mainstream jazz CD was lucky to sell 3,500 and major labels were happy to top 20,000 sales worldwide for an acoustic-jazz CD. Presto: overnight sensation.

Henderson had been making an adequate living, playing top clubs and taking part in all-star affairs at European and Japanese festivals. But suddenly he was making headliner bread, bringing home Grammy Awards, flying first class, appearing on *The Tonight Show*. The irony was monumental. Here was a musician known to colleagues as "the Phantom" because of

Tenor saxophonist Joe Henderson leading his quartet at the Blue Bird Inn in 1958 with pianist Kirk Lightsey, bassist Herman Wright, and drummer Roy Brooks. Photo courtesy Jim Gallert Collection.

his elusive personality, quirky behavior, and analytical mind. On stage he played long solos, dense with ideas, with a soft, reedy sound as mysterious as smoke. Rail thin with a professorial beard and horn-rimmed glasses, he held his tenor upright in front of his body and kept the bell of his horn steady in the face of the microphone. He said little, announcing sidemen with perfunctory efficiency and never introducing tunes or making jokes. He just played his ass off. Every night. Every set. Every tune. For 40 years.

"It's been great, but you know, I've never been in it for the recognition," Henderson said in 1996. "Everybody's got to do something in life, and this was a path I started on a long time ago. I'm still interested in it from a craft point of view, but, you know, if the party ended tomorrow you adjust and count your blessings."

Henderson's initial recordings in the 1960s revealed a synthesis of the discipline of bebop with the exploratory freedom of the avant-garde. Henderson played free *within* structure. He employed an unparalleled flexibility of rhythm and phrasing and explored an expanded harmonic, melodic, and textural landscape that pushed formal boundaries. He honored the fundamentals of blues and swing—his Detroit roots—while abstracting them. A gang of young musicians was working along similar lines in the '60s, among them Wayne Shorter, Herbie Hancock, Bobby Hutcherson, Tony Williams, Andrew Hill, and Sam Rivers. Their artistic victories remain integral to today's post-bop mainstream.

Henderson offered an alternative to the laser-like sonorities and devotional intensity of John Coltrane, the era's messiah. Building on the pliable conception of Sonny Rollins, Henderson's shadowy tone gave voice to unpredictable phrasing, loose rhythm, and a cunning approach to harmony and melody. The combination of his oblique conceptualism, mastery of the saxophone, and Zen-like presence made him an oracle.

"He dares to improvise," said saxophonist Joe Lovano. "There are a lot of cats who play worked-out licks over and over. They play the same solos on every tune, some great players, too. Joe is an improviser. The environment he's in, the tune he's playing, and whoever he's playing with at the moment shapes his solos."

To a degree unusual even for an art based on improvisation, a Joe Henderson solo is an adventure. His ideas burst out of his horn like Silly String. He'll suspend time and harmony in a fog of flickering trills and cockeyed arpeggios. He'll swoop from his altissimo register high above the written range of the saxophone down to the basement of the horn in a blink of an eye. He'll paint each note with its own individualized articulation, color, and texture. He'll play shrieking overtones and seductive purrs. He'll start a phrase in a veiled corner of the beat, hold it up to the light, and then bury it again. He'll play so angular and outside the chords that you can't believe it and then turn around and play a melody so pure and inside the harmony that you can't believe something so simple could sound so hip. He'll play *anything* at *any time*.

Like all players, Henderson had a storehouse of calling-card phrases and ideas that he revisited, but he never stopped tinkering with details and context. They only sound like clichés when others copy them. "I always wanted to be an improviser of the likes that hasn't been seen out here."

Henderson said. "And I learned one thing along the way that served me pretty well: I considered it a sin, in the same way God might consider an act a sin, to ever play an idea more than once. If the world didn't hear it that one time, well, too bad. In trying not to repeat yourself you train your mind not to do that. You're always searching for something new and interesting—not just new and different, but new and *interestingly different*."

The title track of Henderson's 1964 masterpiece *Inner Urge* (Blue Note) defines his aesthetic. Henderson's 24-bar, A-B structure (16 + 8) is built around a corkscrew melody that twists through a cycle of beguiling Lydian harmonies. Pianist McCoy Tyner, bassist Bob Cranshaw, and drummer Elvin Jones create a maelstrom of swirling energy, and Henderson steps into the breach to play eight audacious choruses. Since the development of bebop, soloists had used eighth notes as the basic building block of their phrasing. One Henderson innovation was breaking up his eighth note lines with a barrage of rhythmic abstraction. On "Inner Urge," stuttering repetitions and asymmetric groupings play hide-and-seek with the beat. His slippery rhythms ricochet like a pinball off Jones' cymbal beat. Short musical cells grow into thematic webs. Tension builds. As Henderson's third chorus gives way to the fourth, his zigzagging ambiguity suddenly shifts into a wailing blues call at the 3:35 mark that locks into the groove and brings it all back home to Detroit. *Yeah, Joe!*

No horn player ever played with a looser sense of rhythm and time than Henderson. Where did that concept come from? Henderson said that Sonny Rollins provided key inspiration during his formative years. Early on he also devoured the celebrated 1949 records by pianist Lennie Tristano with tenor saxophonist Warne Marsh that featured circuitous themes and across-the-bar-line phrasing. Tenor saxophonist Junior Cook, who was on the scene earlier than Henderson and preceded him in Horace Silver's band, had a slippery beat and dark sound that ran somewhat parallel and likely had an impact—though by the 1970s, Cook was more influenced by Henderson than the other way around. Henderson considered himself a closet drummer channeling through the saxophone. "I think my concept may have been there from the beginning," he said. "Some of the best compliments I've ever received out here have come from drummers. I used to love how Philly Joe Jones played drums, and every time I'd see him he had something wonderful to say about some solo that I did, starting with the one on the Horace Silver record 'Song for My Father.' Every time I'd see that man, he'd come up and sing that solo."

Henderson's enriched harmonic language employed all the advances of the '60s—increasing chromaticism, modes, pentatonic (5-note) scales.

His formal training was extensive. His teacher at Wayne State University in Detroit was the leading midcentury American guru of the classical saxophone, Larry Teal, and Henderson studied contemporary classical music in the classroom. His personal way of breaking the rules created magic. In an interview on Ethan Iverson's blog *Do the Math*, pianist Jim McNeely remembered hearing Henderson talk at a clinic about how he played outside of standard harmony. Henderson told the class that sometimes he just plays a whole step above the chord changes. "We just started to play," McNeely said, "and he's playing a whole step above, and I thought, 'That sounds like Joe Henderson!'"

Joseph A. Henderson was born April 24, 1937, in Lima, Ohio, 130 miles from Detroit. The son of a steelworker, he grew up in a family of 15 children and was introduced to jazz by an older brother. (Younger brother Leon emerged as a tenor saxophonist in Detroit in the late '60s.) Henderson took up the saxophone around age nine, starting on C melody before quickly switching to tenor and learning Lester Young solos off records with the help of his older brother. Henderson took saxophone lessons and absorbed all kinds of music—bebop, country, R & B, concert band music, classical works. He gravitated initially to tenor saxophonists with lighter sounds, especially Stan Getz, but his most vital influence was alto saxophonist Charlie Parker. At 14, Henderson heard Parker live at the Graystone Ballroom in Detroit while visiting a cousin.

"I was just overwhelmed," Henderson said. "I didn't know what the hell Bird was doing, but he was playing a kind of music that I was familiar with because I had heard the records. He was playing tunes like "Cherokee," "Out of Nowhere," "Indiana," and it was a dance. Guys were swinging these ladies around the floor like a basketball team bounds down from one end of the court to the other."

Henderson worked gigs around Lima as a teenager and started composing. His well-known "Recorda-Me" dates to about 1955. He spent one year at Kentucky State College (now University), a historically black school in Frankfort, before transferring to Wayne State in 1956. Soon he was working with groups led by bassist Ernie Farrow and saxophonist Beans Bowles. Henderson led his own bands from 1958 to 1960 with such peers as pianist Kirk Lightsey and drummer Roy Brooks. Henderson also joined the circle of musicians mentored by Barry Harris. "It was a powerful scene," Henderson recalled. "One of the best learning, growing, getting-it-all-sorted-out scenes you could've been in on at that time."

Henderson said jam sessions would start at noon at one person's home and relocate to a new house every two or three hours. On weekends the hang ended at the West End Hotel, an after-hours spot in southwest Detroit. Saxophonist Joe Brazil hosted sessions at his house in northeast Detroit. Brazil was good friends with John Coltrane, who would stay at the home when in town with Miles Davis. Henderson remembered sitting next to Coltrane on the couch once. "I didn't know who he was, but everyone else did," said Henderson. "Roy Brooks, Hugh Lawson, and Ernie Farrow were there. I remember Roy bowing his head down on the floor and saying, 'Come on, Trane!' He had everybody in a spiritual kind of zone. Going to Wayne University, they filled you up with all this stuff about how you should play, that you should hold the saxophone a certain way and get this kind of sound. I was critiquing John under my breath: 'Wow this guy really moves his fingers fast, but he's got to work on his tone.'"[1]

Henderson's virtuoso technique owed much to his teacher Larry Teal (1905–1984). Teal stressed a warm and centered tone, breath support, and an evenness of sound and articulation. His Tuesday morning lineup of students in 1956–57 was Yusef Lateef at 9:30, Henderson at 10:00, and Donald Sinta at 10:30. "Larry took you back to fundamentals," said Sinta, saxophone professor at the University of Michigan from 1974 to 2014. "He was into the right embouchure and not blowing hard."

Henderson played his entire career on a short-shank Selmer Soloist hard rubber mouthpiece with a "D" tip opening, a setup more typical of a classical player. Many people were shocked when they heard him live for the first time at how soft he played, because records created a different impression. Henderson's sound was indivisible from his broader concept. It's difficult to play with his level of flexibility if you're trying to blow down the back wall. Henderson illustrates the difference between volume and projection. Though he didn't play loud, you could almost always hear him, even in unamplified settings, because his sound was so focused and his intent so strong that he projected throughout a room.

Detroit was a bebop town. If you didn't speak the language of Charlie Parker, you didn't survive. Henderson learned the rules of bebop, but unlike nearly all of his contemporaries in the city, his ears were open to the radical ideas of Ornette Coleman, the saxophonist who in the late '50s upset the jazz world by throwing away traditional markers of harmony and form. Henderson credited his university studies of Hindemith, Stravinsky, and Bartok with keeping his mind open. Those who heard Henderson in Detroit in the '50s say he already sounded like he does on his first recordings in 1963. (There is a homemade tape of a 1958 jam session at Joe Brazil's house with Henderson and Coltrane on it, but the fidelity of the copies I've heard is so poor that it's impossible to discern what Henderson sounds like.)

He also began to get a reputation as an odd duck in Detroit. "You'd go to his apartment, and he had nothing but a mattress, ironing board and a few chairs," said saxophonist Bennie Maupin. By the '80s, students told stories of marathon lessons at Henderson's San Francisco house during which he would slip away into another room for an hour, returning with no explanation. Bassist Marlene Rosenberg recalled how on the road he once tried to engage her in a game of "air chess" without a board by calling out moves. There are stories of him showing up at the last minute for gigs, or not showing at all. "Joe's easygoing, but he runs his world exactly the way he feels at the moment," Rosenberg said. Randy Brecker told *Jazz Times* in 2016 that Henderson failed to show one night in the '80s at 7th Avenue South, the New York club Brecker and his brother Michael then owned. Randy was closing at 4:30 a.m. when Henderson came up the back stairs and slid into the dressing room. Brecker opened the door: "Ahh, Randy, I thought I'd get here early and practice." Henderson thought it was 4:30 in the afternoon. He was only off by 12 hours.

Some of this behavior was likely fueled by drugs. Generally, Henderson kept his personal life separate from the bandstand, but there were exceptions. In vibraphonist Gary Burton's memoir *Learning to Listen*, he tells a disheartening story about erratic behavior by Henderson on tour in 1973 that Burton ascribes to cocaine use. Burton writes that Henderson was disruptive and prickly, didn't show for a couple of concerts, and got into an onstage argument with trumpeter Jimmy Owens.[2] Henderson spoke about drugs in a 1992 interview with the Associated Press. "You're not talking to an angel here," he told the reporter with a laugh, adding that he listened to LSD proponent Timothy Leary in the '60s and '70s and experimented with drugs. "But I never got trapped," Henderson said. "Drugs never interfered with my playing. I was always an after-the-set kind of guy."

Henderson left Detroit in 1960 when he got drafted and spent two years in army bands. Upon his discharge, he headed to New York, arriving in August 1962 at age 25. He was befriended by trumpeter Kenny Dorham, who introduced him to Alfred Lion and Frank Wolff, the pair who ran the elite Blue Note label. Henderson signed a deal in spring 1963, recording five LPs as a leader over two and a half years and appearing on a dizzying number of classics, starting with Dorham's *Una Mas*. It's Henderson's first studio session, and his wildly creative solo on "Straight Ahead" is already peak Joe.

The five Henderson-led Blue Note LPs form a pillar of modern jazz—*Page One*, *Our Thing*, *In 'N' Out*, *Inner Urge*, and *Mode for Joe*. Most of his seminal compositions appear here, among them "Recorda-Me," "Serenity," "Inner Urge," "Isotope" and "Shade of Jade." Henderson's versatility meant he was as comfortable with the after-hours soul of Grant Green's *Idle Moments* as the exploratory contours of Andrew Hill's *Black Fire*, Larry Young's *Unity*, and McCoy Tyner's *The Real McCoy*—the latter including some of Henderson's most indispensable playing. From 1964 to 1966, Henderson toured with Horace Silver and appears on two famous Silver LPs on Blue Note, *Song for My Father* and *Cape Verdean Blues*.

"Recording with Blue Note was like being part of a special family," Henderson said. "Making those records became a way of life. It wasn't about going-to-the-bandstand type of gigs. I did some of that, but at times I was doing more playing in the studio than on the bandstand. Each record brought its own fingerprint with its own compositions. They allowed me a chance to live in several different worlds. It was not just a wonderful pay day; it was a wonderful *play* day."

The late '60s and early '70s found Henderson in flux. He freelanced with Herbie Hancock's Sextet, the Thad Jones–Mel Lewis Jazz Orchestra, and others. He worked a few gigs in 1967 with Miles Davis, joining tenor saxophonist Wayne Shorter in the band—alas, no tapes have surfaced. Henderson tried launching his own group in 1970 but couldn't get traction. He spent four months in 1971–72 with Blood, Sweat and Tears, and relocated to San Francisco, where he was based for the rest of his life. On record he found stability with Milestone from 1967 to 1975, releasing 12 LPs ranging from swinging post-bop to fusion and concept albums. As Henderson's producer Orrin Keepnews once put it, they made every kind of possible record—except a hit. Henderson's best Milestone LPs rank among his greatest work, especially *Power to the People* (1969) with its zeitgeisty jazz-rock elements and peerless rhythm section of Herbie Hancock, Ron Carter, and Jack DeJohnette. *Joe Henderson in Japan* (1971) an incendiary live recording, remains a talisman for saxophonists.

By the '80s, Henderson was traveling from town to town as a single, picking up rhythm sections of varying quality and playing a small group of favorite songs. I heard him often in these years, and when the local sidemen weren't cutting it, he turned out miraculous solos anyway. High-profile albums on Blue Note in 1985, *The State of the Tenor* (vols. 1 and 2) with Ron Carter and Al Foster, jump-started a reappraisal and primed the pump for Henderson's stardom in the '90s—though I find contemporaneous trio records with Charlie Haden and Foster, particularly *An Evening with Joe Henderson* (Red Records), friskier and more fun. Henderson's final recordings for Verve captured public attention, but they often sound overproduced, lacking the unbridled fire and freedom of his best work. The tremendous

Four!, which Verve released in 1994, proves the point. Drawn from a casual one-nighter in Baltimore in 1968, it finds Henderson playing the hell out of standards with Wynton Kelly, Paul Chambers, and Jimmy Cobb.

Henderson's concepts began seeping into the mainstream around 1970, and his influence has shaped multiple generations of saxophonists, among them Bennie Maupin, Dave Liebman, Michael Brecker, Branford Marsalis, Joe Lovano, Rich Perry, Javon Jackson, Mark Turner, and Walter Smith III. "I appreciate them so much for that," Henderson said. "To plant some trees out here, is gratifying." The jazz world got a brilliant reminder in 2024 of how central Henderson was to the music's evolution when Blue Note released *Forces of Nature: Live at Slug's*. Previously unissued, these raw 1966 tapes—visionary, white hot, full of risk—capture Henderson, McCoy Tyner, Henry Grimes, and Jack DeJohnette creating jazz history at ground level one gig at a time.

Henderson's final appearance in metro Detroit came in 1997 at the Michigan Theatre in Ann Arbor with George Mraz and Foster. The last tune was Strayhorn's ballad "Lush Life," deconstructed in rubato time. Henderson floated through the song, ending each phrase with an awe-inspiring cadenza of improvisation that lasted from a few moments to 30 seconds. When it was over, the Phantom slipped into the shadows without saying a word.

Recommended Recordings

Joe Henderson, *Inner Urge* (Blue Note)
McCoy Tyner, *The Real McCoy* (Blue Note)
Joe Henderson, *Power to the People* (Milestone)

Notes

1. A tape from a jam session at Brazil's house was made Sept. 25, 1958, but it seems unlikely Henderson would not recognize Coltrane by this date. Henderson might be conflating two sessions into one in his memory. Or maybe this interaction in fact happened on 9/25/58.

2. Burton mistakenly implies this tour took place in the 1980s, but recordings confirm 1973.

Charles McPherson

REMINISCING BY EAR

Armed with a portable CD player, I arrived at Charles McPherson's hotel suite in Chicago in August 2006. Amid a weeklong stand at the Jazz Showcase, the alto saxophonist agreed to a listening session. I hoped music would spark memories of his formative years in Detroit and professional relationships, and I wanted to prompt a discussion of aesthetic issues surrounding jazz improvisation. McPherson did not disappoint. He responded enthusiastically to the music and spoke insightfully about his mentor Barry Harris, hearing Charlie Parker at a Detroit ballroom, working with Charles Mingus, and his own evolution as a musician and his goals as an improviser.

McPherson, who turned 86 in 2025, has had a major career, but for nearly all of it he has remained a musician's musician rather than a star, better known to insiders than the broader jazz audience. That's a shame, because McPherson's alto in flight has for decades been one of the most exhilarating sounds in contemporary jazz. He is a profound stylist who forged a unique sound and personality within the template of classic bebop. McPherson's playing grows directly out of the breakthroughs of the 1940s spearheaded by Parker.

As he moves through his 80s, his gifts remain undiminished—the luminosity of his tone, rapturous momentum of his improvisations, and cliché-free purity of his melodies and phrasing. McPherson traffics in tradition but not nostalgia. He does not sound like your record collection. His authoritative creativity and spontaneity cast his music in the present tense. The good news is that he has—finally—begun to receive a measure of the critical and public acclaim his brilliance deserves. His most recent recordings, *Jazz Dance Suites* (2019) and *Reverence* (2023), earned rapturous reviews from critics. Meanwhile, the 2020 Jazz Times Readers Poll anointed him Artist of the Year and named *Jazz Dance Suites* the No. 1 New Release.

McPherson, 66 at the time of the interview, settled into the sofa. A resident of San Diego since 1978, he is of medium height, fit, has salt-and-

Alto saxophonist Charles McPherson (*far right*) with the BeBop Boys in Ypsilanti, Michigan, December 1958. Also pictured (*left to right*): Mike Terry, trombone; Lonnie Hillyer, trumpet; Barry Harris, piano; Rudy Tucich, drums; Ira Jackson, alto sax; Bill Stewart, bass; Bill Robinson, friend of the band. Photo courtesy Rudy Tucich.

pepper hair and looked a decade younger than his age. The prodigious Afro he once sported had been shorn, but his bushy mustache remained.

Barry Harris Quintet, "Burgundy," from Newer Than New *(Riverside), September 28, 1961*

No one was more responsible for McPherson's life in jazz than pianist Barry Harris, the bebop sage of Detroit. McPherson was 15 when he began studying with Harris in 1954. *Newer than New* was only McPherson's third recording session after moving to New York in 1960. He was 22. The band includes Detroiter Lonnie Hillyer on trumpet. Harris' breezy original "Burgundy" opens with Latin rhythms before shifting into swing for solos. McPherson hadn't seen the CD cover before the music started, and a look of concern fell across his face. "I haven't heard this in 30 years," he said. "I'm scared to listen to me."

McPherson's playing lacks the strength and individualism of his mature work. He grew uncomfortable listening and made me stop the disc halfway through his solo. "I hear so many things that are immature in my sound and the timidity of the playing," he said. "I hear too much caution, which speaks of an insecurity. It's not easy to sound good young, and some of it has to do with the equipment—the mouthpiece, the horn. I can tell my mouthpiece is too small. I didn't know any better."

Born July 24, 1939, in Joplin, Missouri, McPherson was 9 when he moved to Detroit with his mother. He wanted to play saxophone in his junior high band at 12 but all the saxophones were taken, so he started on trumpet. His mother bought him an alto for his 13th birthday. He took a few lessons and never looked back. In a stroke of good fortune, McPherson and his mother settled on Tireman on Detroit's west side, five blocks from the Blue Bird Inn, the city's top modern jazz club. Harris lived around the corner. "Everybody had a jazz record or two in the house in those days—Duke Ellington, Count Basie, something like that," McPherson said. "It was part of the culture. In junior high an older tenor player told me I should check out Charlie Parker. One day when I was about 14, I was in a candy store and I saw a jukebox and there was a record by this Charlie Parker guy. It was 'Tico Tico,' and when I heard that, it was immediate: I said, 'That's it. That's for me.'

"I didn't know anything about theory or ii–V–I progressions or dominant seventh chords or even that there were such things as chord changes. But I knew that everything I heard Charlie Parker play on that record made perfect sense. I understood the logic. It's like Bach. Perfect. Then I found out that Bird was just one of a group of guys who played in this genre—bebop, modern jazz, progressive jazz; there were a lot of names for it. Then I found out that this music I had discovered was all they played at this bar down the street. That was really it!"

Too young to enter the club, McPherson and his friends soaked up the sounds nightly outside the front window. Harris came outside on breaks and talked to the kids. When he saw they were serious about the music, he invited them to his house. McPherson remembered:

"We'd ask questions like, 'What do you play here and what scales go with this kind of a dominant seventh chord?' He was exploring for himself and showed us what he was finding. Pretty soon I was going over there every day. There was an aura of intellectuality in Barry's house. Barry would do the *New York Times* crossword puzzle every day, and he'd zip through it. He was a reader. One day I came home from school and I had my report card, and he asked to see it. I was a C student; I didn't try for anything more than that. He saw the Cs and he said, 'You're quite average, aren't you?' I said, 'Well, I'm passing.' He said, 'You can't be average and play the kind of music you're trying to learn. There's too much going on. Charlie Parker is not average. Your heroes are above average.' It was like a little epiphany. It totally changed my life. I put in more effort and instead of being a C student I got As. I started getting interested in literature. I started reading philosophers, for instance, Francis Bacon, Kant, Schopenhauer. In Detroit, in this bebop niche we had, to be considered hip meant that you had to know about Charlie Parker and people like that, but you also had to know about Kant and Schopenhauer, Nietzsche and Bertrand Russell, and you had to know about art. We were like 17. People like Barry and Pepper Adams were so smart that we learned about bebop and all that. But they were able to say, 'Oh, Marc Chagall painted that.' That influenced us."

Charlie Parker, "Willis," from The Washington Concerts *(Blue Note), February 22, 1953*

Parker, who died at 34 in 1955, remains a pervasive influence. Modern jazz had many contributing architects in the 1940s, but Bird was its Prometheus and defining virtuoso. Musicians gravitate toward his bootleg nightclub recordings because, unshackled by the constraints of the three-minute record, he stretches out for chorus after chorus and reaches peaks of demonic inspiration and freedom he rarely matched in the studio. Parker's one-nighter with a big band in Washington, D.C. finds him soloing brilliantly without benefit of a rehearsal or music, coping on the fly with unexpected key modulations and breaks in the arrangements. He soars over the pedestrian charts like an Icarus immune from the sun. McPherson's delirious style is rooted in this wilder side of Parker.

McPherson was enthralled by the solo on "Willis," based on the harmonies of "Pennies from Heaven." Parker's wily quote from Stravinsky's *Petrushka* brought a smile, and McPherson marked the end of startling double-time passages by saying, "Beautiful!" Parker's phrases grow astoundingly long and asymmetric. "What can you say?" McPherson said when the song ended. "It's virtuosity. It's musicality. It's imagination. It's intellect. It's emotion. It's perfect instrumental playing and creative spontaneity."

What does McPherson hear in Parker that others may overlook? "I hear the rhythm," he said. "Now, people hear technique and virtuosity, and I certainly hear that. Charlie Parker was so proficient in so many ways you can take your pick. But to me, the area of rhythm and phrasing is what is so spectacular. There are two things that give you variety: sequence and rhythm. When you think about musical phrases, sequence and rhythm give you animation. When you're improvising, you want a balance of tension and release rhythmically but also harmonically and melodically. Bird does all those things well. The balance of tension and release gives you surprise. Starting phrases on odd parts of the beat creates tension—not starting on a downbeat, because that's what people expect. You can slice the beat into little bitty pieces and start a phrase at the 16th-note or 32nd-note level. Bird is great at that. This is what I want to do, and this is what great players do. I like to be totally rhythmically free. I like to think like a drummer. Harmony is a given, but the more important event is how I phrase the rhythm. Most important is how I put everything together and the story I'm telling. The main event is actually the human soul being expressed."

McPherson heard Parker at the Madison Ballroom on Woodward Avenue at Forest on February 5, 1955, just five weeks before his death. He was traveling as a single, backed up in Detroit by saxophonist Candy Johnson's quartet. At 15, McPherson was there on Saturday night. "All of a sudden, I see hordes of people running over to a certain area in this big room," McPherson said. "I could hear people saying, 'He's here! Bird is here!' I elbowed my way over, and there was Charlie Parker taking out his horn. He had on a nice blue suit. I always thought he was short and fat, but he wasn't short. He was like five foot ten or five foot eleven and had beautiful, smooth, clear skin, kind of red-brown color, with no facial hair. He was playing a King Super 20. He hit a low B-flat—really popped it—and then played chromatically all the way to the top of the horn, really fast, *brrrrrrr-rrrrp!!* Clean as whistle! That was his warm-up. The sound was so brilliant it filled the room.

"He went up on the bandstand. He played tunes not too fast, because it was a dance. I remember I was standing there and kind of calling out requests, things that I had heard on records, and I called out 'Kim,' which was this fast 'I Got Rhythm'-based tune. But he was playing for dancers, so Bird said, 'I'm very sorry, but I can't do that at this time.' People clapped really enthusiastically after each of his solos, and he would bow and say, 'Thank you. Thank you very much.' Like Elvis, except Bird was really the King.

"His concentration and focus were unbelievable. I remember thinking that this is one of the smartest cats I've ever seen in my life. The look coming out of his eyes was one of total understanding about everything. He spoke in perfect sentences, with no hemming or hawing, no 'uhs' or pauses. That has something to do with his organization. He had the whole sentence structure and grammar ready in his head—just like his plays.

"I followed him around the room asking him questions. I even followed him into the bathroom. I didn't know enough to ask him about music, so I asked about his father, and whether he had children, and how long he'd been playing the saxophone and things like that. I remember that he didn't answer much directly. Like if I asked him about what time it was, he'd respond by reciting a poem about time. There was a female singer in the audience. She was a black chick, and Bird invited her to sing. When he wasn't soloing, he started dancing with her spontaneously. While he was dancing, Bird took his keys out of his pocket and jingled them. It was like a sly signal, you know, like maybe this was his hotel key or something, but it was playful. He knew the audience could see what he was doing. She took the keys, and Bird turned to the audience very clearly and made a face that suggested, 'Wow, she took 'em!' People just ate that up. It was cute. Plus, he played like a motherfucker."

Charles Mingus, "The Chill of Death," from Let My Children Hear Music *(Columbia), November 18, 1971*

McPherson and Hillyer joined Mingus in September 1960. Detroiter Yusef Lateef recommended the pair to the bassist-composer, who heard them at an afternoon jam session at a coffeehouse. He hired them on the spot and told them to report for work that night. Mingus' aesthetic was gloriously chaotic. Lush Ellingtonian colors collided with roiled textures, searing intensity, and extended forms. Mingus loved Parker and in McPherson found a fresh disciple to fold into his sound world. McPherson's recording debut was with Mingus in 1960, and it was his passionate solos on *Mingus at Monterey* in 1964 that first caught the ears of the cognoscenti. McPherson appeared on *Let My Children Hear Music*, a 1971 masterpiece with a large ensemble of winds, brass, and strings. Mingus recites his own heart-of-darkness poem "The Chill of Death" with brooding musical accompaniment. McPherson improvises freely against a hallucinatory backdrop. "Oh, wow," McPherson said softly at the sound of Mingus' voice: *"The chill of death as she clutched my hand / I knew she was coming so I stood like a man."*

McPherson was given no music in the studio. He was simply told to react to the abstract sound around him. "This is pretty good," he said when the track ended. "It didn't make me cringe. What I'm consigned to do is not easy. There's no (chord) changes or sequential construction. And look what this is about: The emotions are foreboding, mystery, and fear. How do you play that? I don't know if melodicism is what you need. Dissonance might be what's called for. I did some of this fairly well, but there were some areas where I think I get too tonal. If I did this now, I'd be less concerned with trying to be melodic. I'd think about how to melodically handle dissonance."

McPherson worked with Mingus off and on for a dozen years. It was often stressful. Mingus was a large, Buddha-shaped man and volatile, known for firing musicians at will, berating audiences, and carrying a knife. "Our first night at the Showplace, Mingus proceeded to tear up a Steinway grand piano because the club owner owed him money," McPherson said. "He went in and pulled the strings out one by one. Then he wanted to kill Eric Dolphy because he was quitting the band. He reached in his pocket and got his knife and said, 'Eric, get your knife out.' Eric, who was a sweet and intelligent person, said, 'Aw, Mingus, I don't have no knife.' Mingus says, 'Well, wait a minute. I'll buy you one.' And he goes to a store across the street and buys a knife and comes back and says, 'OK, we're each going to kill each other right now.' Eric says, 'Oh, Mingus, c'mon.' Of course, nothing happened. That was my first gig."

Jazz went through many changes in the 1960s. By the middle of the decade the cutting edge was defined on the one hand by the post-bop of John Coltrane and Miles Davis and on the other by the free jazz of Ornette Coleman, Cecil Taylor, and Albert Ayler. McPherson, who turned 26 in 1965, remained committed to bebop. Did he feel out of step with his contemporaries?

"No," McPherson answered. "The world assessing what was in or outdated was the same world that booed Charlie Parker. If it hadn't been musicians insisting he was great, they wouldn't have gotten it. I didn't care for the yardstick for assessing what was hip and what wasn't. I realized that what people like Trane and Miles were doing was different, but I didn't think of it as having higher values. I didn't think those cats were rhythmically more advanced. I didn't think they were more melodically or harmonically advanced. I didn't think they had more virtuosity than Charlie Parker or Dizzy Gillespie, and they didn't. To me the only thing you could say was, 'They're not doing *that,* they're doing *this* instead.' That's fine. I'm sure not going to say it doesn't have value. But some people want to imply that what they were doing was superior, and that's where you get my argument. I knew where the jazz world was, but I was arrogant enough to say, 'So what?' I didn't want to play modally, and I didn't want to play free. I didn't think what I was doing was any more out of date than old wine."

Charles McPherson, "Fire Dance," from Manhattan Nocturne *(Arabesque), April 1997*

McPherson made excellent recordings in the 1990s for Arabesque, including this date with Mulgrew Miller, Ray Drummond, Victor Lewis, and Bobby Sanabria. A whirlpool of Afro-Cuban rhythm colors McPherson's "Fire Dance," and he unleashes a tsunami of melody over a propulsive vamp. "I'm glad I stopped before I ran out of ideas," he said. "I've heard things where I thought it would have been better to stop a chorus or two earlier. If you compare this to that first solo you played, at least I can say that there is a progression toward better playing of the horn and playing music better. I play the language of bebop, but I'm writing my own original tunes informed by that language. I'm playing my own music, which is a branch off the bebop tree. I haven't stopped playing ii–V–I harmony. I haven't stopped being interested in melodicism, and I haven't stopped wanting to be rhythmic."

McPherson agreed that bebop becomes mummified by relying excessively on predetermined patterns—practiced "licks"—rather than improvising spontaneous melodies. He favors players rooted in bebop but broad enough to, as he put it, "take excursions" into other harmonic and rhythmic idioms, even free-form playing. I mentioned Detroit tenor saxophonist Joe Henderson as a potent example. McPherson agreed and put trumpeter Freddie Hubbard on the list. "There are records of me with Mingus where I'm like that too," he said.

"None of that would be possible without the trials of musical fire that bebop exacts. You can't make those kinds of excursions without a thorough understanding of Bird and those guys. Even Trane was like that. That's the core. I'm trying to get better *within* that, trying to be creative and free *within* the constrictions. Not to play Bird or anybody's licks, but to play as creatively as possible within that system and *in the moment*. That's the key. A player who is shuffling licks around can be good but nothing like a player who is still playing within the style and playing new, creative inventions every chorus."

McPherson is best experienced live, where the full force of his creativity and singing quality of his sound electrify the air. Still, his best records capture some measure of this excitement. His jaw-dropping solo on the title track of *Spring Is Here* (Cellar Live), recorded at a Vancouver club in 2002 with an eager but overmatched Canadian trio, attains an airborne euphoria. The best of his earlier records on Prestige, Mainstream, and Xanadu, include *Horizons* (1968), *McPherson's Mood* (1969), *Siku Ya Bibi* (1972), *Today's Man* (1973), *Beautiful!* (1975), and *New Horizons* (1978). He's also in majestic form on the ballad collection *But Beautiful* (Venus) in 2003.

When McPherson is on his game, he sounds timeless and pure. What is going on in his head at those moments?

"You gotta have the wedding of head and heart," he explained. "Your technique has to be up to par so that when inspiration fails, technique saves you. And you may have inspiration but you gotta have the technique to execute. It's left and right brain, intellect and emotion. The combination makes for the best art. When you practice, that's the conscious mind. You're learning mundane things: academics, the idiom, instrumental technique. But when you perform, you should play from the unconscious mind. The act of playing is an act of humility. The conscious mind has to sit to the side and observe the show. When you learn to do that, you are no longer a prisoner of your own empirical experiences—I am a man. I am a white man. I am a black man. You're no longer restricted. Now you can plug into what Carl Jung called the collective unconscious. If you can plug into that, you can play above your empirical experience. The connections are already there. The real act of creation and genius is when you can do that."

McPherson, who turned 85 in July 2024, continues to play (and compose) at a remarkably high level of inspiration and execution. He has—finally—begun to receive a measure of the public acclaim his brilliance deserves. His latest recordings, *Jazz Dance Suites* (2019) and *Reverence* (2023), earned rapturous reviews from critics, and the 2020 Jazz Times Readers Poll anointed him Artist of the Year and *Jazz Dance Suites* the No. 1 New Release.

Recommended Recordings

Charles McPherson, *Horizons* (Prestige)
Charles McPherson, *Siku Ya Bibi* (Mainstream)
Charles McPherson, *Manhattan Nocturne* (Arabesque)

PART THREE
The Jones Brothers

Hank, Elvin, and Thad Jones (*left to right*), backstage at Carnegie Hall in June 1977. Photo by Carol Friedman.

Opening Chorus

Some families really are more musical than their neighbors. Blood relations have made contributions to jazz in every era—from Johnny and Baby Dodds in the early 20th century to the Heath, Adderley, and Montgomery brothers at midcentury to the sprawling Marsalis clan today. The largest of Detroit's jazz families is the McKinney dynasty that includes, among others, brothers Harold, a pianist; Ray, a bassist; and Bernard (Kiane Zawadi), who plays euphonium. Their nephew Carlos is a pianist and Grammy Award–winning producer. Gayelynn (Harold's daughter), a drummer, remains in Detroit.

But when it comes to royal families in jazz, the Jones brothers—Hank, Thad, and Elvin—represent the gold standard. Raised in nearby Pontiac but inextricably tied to Detroit, the brothers have no equal in terms of the range of their careers and individual accomplishments and the pervasiveness of their influence. Eldest brother Hank (1918–2010) was an exalted pianist who set a standard of excellence for 65 years. Middle brother Thad (1923–1986) was a one-of-a-kind trumpeter and one of the greatest postwar big-band composers and arrangers. Elvin (1927–2004) was among the most innovative drummers in jazz history, best known for his historic tenure with the John Coltrane Quartet in the 1960s.

The Jones brothers epitomize Detroit's modern jazz legacy. Each reflects craftsmanship, individualism and versatility raised to the highest level, and all retain an allegiance to swing, blues, and bebop. Hank's eloquent flow of melody, Thad's harmonic imagination, and Elvin's layers of polyrhythms all speak to uncommon musical intelligence wedded to intuition. Their innovations grow out of canny re-orderings of jazz fundamentals. The literal family bond between the brothers also offers a metaphor for the closeness and pride that Detroit jazz musicians across generations feel for each other and their shared legacy.

The Jones family came to Michigan during the first wave of the Great Migration. Hank, the third of 10 children, was born in Vicksburg, Mississippi, and was a few months old when the family moved to Pontiac, 27 miles north of Detroit and a General Motors town. Henry Jones Sr., a tall and lean man, worked as a lumber inspector for GM. Deeply religious, as was his wife, Olivvia, Henry was a deacon in the Baptist church, which he attended seven days a week. He didn't approve of music outside the confines of the church, and he regarded jazz as the devil's music. Still, both parents were musical and neither stood in the way of their sons' creative endeavors. "My mother had a good sense for music and could pick out tunes on the piano," Thad told *Downbeat* magazine in 1956. "My father was a bombastic bass in the church choir." Olivvia was particularly encouraging. "She'd tell you to make up your mind at what you wanted to do and then just do it," Elvin told Whitney Balliett in *The New Yorker* in 1968.

There was a lot of love in the house but also tragedy. Elvin had a twin brother who died of an infection when he was less than a year old, and the eldest daughter, Olive, drowned at age 12, after falling through ice while skating on a lake. She was already playing concerts on the piano when she died, and Hank thought she was the most talented of all the children. The brothers were close, and fellow musicians found it amusing that the pecking order remained in place, even as they moved into middle age and beyond. If, for example, Hank thought Elvin was acting inappropriately, he could shut down the rogue behavior with a stern look of older-brother disapproval.

The six years separating Hank and Thad and nine years between Hank and Elvin represent significant gaps in the context of the rapid evolution of jazz. The brothers all easily crossed stylistic fault lines, but Hank came of age in the swing era in the late '30s. Thad reached maturity as bebop coalesced in the mid-'40s. Elvin emerged as hard bop came into focus in the '50s, before he assumed a leading role in the progressive post-bop of the '60s and the roots of the avant-garde. You can pick any style in jazz history, from ragtime to no-time, and at least one of the Jones brothers will have you covered.

Lots of recordings pair two of the brothers together, but only four LPs lasso all three at once. Best overall is *Elvin!* (1961–62) on Riverside, with attractive material, vivid playing, and a lively hard-bop sextet with Frank Foster on tenor sax and Frank Wess on flute. *Keepin' Up with the Joneses* (Metro Jazz) is a somewhat contrived affair from 1958 that brings the unrelated Eddie Jones into the fold on bass and mixes compositions by Thad with standards by Isham Jones. A year later the brothers backed alto saxophonist Herb Geller on the obscure *Gypsy* (Atco), which covers music from the Broadway hit with feathery vocals by Barbara Long. It's a charming if inconsequential record, but Thad improvises some ear-catching lines.

The three brothers entered the studio together for the last time in March 1965 for Elvin's *And Then Again* (Atlantic). The spontaneously conceived title tune has no written material and unfolds loosely in D minor as Hank and Thad travel deeper into Elvin's milieu than on any earlier record—a forward-looking end to their collaborations on record.

Hank Jones

ONE EXTRA ACE

No jazz pianist in recent decades was more admired by his peers than Hank Jones. Whenever he performed in clubs, he attracted a convention of pianists packed elbow-to-elbow, spellbound by every pirouette of melody and harmony—his musical savoir faire was as slick as a pickpocket on the make. Here's what a few leading pianists said about Jones a few years before his death in 2010 at age 91.

"It's hard to find words for a guy like him because he's so magnificent," said McCoy Tyner. "When you listen to him, it's like you're in a concert hall because he covers so much ground."

"All of us marvel at Hank Jones," said Cedar Walton.

"He's one of the most important pianists in the history of the music, period," said Bill Charlap.

The aristocratic touch, courtly flair, and encyclopedic breadth that defined Jones' playing for more than 65 years never faltered, even if he lost a bit of suppleness in his last decade. His energy level and ambition never waned, and he traveled the world to perform until nearly the end. For decades the subtlety of Jones' pianism, journeyman profile, and modest personality kept him out of the spotlight. He made his primary living in the studios as a pianist-for-hire and staff musician at CBS-TV from 1959 to 1975. His profile rose as he began leading his own trio and recording more frequently as a leader beginning in the mid-'70s. His autumnal collaboration in the early 2000s with tenor saxophonist Joe Lovano—34 years his junior—raised Jones' profile among a new generation of fans. The jazz world also cradled him more lovingly after Elvin Jones died in 2004 and the pianist was the only Jones brother still on the scene.

Jones' resume was without peer. He worked or recorded with just about everybody across the spectrum, including Louis Armstrong, Coleman Hawkins, Lester Young, Billie Holiday, Benny Goodman, Charlie Parker, Miles Davis, Ella Fitzgerald, John Coltrane, Milt Jackson, Wes Montgomery, Stan

Getz, Cannonball Adderley, Dexter Gordon, Sonny Stitt, Ron Carter, and Tony Williams. Still, Jones turned down invitations to join bands led by Parker in the '40s, and Davis in the late '50s, because he considered himself unqualified. "Both times I said, 'I'm not good enough to do that,'" Jones said in 2006. "Isn't that something? I probably missed the chance of a lifetime."

Jones' art was comprehensive. His roots were in the piano kings of the '30s, especially the ornamental sweep of Art Tatum and the refined elegance of Teddy Wilson. But Jones also embraced the rhythmic and harmonic advances of transitional figures like Nat Cole and bebop modernists of the '40s, particularly pianist Bud Powell. The result was an urbane style beyond fashion or category. Liquid single-note lines melted into luxurious chords. Deft interplay between left and right hands animated structure. Luminous harmonies shifted like light in a Turner landscape. Jones' swing was impeccable, his taste unerring, his touch angelic. And there was just enough grease in his ideas to balance his tuxedoed dignity with a taste of down-home soul. Jones' marriage of grace and guts created the basic template for what developed into an informal school of modern jazz pianists from Detroit. Certainly, Tommy Flanagan's lyricism owes part of its origin to Jones, and Roland Hanna's cultivated touch bears a family resemblance. Even Harris, whose percussive attack so differs from his brethren, balances muscle and finesse in ways that make him part of the pack.

Charlap argues that Jones' often overlooked influence has worked its way into the bloodstream of jazz. "His style is as profound and defined as any of the major masters," Charlap said. "It's equal to Teddy Wilson, equal to Bill Evans, equal to Thelonious Monk, equal to Tommy Flanagan. It's as much a unique musical utterance and just as balanced in terms of intellectualism and feeling. With Hank Jones you hear the past, present, and the future of jazz piano. He touched all of the players who came after him, including Bill Evans and Herbie Hancock."

Drummer Dennis Mackrel compared Jones to a quiet hustler. "When we played New York, every great pianist from George Shearing to Kenny Barron would come in," said Mackrel. "Hank was subtle, but when someone of a high caliber came in, he'd get more advanced harmonically or rhythmically. Not to say, 'Look at me,' but just to let them know he was still the cat. He's like a card player where no matter what game you're playing, he's always got a better hand. He'll always have that one extra ace."

Jones was on the brink of his 88th birthday when I arrived at his home in upstate New York on a Saturday morning in July 2006. He lived in a modest white clapboard house on sprawling farmland in Hartwick, New York, near Cooperstown and 215 miles from Manhattan. The remote location suited his demeanor. He lived with his wife, Theodosia, who was six years older. On this morning he wore a houndstooth sport coat and slacks. Jones had a lanky build, long face, deep-set eyes rich with expression, a bald pate with gray trim, and a wispy mustache with an extra dash of whiskers under his chin. His fingers were long and lean and his skin the color of dark caramel. When he laughed, which was often, dimples lit up his face. He was fond of jokes and puns. When asked in later years how he managed to keep such a grueling schedule, Jones would typically reply: "Wheaties."

His health was excellent. When Jones was younger, he was athletically built like his brothers, but by 2006 he was thinner, down to 155 pounds with his doctor's consent. There were two pianos in the house: an upright downstairs and a Baldwin baby grand upstairs. Jones admitted that neither was in tune and the Baldwin needed repair, but he was still practicing at least two hours a day—scales, finger exercises, new songs, old songs, Bach, and other classical composers. "I never tried consciously to develop a *touch*," Jones said. "What I tried to do was make whatever lines I played flow evenly and fully and as smoothly as possible. I think the way you practice has a lot do with it. If you practice scales religiously and practice each note firmly with equal strength, you'll develop a certain smoothness. I used to practice a lot. I still do when I'm at home."

As Cedar Walton put it: "Preparation is his secret weapon!"

Jones considered himself a modern player in the sense that he tried stay abreast of contemporary currents and not play as he did 35 or 40 years earlier. He was a spontaneous musician, and if you listen to the recordings he made with Lovano in the last decade of his life, you can hear him constantly reharmonizing songs and taking risks. "There's this constant process of editing," Jones said. "You retain the things that are consistent with your approach to music and you discard those you don't think are consistent. What resonates with me is harmony. I try to use harmony that seems more innovative, more expressive, more descriptive. I make a conscious effort to do that. The more you practice doing it, the more natural it becomes. I'm always looking to go further and find something else I could do, some other musical color that I can create."

Jones was known as one of the grand gentlemen in jazz, not only for the nobility of his musicianship but for his dignified carriage. He was rarely seen outside of the house without a coat and tie. Even in the 1970s, when he made guest appearances with the Thad Jones–Mel Lewis Jazz Orchestra during the period in which the band wore dashikis, the pianist wore his over a collared shirt and tie. Jones didn't smoke, drink, or swear and believed all good things came from God. But don't mistake a mild countenance for a meek constitution. As Jones recalled traveling with trumpeter Hot Lips Page in the segregated South in the '40s, a flash of anger overtook his face with such intensity that it looked as if he was having an out-of-body experience.

"One time we got into the train station and there was a driveway next to the path when you walked by the station," he said. "We had our bags lined up on the sidewalk next to the tracks and some guy with a truck came along and ran over our bags." Jones' eyes grew large and filled with fire. "We just had to take that stuff. What are you going to do? You were in the Deep South, and all they wanted was an excuse to beat you or lynch you. If I had been like some guys—hot-tempered—I might have gotten killed."

As he got on in years, Jones would not stomach any disrespect. In 2005 he was to receive a lifetime achievement award from the Jazz Journalists Association at the B.B. King Blues Club in Manhattan. A car service was dispatched from New York to pick him up at his home in Hartwick, but upon arriving the driver rudely refused to help Jones with his bags. Jones responded by simply declining to leave the house, and the car returned to the city without him.

Henry W. Jones Jr. was born July 31, 1918. His introduction to music was singing in church, and he started piano lessons at 10. Records by Duke Ellington, Earl Hines, Fats Waller, Louis Armstrong, and blues singers introduced him to jazz. He told writer Gene Lees that published piano versions of Bix Beiderbecke songs like "In a Mist," arranged by Bill Challis, left a lasting impact on his harmonic conception. Jones played in church, accompanying choirs on piano and organ, and began working local gigs as a teenager. After high school he played with a variety of bands in clubs and dance halls from Flint to Detroit. He left Michigan for Cleveland and then Buffalo, where he spent more than a year and first heard Art Tatum in person. Tatum's otherworldly technique and head-spinning modulations left even Vladimir Horowitz shaking his head in admiration.

"After his last set, we'd go hang out at some restaurant or private home and play until daylight," Jones said. "I sat right next to him. Or next to the case of Pabst Blue Ribbon beer. Nobody could get between him and his beer. I'd watch his hands, but you couldn't learn very much from watching because his hands moved so fast. You'd listen to the harmony and what he was playing, and you began to hear certain things and after a while you recognized what he was doing and then why he was doing it, which was more important."

Jones moved to New York in 1944 to join trumpeter Hot Lips Page's band on the recommendation of Detroit saxophonist Lucky Thompson. Jones made his first recordings in November 1944 with Page, including two down-and-dirty blues numbers. Jones' fluid eight-bar solo on "Big 'D' Blues" reveals a sensitive touch, pre-bop rhythm, and impressive facility. Upon arriving in New York, Jones resumed his classical studies with Jascha Zayde, a well-known pianist and teacher. He also came face-to-face with bebop, playing briefly with Billy Eckstine's big band in 1945 and working on 52nd Street with Coleman Hawkins' band that included Miles Davis and Max Roach. Jones started barnstorming with Norman Granz's Jazz at the Philharmonic in 1947 and soon began a five-year stint with Ella Fitzgerald. Meanwhile, he got calls for record dates by young bebop modernists like J. J. Johnson, Leo Parker, Stan Getz, and Detroiter Howard McGhee. Jones' style morphed as he assimilated aspects of the new music, though the charged attack and lightning syncopations of bebop never quite found their way into his unruffled gait. "Even today, I don't think I'm a full-fledged bop player," he said. "When I'm improvising in that vein, I'm reaching out for it. I'm trying to capture the essence of it."

Still, you can hear how quickly Jones grasped the fundamentals on the Dial records he made with McGhee in December 1947. The pianist's 16 bars of improvisation on "Dorothy," an "I Got Rhythm"-based tune, are carried by the right hand in hornlike lines ripe with bebop triplets, off-beat accents, and up-to-date harmony. A few months earlier, Jones had made his first recordings as a leader—six auspicious solo piano tracks for Granz's Clef label later collected on *Urbanity* (Verve). Tatum's shadow hovers, but Jones also plays au courant voicings and jams in a quote from Parker's "Confirmation" on "The Night We Called It a Day." It sounds forced, a sign that all the elements weren't yet balanced within Jones' aesthetic.

Jones recorded just a handful of studio sides with Parker on Clef/Verve, but they're choice, including an expansive minor-key swinger "The Bird" (1947) and debonair blues, "Laird Bird" (1952). Jones' adroit solo chorus and lush chording on the chromatic blues changes show you why Parker wanted him for his group. "Charlie was so brilliant it's hard to put into words," Jones said. "His mind was just so fast, and the music sounded perfect. Every time I played with him I learned something about melody or harmony or rhythm." Jones also appears on film with Parker in 1950, along with

Hawkins, Lester Young, Ray Brown, Buddy Rich, and others. Spearheaded by Granz and directed by Gjon Mili—the pair responsible for the 1944 Oscar-nominated short *Jammin' the Blues*—the 1950 footage was released for the first time in 1996 under the title *Improvisation*. The pantomiming to prerecorded music is awkward, but there are good views of Jones, then 31, in a wide-brimmed fedora, his large hands gliding expressively across the keyboard.

By the mid-'50s, Jones was averaging five or six recording sessions a week. His consistency, sight-reading skills, taste, versatility, and reliability were tough to beat. Of all Jones' sideman appearances on record, he said his two favorites were alto saxophonist Cannonball Adderley's *Somethin' Else*, a lionized 1958 Blue Note LP with Miles Davis is a supporting role, and vocalist Johnny Hartman's *I Just Stopped by to Say Hello* (Impulse), a silky 1963 collection of bedroom ballads.

Jones' five LPs as a leader for Savoy in 1955–56 are beauts, particularly *The Trio* with Wendell Marshall and Kenny Clarke and the exquisite solo LP *Have You Met Hank Jones*. Reissued most recently as *Hank Jones Piano Solo* (Fresh Sound), it's one of the greatest solo piano recordings in jazz, full of truth and beauty. You hear Tatum grandeur, bebop, and a transparent, modified stride with 10ths in the left hand. Jones' right hand plays single-note melodies decorated with waterfall triplets and bell-like thirds. Harmonies change on the fly. On "How About You?" he slips in an impish allusion to Parker's "Scrapple from the Apple" far more smoothly than his awkward gambit nine years earlier.

During his 16 years at CBS, Jones accompanied singers, comedians, jugglers, dancers, and animal acts on *The Ed Sullivan Show*, *The Jackie Gleason Show*, and the like. The pay was good—$250 a week in the early '60s ($2,000 in 2018 dollars). But the music was rarely inspiring. Jones got called for all kinds of gigs. You know the film of Marilyn Monroe singing "Happy Birthday" and "Thanks for the Memories" to President Kennedy in 1962 at Madison Square Garden? That's Jones on piano. Though jazz was the music closest to his heart, Jones' self-identity was less as a jazz musician per se than as a *professional musician*—a pianist whose first responsibilities were to make a living and meet the highest standards of excellence no matter what the job. When he finally left CBS, however, he was ready. "I learned one very valuable thing," he said. "Never do that kind of work again." He burst into a big laugh.

Starting in 1978, Jones worked as the onstage pianist-conductor in the Fats Waller–themed Broadway hit *Ain't Misbehavin'* for more than three and a half years. At one point he did eight shows a week in the theater and then played solo piano sets from 10:30 p.m. to 1:00 a.m. five nights a week at Café Ziegfeld on 45th Street. Jones began expanding his recording and bandleading activities after leaving CBS, and for the last 35 years of his life he made dozens of recordings for a cornucopia of labels in Japan, America, and Europe. His presence at jazz clubs, festivals, and concerts across the globe picked up steam, and he was especially revered in Japan.

Most surprisingly, Jones teamed in the mid-'70s with two younger vanguard musicians, Detroit-bred bassist Ron Carter and explosive drummer Tony Williams. It was Williams' idea to organize the group, and Max Gordon, proprietor of the Village Vanguard, billed them as the Great Jazz Trio. The name stuck as a moniker for a series of subsequent Jones trios, but the original threesome, a true cooperative, remains the most special. Carter and Williams had anchored Miles Davis' pacesetting quintet of the '60s, and their partnership with Jones resulted in the most muscular and forward-looking playing of the pianist's career. At the trio's Vanguard debut in 1975, Jones was 56, Carter was 37, and Williams was 29. Jones loved the challenge of working with musicians with such daring imaginations and fast minds. The trio made a gaggle of records for East Wind (Japan), the best of which is *The Great Jazz Trio at the Village Vanguard* (1977). On Parker's "Moose the Mooche," Jones swings through five feisty choruses, winking at the syncopated melody, dashing off rising and falling triplets, dipping briefly into a cycle of fifths during his second chorus, and spontaneously orchestrating his linear inventions by slipping into thirds or octaves. Williams' crisp cymbal work and breathtaking solo amounts to some of his best pure-jazz playing after leaving Miles Davis. The divine way Jones tackles the superimposed chords atop the pedal-point bass on John Coltrane's "Naima" underscores the timeless modernity of his pianism.

"In the realm of improvisation, if you can conceive it in your mind, you should be able to play it if you have the technique," Jones said. "Then your musical personality will come out. But it takes a long time to do that. In the end, the sum total of all that you've heard and experienced and thought about up to that point becomes your personality."

Outside of the Great Jazz Trio, Jones' best late-period recordings include the 1976 solo piano tribute to Ellington, *Satin Doll* (Japanese Trio), the 1977 trio date *Bop Redux* (Muse) with George Duvivier and Ben Riley, the 1994 recital of spirituals *Steal Away* (Verve) with bassist Charlie Haden, and 1993's *Upon Reflection* (Verve), a heartfelt program of music by Thad Jones with George Mraz and Elvin Jones.

The pianist considered both of his brothers to be geniuses and said that one of his only regrets was that the three of them did not record more together. Just 10 days after Elvin's death in 2004, Jones expanded on his feelings in liner notes for "Collaboration" (441 Records), his last recording with his brother. "I know I have to live on, but quite honestly, I don't think I'll be able to brush away the sadness I feel," Jones wrote. "I'm the only one left of my brothers. Both my older sisters and younger brothers have all passed away. I cannot put into words how lonely I felt after Elvin passed."

Recommended Recordings

Hank Jones, *The Trio* (Savoy)
Hank Jones, *Have You Met Hank Jones* (Savoy)
The Great Jazz Trio at the Village Vanguard (East Wind)

Thad Jones

JONESISMS

Thad Jones was stuck in neutral at the start of 1966. A few months shy of his 43rd birthday, he was toiling in the CBS studios and freelancing in New York as a trumpeter and arranger. He had spent nine years in the cozy nest of the Count Basie band from 1954 to 1963, contributing some potent arrangements and delighting the masses by tossing a mischievous quote of "Pop Goes the Weasel" into his solo on "April in Paris." Jones was known to insiders as a versatile modernist, a thinking man's improviser and composer. But there was also a feeling that for a musician Charles Mingus once called "Bartok with valves," Jones' potential remained unrealized.

That began to change on Monday, February 7, 1966, in a pie-shaped basement below Seventh Avenue in Manhattan: The Thad Jones–Mel Lewis Jazz Orchestra made its debut at the Village Vanguard. Co-led by an A-list drummer, the band was a smash, and Jones was soon recognized as one of the most creative and influential composer-arrangers in jazz. More than anyone else, as musician-scholar Bill Kirchner once wrote, Jones revitalized postwar big-band writing for the conventional ensemble of saxophones, trumpets, trombones, and rhythm section. He created a new template. On top of a Basie and Ellington foundation he added all the harmonic and rhythmic advances since bebop, even venturing into the modal territory of John Coltrane. It was big-band music in the present tense. "Thad was to the modern jazz of the '60s what Dizzy Gillespie was to the late '40s—he gave it a larger framework," said pianist-composer Jim McNeely.

Jones and Lewis parlayed a handshake deal with Vanguard owner Max Gordon for a couple Monday nights into the longest-running gig in jazz history. Fifty-two years and roughly 2,600 Mondays later, the band—which survived Jones' decampment to Europe in 1979 and Lewis' death in 1990—lives on as the Vanguard Jazz Orchestra. The literal birth of the band is documented on *All My Yesterdays* (Resonance), which includes six tracks recorded on that inaugural Monday and 11 taped six weeks later. Execution is not as polished as it would become, but the excitement and spontaneity explode out of the speakers.

The opening-night performance of "The Little Pixie" defines Jones' art. It's a simple form: a 32-bar "I Got Rhythm"-derived tune in A-flat transformed into a symphony of melody and swing. It starts with a burst of muted brass suspended in midair. Saxophones announce the jabbing theme, heavily syncopated, sparkling like pixie dust. Three scampering ensemble choruses follow as reeds and brass (in cup mutes to start, then open) chase after each other in a game of anything-you-can-do-I-can-do-better. They trade 16-bar phrases, then 8s, then 4s. The writing is virtuosic, filled with witty acrobatics, breathless triplets, and colorful chord extensions. Joyous swing is built into every bar. Harmonies bite with dissonance. Tension builds. Fingers fly. Emotions soar. Reeds and brass merge in a rocking climax.[1]

Wow!

The band included mostly midcareer pros with big-band experience and individual personalities as soloists. Section leaders were trumpeter Snooky Young, alto saxophonist Jerome Richardson, and valve trombonist Bob Brookmeyer. Hank Jones was on board, though another Detroit pianist, Roland Hanna, would soon assume his chair. Marvin (Doc) Holladay played baritone sax opening night, but Detroiter Pepper Adams, Jones' first choice, replaced him within weeks. Jones, more than 6 feet tall and built like a linebacker, played unpredictable solos on cornet and flugelhorn and conducted with karate-chop gestures and the charisma of Bernstein. The sidemen made $17 for the night. The Vanguard charged a $2.50 cover. "That first night the place was packed," said alto saxophonist and original band member Jerry Dodgion. "Jazz was alive in New York, but it wasn't thriving. Max wasn't doing great. He said, 'Mondays are a good night to try—nothing's happening.' Pretty soon, Mondays were sustaining him."

Jones, who died in 1986 at age 63, is in the canon, but his brilliance as a composer-arranger and improviser is not as widely understood as it should be. His gifts were multilayered, but as great a trumpet soloist as he was—and Jones remains an underrated school unto himself—his ultimate destiny was the big band.

Born Thaddeus Joseph Jones on March 28, 1923, in Pontiac, he took up the trumpet at 13 or 14 after hearing Louis Armstrong on the radio. Jones taught himself to play from method books. He gravitated to cornet in high school, retaining a lifelong preference for the instrument's darker sound. He was raised on big bands, especially Ellington, and Duke's puckish cornetist Rex Stewart left the biggest imprint until Jones discovered his most important influence, Dizzy Gillespie. Being self-taught reinforced Jones' individuality. "There are certain things I do in certain ways that nobody else does," Jones told *Downbeat* in 1955. "A schooled musician has, I imagine, a crisper style than mine, but there is a freedom in the way I play."

He started playing professionally at 16 and toured the Midwest with bands at 18. Jones told critic Gary Giddins in 1985 that he heard bebop for the first time in the mid-'40s while traveling with a GI show in the Army. Charlie Parker and Gillespie's "Shaw Nuff" thundered out of the radio one night, and Jones was hooked. Years later, Parker and Jones would occasionally have drinks in New York and the saxophonist would always tell him that he wanted to form a band with all three Jones brothers. Jones played with territory bands, revues, and burlesque shows in the late '40s. Trips to the segregated South were rough. Jones and his black bandmates had pistols stuck in their faces by white policemen. Those experiences left scars. Friends remember Jones as generous, gregarious, and funny, but his attitude flipped in a second if he sensed any hint of racism, disrespect, or condescension. "He had antennae up for that," said trumpeter John McNeil. "It came close to having a chip on his shoulder."

Jones told McNeil about an incident in front of Birdland in New York in the '50s in which Jones, wearing a suit and holding his horn case, was standing with friends when two cops approached. One said, "Hey, boys, break it up." Jones' temperature shot up at the demeaning tone, and he barked, "I don't see no boys here!" The cops roughed him up, but Jones didn't retreat. "They had to call for backup," Jones told McNeil. "It took four of them to get me in that car. I got a few bruises, but it was worth it. They charged me with disorderly conduct or some bullshit, and I had to pay a fine."

Jones retained an intense dislike for the South, especially Florida, where, decades later, he split for home in the middle of a couple tours because he perceived racist treatment. He was a complicated man. Mel Lewis told Bob Rusch in *Cadence* magazine that Jones created some scenes himself, situations exacerbated by Jones' alcohol abuse.

Jones settled in Detroit in 1952, joining the house band at the Blue Bird Inn. Led by tenor saxophonist Billy Mitchell, it was the most inventive modern jazz group in Detroit at the city's most vital club—a cozy bar on Tireman on the west side that attracted neighborhood folks, jazz aficionados, and musicians. The band included pianist-vibraphonist Terry Pollard (replaced by Tommy Flanagan when she joined Terry Gibbs in August 1953), bassist James "Beans" Richardson, and Elvin Jones. Mitchell's quintet became the stuff of legend, working on its own and backing Charlie Parker, Sonny Stitt, and Miles Davis. The latter lived in Detroit for five months in 1953–54 as he weaned himself off heroin. Davis played often at the Blue Bird and recorded Jones' enigmatic "Bitty Ditty" in 1955.

In a 1976 interview with *Jazz Magazine*, Davis famously compared Jones' conceptualism with the flash of Freddie Hubbard: "I'd rather hear Thad *miss* a note than Freddie *make* 12." Charles Mingus was so moved hearing Jones in Detroit that he wrote a letter to critic Bill Coss in which he called Jones the greatest trumpet player he ever heard. A decade later in a 1963 profile of Jones in *Downbeat*, Coss quoted the letter: "He uses all the classical techniques and is the first man to make them swing. . . . Here is Bartok with valves for a pencil that's directed by God."[2]

Mitchell's quintet recorded four songs in 1953 for Dee Gee issued on a 7-inch, extended play 45 titled *New Sounds Modern Music*—Jones's slippery "Zec," a blues called "Compulsory," and two standards, "Alone Together" and "Blue Room." The band is as tight as family, its authority the equal of any group in New York. Jones' zigzagging rhythms, piquant note choices, and burnished tone announce a unique voice.

Count Basie hired Jones out of Detroit in May 1954, and he made his first records as a leader for Mingus' Debut label in August and the following March. The highlights of Jones' early discography are his three Blue Note LPs in 1956–57, especially *Detroit–New York Junction*. Half the sidemen were colleagues from home—Mitchell, Flanagan, Elvin, Kenny Burrell, Barry Harris, Paul Chambers—and these were among the first records to draw attention to the burgeoning pipeline of talent from the Motor City. Jones' LPs were part of the emerging hard-bop mainstream, but they also stood apart. Unlike the loose blowing sessions coming into vogue, there is a wealth of organizational detail. Jones' compositions and improvisations are filled with what colleagues called "Jonesisms"—melodic surprises, expressive dissonance, sudden harmonic shifts, rhythmic displacements, curious sequences. He avoided preconceived patterns, and his solos are models of tension-and-release—like Gillespie taken to a higher level of abstraction.

"If you talk about the percentage of true improvisation in a solo—or an entire career of solos—then Thad had one of the highest percentages in jazz history," said trumpeter Tim Hagans. "The quality and percentage of literally new stuff that came out of his horn was astounding. That creative melodic language is what informs his lead lines in his big-band writing. That's why his music has so much warmth and humor."

Jones' "Scratch," which appears on *Detroit–New York Junction*, contains one of his best recorded solos. The song begins with a jaunty introduction landing on a tangy flatted fifth. After the buoyant 36-bar theme, Jones strolls through three choruses with skipping rhythms, bebop curlicues, and double time. Sequences, call-and-response, rhyme, and humor animate his solo; Jones tosses an idea in the air and teases out its implications. In the second eight bars of his final chorus he hits on a flirty two-bar motif that sashays down the scale; he repeats it three more times, starting each recurrence at a higher pitch. Organization and unpredictability stand in teeter-totter balance. "He could make a sequence out of anything," said John McNeil. "He would play a phrase, then play it a minor third away, then maybe a step down; he would move it all over the place. And he would make changes to it as he went along, throwing other notes in or changing the rhythm."

Such a compositional approach to improvising is probably what Mingus meant by "classical techniques," and it's why Jones makes an ideal partner for Thelonious Monk, also a thematic improviser, on *Five by Monk by Five* (1959). "There are no bad notes, just bad organization," Jones told the *New York Times* in 1973.

The first time Jim McNeely played with the Jones-Lewis band at the Village Vanguard in the late '70s Jones called the evergreen "Body and Soul." McNeely played a piano introduction, easing into the E-flat minor seventh chord that starts the song. Jones entered with an outrageous dissonance—a G natural, the major third clashing against the minor third (G-flat) in the chord. "He was sending a message," McNeely said. "'OK, kid, do something with this!' I made up a voicing that had both the major and minor third in it, and I think he liked that. He automatically went for those notes that had a grind to them, a friction."

Jones' first big-band arrangements for Basie in 1958 fit into the band's mold, but there are Jonesisms like the alluring trombone lead over saxophones on "H.R.H.," and the flute, clarinet, and bass clarinet combination in "Speaking of Sounds" At a 1961 recording session pairing the Ellington and Basie bands, Duke's ears perked up when he heard Jones' sumptuous ballad "To You." Ellington hired Jones in March 1963 for what turned out to be just over a week, but included a performance of Ellington's symphonic *Night Creature* at Ford Auditorium in Detroit with the Detroit Symphony Orchestra led by associate conductor Valter Poole.[3] Jones, who revered Ellington for the panoramic colors and emotional ambrosia of his scores, regarded the experience as a highlight of his life. But having just left Basie to spend more time with his family, Jones decided he couldn't keep the gig. Five years later, Ellington veterans Britt Woodman and Jimmy Hamilton dropped by the Village Vanguard one Monday. When they left, Jones turned to David Berger, an aspiring composer-arranger: "Duke Ellington—greatest band in the world," said Jones.

Berger protested: "Your band's the greatest!"

"No, no, no!" Jones said. "My band's not one-tenth of what Duke Ellington and Count Basie are and never will be."

Jones and Mel Lewis first met in Detroit on a sweltering August night in 1955 when Jones was with Basie and Lewis was with Stan Kenton.[4] The groups were booked for a battle-of-the-bands dance at the Graystone Ballroom, and after the dance was over, Jones took Lewis to the jam session at the West End Hotel. They later crossed paths in New York and in the fertile Gerry Mulligan Concert Jazz Band, where they plotted their own group. Fate and the demise of Mulligan's band in late 1964 set the stage. Basie commissioned an album's worth of material from Jones in 1965, but the arrangements proved too adventurous and the recording was scuttled. Jones and Lewis now had the foundation for their own book. (Bob Brookmeyer also contributed a few key arrangements in the early days.)

The co-leaders were a curious pair: one black and Baptist, the other white and Jewish. Jones was genial, Lewis rather brusque and a talker of rabbinical proportion. But they were as close as twins. They insisted on rooming together on the road, even though Jones was an inveterate ladies' man and Lewis was often left biding his time in hotel lobbies while Jones entertained a new friend. Both wanted a disciplined band committed to the grandeur of the ensemble but with unfettered freedom granted to soloists. They insisted on an integrated band. The group was half black and half white, a notable symbol of harmony in an era in which Black Power politics gained currency. When the balance tilted toward white players in the late '70s, Jones and Lewis candidly complained to critic Leonard Feather in the *Los Angeles Times* about the relative scarcity of young black musicians willing to commit to straight-ahead jazz in the fusion era and the irony of losing black players to studio and Broadway gigs once denied African Americans.

For all of Jones' originality, it's instructive how many of his seminal pieces are built on basic forms and saturated with the blues. "The Second Race," "Big Dipper," "Backbone," and "Tow-Away Zone" are all 12-bar or 16-bar variations on the blues. Even "Central Park North," one of Jones' most formally complex works, mutates into a boogaloo blues. His melodic imagination and reservoir of swing are inexhaustible. The theme of "Mean What You Say," as memorable as a Gershwin tune, gives way to oodles of fetching countermelodies, ornamentation, interludes, and backgrounds. You could draw a frame around any detail and call it a song.

There were other innovations and Jonesims: He set a new standard for the saxophone section "soli"—a written passage that mirrors an improvised solo, such as the bebop joy ride in five-part harmony on "Three and One." He reintroduced the soprano saxophone into big bands. His climactic shout choruses roar with expressive dissonance. In the '70s, he explored woodwind colors and denser harmony. When you take the scores apart, you see the craftwork, but there's a soulful resonance beyond technique. Jones tells stories. He gets under your skin where your emotions live. He excites the imagination, elevates the spirit. Only uneven ballads like "All My Yesterdays" and "Yours and Mine" suggest a relative weakness. David Berger suggests that for all of Jones' genius, his music lacks romance. More successful are his lyrical pieces with extra punch, such as the bewitching "Quietude" and the robust "Kids Are Pretty People." (Though Jones is credited as the composer of "A Child Is Born," a tender waltz that's become a standard, it was almost certainly written by Roland Hanna. See the chapter on Hanna for full discussion.)

Lewis was a secret weapon. The most musical big-band drummer of the modern era, he swung in relaxed fashion, set up the ensemble with a minimum of fuss, and transformed into a fine small-group drummer behind soloists. He forged a special bond with idiosyncratic bassist Richard Davis. Lewis' drums laid behind the beat and Davis' bass pushed ahead: Imagine the back and front legs of a chair moving in unison, the band riding on a wide cushion in between.

Audiences at the Vanguard never knew what was going to happen. Neither did the players. Jones cued the rhythm section in and out in unpredictable fashion, letting a soloist go it alone or putting a horn in motion with, say, just bass behind him. Background riffs and dynamics were improvised on the spot. Jones had fun, and if you were in his orbit, you did too. Miles Davis was in the club one night, and between tunes asked Jones to play a ballad. "Sure!" said Jones. He turned to the band and counted off one of the fastest numbers in the book. The *next* tune was a ballad.

The band recorded five indispensable LPs between 1966 and 1970 on Solid State and Blue Note—*Presenting Thad Jones–Mel Lewis & the Jazz Orchestra*, *Live at the Village Vanguard*, *Monday Night*, *Central Park North*, and *Consummation*. There are also tremendous video and audio bootlegs from a 1969 European tour with former Detroiter Joe Henderson blowing up a storm on tenor sax. *New Life* (Horizon) from 1976 introduces two of Jones' most enduring later-period charts, the beguiling "Little Rascal on a Rock" and the burner "Cherry Juice." Jones made relatively few small-group records after 1965, but *Mean What You Say* (co-led with Pepper Adams in 1966) and *Thad Jones–Mel Lewis Quartet* (1977) are keepers.

The '70s were frustrating for Jones. He and Lewis were unable to parlay their acclaim into higher fees, steady recording, and consistent touring. A *New York Times* story in 1973 gives a picture of Jones' harried life: He taught at William Patterson University in Wayne, New Jersey, on Mondays, Tuesdays, and Thursdays. He played seven shows a week in a Broadway pit for *Two Gentlemen of Verona*. On Fridays he flew to Boston to teach at the New England Conservatory. Monday nights were reserved for the Vanguard. "America makes a mockery of higher aesthetic yearning," Jones told *Jazz Journal International* in 1979.

By the late '70s, Jones had reached another crossroads, and there was a new woman in his life from Denmark. He began a partnership with the Danish Radio Big Band in 1977 that called for well-paid, two-month residencies in Copenhagen in the fall and spring. He re-upped the next year, secretly laying the groundwork for a permanent move. Then came a bizarre incident whose details remain elusive. While on tour in 1978, Jones was in a taxi in Yugoslavia when a bystander shoved his fist through the window. The shattered glass cut Jones' lip, and it took three years and several surgeries before he returned to steady playing. Jones blamed the incident on a random act by a drunk, but given Jones' volatile history, it's more likely words were exchanged before the punch.

Jones left New York without warning in January 1979 to start a new life in Denmark. Deeply hurt, Lewis never got over the bitterness, although he and Jones eventually reached a détente. When Jones' radio contract ended, he started a big band, Eclipse, with Scandinavians and expatriate Americans. He returned to America in 1985 to take over the Count Basie band after Basie's death, but within a year, exhausted, he returned to Copenhagen and died of cancer in August 1986 at age 63.

Jones remains central to the big-band tradition, His music is widely performed, and his arrangements are considered foundational texts within jazz education. Nearly all the mainstream big-band arrangers and composers to emerge in the 1970s and '80s bore his influence, among them Jim McNeely, John Clayton, and Bob Mintzer. Jones' use of dissonance touched writers as different as Bob Brookmeyer and Muhal Richard Abrams. Of the younger generation, composer-bandleader Darcy James Argue grew up worshiping Jones. Countless once-a-week big bands across the country grew out of the Jones-Lewis model. Jones' trumpet playing remains a gold mine of ideas and inspiration for anyone who discovers it.

Ultimately, however, Jones' legacy transcends aesthetic bloodlines and musicology. The key lesson of his career is that his work embodies a spirit of individualism as adamantly as any in jazz. "Each person has his or her own voice that they have to speak with if they want to speak the truth," Jones once said. That's it exactly: The music of Thad Jones spoke the truth. The whole truth and nothing but.

Recommended Recordings

Thad Jones, *Detroit–New York Junction* (Blue Note)
Thad Jones and Mel Lewis, *Presenting / Live at the Village Vanguard / The Big Band Sound* (BGO)
Thad Jones and Mel Lewis, *Monday Night / Central Park North* (BGO)

Notes

1. The tape runs out before the end of "The Little Pixie," and the producer, regrettably, has spliced the opening chorus onto the end of the performance with no explanation. Jones' arrangement actually concludes with a brilliant shout chorus and coda.

2. Sy Johnson, "An Afternoon at Mile's," *Jazz Magazine* (Fall 1976); Bill Coss, "Thad Jones: Horn of Plenty," *Downbeat* (May 9, 1963), 16.

3. Jones rejoined the Ellington band in Detroit for a week-long engagement at the Michigan State Fair in August 1963. Ken Vail, *Duke's Diary, Part 2: The Life of Duke Ellington, 1950–1974* (Scarecrow Press, 2002), 215–216, 224.

4. In Chris Smith's *The View from the Back of the Bus: The Life and Music of Mel Lewis* (University of North Texas Press, 2016), the author quotes from a radio interview in which Lewis said he met Jones in July. However, an advertisement in the Detroit Free Press (August 28, 1955, C15), confirms the Battle of the Bands concert took place on August 29, 1955.

Elvin Jones

PHILOSOPHER KING

Faced with the animalistic intensity and rhythmic innovations that drummer Elvin Jones brought to jazz, critics often retreat into dry technical analysis or force-of-nature metaphors comparing his style to a tornado or hurricane. But neither captures the full measure of what Jones meant to the music. Yes, he was one of the most influential drummers in jazz history and helped elevate the music to new peaks of creativity and expression in the 1960s with the John Coltrane Quartet. But Jones, who died of heart failure in 2004 at age 76, was not just a trailblazer. He was a philosopher king, venerated for his hard-knock wisdom, charisma, spiritual aura, personal warmth, and the respect he accorded fellow musicians and everyday fans. He was famously supportive of colleagues and newcomers and generous with bear hugs. The contrast between his sweet disposition and violent physicality of his playing—his forearms and biceps were as big as a bodybuilder's—was part of his vibe. To see waves of polyrhythms crash across his drums, sweat pour off his drenched frame, and his face contorted into a shaman mask—and then experience his 1,000-watt smile and humanity off the bandstand was to witness a sage in a state of grace.

Jones signed autographs: "Love and Peace, Elvin Jones." He meant it.

"His ability to communicate with people from the drum stool was amazing," said saxophonist David Liebman. "He hypnotized people. It was because of this immense reservoir of energy, the way he played, the way he looked—the sweat, the cigarette dangling from his mouth. He was super expressive, and then he'd walk off the stand and talk to anyone. That reflected his generosity of spirit, his desire and ability to warm you up, to involve you with the music."

Jones took nothing for granted in music or in life. He played every night as if it might be his last, and he gave the impression of a man ready to die for his art. Jones took tremendous pride in his heritage as a jazz musician. In a 1971 interview with drummer Art Taylor published in *Notes and Tones*,

Jones spoke of jazz as a profoundly humanist calling: "It's a pure art form developed here in this country by black artists and which is continuing to be developed by everybody that has any musical aspirations at all or who has even thought about becoming a musician, whatever color they are. I think the fact that it's pure transcends all colors and races."

Musically, Jones represented the next great leap forward in jazz drumming after bebop innovators Kenny Clarke and Max Roach in the '40s ushered in the ride cymbal as the main carrier of the beat and employed more intricate syncopation than earlier drummers. Art Blakey, Philly Joe Jones, and Roy Haynes pushed the drums ahead in the 1950s; Haynes' conversational approach and way of breaking up the time proved especially forward-looking. But Elvin Jones had the most individual take of all. Fiercely aggressive, he created a pulsating web of shifting accents and meters that echoed the multilayered complexities of African drumming.

The result was a visceral and loose post-bop, a new and deeper way to swing that implied the beat instead of stating it outright. At full throttle, the ferocity and volume of Jones' playing bordered on maniacal. But it was also musical and disciplined, varied in dynamics, texture, and color. Jones erased the line between foreground and background, elevating his accompaniment to a kind of continuous solo that remained complementary and supportive. Musicians often said that playing with him was like feeling the vastness and power of the ocean behind them. Jones reconciled opposites. In the same way that Miles Davis married virility and vulnerability and Billie Holiday encompassed joy and suffering, Jones embodied a push-pull between kinetic fury and a mystical feeling of relaxation. The result was an emotional breadth unique among drummers.

Jones' unorthodox approach was present in embryo before he left Detroit in 1955 and he hit an early peak on records in the late '50s. But it was during his five and a half years with John Coltrane, from 1960 to 1966, that Jones reached full maturity. The quartet—Coltrane on tenor and soprano saxophones, McCoy Tyner on piano, Jimmy Garrison (who joined in 1961) on bass—pioneered a freer approach to jazz. On epochal records such as *Impressions*, *Live at Birdland*, and *A Love Supreme* the group explored more open forms, modal and pedal-point harmony, and incantatory improvisations that crested on Jones' waves of thunder. Anthems like "Impressions" or "One Down, One Up" could last an hour and include 30- or 40-minute duets between tenor sax and drums that were cathartic rituals.

On a technical level, Jones reinvented the fundamental bebop ride cymbal beat with his right hand. He reorganized the standard ding-dinga-ding pattern, breaking up the beat with fluidity and phrasing over bar lines. Jones scattered triplets across the drum kit with his left hand and integrated all four limbs into a churning undertow. He further unshackled the beat by abandoning the conventional practice of accenting beats 2 and 4 in every bar of 4/4 time on the hi-hat. Instead, he folded the hi-hat into his vortex.

The floating-triplet feel is Jones' most recognizable calling card. Triplets are three evenly spaced notes squeezed into the space of two—think da-da-da/da-da-da/da-da-da. That's the ubiquitous rhythm that "floats" through Jones' playing and implies constant motion. One clear example is the 1962 Coltrane recording of "Tunji." Jones plays eddies of triplets across the snare drum and tom-toms with his left hand.

"I especially like his ability to mix and juggle rhythms," Coltrane once said. "He's always aware of everything else that's happening. I guess you could say he has the ability to be in three places at the same time."

The unusually wide spaces between Jones' cymbal strokes stretched out the beat. As Liebman once wrote, this gave the appearance that Jones played behind the stated pulse. At faster tempos, the variety of articulation of his cymbal strokes made downbeats less discernable and difficult to follow for musicians whose internal time wasn't secure. Jones' solos were also challenging to follow. Sometimes his breaks gave the impression of a drum set crashing down a flight of stairs, only to somehow land standing right side up. "I can see forms and shapes in my mind when I solo, just as a painter can see forms and shapes when he starts a painting," Jones told Balliett. "And I can see colors. My cymbals will be one color and my snare another color and my tom toms each a different color. I mix these colors up, making constant movement."

Other widely copied elements of Jones style include the elliptical swirl he brought to Latin rhythms—a kind of surreal and swinging mambo—and his loose approach to waltz time heard on "My Favorite Things," "Afro-Blue" and "Chim Chim Cheree" with Coltrane. Though Jones' bashing volume became part of his legend, he had masterful control over dynamics, and his eloquent playing with wire brushes is part of his legacy too. On recordings you can often hear Jones' involuntary vocalizing in the mix with the swooshing brushes—a growling cackle that became a defining sound in jazz all on its own.

Elvin Ray Jones was born in Pontiac on September 9, 1927. His fascination with the drums dated back to seeing the Ringling Bros. circus train in Pontiac when he was five. By his early teens he had acquired sticks, wire brushes, a drum pad, and a standard Paul Yoder method book from which he learned the 26 basic rudiments. Jones always credited the instruction he received from his band director at Washington Junior High School, Fred Weist, a former drum major, for teaching him that the drums were a musical instrument and not a noisemaker. At Pontiac Central High School he led the marching as a drum major (twirling baton and all), and he played percussion in the concert band. When older brother Hank was around, the pianist would put on records by Art Tatum on a wind-up Victrola and have his brother play along with brushes on a book.

Jones quit school after the 10th grade and unloaded boxcars for General Motors. He joined the Air Force in 1946, receiving eight weeks of musical instruction after basic training, and he played with company bands while stationed near Columbus, Ohio. He returned to Detroit in 1949, bought his first drum set, and began woodshedding. The city's leading bebop drummer, Art Mardigan, took a shine to Jones and offered friendship, advice, and inspiration. Jones worshiped Mardigan, who worked regularly at the Blue Bird Inn. When Billy Mitchell took over the house band at the club in 1952, Jones assumed the drum chair and stayed three years. "That's where I really got settled," Jones told the *Detroit Free Press* in 1991. "I seemed to be welcomed in there among those highly skillful musicians. They took me in as one of their own, and I began to learn how to use my abilities."

Jones spoke fondly about many drummers—modernists like Roach, Clarke, Haynes, Blakey, Philly Joe Jones, and Mardigan, as well as pre-bop drummers Baby Dodds, Sid Catlett, Jo Jones, Sonny Greer, Gene Krupa, Chick Webb, and Buddy Rich. Jones knew his history, but his playing was fundamentally without precedent. "I figured that a lot of things drummers were doing with two hands could be done with one—like accents with just the left hand on the snare, so you wouldn't have to take your right hand off the ride cymbal," Jones told Balliett. "And it didn't seem to me that the four-four beat on the bass drum was necessary. What was needed was a flow of rhythm all over the set."

An early version of that flow can be heard on his first recordings—the Dee Gee sides circa 1952–53 with Mitchell's quintet. Jones' unbound ride cymbal, left-hand chatter, and triplet rhythms are audible on the shuffling blues "Compulsory." On "Zec," the drummer's aggressiveness with brushes and sticks and the displaced rhythms of his eight-bar solo predict the future.

Friends remember that Jones was always smiling, always upbeat, always making friends. Detroit drummer Rudy Tucich said Jones shared an apartment with a white woman on the city's west side on Linwood near

West Grand Boulevard—a bold lifestyle choice at the time, and Tucich recalled hearing neighborhood police curse the couple in racist language. Hank Jones arranged for an audition for his brother with Benny Goodman in New York in 1955. Though he didn't get the job, Jones landed a gig with bassist Charles Mingus and in July recorded with Miles Davis.

By 1956, Jones was playing with Bud Powell, and for the next four years worked or recorded with a cross-section of the scene, including Sonny Rollins, J. J. Johnson, Gil Evans, Steve Lacy, Randy Weston, Sweets Edison, Tyree Glenn, and many former Detroiters—his brothers, Kenny Burrell, Paul Chambers, Tommy Flanagan, Donald Byrd, and Pepper Adams. Jones' growing mastery is heard most clearly on Rollins' landmark 1957 trio record *A Night at the Village Vanguard* (Blue Note). On "Old Devil Moon," "Sonnymoon for Two," and "Striver's Row," the drummer's surging momentum and liberated rhythms mesh with Rollins' loose phrasing on tenor sax and Wilbur Ware's emancipated bass lines to create a beat as elastic as a rubber band.

Jones' style made him a rebel. Detractors said he was loud and confusing, and it took a while for many musicians to feel comfortable with him. "He played so many strange overlapping rhythms that I found it hard to hear the basic tempo," saxophonist Bobby Jasper wrote in the *Jazz Review* in 1959. "I thought that he was in poor form and just couldn't keep time. . . . Then, little by little, I began to understand the mysteries of Elvin's playing."

Like many of his contemporaries, Jones fought a drug problem—heroin—that led to two stays in prison. He told Balliett that he got started using drugs in Detroit in 1949 to join the insiders club and escape the slog of everyday life. Jones mentions a run-in with the law in Detroit without offering specifics, and he describes his arrest for possession at a New York hotel in 1959. (This may have taken place in 1960.) He told Balliett that he served six months at Rikers Island and there's a conspicuous hole in his discography from the end of April 1960 through September of that year. While Jones told Balliett he had been clean ever since, another possession charge in late 1962 led to a three-month incarceration in mid-1963 at the federal prison and rehabilitation center in Lexington, Kentucky, the so-called "Narcotic Farm" where many jazz musicians put in time.

Coltrane biographer Lewis Porter writes that Jones told an interviewer he first played with the saxophonist as a sub for Philly Joe Jones with Miles Davis' band in Philadelphia or on a Coltrane-led gig with a pickup band, probably in 1958 or '59. Prison prevented Jones from joining Coltrane's first quartet in spring 1960, but he joined upon his release. He was

33. "It seemed that all my life was a preparation for that period," Jones told Balliett. "Right from the beginning to the last time we played together, it was something pure. The most impressive thing was a feeling of steady, collective learning. Every night when we hit the bandstand—no matter if we'd come 500 or 1,000 miles—the weariness dropped from us. It was one of the most beautiful things a man can experience. If there is anything like perfect harmony in human relationships, that band was close as you can come."

The quartet's first recordings for Atlantic in October 1960—*My Favorite Things*, *Coltrane Plays the Blues*, and *Coltrane's Sound*—retain links to Coltrane's advanced bebop idiom while pushing forward into vamps and modes. The band turned another corner when Jimmy Garrison joined on bass in December 1961. The quartet's entire Impulse catalog is worth owning, but the clarified lyricism of *Crescent* (1964) make it a good starting point for newcomers, followed by the all-embracing masterpiece *A Love Supreme* (1964). The heroic title track on *Transition* (1965) captures the quartet at its apex. Videos and incendiary concert and club recordings issued long after Coltrane's death in 1967 fill out the story, especially the epic *One Down, One Up* taped at the Half Note in New York in spring 1965. There's also a version of "Bye, Bye Blackbird" recorded in Stockholm, Sweden, in 1962 issued on Pablo that includes a delirious five-and-a-half-minute tag ending driven by Jones that sounds, to borrow a phrase from Amiri Baraka, like the wild pulse of all living.

Beyond Coltrane, Jones played on countless records in the '60s that entered the canon. A short list: McCoy Tyner's *The Real McCoy*, Wayne Shorter's *Speak No Evil* and *Juju*, Joe Henderson's *Inner Urge*, Larry Young's *Unity*, Freddie Hubbard's *Ready for Freddie*, Grant Green's *Street of Dreams*, Andrew Hill's *Judgment*, Lee Konitz's *Motion*, and Ornette Coleman's *New York Is Now!*

Jones left Coltrane in January 1966 when the saxophonist added a second drummer and turned a steady pulse toward more avant-garde realms. Given Jones' history with the darker side of the jazz life, the success of his post-Coltrane career was not guaranteed. Fortune smiled when on a trip to Nagasaki, Japan, in 1966 he reunited with a woman named Keiko whom he had met in New York a year earlier. They married in 1966. A small Japanese woman of indomitable will, Keiko became his field general and gatekeeper. Fiercely protective, she managed his business, kept him on the straight and narrow as best she could, tended to his diet, and even set up and tuned his drums before performances. In later years they lived in New York and Nagasaki. Jones had been married previously to a woman named Shirley DeFranco, with whom he had two children.

Jones, now 40, settled into a productive career as a bandleader. He typically fronted ensembles that showcased one or two Coltrane-inspired tenor saxophonists, among them Joe Farrell, Frank Foster, George Coleman, Dave Liebman, Steve Grossman, Pat LaBarbera, Sonny Fortune, and Ravi Coltrane (John's son). Jones' presence was so strong that even though he only wrote a few pieces, all the music owed its character to his interpretive stamp. Liebman, who toured with Jones for a year and a half in 1971–72, said that if he was noodling around too much on a ballad, Jones might growl over his brushes, "Play the melody!" Liebman complained once that he was tired of playing the same ballad every night—"I'm a Fool to Want You"—and stuck for fresh ideas. Jones' reply was essentially, "*You're stuck, but it's the tune's fault?*" Liebman got the message: The problem was his attitude. Jones told him audiences don't know or care whether he played the same song every night, and it was Liebman's job to communicate to people who had paid to hear him—to play more meaningfully, with more focus or cleaner execution. Jones' bottom line: "Just keep playing that goddamn ballad."

Jones was in a good personal space. Keiko took care of him, and his drug issues were behind him, although he was enrolled in a methadone program in the early '70s. He mostly stayed away from hard alcohol but on an average night in a club might go through eight to 12 bottles of Lowenbrau beer—and sweat it all out while playing. On the road, Jones would settle into the hotel, stay in his kimono until late afternoon, read voraciously—science fiction, nonfiction, biographies—watch TV and smoke pack after pack of Newport cigarettes. He stayed plugged into current events and politics.

Jones' finest body of recordings as a leader were the 10 albums he made for Blue Note from 1968 to 1973. The bands range from lean trios to 11 pieces and sweep through an impressive diversity of material. Of the two initial LPs from 1968 showcasing his first working group with Joe Farrell and Jimmy Garrison, *Puttin' It Together* has an extra snap heard in the bacon fat Jones slaps on "Keiko's Birthday March" and the driving tom-toms on "Gingerbread Boy." From 1971, *Merry-Go-Round* stands out for its thoughtfully arranged material, mix of veterans and newcomers (including Chick Corea and Jan Hammer), and hints of the eclecticism entering jazz. The generational shift was complete by *Live at the Lighthouse* (1972), recorded by Jones' working band with bassist Gene Perla and young saxophonists Liebman and Steve Grossman tearing into a post-Coltrane language.

Of the post–Blue Note dates as a leader, two stand out: The bristling *Elvin Jones Is on the Mountain* (PM) from 1975 with Hammer on keyboards and Perla, and *Earth Jones* (Palo Alto) from 1982, with a mature quintet including Liebman, Terumasa Hino, Kenny Kirkland, and George Mraz. At 70, Jones made his most adventurous album, *Momentum Space* (Verve), with a cooperative trio including the incomparable free-jazz pianist Cecil Taylor and gutsy saxophonist Dewey Redman; the roiling music is ballet-like in movement. Jones also recorded prolifically as a sideman, bringing a sense of occasion to dates by McCoy Tyner, Art Pepper, Benny Wallace, Robert Hurst, and others.

Jones remained a marvel of undiminished energy and creativity through his 60s and early 70s. The quality of the Elvin Jones Jazz Machine, as his band was called, was hit or miss, but Jones never sounded anything but amazing. His most memorable appearance back home in later years was at the Detroit Jazz Festival in 1999. He greeted old friends backstage with smiles and hugs, and his quintet—Antoine Roney, Robin Eubanks, Carlos McKinney, Cecil McBee—caught fire. Perched high behind his set, Jones presided like an omnipotent deity. The music poured out of him, his spirit channeling everything jazz can be musically, creatively, and emotionally. A revival-meeting vibration spread through the audience, and some people stood and shouted. At the end of the set, Jones was soaked in sweat and the world had been made a better place.

Recommended Recordings

Wayne Shorter, *Juju* (Blue Note)
John Coltrane, *A Love Supreme* (Impulse)
Elvin Jones, *Merry-Go-Round* (Blue Note)

PART FOUR
Taking Control
Self-Determination in the 1960s and '70s

Opening Chorus

Around 3:30 a.m. on July 23, 1967, Detroit police raided an after-hours club selling booze near the corner of 12th and Clairmount in an African American neighborhood on the west side. Detroiters called such joints a "blind pig." More than 80 people were arrested, and a crowd gathered. Tempers flared, and long-simmering tensions between black residents and the mostly white cops turned violent. Someone heaved a bottle, and—just like that—bricks, sticks, and other objects began smashing windows of police cars and storefronts of mostly black-owned businesses. As the violence escalated in the coming days, Governor George W. Romney activated the Michigan National Guard and President Lyndon Johnson sent in federal troops and tanks to quell the protests.[1]

Pianist Kirk Lightsey lived close to ground zero, and at one point he headed up to the roof to survey the scene. He was soon confronted by National Guardsmen, guns drawn, mistaking him for a sniper. Lightsey talked himself out of the situation, and headed back to his apartment, where another soldier had a bayonet against the neck of pianist David Durrah. "We were almost dead," Lightsey said. Later, flames from a fire behind Lightsey's apartment reached through a window and burned his Steinway.

The events of 1967 are usually referred to as a "riot," though many today prefer "rebellion" in deference to the root causes of systemic discrimination faced by blacks in housing and employment and racist behavior of police. The destruction of Paradise Valley and Black Bottom to build the interstate highways played a role too, pushing thousands of blacks into the increasingly overcrowded neighborhood around 12th Street and exacerbating the conditions that led to the eruption of violence. Order was restored after five days of bloody chaos. The damage was almost incomprehensible: 43 people died, 33 of them black and 10 white, most shot by police or military. Nearly 1,200 were injured. More than 2,500 stores were burned or looted. Nearly 400 families lost homes and nearly 700 buildings were destroyed. Estimated monetary losses reached as high as $333 million in 2018 dollars. It remains one of the deadliest and costliest civil disturbances in American history.[2]

The violence of 1967 forever altered the physical, psychological, and cultural landscape of Detroit. The city had been losing population since the mid-1950s, but the exodus picked up speed in the late '60s and '70s, and the city's economic decline accelerated—a process that took decades to run its course. Census figures show that between 1960 and 1970, population in the city dropped by 10%. Between 1970 and 1980, population dropped an additional 20% to 1.2 million.

Detroit's jazz club scene began to splinter after 1967. The process was gradual, part of a long arc of change that had started in the early '60s, when urban renewal destroyed Black Bottom and Paradise Valley. "Things didn't completely stop, but they slowed down after 1967," said drummer Doug Hammond. A further blow came in 1972, when Berry Gordy moved his Motown empire to Los Angeles. The shift deprived Detroit jazz musicians of studio work and touring opportunities that had helped sustain many of them.

Detroit musicians increasingly took matters into their own hands to counter diminishing opportunities. The 1960s and '70s saw the rise of numerous artist-driven cooperatives and self-determination efforts. The best known of these were Strata Corporation (1969–76) and Tribe (1971–77), influential ventures that still loom large in the city's cultural mythology. At their peak in the first half of the '70s, Strata and Tribe produced recordings and concerts, marketed and distributed their work, and, in the case of Tribe, published an Afrocentric magazine. The records are now collectors' items; the original LPs often sell for hundreds of dollars. The Contemporary Jazz Quintet, the leading Detroit band of the era and associated with Strata, continues to inspire musicians in the 21st century. Lesser-known ventures like the Detroit Creative Musicians Association (1967–69) and the Detroit Artists Workshop (1964–67) left behind no commercial recordings but remain a key part of Detroit jazz history. In an age when the city was losing power and population, self-determination efforts encapsulated the stubborn resolve of the jazz community to build on its storied history.

"We just wanted to find a way to get our music played," said trombonist Phil Ranelin, who cofounded Tribe with tenor saxophonist Wendell Harrison. "We didn't have a lot of money to pay guys, but we found ways to make it work. Our number one priority was artistic expression, but nobody was doing it for us, so we had to do it ourselves."

The Detroit collectives of the 1960s and '70s were in spirit linked to the New Music Society, which produced jam sessions and concerts at the World Stage theater in the 1950s. But the 13 years from 1964 to 1977 in which the do-it-yourself imperative flowered most intensely in Detroit represented a new kind of artistic and entrepreneurial ambition. The Detroit Artists Workshop brought together poets, jazz musicians, painters, and filmmakers. The Detroit Creative Musicians Association produced interdisciplinary works merging composed and improvised music, dance, and spoken word. Strata and Tribe were business ventures investing in musicians and community development.

The Detroit collectives bubbled up from the street as part of the zeitgeist that saw similar ventures form across the country in the 1960s and '70s. The Detroit groups were the city's answer to organizations like the Association for the Advancement of Creative Musicians (AACM) in Chicago, the Black Artists' Group (BAG) in St. Louis, the Collective Black Artists in New York, and the Union of God's Musicians and Artists Ascension (formerly Underground Musicians Association) in Los Angeles. Many of these groups can be seen broadly as part of the Black Arts Movement, which started in New York and spread to other cities, including Detroit, where, for example, Dudley Randall founded Broadside Press as a means of publishing African American poets.

As usual, however, Detroit musicians put their own spin on things. By the mid-'60s, the jazz avant-garde was in full swing. Figures like Ornette Coleman, John Coltrane, Cecil Taylor, and Albert Ayler pursued a variety of free-jazz idioms that overturned conventional ideas of rhythm, harmony, and form. While groups like the AACM and BAG were hotbeds of the avant-garde, the cooperatives in Detroit were melting pots for the assimilation of advancing post-bop, free-jazz, and fusion styles that were coursing through jazz. Detroit organizations cultivated progressive profiles and pushed against convention but remained on speaking terms with the mainstream musical values that defined jazz in the city in the '50s. The familiar components of '60s idealism, consciousness-raising, and political activism were in the mix. Yet even as the civil rights movement grew more militant after 1965, there were fewer divisions and less tension between black and white musicians in Detroit than other cities. Tribe and Strata were predominantly black organizations, but white musicians were a visible presence in ways they were not in Chicago's AACM, where the marriage of musical experimentalism and black cultural nationalism created a more separatist dynamic.

The warm camaraderie of black and white players had long been a part of Detroit jazz. Detroit's Local 5 of the American Federation of Musicians was one of the rare locals integrated from the start in the early 20th century. Even more important were integrated schools. "All the guys who went to school in the 1940s and '50s went to integrated schools in Detroit with great music programs," said John Dana, a white bassist and part of several Detroit cooperatives. "They all played together in school bands, and they all got together after school to play and learn together. That attitude never went away."

There were still cliques that broke down along racial lines, and white musicians dominated high-paying society gigs and lucrative commercial theater and studio work. But Ranelin said that among the city's most creative jazz musicians, whoever was most capable and available got the gig, regardless of race. The charged racial politics of the era, however, created some awkward moments. One night around 1969, white guitarist Ron English was hanging out with four or five black musicians in somebody's living room. One of English's best friends, the African American drummer Bobby Battle, was holding court and quoted an incendiary line by poet Amiri Baraka: "The white man, at best, is merely corny!" Battle turned quickly to English: "No offense, Ron."

Notes

1. Details drawn from *The Detroit Almanac: 300 Years of Life in the Motor City*, edited by Peter Gavrilovich and Bill McGraw (Detroit Free Press, 2000).

2. Figures from *Detroit Free Press*, July 22, 2017.

Detroit Artists Workshop, Detroit Creative Musicians Association, and Focus Novii

In November 1964, 16 young writers, musicians, and artists living near Wayne State University came together to form the Detroit Artists Workshop. Among the founders were poet and social activist John Sinclair, trumpeter Charles Moore, drummer Danny Spencer, painter Ellen Phelan, photographer Magdalene Arndt (later Leni Sinclair, after marrying John), poets George Tysh and Jim Semark, and poet-filmmaker Robin Eichele. All except Moore were white, though many black musicians became integral to the workshop, among them drummer Ronnie Johnson, pianist Stanley Cowell (then a graduate student at the University of Michigan), drummer Doug Hammond, and pianist Harold McKinney.

"There were a handful of people who were interested in different things in the arts—the avant-garde, jazz, poetry," said Sinclair. "We hooked up because we were looking for people like ourselves. Mentally, we were avant-garde. We wanted to be different. We studied what people were doing across the country and tried to bring that to Detroit. We wanted our art to reflect life around us, and to help create a community. The main thing was having a place we could perform and exhibit work."

Each founder put up $5 to cover the $65 monthly rent for a two-story house at 1252 W. Forest, just west of the Lodge Freeway. They sublet the top floor for additional cash flow. Subsequent members paid $5 to join, and there were $3 monthly dues for rent and utilities. Performances were held Sunday afternoons—informal concerts, jam sessions, poetry readings—in an L-shaped living room with a fireplace. There was no admission charge, and audiences ranged from 15 to 50 people or more. Members could hang paintings or photos, stage plays, show films, work on poetry, or conduct workshops. They would also sit on the porch and smoke pot. The bohemian vibe was post-beat but pre-hippie.

Sinclair, a 23-year-old graduate student in American literature in 1964, was a key catalyst, organizer, and advocate. Beyond the Artists Workshop

The Detroit Contemporary 5 at the Detroit Artists Workshop in 1965 (*left to right*): drummer Danny Spencer, bassist John Dana, saxophonist Larry Nozero, trumpeter Charles Moore, guitarist Ron English. Photo by Leni Sinclair,

and activities as a poet and performer, he was Detroit correspondent for *Downbeat*, managed the proto-punk MC5 in the late '60s, and did promotion and production work for Strata in the '70s. Sinclair, who died in 2024 at age 82, became famous for his influential role in the counterculture, was a cofounder of the radical White Panther Party, and a cause célèbre after multiple marijuana arrests led to a draconian 10-year prison sentence in 1969. He served two and a half years before the Michigan Supreme Court ordered him released and eventually overturned his conviction. Pianist Harold McKinney, who turned 36 in 1964, was a mentor to Sinclair and the other young artists in the workshop. McKinney, who had come up with Kenny Burrell and cut his teeth at the World Stage, was a direct link to Detroit's modern jazz community and his encouragement, a benediction from a leading African American musician, carried weight. It legitimized the enterprise and reminded everyone of their connection to the city's jazz legacy.

In addition to Sunday jam sessions, the Artists Workshop produced formal concerts on the Wayne State campus with paid admission. There were mini-festivals that combined jazz, contemporary classical music, electronic music, rhythm and blues, and poetry. Sometimes concerts included guest performers like tenor saxophonist Archie Shepp or pianist Paul Bley. One Sunday in 1965, tenor saxophonist Charles Lloyd, in town with Cannonball Adderley's sextet, jammed at the house. Members started a newsletter and Sinclair eventually spearheaded the Detroit Artists Workshop Press, which published stapled periodicals and poetry volumes. The short-lived journal *CHANGE* (just two issues) was devoted to the jazz avant-garde. The first issue (Fall–Winter 1965) featured Leni Sinclair's cover photo of Shepp and John Sinclair's poem "Songs of Praise for John Coltrane."

The most important band that grew out of the Artists Workshop was the Detroit Contemporary 4, which initially included trumpeter Charles Moore, drummer Danny Spencer, guitarist Ron English, and bassist John Dana. Stanley Cowell and Ronnie Johnson eventually replaced English and Spencer. (The band was billed as the Detroit Contemporary 5 whenever saxophonist Larry Nozero joined for gigs.) The DC 4 is considered Detroit's first avant-garde jazz group. Its avatars were Miles Davis, John Coltrane, and left-leaning Blue Note albums by Jackie McLean, Grachan Moncur III, Andrew Hill, and Eric Dolphy. The band played originals like Moore's "Stan" (written in 7/8) and Cowell's "The Killers" (based on a 12-tone row); modal anthems like Davis' "So What" and Coltrane's "Impressions"; and expressionist pieces like Dolphy's "Gazzelloni" and Moncur's "The Coaster" and "Twins." There was also free-form playing, especially when Chicagoans such as saxophonists Joseph Jarman and Roscoe Mitchell and others associated with the AACM came to perform.

Frequent visitors, the exploratory Chicago musicians were impressed to find kindred souls probing unconventional ideas at the Artists Workshop. "I was amazed at the energy these people were putting out," Jarman told the *Ann Arbor Sun* in 1972. A proto-version of the Art Ensemble of Chicago appeared in Detroit in 1966 or '67 with Mitchell, trumpeter Lester Bowie, bassist Malachi Favors, and drummer Phillip Wilson. The audience that day included a student drummer, Don Moye, barely into his 20s, who had recently transferred to Wayne State from Central State University in Ohio. Moye would come to fame as a member of the Art Ensemble a few years later, but this was the first time he met his future colleagues. Moye spent only 20 months in Detroit but the time proved crucial to his development. He fell into the orbit of the Artists Workshop, and Moore became a particularly important mentor. Moye went to the trumpeter's home nearly every day to study music, listen to records, and play.

"I wasn't in Detroit long enough to develop a self-identity as a Detroit musician, but my time and experiences there changed my life and set me firmly on my life-long journey and odyssey as a professional musician," Moye said.[1]

Few recordings of workshop performances have circulated. A handful were included on CD in *The Work Box*, a limited-edition 2014 publication issued by the Museum of Contemporary Art Detroit collecting Artists Workshop memorabilia and reprints. A DC 4 version of "So What," taped at the first gathering on November 1, 1964, reveals young musicians feeling their way forward. By January 1965, the group sounds more confident on "All Blues," and Moore stands out for the aggressive smears and dark complexion of his Davis-inspired soloing. At a concert at Wayne State in November 1965, a nine-piece band explores an abstract idiom on "Adolescence," a freely improvised piece on a scenario conceived by Sinclair with Moore cast as the teenage protagonist. It's an angst-filled trumpet concerto, with chaotic ensemble explosions setting off Moore's existential musing.

Recorded in 1967, organist Lyman Woodard's abstract "Prayer for the Future" unfolds in meditative rubato. It showcases the obscure alto saxophonist Charles Miles, who plays with a bright sound without edge, almost classical in its fast vibrato. His discursive solo mixes vocalized yearning, false-fingered overtones, expressive sequences, and a sardonic quote of Kurt Weill's "Speak Low." Though the Detroit Artists Workshop ran out of steam in 1967, many of its musicians remained key figures in Detroit during the next decade and beyond. Miles, who died young, should have been among them.

Detroit Creative Musicians Association and Focus Novii

With the city still smoldering in early August 1967, a few members of the newly formed Detroit Creative Musicians Association (DCMA) decided to make a statement. "We cannot let such violence stop the music," guitarist James "Blood" Ulmer told drummer and composer Doug Hammond. Ulmer, Hammond, and bassist John Dana found a storefront on 12th Street not far from where the riot erupted and played several nights as a gesture of goodwill and healing for neighborhood residents. "People came and were glad to have the music," Hammond remembered. "It was what we could do as musicians."

Drummer and percussionist Doug Hammond in 2009 with a *sanza* (an African thumb piano). Photo by Jon Sokol / Courtesy Doug Hammond.

The DCMA was a loose federation that came together after the Detroit Artists Workshop folded. It provided a forum for musicians to explore new directions as composers and improvisers. Henry Hence, an African American factory worker who played tenor sax, came up with the idea and functioned as the organization's manager. Drummer James Brown, who made his primary living in R & B, was president. Hammond became vice president and coordinator of concerts and programs. Rosetta Hines, who would later become a prominent radio personality, was a secretary. Bruce Millan, founder of Detroit Repertory Theatre, allowed the musicians to use the company's theater on Woodrow Wilson on the near west side for concerts and taught them to print their own silkscreen posters. Many of Detroit's top musicians performed under the DCMA umbrella, among them Marcus Belgrave, Harold McKinney, and the Contemporary Jazz Quintet. After a while, the group moved its base to a nearby house, and there were occasional concerts at Cranbrook Art Museum in Bloomfield Hills and Wayne

State. At its peak in 1968–69, DCMA sponsored two performances a week by local bands and paid players modest fees from door receipts.

DCMA gave birth to one of the most significant Detroit bands of the era, Focus Novii, which nurtured two player-composers, Ulmer and Hammond, whose influence would carry far beyond Detroit. Focus Novii was an experimental quintet, synthesizing post-bop, avant-garde, and multimedia elements. In addition to Ulmer and Hammond, the group included trombonist Patrick Lanier, a regular in the Motown studios; saxophonist and flutist Bill Wiggins, who had worked with Aretha Franklin but was versed in extended classical techniques; and bassist John Dana, a studious and sensitive musician. The lack of recordings by Focus Novii, even bootleg tapes, leaves a mysterious haze around the band, and it remains all but unknown.[2]

Ulmer and Hammond, two transplants from the South, drove the group. Ulmer, born in South Carolina in 1940, settled in Detroit in 1967. He became a fixture on the blues and jazz scenes and worked occasionally at Motown. In Detroit he was still forming his rough-hewn, jagged guitar style. A decade later Ulmer connected the dots between funk and free jazz and collaborated with Ornette Coleman. Hammond, born and raised in Florida, was 22 when he relocated to Detroit in 1965 to hone his skills for an eventual move to New York. Hammond jumped into the Detroit Artists Workshop, played with jazz veterans like pianist Bu Bu Turner, worked the blues clubs along 12th Street, and backed acts auditioning for Motown. Hammond codified his original ideas about rhythm and form after leaving Detroit, and by the early '80s, his compositions would deeply influence the innovative alto saxophonist and composer Steve Coleman. "Detroit was my university," Hammond said. "The scene was still indescribable in terms of the wealth of musicians, the variety of styles—an intact jazz scene, blues scene, Motown, and rock. It was a place where you could do and hear it all and get the highest quality."

Focus Novii rehearsed nearly every day for five months before performing in public. The group played all original music in myriad idioms—meticulously notated compositions, open forms, swinging time, no time, odd meters, homespun counterpoint, collective improvisation, complex or simple harmony, idiomatic jazz performances, and large-scale collaborations with artists, dancers, and poets. One multimedia production was called *Tangential Diorama*. The stage included massive paintings by a local artist, and a sculpture-like bandstand that Hammond built from a design that came to Lanier in a dream. The pieces by Hammond and Lanier included spoken text and dancers. Group members composed classical pieces that they recorded and played on tape at intermission. "Focus Novii is the highest-level band I've ever been a part of," Hammond said.

Repertoire included Ulmer's "Raw Groove" (a swinger with simple harmony and open form); Hammond's "Before and After the Fact" (built on a repeating bass ostinato in 5/4); and Dana's intricate "Sneakin' and Peekin' (with Bartok-inspired symmetric properties). Experiments with rhythm and pulse were central. Some pieces were written with bars that had eleven and a half, four and a half, or two and a half beats. One composition by Ulmer had a steady pulse of two slow beats per bar, but on top of that were superimposed rhythms that shifted between 5 over 2, 6 over 2, 3 over 2, etc. "If you can lay things out in a particular space, it can feel like it's in 4/4 even if it isn't," Hammond said.

DCMA and Focus Novii came to an end in 1969. Hammond took a job touring with Smokey Robinson to make a living and moved to New York in 1971. Hammond played and recorded with Charles Mingus in 1973, and Dave Holland recorded several Hammond compositions in the '80s. Hammond still stayed connected to Detroit, returning in 1988–89, before heading to Linz, Austria, where he taught for two decades at the Bruckner Conservatory. Hammond recorded *We People* (Idibib) and *It's Born* (JPC) in Detroit in 1988 and 1996 with homegrown musicians, among them violinist Regina Carter, trumpeter Dwight Adams, and saxophonist-clarinetist Wendell Harrison. In addition, the Hammond-David Durrah LP *Reflections in the Sea of Nurnen* was issued on Detroit's Tribe label in 1975, though it was recorded in San Francisco.

Notes

1. Moye and other area musicians left Detroit for Europe in April 1968, touring for nearly a year with a band under the name Detroit Free Jazz. Other members were Arthur Fletcher Jr., alto sax, flute, congas; Bill Hagans, tenor and soprano saxes; Bob Sklar, piano; Ron Miller, bass; and Billy Banks, manager.

2. Hammond has tapes of Focus Novii, but there were no definitive plans to release them as of 2018.

Contemporary Jazz Quintet and Strata Corporation

The most celebrated jazz band in Detroit in the late 1960s and '70s was the Contemporary Jazz Quintet (CJQ)—Kenn Cox on piano, Charles Moore on trumpet, Leon Henderson on tenor sax, Ron Brooks on bass, and Danny Spencer on drums. The group explored the up-to-date modal harmony, shifting meters, and broken rhythms of the Miles Davis Quintet of the '60s that included Wayne Shorter, Herbie Hancock, Ron Carter, and Tony Williams. Most significantly, the CJQ absorbed in real time Davis records like *Nefertiti*, *The Sorcerer*, and *Miles in the Sky*. The influence of Davis' '60s quintet is ubiquitous today. But the CJQ was there at ground zero, creating a compelling book of original material rooted in compositions like Shorter's "Paraphernalia" and Williams' "Black Comedy." The band recorded two LPs for Blue Note in 1968–69 and a third in the early '70s for the homegrown Strata label.

"It was the first band to take in all the innovative time and tempo changes incorporated by Miles' rhythm section and compose music that incorporated these ideas," said trumpeter David Weiss, who has recorded several Moore compositions. "They also ran with the then-innovative use of cueing systems from Wayne Shorter's 'Paraphernalia' where the soloist would cue going into the next section by playing a particular phrase."

The roots of the CJQ date to spring 1966. Cox got a call from Brooks asking if he would replace Stanley Cowell (who was moving to New York) in the bassist's trio working six nights a week in Ann Arbor; Spencer was already on board. Cox leapt at the job and within a couple weeks, Moore and Henderson were coming by to sit in. The chemistry was so strong that they began rehearsing as a quintet, coalescing as a group in 1967 and incorporating formally around the start of 1968. "We were so excited about the music that during the riots we were breaking the curfew and dodging tanks and National Guard to get to our gigs," Cox said.

CJQ members were in their mid-20s to early 30s in 1968. Cox and Brooks

The Contemporary Jazz Quintet c. 1970 (*left to right*): pianist Kenn Cox, saxophonist Leon Henderson, bassist Ron Brooks, trumpeter Charles Moore, drummer Danny Spencer. Photo by Clyde Stringer.

were the most experienced, the only two to have previously recorded. Born in 1940, Cox, a Cass Tech graduate, had spent three years in New York and touring with vocalist Etta Jones—he's tasteful and supportive on her *Love Shout* (Prestige)—before returning home in 1964. He worked with local bands and backed up visiting stars like Wes Montgomery and Roy Haynes. Initially inspired by Horace Silver, Barry Harris, and Tommy Flanagan, Cox was assimilating Hancock's harmonic ideas by the mid-'60s. Brooks, born in Chicago in 1936, was the senior band member. A versatile bassist, he was comfortable in straight-ahead and more open settings. He attended the University of Michigan in Ann Arbor, where he worked with budding pianist Bob James and played on James' first LP in 1962; Brooks also worked with leading-edge alto saxophonist Eric Dolphy at the 1964 Once Festival of avant-garde music in Ann Arbor.

Both Moore and Spencer were among the founders of the Detroit Artists Workshop and part of the DC 4. Moore (1940–2014) was born in Alabama and migrated to Detroit in 1958 to study music, first at the Detroit Conservatory of Music, then Wayne State. His pensive moodiness on ballads and slashing attack on faster tunes were indebted to Miles Davis, but Moore brought his own blunt and intelligent personality to the music. Spencer, the only white musician in the CJQ, was born in 1942 in Michigan's Upper Peninsula but raised in Lansing and relocated to Detroit after high school to play jazz. His loose but driving beat, imagination, and interactive sparring distilled the advances of the '60s. Leon Henderson (1940–2016), like older brother Joe Henderson, grew up in Lima, Ohio. The younger Henderson moved to Detroit in 1965, after attending Kentucky State College. Curiously, his dominant influence wasn't his brother but rather Wayne Shorter.

The CJQ caught the ear of Detroit disc jockey Jack Springer, who alerted pianist Duke Pearson, who worked for Blue Note as a talent scout and producer. Pearson signed the band to a contract, a coup for young Midwesterners. Blue Note was past its peak—visionary cofounder Alfred Lion had recently sold the label and retired—but it still marshaled significant credibility in the marketplace. Blue Note billed the band as Kenny Cox and the Contemporary Jazz Quintet, because the label thought a front man was needed to sell an unknown group.

Recorded in December 1968, *Introducing Kenny Cox and the Contemporary Jazz Quintet* opens with Cox's blistering "Mystique," a provocative 28-bar ABA form (10-8-10) with weightless harmonies and a maniacally fast, swinging tempo. Cox's alluring "Trance Dance," which had already been recorded by the Jazz Crusaders, is the CJQ's least abstract piece—a minor blues with a contemporary dance beat. Moore's "Number Four," with its corkscrew theme, alternating 3/4 and 4/4 meters and cueing system, is the most challenging piece. The group interplay is electrifying, though there are also shaky moments when the players sound as if they're in over their heads. *Multidirection*, taped in November 1969, exhibits more cohesion. Moore's beguiling steeplechase "Snuck In" is a highlight with its urgent, staccato repetitions, dramatic suspensions, acidic dissonance, and shifting 6/4, 3/4, and 4/4 meters. Cox's gift for writing hummable melodies comes to the fore on the evocative "Spellbound."

Unfortunately, the relationship between the CJQ and Blue Note soured quickly, and the band never translated its brief fame and good reviews into touring outside the Midwest. A huge source of tension with Blue Note was that the label refused to fly the CJQ to the East Coast to record, relying instead on ill-suited Detroit studios and engineers with little sensitivity to jazz. The CJQ records lack the larger-than-life sonic presence and warmth of typical Blue Note LPs recorded by engineer Rudy Van Gelder. Cox said there was also friction because producers Duke Pearson and Francis Wolff never understood the band's aesthetic and rejected artistic ideas concerning performance lengths, segues, and sequencing. The CJQ tried unsuccessfully to have Blue Note halt release of *Multidirection*. Cox and Moore each wrote letters to critic Nat Hentoff—whom Blue Note had engaged to write liner notes—to lobby for his support.

"We feel that the recording media is one that has a responsibility to its consumers and contracted artists to produce recordings that capture the essence of a performer's musical character and his current music attitude i.e. current concept, direction and technique," Cox wrote to Hentoff on June 6, 1970.[1]

The CJQ and Blue Note went their separate ways. By the time the band recorded *Location* for Strata between 1970 and '72, its aesthetic had shifted toward more amorphous structures, coloristic textures, and collective improvisation. Adventurous early jazz-rock was in the air, and *Location* walks an acoustic-electric fault line in the general neighborhood of early Weather Report and Herbie Hancock's Mwandishi sextet. Electric piano and electric bass color the palette, and some pieces include a guitarist, second keyboard player, or second drummer. The music alternates between heated aggression and lush avant-gardism. There's a stylistic independence that makes this the CJQ's most personal statement.[2]

The CJQ called it quits in the mid-'70s, though there would be periodic reunions. Cox remained a stalwart pianist, bandleader, and mentor in Detroit. Moore left for Los Angeles, earning a doctorate in ethnomusicology, teaching at universities, and performing. Henderson's life took a tragic turn as he suffered from mental illness and stopped performing after the early '80s. Brooks, who earned advanced degrees in educational psychology and made his primary living as a mediator, remained on the local scene as a bassist and owned the beloved Bird of Paradise jazz club in Ann Arbor from 1985 to 2004. Spencer anchored numerous local bands and backed big names like Art Farmer and toured with Joe Henderson before relocating to San Francisco in the 1990s.

Strata Corporation

As the Contemporary Jazz Quintet's frustrations with Blue Note intensified, Kenn Cox and Charles Moore, both strong-willed, began plotting an organization that put musicians in control of their own artistic and financial destinies. Cox had been working clerical and administrative jobs at banks for the previous few years to make ends meet. In 1969 he took a position at the Inner City Business Improvement Forum, a nonprofit business development organization. Moore's history of community activism dated back to the Detroit Artists Workshop. The musicians envisioned a for-profit business, believing a corporate model was the best way to support their artistic goals. They issued stock to raise capital and formed a company with three divisions to produce concerts and recordings, publish music, and manage, book, and market artists. There were even plans to develop satellites and subsidiaries across the country. They called their venture the Strata Corporation after pedagogue Joseph Schillinger, who used "Strata" to refer to layers of compositional elements.

There had been musician-run record labels before in jazz, including Dee Gee Records in Detroit (1951–53). But the scope of Strata's vision, which stretched into all aspects of the music business, was audacious, even arrogant. It merged capitalist fundamentals, do-it-yourself grit, and utopian confidence in artists. The Strata Corporation was chartered on July 15, 1969. "Artisans as administrators may appear incongruous with the ultimate motive of the stockholder—profits," Cox and Moore wrote in the first stockholders' report in May 1970. "Yet we can assure you that there is expertise within our ranks and at our disposal which will guide your staff in matters of good business practices. This combined with the innovative talents, self-discipline and self-motivation which is typical of creative people, will bring unquestioned and unprecedented success to the company."

The report predicted $10,000 in earnings by end of 1970. This proved laughingly naive. Strata generated a surplus of a few hundred dollars in 1970 on concerts, while overall operating costs led to a loss of about $600.[3] Strata was perennially undercapitalized and struggled with cash flow during its seven-year lifespan. But if the company never fulfilled its grandest ambitions, its accomplishments were significant: It produced concerts for more than four years including national and local artists. It released several memorable LPs. It created the first courses in African American music at the Oberlin (Ohio) Conservatory. Strata made a difference in the lives of musicians and audiences in Detroit and inspired others to action—

including the East Coast musicians who created Strata-East Records and the Detroiters who created Tribe.

Strata's initial leadership team included Cox as chairman and president, Moore as vice chairman and executive vice president, and Harold Gardner as treasurer and vice president. Gardner, who handled the financial books, was a young accountant whom Cox worked with at the business forum. No one drew a salary. Strata authorized 5,000 shares of capital stock at $1 per share and initially offered 1,449 shares to investors. But strong community buzz and pledges did not translate into hard cash. By the start of 1971 the company had just $1,429 in cash on hand. Strata leaders had already begun seeking a government-backed Small Business Administration loan for $5,000. The process dragged on for years and ultimately proved futile.

Strata started producing concerts by local bands at the Detroit Institute of Arts and representing clients such as saxophonist Larry Nozero, organist Lyman Woodard, and the CJQ. In July 1970, the organization put down roots at 2554 Michigan Avenue in the Corktown neighborhood, west of 17th Street. The Strata Concert Gallery, a 5,000-square-foot second-floor space, became the epicenter of the scene for Detroit's most progressive audiences and musicians. There were multi-night engagements by the Herbie Hancock Sextet, Chick Corea Trio, Joe Henderson Sextet, Sam Rivers Trio, and Archie Shepp. In July 1972, the gallery moved to 46 Selden, a former photography studio on a gritty block in the shadow of then-abandoned Orchestra Hall, where it remained open until 1974. Among the performers were Hancock, Ornette Coleman, Weather Report, Keith Jarrett, Charles Mingus, Elvin Jones, and McCoy Tyner. Portions of some performances were broadcast live on WDET-FM.[4] "Most of these bands had no other place to perform in Detroit at the time," said guitarist Ron English. "A club like Baker's wouldn't take a chance on somebody like Ornette, Mingus or Sam Rivers."

The concert gallery also provided work to Detroiters, including the CJQ, Tribe, Nozero, English, Woodard, and others. Sometimes a guest such as drummer-composer Joe Chambers would team with local players. To help underwrite performances at the gallery, Strata started a nonprofit subsidiary, Allied Artists Association of America, headed by English, to target grants from the state arts council.

On another front, Strata was contracted by the Oberlin Conservatory to create a curriculum for what was called Afro-American music. There had been growing pressure from students to add classes in jazz, and Strata was on the school's radar because its musicians had appeared on campus. Journalist, scholar, and activist Herb Boyd, who taught black history at Wayne State, worked with Cox and Moore to develop courses in jazz history, aesthetics, improvisation, theory, and composition. For two years from 1971 to 1973, Boyd taught history and Moore taught music at Oberlin; they drove to Ohio on Thursdays and returned Fridays. They were paid $5,100 each for the first year—$32,000 in 2018 dollars.[5]

Musicians elsewhere took note of Strata. Trumpeter Charles Tolliver and pianist Stanley Cowell had already self-produced a big-band recording in New York but had no luck shopping it to established labels. Inspired by Strata, they discussed a partnership with Cox and Moore. In the end, the New Yorkers decided to go it alone. They were wary of the burden of selling stock in a Strata-like corporate structure, but they retained the name Strata-East to honor shared values.[6] "The connection to Strata was separate from what Stanley and I created with Strata-East but shared one important thing in common—self-determination," Tolliver said.

Strata-East focused narrowly on recordings, adopting a model in which artists financed production and manufacture of their own records and retained ownership of the master tapes. The company then sold the records via a growing distribution network. Most of the revenue flowed back to the artists. Strata-East was a mechanism to get records into the marketplace, and from 1971 to 1982 the label issued roughly 50 LPs, many by nationally known artists. In contrast, prohibitive up-front costs prevented Strata from releasing its first LP, the CJQ's *Location*, until 1973. Ultimately, only five records were issued before Strata ceased operations, though five more were in the pipeline. The entire catalog, including the five previously unreleased LPs, has been reissued in recent years on the 180 Proof label.

Strata's catalog spans hard bop, post-bop, funk, fusion, and songful crossover. Other than *Location*, the most rewarding of the five original LPs is *Live 'n Well*, released in 1974 under drummer Bert Myrick's name but featuring what was the George Bohanon–Ronnie Fields Quintet taped live at the University of Michigan student union in Ann Arbor in 1965. Its aggressive brand of hard bop made it the best straight-ahead group in the city in the mid-'60s. The underrated Bohanon plays fleet and lucid solos. Born in Detroit in 1937, he had previously toured with Chico Hamilton and appeared on two LPs for Motown's short-lived subsidiary Workshop Jazz—his own *Boss: Bossa Nova* (1962) and Detroit-born drummer Roy Brooks' *Beat* (1963).[7] Bohanon moved to Los Angeles in 1968. Fields, a now-forgotten tenor saxophonist, plays with a careening, Coltrane-like tone on

Alive 'n Well. The frisky rhythm section includes Cox, bassist Will Austin, and Myrick, and some of the original material recalls Horace Silver's more advanced writing.

Recorded in 1970 and released in 1974, *Inside Ourselves* by Sphere—a quintet with Larry Nozero, John Dana, Ed Nuccilli, Keith Vreeland, and Jim Peluso—offers a view of the evolving mainstream. Chicago-based saxophonist Maulawi Nururdin's soul-jazz date *Maulawi* is the only Strata record by a non-Detroiter. The label's final official release, Lyman Woodard's *The Saturday Night Special*, was issued in 1975. A melting pot of jazz, funk, and Latin idioms, the record's compositional flair and dollops of studio sweetening helped make it the best-selling Strata LP. The higher production values were a result of Strata borrowing a mobile recording studio at the end of 1973—a small truck with 16-track capability—and punching a hole in the back wall of the concert gallery to accommodate it.

Of the previously unreleased recordings, Ron English's *Fish Feet* and Sam Sanders' *Mirror Mirror* mine funk and fusion. Cox's *Clap Clap! The Joyful Noise* aimed for airplay with breezy melodies and island rhythms. Nozero's *Time* places his tenor and soprano sax and flute in the company of strings, rhythm section, and Swingle Singers–inspired voices arranged by pianist Dennis Tini. Nozero, who died in 2005 at age 61, was one of Detroit's off-the-radar treasures, though untold millions have heard him play the soprano sax intro on Marvin Gaye's "What's Goin' On." (For a discussion of the CJQ's *Black Hole*, see Note 2 on page 196.)

By the mid-'70s, Strata was desperate for cash and unable to provide distributors with product. Commercial banks declined to provide credit. While waiting for final dispensation about a Small Business Administration loan, Strata tried to finagle a licensing-distribution deal with a major label or sell the catalog outright. Arista, A&M, and ABC Records all passed. When the SBA denied financing, Strata shut its doors in 1976. "The scale of what we tried to do was too big, and it cost us," Cox said. "But we made great music."

Recommended Recordings

Contemporary Jazz Quintet, *Introducing Kenny Cox and the Contemporary Jazz Quintet* (*Multidirecton* included as bonus tracks on CD) (Blue Note)
Contemporary Jazz Quintet, *Location* (Strata; 180 Proof/BBE)
Bert Myrick, *Alive 'n Well* (Strata; 180 Proof/BBE)
Lyman Woodard, *Saturday Night Special* (Strata; 180 Proof/BBE)

Notes

1. Correspondence included in John Sinclair Collection at Charles H. Wright Museum of African American History in Detroit.

2. The CJQ's final recording, *The Black Hole*, was slated for release in 1975 on Strata but not issued until 2020 on the 180 Proof label. Recorded live at the 1973 Ann Arbor Blues & Jazz Festival, the double LP features an expanded, 10-piece ensemble with a second drummer, conguero, two additional keyboard players, and guitarist. In the vein of early '70s electric Miles Davis, the music unfolds in a suite-like, improvised sprawl with no written material and bass-heavy grooves alternating with spacy episodes; trumpeter Charles Moore is the most compelling soloist. In addition, one song by the CJQ was included on an Atlantic Records compilation from the 1972 Ann Arbor Blues & Jazz Festival.

3. Strata financial figures and operational details found in documents in Sinclair Collection at Wright Museum.

4. In 2018, BBE Music and 180 Proof Records released *Mingus: Jazz in Detroit/Strata Concert Gallery/46 Selden*, recorded February 13, 1973, and sourced by WDET. No other Strata broadcast tapes have surfaced, except for a bootleg of the Herbie Hancock Sextet from 1973.

5. Herb Boyd column in *Amsterdam News*, Jan. 28, 2016, provided background. A letter to Strata from Oberlin's dean Emil Denenberg, June 17, 1972, confirms salary figures for 1971–72 (Wright Museum).

6. Cowell was an original member of Strata's board of directors and first executive director of the publishing division.

7. Bohanon's *Bold Bohanon* was recorded October 30, 1962, for Workshop Jazz and given a cover and a catalog number (214) but never issued. Universal Music Group released it as a digital download in 2014 as *Motown Unreleased 1962: Jazz, Vol. 1*.

Tribe

Wendell Harrison's life reached a turning point in 1970. At age 28, the Detroit-born tenor saxophonist and clarinetist had completed a two-and-a-half-year stay in Santa Monica, California, at Synanon, a drug rehabilitation and residential center.[1] Harrison, who had come of age under the tutelage of pianist Barry Harris, moved to New York in 1960 and worked steadily in jazz, blues, and R & B circles. He also spent time in the orbit of Sun Ra, the iconoclastic pianist and Afrofuturist. But while touring with Hank Crawford in 1963, the grind of the road and proximity to junkies in the band led to addiction to heroin.

"I'm thinking I'm young and strong and can't be defeated," Harrison said. "At first it was once a week, then every other day, then every day. When I got back to New York, I had a habit."

Harrison spent his time at Synanon reading and learning about business and fundraising. He drove supply trucks and jammed with fellow inmates, including star alto saxophonist Art Pepper, who noted in his autobiography that Harrison "really played well." Harrison landed in Detroit in 1970 for what he thought would be a pit stop, but fearful of slipping back down the rabbit hole of addiction in New York, he decided to stay put. He got a job teaching at Metro Arts, an inner-city youth organization, where he connected with trombonist Phil Ranelin, an Indianapolis native who moved to Detroit in 1968. Ranelin found studio work at Motown, toured with Stevie Wonder and Gladys Knight, and played with small jazz groups, big bands, and Latin groups. Ranelin was impressed by Detroit's musical richness and black community pride. "There was not a lot of black awareness in Indianapolis, but there was in Detroit," Ranelin said. "There were still blocks and blocks of black businesses, even though a lot had been destroyed in 1967. I felt a unity there."

Metro Arts, which received federal Model Cities funding, was an important income source for musicians who taught there in the early '70s, including Harrison, Ranelin, pianist Harold McKinney, and trumpeter Marcus Belgrave. Harrison and Ranelin talked about shared goals and

Key members of the Tribe collective in 1975, including cofounders Wendell Harrison, saxophone, and Phil Ranelin, trombone, with trumpeter Marcus Belgrave (tambourine) and an unidentified bassist. Photo by Leni Sinclair.

documenting their original music. They admired Strata, but the corporate model wasn't for them, and other influences hovered: Black Power, the counterculture and antiwar Left, urban poverty, and the shock waves from 1967. McKinney (1928–2001) was again a consigliere, broadening their vision the way he previously mentored founders of the Detroit Artists Workshop.

This foment gave birth to Tribe. At first it was a band with core members Harrison, Ranelin, McKinney, and Belgrave. The name was chosen for its allusions to mother Africa and collectivism. Harrison's then wife, Patricia, a graphic designer, created a provocative logo—an elongated head with two opposing faces bisected by a spear and T-R-I-B-E spelled top to bottom. The group's first major concert was on November 26, 1971, at the Detroit Institute of Arts. The program, "An Evening with the Devil," included music by Harrison and Ranelin that reflected themes of social justice and cultural identity. Eight weeks later in January 1972, Ranelin and Harrison registered Tribe as a new business at city hall.

Around the same time, the group began recording, playing concerts, and making radio and TV appearances; Harrison and Ranelin created a joint publishing company. (Later they formed individual publishing companies too.) Tribe was back at the DIA in August with an evening-length play with music, *Wait Broke the Wagon Down*, a collaboration with the Black Messengers, a black arts theater company. Harrison's pieces were titled "Farewell to the Welfare" and "Tons and Tons of Bull Shit" (*sic*). The fall saw the release of the inaugural Tribe LP, *Message from the Tribe*, and the first issue of *Tribe* magazine.[2]

Tribe operated out of the Harrisons' house in the North End, where the couple and Ranelin shared organizational and administrative duties. Ranelin's liner notes for his LP *The Time Is Now!* capture the mood: "The time is now for oppression, racism, greed, hate and poverty to end! The time is now for revolution! This record itself is part of the revolution, and the whole purpose behind this self-determination venture is survival."

Tribe magazine was a phenomenon without precedent for a musicians' cooperative. As Tribe leaders solicited program ads from black businesses, sales were so strong that the organization parlayed interest into a glossy magazine to address political, cultural, and community issues from a black perspective. Harrison was editor and publisher on the masthead, though journalist Herb Boyd was credited as guest editor in the first issue and remained active as the enterprise grew to encompass a pool of freelance writers, graphic designers, copyeditors, and sales staff. Circulating only in metro Detroit, Tribe was published quarterly at first, then bimonthly. Harrison's photo adorns the cover of the first issue (November 1972), and among the articles is an essay arguing in favor of a state referendum to legalize abortion in Michigan. Later issues feature hefty pieces on school busing in Detroit and racist tactics of the Detroit Police Department (under the provocative headline "Nigger Beaters"). There are stories about Jesse Jackson and Detroit's first black mayor, Coleman Young, as well as features about local musicians and interviews with Donald Byrd and Redd Foxx.

Tribe's politics cut a guerrilla profile compared to Strata's quasi-corporate strivings. Yet, *Tribe* magazine became the most successful business created by either organization. Profits helped subsidize recording, printing, and administrative costs. Harrison kept the magazine going until 1977. "My interest was in music, not publishing," Harrison said. "This thing popped up, and I took it as far as I could."

Tribe artists financed their own recordings, including production and

The debut issue of *Tribe* magazine in November 1972 featured saxophonist Wendell Harrison on the cover. Photo courtesy Wendell Harrison.

manufacturing, and retained ownership of master tapes. The label handled distribution. Tribe released eight LPs between 1972 and 1976 and forged dozens of distribution deals to sell records across America and overseas. Getting paid, however, was never guaranteed, and Tribe was often stiffed by distributors.

While Strata LPs vary enormously in style, Tribe records project a consistent aesthetic borne of a repertory company. Some combination of Harrison, Ranelin, McKinney, and Belgrave appear on all but two albums. The flavor shifts depending upon the leader, compositions, and rhythm section. Overall, the Tribe sound affirms a fundamental grittiness, a consciousness-raising vibe, and idiosyncratic mélange of modal post-bop, populist hooks, and streaks of free-jazz abstraction. It is local music, forged in isolation from industry centers New York and Los Angeles, but in touch with the au courant spiritualism and Afrocentrism heard in Pharoah Sanders and Alice Coltrane. The records offering the purest expression of Tribe's house style are Harrison's *An Evening with the Devil* (c. 1972–73) and Ranelin's *The Time Is Now!* (1973–74). Harrison's LP includes Ranelin, Belgrave on flugelhorn, Charles Moore on trumpet, Charles Eubanks on electric piano, Will Austin on bass, and Ike Daney on drums. Everyone also plays "little" instruments and percussion, and poets from the Black Messengers appear. Harrison's title suite opens with "Mary Had an Abortion." Austin's agitated, bowed bass and rumbling percussion set the scene. A poet enters: "*Mary had a little lamb, her fleece was black as coal / No matter how hard they tried / They could never reach their goal.*" Roiling instrumental passages of collective improvisation slide into a Latin vamp and the inquisitive melody of "Where Am I." The finale, "Angry Young Man," sways in waltz time. Harrison's brusque tenor barks low and screams high.

A similar, feral intensity pervades Ranelin's *The Time Is Now!* On the extended title track, bassist John Dana and electric pianist Keith Vreeland play fast, jagged patterns that loop and interlock while two drummers, George Davidson and Billy Turner, create a vigorous, polyrhythmic boil. The horn melody floats loosely, breaking free into expressionist gestures. Ranelin solos passionately, mixing fluid passages, punchy jabs, and whooping calls. Ranelin's *Vibes from the Tribe* (1975) folds fusion and the leader's wobbly vocals into the mix.

Belgrave's *Gemini II* and McKinney's *Voices and Rhythms of the Creative Profile* (both recorded in 1974) are adventurous if inconsistent records. On the former, the trumpeter's spirited playing has aged better than the spacey electronics. McKinney's eclectic LP sometimes sounds like it's going in too many directions at once—ritualistic chanting, choral singing, rock, fusion, hard bop, funk—but the leader plays electric piano and moog with two-handed, rococo flair. The last Tribe release, *Mixed Bag's First Album*, a fusion record issued in 1976, featured, among others, Larry Nozero and keyboardist Eddie Russ (under the pseudonym Gaff Dunsun).

Tribe disbanded in 1977 after Ranelin decamped for Los Angeles. Harrison created the nonprofit Rebirth in 1978 as an umbrella for his performing, recording, and teaching, and four decades later, it's still going. At 75, Harrison was named the 2018 Kresge Eminent Artist, a $50,000 lifetime achievement award from the Kresge Foundation in metro Detroit. Tribe became a cult brand as numerous licensing deals kept CD reissues circulating in Japan, Europe, England, and America—and made far more money for the artists than the original LPs ever did. Tribe principals reunited occasionally, including at the 2008 JVC Jazz Festival in New York, and Detroit techno producer Carl Craig championed Tribe's legacy with concerts and recordings.

Recommended Recordings

Tribe, *A Message from the Tribe* (Tribe/Scorpio)
Wendell Harrison, *An Evening with the Devil* (Tribe/Hefty)
Phil Ranelin, *The Time is Now!* (Tribe/P-Vine)

Notes

1. Founded as a respected drug rehabilitation center and utopian community, Synanon became infamous in the late 1970s after devolving into a criminal and violent cult.

2. Three versions of *Message from the Tribe* were released. The first included Harrison's suite "An Evening with the Devil" and Ranelin's "What Now? (Freedom Suite)" and the cover was a photo of the ocean. Tribe issued a second version with a black-and-white cover drawing of the Earth, a tweaked title (*A Message from the Tribe*), three different Harrison compositions in place of his suite, and additional performances of two of Ranelin's compositions outfitted with lyrics and sung by Jeamel Lee. A third version was later issued with a colorful cover painting of Harrison, Ranelin, and Lee.

Coda

The end of Strata and Tribe brought a golden age of self-determination in Detroit jazz to a close, but the impulse stayed embedded in the scene. Beyond Harrison's Rebirth, other manifestations include the nonprofit Detroit Jazz Center run by John Sinclair (1979–81), Detroit Jazz Composers LTD in the '70s, Belgrave's Jazz Development Workshop, and saxophonist Donald Walden's New World Stage in the '80s. One of the most enduring organizations has been the Creative Arts Collective (CAC), founded in 1978 by A. Spencer Barefield and still active 40 years later. An exploratory guitarist and composer, Barefield has worked and recorded extensively with Roscoe Mitchell and produced an exceptional series of concerts at the Detroit Institute of Arts from 1979 to 1992 in which cutting-edge national artists like Mitchell and Muhal Richard Abrams mixed it up with Detroit musicians.

Detroit-born saxophonist and poet Faruq Z. Bey (1942–2012) was not specifically associated with any organization, but Griot Galaxy, the creative ensemble he led for more than 15 years starting in 1972, grew out of the musical and cultural radicalism of the 1960s and '70s and came to embody the city's collectivist legacy. Bey (born Jesse Davis) was a regular at Focus Novii performances in the late '60s, and he and several Griot Galaxy members were introduced on Phil Ranelin's *Vibes from the Tribe*. The most vital edition of Griot Galaxy emerged around 1980 with Bey joined by fellow saxophonists Tony Holland and David McMurray and the bass-and-drum team of Jaribu Shahid and Tani Tabbal.

Griot Galaxy was Detroit's leading avant-garde ensemble in the late '70s and '80s. Bey's personal charisma, Afrofuturist ideas, and a philosophy of music-as-language that was both studied and homespun all suggest parallels to Sun Ra. The Detroiters also reflected the influence of the Art Ensemble of Chicago, donning face paint and infusing performances with ritual. But Griot Galaxy was no copy. Bey's marriage of composition and improvisation was his own, and the woolly ensemble moved easily between collective, unstructured improvisation, odd metered romps, and emergent grooves that grounded abstract flights with the earthy spirit of Detroit.

Live at the DIA (Entropy) from 1983 captures the band's aesthetic. A ritualistic gong opens "The Z Series," giving way to a fragmented theme that saxophones, flute, and bowed bass paint against a blank canvas of air. Textural group improvisation builds toward unison, stop-and-go written material until the 9:30 mark, when a walking bass line and swinging drum announce a good-time beat and welcome Bey's garrulous tenor saxophone solo. "After Death" opens with a repeating bass vamp in a slow six-beat pattern, while Tabbal's drums superimpose a faster meter on top. A unison saxophone riff adds another layer of rhythm in between and a lone soprano incants a melody. Of the saxophonists, David McMurray, who has worked with everyone from Geri Allen to Kid Rock, brings a muscular fluidity to the table that contrasts with the more primal excursions of Bey and Holland. The insoluble partnership of Shahid and Tabbal was the group's spine. Later, they recorded with Geri Allen, became the battery of James Carter's first working band, and have worked on and off with Roscoe Mitchell for more than 35 years.

From the vantage point of the early 21st century, Strata and Tribe appear prescient. The traditional recording industry has mostly collapsed in the wake of digital technology, downloads, and streaming. Yet the same technology has unleashed an ocean of self-released recordings and musician-founded labels. Dave Douglas' Greenleaf Music and John Bishop's Origin Records, for example, have found ways to make it work. A. Spencer Barefield considers Tribe and Strata as "prototypes" and part of what musicians across the country always admired about Detroit. "The idea at the time was you needed to go to New York to get discovered," Barefield said. "But it was Detroit musicians who said, 'Screw New York, we'll do it without them.'"

Recommended Recordings

Griot Galaxy, *Live at the DIA* (Entropy)
A. Spencer Barefield, *Xenogenesis 2000* (CAC)

PART FIVE
Marcus Belgrave and His Children

Marcus Belgrave at the Carr Center, Detroit, in October 2009. Photo by Patricia Beck / Detroit Free Press.

Marcus Belgrave

THE NURTURER

In a metro Detroit recording studio in July 2012, Marcus Belgrave, flugelhorn in hand, eyed his quintet and said, "I want you to know that you're all composers now." He was offering a shrewd challenge, nudging his charges to a higher plane of invention by reminding them that jazz improvisation is instant composition.

The quintet launched into a sinuous piece with a Latin beat called "Lottie the Body's Mood," written by Detroit drummer Lawrence Williams and named for a legendary exotic dancer in the city. At 76, Belgrave navigated the tricky intervals with a firm tone and confidence that belied his lung problems. He sculpted an improvisation full of surprise, songful expression, and probing rhythms. Pianist Mike Jellick, bassist Marion Hayden, and drummer Gayelynn McKinney played with more authority than they had before Belgrave made his speech. Belgrave smiled after the take. "Perfect," he said. On the other side of the glass in the control room, Grammy Award–winning producer Don Was, his long hair topped by a custom cowboy hat, smiled through a scraggly beard. "Beautiful," he said.

Belgrave was recording a track for *Detroit Jazz City*, issued in 2015 and conceived as a valentine to the city's jazz legacy by Was, president of Blue Note and a Detroit native. The album featured national stars with local roots, leading lights on the contemporary Detroit scene, and classics from the Blue Note catalog by Detroit musicians. The most significant new track was by Belgrave, because it offered a rare moment in the national spotlight for the most important and influential jazz musician in Detroit during the last 45 years.

Belgrave, who died of heart failure at age 78 in 2015, was the reigning patriarch of Detroit jazz. It's impossible to overstate the impact he had on musical culture in the city as a performer, teacher, and standard bearer. Like an African griot, he embodied the soul, conscience, and mythology of Detroit jazz history, handing down the values of blues and swing forged through a lifetime in the trenches and associations with Ray Charles, Max Roach, Charles Mingus, Wynton Marsalis, and others. Even as Detroit declined as an urban metropolis in the 1970s and '80s, Belgrave remained a direct link to the jazz aristocracy and a potent symbol of Detroit's ongoing vitality as a jazz incubator.

To put it another way, one answer to the question of how Detroit sustained its jazz culture during the late 20th and early 21st centuries is this: Marcus Belgrave.

He was certainly not the only important mentor to young jazz musicians during these years. Pianists Kenn Cox, Harold McKinney and Matt Michaels; tenor saxophonist Donald Walden; pianist and saxophonist Teddy Harris Jr.; drummer J. C. Heard, baritone saxophonist Marvin (Doc) Holladay; and public school teachers Donald Washington, Bill Wiggins, Ernie Rodgers, and Jack Pierson all trained multiple generations of students. But Belgrave cast the largest shadow. With many public schools in Detroit still boasting quality music programs into the early 2000s, the city's powerful marriage of formal and informal musical education that proved so fruitful in the 1940s and '50s remained in effect. Except Belgrave was now cast in the Barry Harris role.

Belgrave's best-known protégés—his de facto children—have left a substantial mark. Pianist Geri Allen was a defining voice of her generation, reconciling progressive, avant-garde, and mainstream traditions. Alto saxophonist Kenny Garrett and bassist Robert Hurst were charter members of the "young lions" generation of jazz traditionalists in the '80s, but their careers have since led in many directions and both have left a trail of disciples. Violinist Regina Carter, bassist Rodney Whitaker, and drummers Gerald Cleaver, Ali Jackson, and Karriem Riggins all developed distinct identities in idioms ranging from the swinging mainstream to free jazz and hip-hop. Belgrave's students inherited from him the Detroit DNA—a core understanding of the tradition (especially bebop), high standards of craft and musical intelligence, versatility, and a passionate and personalized approach to a shared heritage. Even Detroiters who did not come up directly under Belgrave's wing—tenor saxophonists James Carter and JD Allen, for example—were inspired by him and absorbed his values.

Belgrave created the nonprofit Jazz Development Workshop on a shoestring in the early '70s as an umbrella for his teaching, and there were sometimes formal posts with Oakland University, the Detroit Symphony Orchestra, and the Oberlin Conservatory in Ohio. But Belgrave also hired advanced students for gigs, placing them within the crucible of the bandstand, where true jazz education takes place. "With Marcus there was a pipeline from high school right into a safety zone in the scene," Geri Allen said in 2012. "We saw the passion and professionalism up close. What Marcus has done for Detroit and what he's done for all of us—he truly is a national treasure. How much we love him can't be expressed in words."

Belgrave, to borrow the title of an Allen recording, was *The Nurturer*. Protégés who became stars are by no means the whole story. Many former students became pillars in Detroit as players and teachers. Countless kids never became professional musicians, but Belgrave kept them on the straight and narrow. And it's no coincidence that Allen, Whitaker, and Hurst all became college professors. "If you factor in those of us who also became mentors because of his example, Marcus changed the lives of thousands of students," said Whitaker, who directs the jazz program at Michigan State University.

Not long after the recording session for Blue Note, Belgrave talked about his life in the Ann Arbor home he shared with his third wife, singer Joan Belgrave. An elfin 5-feet-4, he had the face of a cherub, a bebopper's beard more salt than pepper, and a smile that could light up the dark side of the moon. His eyes were locked in a permanent twinkle, and he spoke in a cool sandpaper rasp the ladies loved. "We'll be on the airplane and a stewardess will walk by and hear him say something, and she'll take a step back," Joan said. "I'll look at her and say, 'I know!'"

Joan was 21 years younger than her husband, and their 2007 marriage stabilized his life. She helped manage his business affairs and monitored his health. They wintered in Los Angeles or Barbados (the home country of Belgrave's father), because warm climates were easier on his lungs. Belgrave smoked cigarettes for decades and used oxygen 24 hours a day during his final years to deal with chronic pulmonary disease—though you wouldn't have known it to hear the strength with which he played until the end. Pneumonia and related issues stalked Belgrave like a mugger. It was not uncommon for him to land in the hospital for a few days or a week. The trumpet literally kept him alive. He practiced religiously, two hours a day including an hour of long tones. Doctors told him the calisthenics kept his lungs functioning. Even in the hospital he worked out with a muted pocket trumpet. "I always think of Dizzy Gillespie saying, 'If you skip a day, you notice. If you skip two, everybody notices,'" Belgrave said.

His work ethic offered lessons for a lifetime. Wynton Marsalis recalled that Belgrave, then in his '50s, once stayed up all night to transcribe Clark Terry's wily flugelhorn solo on the Ellington-Strayhorn waltz "Lady Mac" so he could better understand the piece before rehearsing it with the Jazz at Lincoln Center Orchestra.

"Marcus Belgrave is the epitome of soul and taste," Marsalis said in 2009. "His sound is just so evocative, and he's a master of swing and blues. When he walks into a room, he brings a good time with him."

Belgrave's decision to remain anchored in Detroit prevented his national profile from rising higher, but his cult status grew once his protégés began championing his name in interviews and liner notes. Work with Marsalis, a handful of New York gigs, and some sideman appearances on CDs bumped up his visibility in the 1980s and '90s, but his best recordings as a leader were self-produced with limited circulation. The jazz life is never easy, and Belgrave scuffled at times. A post at Oberlin (2001–2010) brought some financial security, and a $50,000 Eminent Artist award from the Kresge Foundation in 2009 raised local awareness beyond the jazz community. "I feel famous, because I've been able to survive playing music in Detroit," Belgrave said. "Major musicians would say, 'What is Marcus doing in Detroit?' But I had to find a place where I belonged, and where I could have an impact. Being around all this young talent gave me a sense of community and a purpose. I became a catalyst."

Marcus Batista Belgrave was born into a family of 12 children on June 12, 1936, in Chester, Pennsylvania, a small manufacturing town near Philadelphia and Wilmington, Delaware. He started blowing a bugle at four and a trumpet at six, taught by his father, who made his living in a steel mill but also played baritone horn. Belgrave's cousin was baritone saxophonist Cecil Payne, who played with Dizzy Gillespie's big band. One of Belgrave's early musical memories was listening to Gillespie's saxophone section rehearse in Payne's home in Brooklyn. Payne soon taught him to play Charlie Parker's "Chasin' the Bird."

At 12, Belgrave began studying with a local teacher and performing with a small concert band in Wilmington that included Clifford Brown. Six years older than Belgrave, Brown was on his way to becoming one of the most influential trumpeters in jazz. Belgrave watched Brown's every move, noting the precision of his execution and how he wrote down ideas at the piano. Brown put in a mute once during a performance and began to improvise around the melody of "Some of These Days." Belgrave was so moved by the beauty that he choked up and missed his entrance.

Brown took a shine to his young colleague and helped teach him to improvise by writing out a solo for him on the chords to "How High the

Moon." One day Belgrave asked Brown why he was playing marches and overtures in a community band. "He told me he liked to play all kinds of music," Belgrave said. "That opened my eyes to how valuable all music was. I've never forgotten that."

Belgrave joined the Air Force after high school to escape the mills. He played in a service band stationed in Wichita Falls, Texas, where he met Ray Charles one night at a concert and sat in with the band. By early 1958, Belgrave was back in Chester, married with an infant daughter. Charles came to the area for a two-week gig and on the final night offered Belgrave, 21, a job as second trumpet. Charles was in the throes of inventing soul music, grafting gospel influences onto rhythm and blues, but jazz—Count Basie, Nat Cole, bebop—was embedded in Charles' aesthetic. It was a hot band: a septet with two trumpets and two saxophones that grew to an octet with the addition of a third saxophone in 1959. The booting saxophonists David "Fathead" Newman and Hank Crawford were in the mix, and the tight arrangements were soulful, sassy, and swinging.

"I had to learn patience," Belgrave said. "I wanted to play bebop, but I had to learn to play the blues. I played too many notes. Ray would play such slow ballads that I'd be through eight bars before he got through one. But eventually he let me play obbligatos behind him on a ballad."

The road was brutal. Six-hundred-mile days. Sleepless nights. The segregated South. Twenty-five bucks per gig minus expenses. But the steady work, camaraderie, and Charles' genius were compensatory rewards. Charles was a taskmaster. His sharp ears caught every mistake, and his straw bosses were his eyes. Belgrave was once fined $25 because his black shoes weren't the patent leather pair required. But Belgrave managed to avoid the scourge of hard drugs, which was not always easy on a band in which several musicians were heroin addicts, including Charles. "I was the youngest guy in the band, and I was scared of that stuff," said Belgrave.

Belgrave made his first recordings with Charles on two classic Atlantic LPs, *Ray Charles at Newport* (1958) and *The Genius of Ray Charles* (1959). His brassy sound and coiling lines seize the moment on Max Roach's "Blues Waltz," which Belgrave brought into the book, and Quincy Jones' rambunctious big-band chart on "Alexander's Ragtime Band." Belgrave's most extensive soloing of the period is on Newman's *Fathead* (Atlantic) in 1958. The trumpeter's flowing phrases are rooted in Clifford Brown, but there's more grease in Belgrave's tone and a bubbling articulation that has a rougher edge than Brown's polished perfection. "Willow Weep for Me," a walking ballad, offers 16 eventful bars of trumpet preaching with shifting melodic and rhythmic accents, amen stutters, and detached articulation that falls behind the beat in the manner of Kenny Dorham.

Belgrave worked with Charles from 1958 to 1963, except for 18 months in 1960–61, when he gave New York a go. He found the city cold and cliquish and didn't work much. He said things might have gone differently had he not turned down high-profile gigs with Duke Ellington and Horace Silver during this era, but when the offers came, Belgrave didn't want to return to the road so soon after unpacking his suitcases. Still, Belgrave toured briefly with Max Roach as a sub for an ailing Booker Little and recorded with Mingus on *Pre-Bird* (Mercury).

Belgrave would later make a cameo at the December 1974 sessions that produced the Mingus LPs *Changes One* and *Changes Two* (Atlantic). "If I had Marcus Belgrave, I'd have the greatest band going," Mingus told *Downbeat* magazine in fall 1974. In the interview, published in February 1975, Mingus lamented that he couldn't pay Belgrave enough to pry him out of Detroit. A Mingus-Belgrave partnership could have been special. Mingus' affection for Belgrave notwithstanding, the backstory opens a window on the bassist's pugnacious personality and the difficulty of parachuting into his sui generis sound world. Trumpeter Jack Walrath joined the band shortly before the *Changes* recording sessions, and Mingus often bullied new band members. He told Walrath that Belgrave would play four nights at New York's Five Spot and then do the recording. But after the first set on the first night, Mingus, disappointed in Belgrave's stamina, called Walrath to play the rest of the gig. "Marcus has no chops," Mingus told Walrath.

"Of course, Marcus had chops," Walrath explained in 2017. "But it isn't easy for a trumpet player to jump into Mingus' stuff. On that gig, you don't reach that level beyond all limits until you have done a string of two or three weeks of one-nighters."

Mingus told Walrath that he would play the written parts and Belgrave would play the solos on the recording. But once the session started, Belgrave only played an ensemble part on "Duke Ellington's Sound of Love." Walrath played the rest of the session, though Mingus still cut his trumpet solos in the editing. (The bassist later apologized to Walrath.)

In the early '60s, Belgrave also played gigs with Yusef Lateef and drummer Charli Persip, made rehearsals with multi-reedman Eric Dolphy, and appeared on recordings by Persip, singer Betty Blake, and tenor saxophonist Roland Alexander. On *The Soul of Jazz Percussion* (Warwick), Belgrave holds his own in the fast company of fellow trumpeters Booker Little and

Donald Byrd on a rousing "Chasin' the Bird." Belgrave also plays charged solos on Fathead Newman's *Fathead Comes On* (Atlantic) and Curtis Amy's *Way Down* (Pacific Jazz).

When Belgrave tired of the road for good in January 1963, he settled in Detroit. He was lured by the city's reputation as a jazz mecca, by the promise of studio work at Motown, and because a hero, Thad Jones, had come from the city. Belgrave played on numerous Motown records during the label's heyday. He also led unreleased sessions on June 20 and 26, 1963, for Motown's short-lived Workshop Jazz label. The players included Pepper Adams, Bennie Maupin, George Bohanon, Paul Riser, Kirk Lightsey, Cecil McBee, and George Goldsmith. Adams scholar Gary Carner said the tapes remain buried in vaults at Universal Musical Group in Los Angeles.

Belgrave's trumpet sound is broad and lustrous, and his solos unfold in complete paragraphs of cogent melody, rhythmic wit, and variegated emotions. Improvising is about making choices, and Belgrave favors the road less traveled. The marriage of down-home blues and offbeat tangents reflects his love for Thad Jones, whose unpredictable phrasing had a big impact on Belgrave's maturation in the '70s. The spontaneity and rhythmic variety of saxophonist Sonny Rollins also impacted Belgrave. "I'm trying to hear the whole picture of the piece," Belgrave said. "The improvisation comes in as a part of being able to feel the whole framework of a song, and then you work your way into the flow. I want to play like a singer and feel the rapture of the song. I'm hearing melody first and how that relates to the overall structure in terms of the continuity of phrases."

Belgrave sounded like himself in any setting. He recorded bebop, blues, ballads, post-bop, funk, fusion, and free jazz. Later in his career he traveled the country playing and singing the Louis Armstrong songbook with authenticity. "There's nothing you can throw at him that he can't handle," Geri Allen said. "I've seen him sight-read some things that are just ridiculous and negotiate really complex harmony."

The two Belgrave-led recordings that best capture his artistry were made in the 1990s for his own Detroit Jazz Musician Co-Op label. *Live at the Kerrytown Concert House* features three ensembles, each built around a different Detroit pianist—Allen, Tommy Flanagan, and local hero Gary Schunk. Belgrave plays dew-fresh solos on Thad Jones' "Mean What You Say" and "Zec" with aristocratic support from Flanagan, Peter Washington, and Lewis Nash. The trumpeter delivers his buoyant composition "All My Love" with charm and whimsical half-valve glissandos squeezed out of his horn. Three duets with Allen include a joyous "Sweet Loraine"—Belgrave

Marcus Belgrave with three of his most famous protégés at Kerrytown Concert House in Ann Arbor on March 21, 2014 (*left to right*): Karriem Riggins, Belgrave, Geri Allen, Robert Hurst. Photo by Mark Stryker.

impishly teases his student by singing the lyric "Sweet Geri"—along with Allen's challenging "Dolphy's Dance" and a nostalgic ballad by Lawrence Williams, "It's Good to Be Home Again." Co-led by Belgrave and Williams, *Working Together* documents the trumpeter's long partnership with an animated drummer and absorbing post-bop composer who was a force on the Detroit scene in the 1980s and '90s. (He died in 2006 at age 67.) Williams' songs have unclichéd melodies and intriguing structures and vary widely in mood. Among the rotating cast are pianists Allen and Lightsey and bassists Ralphe Armstrong, David Williams, and Rodney Whitaker.

Belgrave's first record under his own name, *Gemini II* (Tribe) a progressive fusion album from 1974, represents his association with Detroit's Tribe collective. His recording activities picked up around 1980, and over the next 30 years he appeared on dates by Mickey Tucker, Junko Onishi, Fathead Newman, Geri Allen, Horace Tapscott, George Gruntz, Robert Hurst, McCoy Tyner, Wynton Marsalis, David Murray, Kirk Lightsey, Cecil Payne, and Lenny White.

Belgrave fell into teaching in 1970. His friend Harold McKinney recruited him to work for Metro Arts, an antipoverty initiative. Belgrave found the energy and excitement of the students irresistible. Suddenly, he had a calling. When Metro Arts closed in 1973, Belgrave created the Jazz Development Workshop, went into schools to teach, and organized after-school programs and summer initiatives. His most promising students began rehearsing and performing with him at concerts, hotel and restaurant gigs, weddings, even European tours. "Marcus didn't treat me like a student," said Robert Hurst, who started working with Belgrave at 15. "He treated me like a fellow musician and a man. In classical music there's this hierarchy with the teacher up here and the student down there, but we're all students and we're all teachers. That's the most beautiful thing Marcus instilled in me—that you're a perpetual student."

Belgrave was a natural communicator. Hurst remembered playing educational concerts in school gymnasiums across the city for unruly junior high and high school students. "I'd say, 'Oh my God, this is an impossible environment,' but Marcus would bring them down," said Hurst. "He would either talk to them right off the bat, or he would just play. At first, I thought it was arbitrary, but Marcus would really survey the situation, and he was so in tune with the mood of those kids. Sometimes he would just call them out—not violent but confrontational. I would kind of crawl behind my bass! But he would pull them in, and by the end of the day he would have them singing on the blues form, responding and involved."

Belgrave did not have a formal system of teaching. He offered specific technical instruction when needed but left lots of room for intuition and osmosis. One day a few years before his death, I watched him rehearse a small group of high school and college students in Detroit. The band included his son, Kasan, then 14, on alto saxophone. The rehearsal was supposed to start at 1:00 p.m., but Belgrave, wearing a jaunty leather cap and olive-brown paisley vest, arrived at 1:15. Punctuality was a lifelong challenge. "Y'all have to excuse me for being tardy," he said, sheepishly, removing his trumpet from its leather case.

Belgrave called up "Cool Eyes," a bebop tune by Horace Silver with a serpentine melody and cagey rhythms. Belgrave set a deliberately slow tempo and played through the song with the students. There were lots of mistakes. He said little but kept playing the tune with them over and over. Each repetition brought greater clarity as the students' awkward attack began to mimic the fluency and feeling of Belgrave's phrasing. "Put that accent on the upbeat," Belgrave said. "I want the notes to sing; I want them to have a *beat* to them." Belgrave was teaching the language by ear. An academic watching might have complained about the lack of structure: *He's not really teaching them anything.* In fact, Belgrave was teaching them *everything.*

"He's got a focus on the universal truth that's always in his sight, even if he veers off the path a bit," said Hurst. "If I knew what that was I could solve all the problems in the world."

For Belgrave, truth was located within the continuum of history. What connected his trumpet playing and teaching was a belief in the past as a springboard to the future. "You learn from the masters in your presence and go back and forward from there," Belgrave said. "In order to find yourself, you have to be cognizant of what went down before you. That's my philosophy."

Recommended Recordings

Marcus Belgrave, *Gemini II* (Tribe/P-Vine)
Marcus Belgrave, *Live at the Kerrytown Concert House* (Detroit Jazz Musicians Co-Op)
Marcus Belgrave, *Working Together* (Detroit Jazz Musicians Co-Op)

Geri Allen

BACK TO THE FUTURE

Geri Allen was feeling pretty good about herself. She was a teenager in the mid '70s and playing her first professional jazz gig at Dummy George's in northwest Detroit. Things were going well until the group started to play a standard and veteran pianist Teddy Harris walked over to Allen, plopped down next to her, and literally slid her off the piano bench because she wasn't playing the correct chord changes.

"I knew right away that if I was gonna be around these guys, I had to have a thick skin, and I also had to do the work," Allen said in 2015. "Now, Teddy came from a place of love—tough love—but it was fair. I learned there was a criterion in this music and high expectations. I never forgot that lesson. I understood that Detroit was, and still is, at a high level. The ideology was that this music is a representation of the best we have to offer as people."

That's a high bar—"the best we have to offer as people"—but Allen took the charge seriously. She spent her career reaching for the stars, grounded by the tradition defined by her Detroit roots and hometown mentors, particularly Marcus Belgrave. A pianist, composer, conceptualist, and teacher, Allen, who died of cancer at age 60 in 2017, was a game changer. The innovative bite of her music during the first flush of her career in the 1980s and early '90s remains a key influence on progressive pianists in the 21st century, among them Craig Taborn, Vijay Iyer, Jason Moran, Kris Davis, Matt Mitchell, and numerous others. "She was the one who pulled together all of the histories," Moran wrote in tribute after her death.

Allen sounded like herself from the start. On her landmark 1984 debut LP *The Printmakers*, as well as follow-ups *Homegrown*, *Open on All Sides* and *Twylight*, she assimilates swing, blues, funk, free jazz, atonalism, fusion, and African music into a singular voice—while avoiding superficial pastiche. Her puzzle-box compositions and improvisations are rife with veiled riddles, secret passageways, and unexpected silences. Spellbinding

Geri Allen performs at the Detroit Jazz Festival on September 4, 2005. Photo by Eric Seals / Detroit Free Press.

vamps and bass lines support brittle melodies, jabbing rhythms, disjunctive counterpoint between her hands, odd meters, and night-music harmony. The skittering attack and asymmetry of her phrasing on a composition like "A Celebration of All Life" suggests music moving forward and backward at the same time.

Iyer put it this way in a social media post after Allen's death: "Her improvisations were full of space, thought, and listening, as well as a liberatory quality; her groove was deep, her contrapuntal independence often shocking; her lines and voicings were fresh and unique; she would seem at times to play with great reserves of calm, but when she chose to step up, she would dazzle with fearless virtuosity. She was at home with experimentalism and tradition, embracing new technologies and old."

Allen grew up on bebop in Detroit, but she avoided mainstream orthodoxies that defined most young pianists of her era—Bill Evans impressionism, hard bop, the Herbie Hancock–McCoy Tyner–Chick Corea post-bop axis. Allen took as her avatar the craggy modernist Thelonious Monk and the line of percussive, idiosyncratic pianist-composers that he begat, including Herbie Nichols, Randy Weston, and Andrew Hill. The first jazz tribe Allen connected with in New York was the musical left wing. She worked and recorded with established avant-garde figures like saxophonists Oliver Lake and Joseph Jarman, and she joined bassist Charlie Haden and drummer Paul Motian in a celebrated cooperative trio starting in 1987. Allen also joined her peers in the eclectic M-Base collective that circled around alto saxophonist Steve Coleman. In the mid-'90s she become the first pianist since the 1950s to play and record with free-jazz pioneer Ornette Coleman.

But as Allen reached her middle 30s, she sought a rapprochement with the mainstream. She consciously channeled the influence of Herbie Hancock, and her touch and technique turned more pianistic, smoother, and capable of a wider range of articulation, color, and harmony. An extended tour and recording in 1993 with Betty Carter—the daredevil singer from Detroit, who demanded a no-nonsense, swinging groove—was a catalyst. So was Allen's husband at the time, trumpeter Wallace Roney. He was her portal into the orbit of the canonical bass-and-drum team of Ron Carter and Tony Williams, with whom she made a mighty trio album, *Twenty-One* (Blue Note), in 1994. She hired drummer Jimmy Cobb, a hero of hard bop, for her trio. She joined the quartet of tenor saxophonist Charles Lloyd, a veteran of the jazz wars of the 1960s and '70s. She burrowed deeper into jazz history, championing the music of pianist-composer Mary Lou Williams (1910–1981). Allen wrote choral works and a commissioned orchestral piece for the New Jersey Symphony celebrating Martin Luther King. She added a tap dancer to her group to reconnect jazz and dance. She collaborated with visual artist Carrie Mae Weems and writer Farah Jasmin Griffin on multimedia and theatrical works.

Though Allen would not have put it in these terms, she was wrestling with the central dilemma facing all artists, including jazz musicians, in our postmodern age: How do you adopt a healthy relationship with the past, rather than a parasitic or superficial relationship with tradition? Allen's career arc illustrates the special challenge facing a musician who cuts an innovative profile right out of the gate. What do you do for an encore? There are no universal answers. Allen's response was to walk a tightrope between experimentalism and historicism. Her choices left some acolytes and critics wondering if she had lost her edge. Jason Moran, who worships Allen, lamented to fellow pianist Ethan Iverson in a 2006 interview that she "retreated." But that's too reductive. Allen was following her muse, reconnecting with her own history as a Detroiter and trying to reconcile all her influences and creative impulses into a grand synthesis.

Allen said that she had consciously suppressed some of her mainstream influences during the 1980s—particularly Hancock's Mwandishi and Head Hunters bands of the '70s—because the progressive profiles of the musicians with whom she was working demanded a different approach. By the mid-'90s, she had come to regard Hancock, McCoy Tyner, and avant-garde hero Cecil Taylor as the three pianists who defined the outer edge of where the instrument had gone. Her challenge, she said, was to find her voice "within the context of those three voices" and make the best music she could along the way.

There were trade-offs. In search of a broader palette, Allen sacrificed the idiosyncratic clarity of her early work. Sometimes she lost her balance. Her Hancockisms, for example, could come off as generic. But Allen's best work during the last 20-plus years of her life revealed a deeper musicianship for having gone back and dealt with mainstream fundamentals. Two wildly different solo piano discs for Motema are revelatory. Recorded in 2008, the spectacular *Flying Toward the Sound* includes some of the most abstract music of Allen's career; yet there are nuances of color, texture, and expression that she could not have accessed when younger. On *Grand River Crossings* (2012), disarmingly straightforward interpretations of Motown hits like "That Girl" and "Tears of a Clown" achieve a glowing transparency.

"My goal has always been to serve the music, but at the same time to understand that this is all my palette," Allen said. "When you sit down to play with certain musicians, what is going to make the music thrive in that moment? With time you become more adept at being able to access a whole range of possible answers in the moment. I enjoy the variety and the opportunities these different points of view allow in improvising. For me, it's always helped to have choices."

Because of Allen's early radical attachments, pockets of mainstream musicians at first viewed her with suspicion, though she eventually won over just about everyone. Interestingly, a 22-year-old Allen got the call all young hard boppers dreamed about. It was 1979 and legendary drummer Art Blakey was on the phone: *Hey, Geri! Come on and join my band.* As the leader of the Jazz Messengers, Blakey had launched dozens of major careers. Playing with him would have engendered immediate respect from the entire jazz community. Reluctantly, Allen turned him down. She had already accepted a scholarship to graduate school at the University of Pittsburgh to study ethnomusicology. Coming from a family of educators, she wanted the degree, and her parents wanted her to stay in school. "I'm glad I went to school, but I'm also sorry I didn't play with Art," Allen said in 1996. "I can't imagine what would have happened, but I know it would have changed a lot. But who am I to complain?"

One cold day in January 2015, Allen met me for coffee at a restaurant in Ann Arbor, where she had taught at the University of Michigan for a decade, before leaving in 2013 to head jazz studies at the University of Pittsburgh. Allen had a round, soft face with saucer eyes, and she wore her shoulder-length hair in locs. She was dressed casually in black, with a long, stylish scarf of multiple hues draped around her neck. She looked good. She *always* looked good, with a reputation for eye-catching outfits on and off stage. Back in 1996, she traced her fashion flare to the six months she spent touring with former Supreme Mary Wilson in the early '80s to pay the rent. "I watched them make themselves up and I got all kinds of great ideas and tips," Allen said. "That influenced me, because jazz was always like that. Until the '60s, it was very fashion-oriented and glamorous. I wanted to project that in my stage appearance."

Allen was described by friends, colleagues, and former students as warm, nurturing, and sweet. But she was fundamentally shy and guarded in interviews, wary of being pigeonholed and reluctant to talk about her personal life. Each of her three marriages ended in divorce, and two of her husbands were famous jazz musicians: Roney and Steve Coleman. She had three children.

Pianist Ellen Rowe, a colleague at U-M, recalled that Allen did not come off as warm and friendly when they met. Allen had come to campus to interview for the job, and Rowe was nervous and intimidated. "After I really got to know her, I learned that she had been nervous too and a little insecure," Rowe said. "Sometimes she'd come off stage after a performance and say to me, 'What did you think? Did I use too much pedal?' She'd ask advice about her playing, and I'd think, 'You're asking me?' To see her teach was to get to know her. She had a quiet authority and was so invested in her students. She never criticized them. She'd say, 'You might want to think about this approach.' But she always challenged them to do things they thought impossible—like transcribe an Andrew Hill solo or something by Art Tatum. She'd help them with it, and I might help a bit too, but they'd end up doing it and gain a new belief in themselves."

Geri Antoinette Allen was born north of Detroit in Pontiac on June 12, 1957. She grew up in northwest Detroit. Her father, Mount Allen, was a teacher and principal in the Detroit Public Schools. Her mother, Barbara Allen, was a defense contract administrator for the federal government. Allen's parents exposed her and her brother to all the arts. She took dance, art, and, starting at age seven, piano lessons. Her parents instilled discipline, requiring she practice and do her homework before going outside to play.

Allen's father loved jazz, and she grew up listening to his records by Charlie Parker, Duke Ellington, and others. By the time she entered Cass Tech, she knew she wanted to be a jazz musician.

Allen met Belgrave when his community-based Jazz Development Workshop was engaged at Cass Tech. He taught her harmony and standards and soon hired her for gigs ranging from jazz concerts to Jewish weddings. Belgrave also took her to pianist Bess Bonnier for jazz piano lessons. "Geri absorbed the music as swiftly as any student I've ever had," Belgrave said. She had to cope with dismissive attitudes from of some of the boys in school, but Belgrave created a protected lane in which she could develop. Her first composition, "Minor Complication," was in an odd meter. Forty years later, Allen could no longer recall the exact time signature, but she remembered that Belgrave assembled a group of professionals to rehearse her music. "He was so generous to me and other students," she said. "Marcus heard all the clunkers."

Belgrave wasn't Allen's only guru. Detroit drummer Roy Brooks, best known for his tenure with Horace Silver in the early '60s, pushed her to explore Thelonious Monk's singular style: "I was playing 'Round Midnight' with Roy, and he said, 'This is Monk's song. Let's hear you use Monk's language.' I had to go back to the drawing board. I spent a lot of time internalizing what he meant in terms of the weight of the attack, the space, Monk's unique voicings and colors."

Allen majored in jazz studies at Howard University, where one of her teachers was pianist John Malachi, who had worked with Billy Eckstine and Sarah Vaughan. The summer after graduating she studied with Kenny Barron in New York. At the University of Pittsburgh, she studied with saxophonist Nathan Davis and wrote her master's thesis on saxophonist Eric Dolphy. Bassist Robert Hurst remembered paging through Allen's thesis and marveling at how studied she was in her analysis of harmony.

"I felt like I could play anything with her and she'd make it sound good—I never felt like I could play a wrong note," Hurst said. "I got a chance to play with my Mount Rushmore of '80s-generation piano players in Geri, Kenny Kirkland, and Mulgrew Miller. With Kenny and Mulgrew I did feel like something I might play could sound wrong. Maybe they'd find a note or voicing to help, but it wasn't like that with Geri. I felt a complete freedom with her to play anything."

Allen's recordings under her own name and with others are dizzyingly varied. Start at the beginning with her first two LPs on Minor Music: *The Printmakers* with bassist Anthony Cox and drummer Andrew Cyrille, and the solo record *Homegrown*. Of her five recordings with Charlie Haden and Paul Motian, the first, 1987's *Etudes* (Soul Note), best captures their special chemistry. "The thing that is so interesting is that the core of Paul and Charlie was bebop," Allen said. "You feel that sense of dedication to the time. The music would levitate, yet it still had this foundational connection to what swing is. The pulse was designated but within a wash of a free expanse."

Like *Etudes*, Allen's first two Blue Note recordings in 1990–92 had a big impact on musicians. *The Nurturer* showcases a mostly Detroit cast including Belgrave and three of his protégés—Allen, Hurst, and Kenny Garrett. *Maroons* (1992) includes some of Allen's most beloved compositions—"For John Malachi," an enigmatic ballad; "Feed the Fire," an exuberant, abstract blues that unfolds in a 20-bar rhythmic loop; and "Dolphy's Dance," a scampering 64-bar melody full of leaping intervals, hairpin turns, and dissonance over basic "I Got Rhythm" chord changes.

Twenty-One (1994) was the recording that most clearly announced Allen's growing mainstream bona fides, but she pointed to her 1993 tour with Betty Carter and live recording *Feed the Fire* (Verve) as her turning point. Allen's accompaniment bounces off the upbeats in a more conventional manner than in her earlier work. Still, her solos often retain her previous rhythmic rumble, and Carter responds with some of her most inspired singing. "I don't know if my playing changed as much as it crystalized with Betty," Allen said. "She wanted a certain fleetness and snap. She was coming from a place where the trio was a well-honed, well-rehearsed, well-oiled sports car. She made me realize that how I positioned myself philosophically as a pianist had a lot to do with who would call me and who wouldn't. I started to really understand what it was the bandleader was interested in—what kind of personality the core trio should represent. That's helped me move in and out of different settings. Betty introduced me to the broader jazz community."

The Gathering (Verve) from 1998 marks Allen's evolving style with compositions that mix ostinato bass lines with liquid pianism, modal harmonies, and pastel colors voiced in the manner of Hancock's early '70s Mwandishi band. Allen's rowdy-but-respectful interpretation of Mary Lou Williams' album-length *Zodiac Suite: Revisited* (Mary Records) with Buster Williams and Billy Hart ranks among the glories of her later discography. Among Allen's recordings with others, Oliver Lake's *Gallery* (Gramavision), drummer Ralph Peterson Jr.'s *Triangular* (Blue Note), Charles Lloyd's *Jumping the Creek* (ECM) and Ornette Coleman's *Three Women* and *Hidden Man* (Verve) find her fitting into disparate settings. Trumpeter Woody Shaw's *Bemsha Swing* (Blue Note) has special significance for having been recorded live at Detroit's historic Baker's Keyboard Lounge in 1986. The multigenerational hometown rhythm section—Allen, Hurst, Brooks—makes a heavy statement about the regenerative capability of the city's jazz scene.

Allen's death two weeks after her 60th birthday in June 2017 hit the jazz community with a thunderbolt of grief. Only a few confidants knew she was ill, and she had been such a creative force for so long that it was difficult to process her sudden passing. It said something profound about her impact that online tributes after her death came from pianists as stylistically diverse as Vijay Iyer, Kenny Barron, Ethan Iverson, Jason Moran, and Mike LeDonne. The Detroit jazz scene had lost its big sister. More than any other musician of her generation or younger, Allen was revered as the contemporary embodiment of the city's jazz legacy. She took pride in her roots, championing her hometown in interviews and often hiring Detroiter musicians. Only a year before her death she assumed the role of artistic director of the Carr Center, a Detroit nonprofit focused on African American culture and arts education. Allen saw her appointment as coming full circle, a way to give back to the community that nourished her.

She came to see her life as one of service. In 2014 she became the founding director of the New Jersey Performing Arts Center All-Female Residency, a summer camp for young women interested in jazz. Allen made sure that the camp not only addressed musical matters but also issues like building a sustainable career and gender bias. Where would her music have gone had she lived? It's impossible to say for sure, but it's likely she would have continued to look to the future while deepening her understanding of the past. On one of her last recordings, *Perfection* (Momenta), with a power trio including saxophonist David Murray and drummer Terri Lyne Carrington, Allen raises a ruckus akin to her wild early days. Detroit would certainly have retained primacy in her vision. In 2015, Allen entered the studio with Hurst and drummer Karriem Riggins—three former Belgrave students who had been performing as D3.[1]

"This is something we all really wanted to do," Allen said. "There's something special about the Detroit legacy and the rhythm section particularly. It's foundational. Detroiters are a proud group, and we have a lot to be proud of."

Recommended Recordings

Geri Allen, *The Printmakers* (Minor Music)
Charlie Haden and Paul Motian, *Etudes* (Soul Note)
Geri Allen, *The Nurturer* (Blue Note)

Note

1. As of 2018, no material had been released from this session.

Kenny Garrett

SOUND AND SPIRIT

Sometimes fathers dispense paternal wisdom with a pat on the back, sometimes with a kick in the rear, and sometimes with a scoop of ice cream. Kenny Garrett was about 10 when he and his dad stopped at a Dairy Queen on the east side of Detroit. Stanley Turrentine's burly tenor saxophone came barreling through the car radio speaker. The elder Garrett, who made his living as a carpenter but also played tenor, turned to his son and asked, "Who's that?"

"I don't know."

"Well, *everybody's* got a sound."

Garrett, who turned 64 in October 2024, never forgot the lesson. As one of the most compelling and influential alto saxophonists of his generation, he brings a lot to the table—brushfire intensity, a personal melodic and harmonic language, and a feverish spirituality that reaches across the footlights and brings audiences into the fold like a charismatic preacher. The individuality of Garrett's expression, however, starts with his sound: a brawny roar that radiates in equal measure the high-wattage warmth of the jazz tradition and the impassioned grit of the Detroit streets. Garrett's sound distills his varied influences, among them alto saxophonists Charlie Parker, Cannonball Adderley, Sonny Stitt, Hank Crawford, and Maceo Parker and tenor saxophonists John Coltrane, Sonny Rollins, and Joe Henderson. But Garrett's sound also makes a statement about the continuum of African American culture.

"It's a sound in which you hear not just jazz history but the history of black music," said alto saxophonist Steve Wilson. "You hear the whole lineage in Kenny's sound and language—the noncodified blues up through bebop, R & B, Coltrane, gospel. I think Kenny was a game changer in the 1980s. Most of us growing up in the '60s and '70s weren't just jazz babies. We grew up on P-Funk, Motown, Stax, soul-jazz, James Brown. All of that is encompassed in what Kenny does. Before he hit the scene, there was a

Kenny Garrett performs at the Detroit Jazz Festival on September 3, 2012.
Photo by Mandi Wright / Detroit Free Press.

tendency for us to compartmentalize, but Kenny was an affirmation that this could all be a part of one sound."

The essence of Garrett's tone has been with him since he was a teenager in Detroit under the tutelage of Marcus Belgrave. It gained polish and nuance through Garrett's three-year apprenticeship with the Duke Ellington Orchestra (led by Mercer Ellington), which he joined out of high school at age 17 in 1978. Garrett's sound matured further in the 1980s, accumulating strength and weight as he worked with Freddie Hubbard, Woody Shaw, Art Blakey, and, finally, Miles Davis from 1987 until the trumpeter's death in 1991. Since then Garrett has led his own bands, traveling the world, recording extensively, and nurturing young talent in the manner of his elders. He's also contributed to high-profile Chick Corea projects and lit up recordings by Roy Haynes, Bobby Hutcherson, Marcus Miller, and others.

Garrett has always been determined to find his own voice within the jazz tradition with which he grew up in Detroit. His bands for the most part explore the post-bop territory mapped out by the John Coltrane Quartet in the 1960s. Garrett, who doubles on soprano saxophone, is hardly alone in this, but one of his primary achievements has been to absorb Coltrane's ubiquitous influence without copying licks or mortgaging an identity that happily assimilates a broad spectrum of idioms and ideas. Garrett likes to weave into his music the flavors of Asian and African cultures, and his fondness for pop melody, funk, and hip-hop grooves are in the mix too. "The spirit of the music is what's most important," Garrett said in 2017. "I used to have these conversations with Brother Yusef Lateef—he's 40 years my senior and we have the same birthday. Afterward I realized that we were searching for a similar quality of spirituality. There was an aura about Yusef and all the older guys I respected. They all had this searching and sophisticated blues quality in what they played. That's what we had in Detroit in people like Marcus Belgrave, saxophonist Lamont Hamilton, and others. That's what I wanted."

Garrett's association with trumpeters has also left a unique stamp. His crackling articulation and the way his notes lock inside the beat, generating tremendous momentum and swing, recall Freddie Hubbard. The way Garrett leans on pentatonic scales and chromatic side-slipping to create tension reflects Woody Shaw. From Miles Davis came the lesson that music wasn't simply a mass of scales and chords but a stage for storytelling and drama. "What I like about the trumpet is that it's a powerful instrument," Garrett said, speaking in the swift tempo of bebop. "I always wanted my saxophone to have that power. Standing next to Freddie Hubbard and he'd go *be-do WHEE!*—I mean, that's power! I had to work to get meat in my sound to match that intensity."

Garrett's solos have a shock-and-awe impact. At a 2015 concert by his quintet at Orchestra Hall in Detroit, he played his original "J-Mac," dedicated to alto saxophonist Jackie McLean. It's a simple AB form comprised of repeating melodic calls, modal harmony, and contrasting rhythm. The band shifted into fierce swing for the improvisations, and Garrett played a caterwauling solo of scorching runs, cathartic wails, and stuttering riffs that cracked against the beat. Piano and bass dropped out along the way, leaving Garrett to spar with drummer Marcus Baylor. Wearing stylish glasses and one of his trademark hand-stitched African skullcaps, Garrett entered an incantatory trance. He rocked up and down like a shaman in flight. High-register squalls climbed toward the heavens one half-step at a time. Baylor threw everything he had at his boss, but Garrett never flinched. Audience members shouted as if at a revival meeting, and when it was over the crowd roared and rose to its feet.

Garrett is such a beast with a saxophone in his mouth that his mild-mannered presence offstage suggests a Jekyll-and-Hyde duality. Garrett—who is of medium height, trim, with round cheeks and a close-cropped beard—keeps to himself on the road. He can usually be found reading a book, often about foreign cultures and languages. He's fluent in Japanese, commands a fair amount of Chinese, and can say "Thank you," "Good morning," and other everyday phrases in some 40 languages. After Garrett first went to Japan with the Ellington band, he was so taken with the culture that he hired a private tutor to learn the language. Part of his initial intrigue was he met people for the first time who were shier than he was. The experience pulled him out of his shell. Garrett found that being able to say just a few words in the native tongue of the countries he visited forged deeper connections with people and music.

"Everywhere I go to I try to hear the indigenous music," he said. "I want to study it, to hear the spiritual connection. When I started to study Japanese, it changed the way I heard music. It made me more aware of sounds and rhythms. . . . Everyone can play a B-flat, but what are you going to do with that B-flat to make it sound different than the other guy?"

Garrett's fundamental curiosity means that he's constantly asking questions, even when he likely already knows the answer. He doesn't want to lose any detail. On the road with Chick Corea, for example, Garrett is forever picking the pianist's brain. "Kenny will say, 'Chick, you always play that sharp-5 sound—what scales do you usually play over that?'" bassist

Christian McBride said. "Chick would say something like, 'C'mon, man, you know this. You could show me some things!' But Kenny would say, 'Nah, I want to learn some more!'"

Off the bandstand, Garrett leads a quiet life. He lives near Manhattan in Glen Ridge, New Jersey, with his wife of 33 years, Sayydah Garrett. She teaches English as a second language and is founder and president of the Pastoralist Child Foundation, a nonprofit dedicated to eradicating female genital mutilation and early marriage in parts of Kenya. The couple has a grown daughter, Halima, who works as a nutritionist.

Kenneth Garrett was born in Detroit on October 9, 1960. He grew up on the west side in a house saturated with music, from Joe Henderson and Stanley Turrentine to Maceo Parker and Gladys Knight. Garrett loved listening to his father practice the tenor saxophone, and when Garrett was nine or 10 his dad gave him a toy saxophone for Christmas. Shortly thereafter his father bought him his first horn—a used alto that had a literal bullet hole in it that had been soldered. His father got him started on the horn, before sending him off for private lessons.

Garrett focused on music at MacKenzie High School, where the band director was Bill Wiggins, a versatile saxophonist who had worked with Aretha Franklin and the cutting-edge Detroit band Focus Novii. Wiggins had also studied with the classical saxophonist Larry Teal (who also taught Joe Henderson and Yusef Lateef). Wiggins gave Garrett private lessons, providing a thorough grounding in the fundamentals of sound production and technique. It was Wiggins who would later calm Garrett's anxiety about moving to New York by dropping advice on him like, "A seventh chord is the same all over the country." Wiggins eventually sent Garrett to Marcus Belgrave for more intensive tutoring in harmony and improvisation. The lessons went beyond music theory and even the gigs he played with his mentor. "Mainly, I learned about sharing and giving back," Garrett said. "The lesson was just being with Marcus, watching him practicing and rehearsing, trying to make all of these gigs, working with peers and young musicians."

Garrett found his comfort zone practicing seven hours a day. Soon he was also working weekends with the organist Lyman Woodard. Heads turned when he started playing in clubs. "Kenny's main thing was that he could take over any situation," Belgrave said. "He had such a strong sound and inner concept that though he didn't have control of bebop yet, what he did play he mastered. He got to people."

A bootleg recording that captures Garrett at age 17 in 1978 proves the point. He plays a dozen scorching blues choruses on Charlie Parker's "Billie's Bounce" at Cobb's Corner, a bustling club in those years at the corner of Cass and Willis in what used to be called the Cass Corridor but has since been rebranded as Midtown. The local ii-V-I Orchestra was playing that night, and singer Eddie Jefferson and alto saxophonist Richie Cole, in town to perform elsewhere, sat in with Belgrave, Garrett, and the rhythm section. Garrett destroys. His playing is raw, and his note choices are still awkward, but the essence of his sound—robust and wailing—and his passionate will to communicate are already in place. The audience explodes when he finishes.

Garrett was preparing to attend the Berklee College of Music in Boston when the Ellington band arrived in Detroit in 1978 in need of a second alto player. Wiggins recommended Garrett, and he ended up staying three years and rubbing shoulders with history. Lead alto Harold Minerve taught Garrett how to blend his sound with the ensemble, and trumpeter Cootie Williams, whose history with Ellington dated back to 1929, was a living link to the earliest days of jazz. Garrett also grew close to the Ellington band's pianist, Mulgrew Miller, who would later use the saxophonist in his own group and recommend him to Woody Shaw.

Garrett landed in New York in the early 1980s. He got an early wake-up call from the protean tenor saxophonist George Coleman at a jam session at the Tin Palace. "He was taking 'Green Dolphin Street' through all the keys," said Garrett. "I had heard about that from people in Detroit, but I didn't really believe it until I saw it live. It was *serious*."

Garrett took every gig he could. He won a spot in the Mel Lewis Jazz Orchestra, and he played jobs with big bands led by Charli Persip, Frank Foster, and Lionel Hampton. He toured Europe in 1981 with drummer Dannie Richmond's quintet alongside trumpeter Jack Walrath and two other native Detroiters, pianist Bob Neloms and bassist Cameron Brown. A recording of the band performing in Germany, *Three or Four Shades of Dannie Richmond Quintet* (Tutu), was issued years later. It's the earliest Garrett on record, and at 20 he sounds more than ready.

Garrett worked some Broadway shows in New York and on tour, and he learned to play flute, piccolo, and clarinet. He left Broadway behind as his jazz career took off. He won a spot in Out of the Blue (OTB), a band of young lions sponsored by the Blue Note label, and he made three records with the group in 1985–86; fellow Belgrave student Robert Hurst was also a charter member on bass. Garrett worked and recorded in this period with Freddie Hubbard, Woody Shaw, and Art Blakey. (Belgrave had first introduced Garret to Hubbard in Detroit.)

Garrett's first recording as a leader, *Introducing Kenny Garrett* (Criss Cross) was taped in December 1984 with Shaw, Mulgrew Miller, Nat Reeves, and Tony Reedus. It's one of the strongest debuts of the era. Garrett's commanding sound, harmonic savvy, rhythmic pop, and original compositions make a striking impression for a 24-year-old. Shaw adds the imprimatur of a master. Garrett's solo on "Have You Met Miss Jones" speaks to the breadth of the tradition in his playing. His double-time lines chew up the harmony with a contemporary bite, but he lays into the blues with a Stanley Turrentine–like strut in his final eight bars and sings out several high Ds with a butter-and-sass vibrato winking at his Ellington apprenticeship.

Miles Davis called Garrett in 1987 and requested an audition tape. Davis called back after listening and said, "You sound like you're wearing Sonny Stitt's dirty drawers." The final chapter of Davis' career was pop and funk influenced, simmering with the rhythms of Prince and a cover of Cyndi Lauper's "Time After Time." Unlike other saxophonists who worked with Davis in later years, Garrett didn't just layer stacks of harmony on the simple structures. Instead, he played melody and engaged Davis in call-and-response dialogue. Garrett enjoyed a warm relationship with Davis. Whenever Garrett wanted to hear stories about the old days, he'd take out his horn within earshot of the boss' dressing room and play bebop tunes. Invariably, Davis would send for Garrett and growl, "That's not right," before launching into a tale about Charlie Parker, Dizzy Gillespie, Sonny Rollins, or Coltrane.

"What surprised me was how friendly Miles was," said Garrett. "I heard all the stories, but Miles had changed by the time I got in the band. I would go to his house and hang out, and he'd paint, and we'd talk, not about music but about things like cars. The coolest thing was he just let me hang in his presence. He didn't have to say much. We had this communication without having to say anything. But one time he wanted me to go with him to get a Ferrari, and I said, 'Man, I am *not* driving in a Ferrari in New York.' I didn't care if it was Miles Davis."

Garrett's first recording as a leader after joining Davis, *Prisoner of Love* (Atlantic), a smooth crossover date in 1989, hasn't aged well, and there is still an occasional tension between Garrett's straight-ahead core and more populist ambitions. *Seeds from the Underground*, a 2011 release on the Detroit-based Mack Avenue label, threads the needle in savvy fashion.

"Boogety, Boogety," for instance, goes deep without mortgaging a common-man touch. The breezy melody, vamp, and Afro-Cuban rhythms will enchant newcomers, while Garrett's expansive improvisation has all the meat a connoisseur could want. The standouts of Garrett's earlier recordings on Warner Bros. are *Triology* (1994) with a lean trio anchored by Brian Blade on drums; *Pursuance: The Music of John Coltrane* (1996) with guitarist Pat Metheny and Detroit bassist Rodney Whitaker in the band; and *Songbook* (1997), which includes some of Garrett's most attractive compositions.

By the mid-'90s, Garrett was influencing his contemporaries and those coming up behind him. Alto saxophonists such as Steve Wilson, Antonio Hart, and Stefano Di Battista are among those who absorbed elements of his aesthetic. Garrett's solos were dissected at a fever pitch by players at the top jazz schools across the country, and he's still a popular model in terms of sound and ideas. Garrett has also become a bandleader known for nurturing young talent, and his groups have included pianists Robert Glasper, Benito Gonzales, and Vernell Brown Jr., bassist Corcoran Holt, and drummers Brian Blade, Marcus Baylor, Chris Dave, and Ronald Bruner Jr. "I really want to share the information," Garrett said. "What I got from Marcus or Freddie or Miles, I'm doing that too, but in a different way."

In 2023, the 45th anniversary of Garrett leaving Detroit with the Ellington band, his impact and influence were recognized by the National Endowment for the Arts with a Jazz Master award. When he talks about his priorities, you hear the legacy of Detroit and Belgrave's mentorship in the message: "I'm always thinking about where I want to take the music. We never completely figure this thing out. I'm still trying to connect the music spiritually to my travels, still trying to practice and work out things. As you get older you start to reflect on the past. You also reflect on the future, but you do it with a clearer understanding of what happened before you."

Recommended Recordings

Miles Davis, *Live Around the World* (Warner Bros.)
Kenny Garrett, *Songbook* (Warner Bros.)
Kenny Garrett, *Seeds From the Underground* (Mack Avenue)

Regina Carter

SEARCHING FOR ROOTS

Most of the young jazz musicians from Detroit who came to prominence in the 1980s and '90s sprinted out of the blocks. Geri Allen, Robert Hurst, Kenny Garrett, Rodney Whitaker, James Carter, and Karriem Riggins all were precocious teenagers and making marks on the national scene by their mid-'20s. Regina Carter? Not so much. Though she took up the violin at age four, Carter's destiny took a long time to reveal itself. She battled self-doubt and struggled to find her footing. It wasn't until she was about 30 that her career picked up momentum, and she didn't start headlining major jazz clubs and festivals until she was 35. She has since been widely acclaimed as the leading jazz violinist of her generation, and she reached a pinnacle in 2006 when she received a prestigious $500,000 MacArthur Fellowship.

Carter, who turned 63 in 2025, is a versatile and communicative musician of eclectic tastes with a large and diverse fan base. She's played everything from straight-ahead jazz to R & B, funk, avant-chamber music, and new arrangements of traditional African songs. She's also performed jazz-tinged classical concertos by David Schiff and Billy Childs with her hometown Detroit Symphony Orchestra. Regardless of idiom, Carter's playing boasts an exuberant, openhearted spirit that can turn a cloudy day sunny in a few bars. Her high profile—she was named an NEA Jazz Master in 2023—is the most public sign of the slow-but-steady-wins-the-race arc of her career.[1] But there's another, more personal story to her trajectory. More than most musicians, her musical journey has been a voyage of self-discovery. Her recording projects have favored autobiographical themes—her Detroit roots, classical music training, West African heritage, familial legacies in the American South, and midcentury popular songs adored by her mother. Ultimately, making music has been a way for Carter to better understand herself, her relationship to the world, and her connection to others.

"I didn't consciously start out feeling that way," Carter said in 2017.

Regina Carter performs at the Detroit Jazz Festival on September 1, 2002. Photo by Mandi Wright / Detroit Free Press.

"But now that I'm at this point in my life and looking back, yes. Having so many different musical experiences, particularly in Detroit, really opened me up so when I got to New York, I didn't limit myself to one style of music. I was curious about so much music. With each project and with maturing, I began to realize that I was finding out more and more about myself and my family. That made me even more curious to keep looking and digging even deeper."

At the same time, music has also led Carter outside of herself to a place of greater empathy and responsibility. In Detroit she used to play small gigs in the community with trumpeter Marcus Belgrave—nursing homes, hospitals, schools, and the like. Those performances planted a seed. Carter saw the impact that music had on people desperate to have their spirits lifted. She didn't think much about such things at the time, but as the years accumulated, Belgrave's implicit lessons about community service grew into an imperative.

When Carter's mother, Grace, was dying of cancer in 2005, Carter was heartbroken to see other patients alone in the hospital for lack of family. She also noticed how her mother's vital signs improved when recordings were played in the room. After her mother's death, Carter enrolled in an online course in music therapy through Western Michigan University. When it became clear that this wasn't quite the right path for her, she signed up for hospice training and later worked as a volunteer near her home in Maywood, New Jersey. Carter found the experience so fulfilling that she's begun examining ways to do professional work in the field, even if it means touring and performing less.

"There's something about being around people who know they are dying," she said. "The little stuff becomes *really* little. It just puts life in perspective. It's not only playing music for them. I love just being with them. I've been talking with people and reading books and trying to figure out how I can spend more time being there for people when they're in their last stages of life, to be a comfort hopefully. I've felt guilty sometimes, because I thought, 'Oh, you're just supposed to play.' But, no, everyone has many sides to them, many gifts. This will balance me out."

When Carter arrived on the national scene in the 1990s, she stepped into a vacuum whose existence was only obvious once she had filled it: There were no young violinists around at the time who knew their way around the swinging mainstream like Carter but also sounded at home in funk, fusion, or more exploratory idioms. The violin has had a now-you-see-it, now-you-don't history in jazz. Joe Venuti had a distinctive and visible voice in the 1920s. Two of Carter's idols, Stuff Smith and Stephane Grappelli, kept the instrument on the front lines through the swing era and beyond. Ray Nance played violin solos with Duke Ellington at midcentury. But the beboppers of the '40s and their progeny had little use for the violin. Save a rare exception like Michael White, the instrument disappeared from the jazz vanguard until the 1970s, when it reemerged as a fusion staple (Jean-Luc Ponty, Michael Urbaniak, Noel Pointer, Didier Lockwood) and free jazz (Leroy Jenkins and Billy Bang). John Blake—with whom Carter studied—played modal-driven post-bop with McCoy Tyner in the 1970s and '80s.

As Carter's career picked up steam in the 1990s, she attracted some high-profile champions, among them Wynton Marsalis, who featured her on the 1996–97 national tour of *Blood on the Fields*, and pianist Kenny Barron, with whom she began a periodic partnership in the late '90s that continues to this day. "Regina's got an incredible ear," said Barron. "She's extremely creative and has a great imagination. She's open and can hear anything, so wherever I want to go, she's right there with me."

On *Freefall* (Verve), Carter and Barron's duet recordings from 2000, she plays with a mahogany tone, dark and sensuous, with little vibrato except an extra dollop on ballads. Her phrasing is direct, ardent. She doesn't weave in and out of the chords with elaborate bebop melody—that's not her strength. Instead, her solos unfurl in punchy riffs and declarative phrases. Trills, bluesy slides, gruffly articulated double stops, vocalized sighs and shouts add color and drama. On a swinger like "Squatty Roo," Carter's ebullient bounce evokes her love for Stuff Smith. On her ballad "Shades of Gray," she and Barron circle the fine-spun melody in a dance tempo, singing sweet embellishments to each other. Barron sets the mood on "Softly as in a Morning Sunrise" with a lively Afro-Cuban vamp and propulsive solo. Carter rides the wave, and the music soars.

Carter shares her home in Maywood, about an hour outside of New York, with her husband, drummer Alvester Garnett. The couple have no children. "*We* are the children," Carter said, laughing. She is a compact woman, five feet tall, with a face that lights up with a toothy grin. She wears two tiny nose rings, and in the past has sported locs, though she's currently rocking a close-cropped cut. In the throes of performing she tends to close her eyes and rock side to side on her heels. At her most involved, she furrows her brow into what her mother used to affectionately call her "ugly face."

Carter was born into a family of three children in Detroit on August 6, 1962. Her father, Dan Carter, worked on the assembly line at Ford. Her mother, Grace, was a kindergarten teacher. Carter grew up mostly in a two-story house on the west side. Her ear for music revealed itself at the age of two, when she walked over to the piano and plunked out her older brother's lessons. She started taking piano lessons herself, but instead of playing her prepared material she'd present her teacher with homemade drawings of large circles and say, "Here's my song I wrote." The Detroit Community Music School offered Suzuki violin lessons, and Grace signed up her daughter at age four.

The Suzuki method stresses playing by ear, repetition, and imitation. Those skills paid dividends when Carter started to play jazz, but her ear developed so acutely that she had difficulty learning to read music—a not uncommon bugaboo of Suzuki training.

Her introduction to jazz came at age 16 at Cass Tech. Classmate Carla Cook, a terrific singer who would later record for the MaxJazz label, gave Carter records by Jean-Luc Ponty and Noel Pointer. Carter then went to hear Stephane Grappelli in person. The French-born master was about 70 and appeared elderly, but the years fell away when he played. "The person that walked out and the person that played were two different people," Carter said. "He transformed into something else. It was amazing; it was magical. Like when you watch cartoons and the characters come out and change into their superhero thing. It just took hold of me, and I said, 'OK, you've been chosen.'"

What Carter found so enthralling about jazz was its surge of freedom. Her classical lessons were regimented: Stand this way. Hold the bow this way. Don't smile. But Grappelli broke these rules. He played with winking charm, twinkling eyes, and joie de vivre. Carter was captivated. She never cared much for school. By the time she was a sophomore, she was playing in the pop-funk group Brainstorm, and her mother said that her daughter used to skip Spanish class and hide out in the music room, playing the violin and telling anyone who would listen that she was going to get a record deal.

Carter's mother all but forced her daughter to go to college. She attended the New England Conservatory in Boston, and it was a disaster. She was uncomfortable in the orchestra, had a prickly relationship with her violin teacher, and recoiled at school politics. She transferred into the jazz department but felt lost without the step-by-step method books she was used to. "It was like everybody was keeping a secret from me," Carter said. "I did some studying with the pianist Fred Hersch in Boston, and that ended up being more like therapy than lessons," she said, laughing (again).

Carter's fundamental insecurity stemmed from her inability to process information like her peers. She plays almost entirely by ear. The music theory most musicians use as a blueprint for improvisation is as unintelligible to her as Latin. The paradox is that Carter's weakness is her strength. The conversational flow of her playing is partly a by-product of the inability to create the surface complexities of theory-obsessed players. A parade of teachers threw up their hands and told Carter not to worry and just keep doing what she was doing. But even today doubts linger. "I sometimes think, 'Are you ever going to let this go?' Carter said. "I learn differently, but instead of accepting that and going about it my way, I still try and force myself to learn like those people over there. I'm still trying to make peace with all of that."

Only after Carter transferred to Oakland University in suburban Detroit for her final two years of college did she begin making real progress. Marvin (Doc) Holladay, the veteran saxophonist who ran the OU jazz program, pushed her to listen to horn players and study how they phrased and when they breathed. She started learning Charlie Parker songs and solos. She also began working around town with leading local figures like organist Lyman Woodard, who awakened her passion for Afro-Cuban music, and Marcus Belgrave, who became her employer and mentor. "Regina always played great, and her spirit always made an impact on people," Belgrave said in 2014. "But she still lacked confidence."

After graduating in 1985, Carter moved—on a whim—to Germany for two years, settling in Munich. She wasn't playing much violin, but there were other life lessons: Work as an au pair convinced her that the only place you could start a music career and raise children at the same time was in fantasyland. She reentered the Detroit scene upon her return and came alive, joining the city's popular all-female band Straight Ahead. The group included flutist and vocalist Cynthia Dewberry, keyboardist Alina Moor (Eileen Orr), bassist Marion Hayden, and drummer Gayelynn McKinney. Straight Ahead's populist mix of fusion, R & B, Latin, and jazz caught the attention of Atlantic Records. The label issued three CDs by the band between 1992 and '95, the first two with Carter, and the group had a nice if brief run of national touring. Meanwhile, she received a National Endowment for the Arts grant to study with John Blake for about 18 months, and she moved to New York in late 1991.

Carter worked with all kinds of bands, from a Cuban *charanga* orchestra to the String Trio of New York, a long-running progressive ensemble founded by bassist and metro Detroit native John Lindberg. The trio, which included James Emery on guitar, played jazz classics by Monk, Mingus, and others but sounded most vital addressing originals from within the group and by avant-garde composers Muhal Richard Abrams, Wadada Leo Smith, and Anthony Davis. Carter made five CDs in four years with the trio, and the experience challenged her to deal with extended violin techniques, graphic notation, and free improvisation. The brambly chamber music landscape and bracing violin solos heard on 1992's *Octagon* (Black Saint) will surprise anyone who only knows Carter's work in more conventional settings. "It really stretched my playing and thinking," she said.

Carter parlayed her rising profile with Straight Ahead into a solo contract with Atlantic in 1995. Her first two CDs were unapologetically commercial, aimed at the "smooth jazz" market. She reoriented to the acoustic mainstream with her leap to Verve in 1998. Her recordings were mostly high-concept affairs. *Motor City Moments* (2000) features a revolving cast and program anchored in Detroit's popular and jazz traditions. *Paganini: After a Dream* (2003) deploys Jorge Calandrelli's string orchestra arrangements of classical themes; Carter performs on Niccolo Paganini's 1743 Guarneri de Gesu, owned by the city of Genoa, Italy. She was the first jazz musician invited to play the instrument, and her tone has never sounded more luscious. Still, the CD's moody reverie grows sleepy.

More recently, the projects have had greater weight and bite. The African-themed *Reverse Thread* (E1) from 2010 relied on a folkloric ensemble including guitar, accordion, and the kora, a West African string instrument. *Southern Comfort* (Sony Classical) from 2014 collects music of the rural South and grew out of Carter's genealogical research. She discovered, for example, "Shoo-Rye" at the Library of Congress among field recordings from Alabama, the home of her paternal grandparents. The tune finds Carter in fiddling mode, blending evocatively with accordion and improvising with focus over roiling bass and drums. The music sounds at once contemporary and authentic to its source material.

As Carter made musical connections to her roots, she also began to fill the holes in her family tree. Her paternal grandfather died before she was born and all she knew was that he had been a coal miner in Alabama. She had never seen a photo of him. Whenever she asked aunts and uncles about him, they shut down the conversation by saying they didn't remember him. "When you get that kind of response more than a couple of times, you know there's definitely something more to it," Carter said. "I still had boxes from my mother's house that I hadn't unpacked. I opened one and right on top was a photograph of both my grandparents and all 14 of their children. That was huge. I finally started to get some information."

She discovered a dark family secret related to her grandfather—she declined to elaborate—but allowed that the information was cathartic. "It was an aha moment for me," she said. "It explained a lot about things I had experienced growing up. It helped me to understand and say, 'I don't have to carry this around anymore.'"

Carter's deep dive into her family and hospice work has led to musical and personal growth. She understands now that she's not competing with anyone but herself—in music or in life. A more nuanced range of emotion has settled into her music that you can hear on *Accentuate the Positive* (Okeh), an Ella Fitzgerald tribute released in 2017 that finds unexpected rewards amidst a postmodern parfait of soul, R & B, and rootsy grooves. Carter has also recently upped the ante on teaching, succeeding the late Geri Allen in 2018 as director of the New Jersey Performing Arts Center All-Female Residency, a camp for young women in jazz. At 56, Carter is in a different place than she was at 36.

“Every experience has some impact,” she said. “I used to be concerned about wowing the crowd—you gotta play this fast lick or whatever. But now I just want to play something that’s beautiful and that touches someone.”

Recommended Recordings

String Trio of New York, *Octagon* (Black Saint)
Regina Carter, *Freefall* (Verve)
Regina Carter, *Southern Comfort* (Sony)

Note

1. Since the National Endowment for the Arts began the Jazz Master awards in 1982, roughly 10% of the winners—18—have been Detroiters, a reflection of the city’s enduring influence. The 2023 class alone included three of multiple generations: Louis Hayes, Kenny Garrett, and Regina Carter.

The others: Barry Harris, Hank Jones (1989); Gerald Wilson (1990); Betty Carter (1992); Tommy Flanagan (1996); Milt Jackson (1997); Ron Carter (1998); Joe Henderson (1999); Donald Byrd (2000); Frank Foster (2002); Elvin Jones (2003); Kenny Burrell (2005); Curtis Fuller (2007); Yusef Lateef (2010); Sheila Jordan (2012).

Gerald Cleaver

THE BIG PICTURE

More than any other Detroit jazz export of his generation, drummer Gerald Cleaver has earned his reputation on the cutting edge. But if you ask Cleaver, who turned 62 in 2025, the secret of his originality, the first thing he'll tell you is that he's not trying to do anything new. To put it another way, Cleaver sees the big picture, and he's interested in everything except novelty.

"I'm just continuing in my personal fashion with what I grew up with," Cleaver said one summer afternoon in 2013 at a coffee shop in Manhattan. "I think that's all anybody really does. No matter what I'm playing, I'm looking for a connection to infinity. I think getting preoccupied with creating something new handicaps you from doing it. That's one of the main problems I have with younger musicians I've come into contact with while teaching. They don't particularly connect with what happened before. They want to do something new and different and want to play themselves, but I feel like you actually have to become intimate with the language before you can actually say something that makes sense."

This was all driven home for Cleaver years ago when he heard drummer Rashied Ali, best known for working with John Coltrane in the late, radical stage of the saxophonist's career. Cleaver said: "I shook his hand and said, 'Thank you so much for the music. That was some different shit you played.' He looked me in the eye and grabbed my hand with this intense handshake and said, 'Ain't nothing new under the sun.'"

Cleaver, who lived in New York for two decades before spending a few years in the San Francisco Bay Area, resettled overseas in Graz, Austria, in late 2024. Of medium build, Cleaver looks like a cool college professor. There's a quiet intensity about him, from penetrating eyes to his finely tuned conversation. He was dressed casually at the coffee shop, sporting stylish horn-rimmed Legre glasses and a sharp Diesel watch loaded with enough technology to launch missiles.

Drummer Gerald Cleaver performs with the Craig Taborn Trio including bassist Thomas Morgan at Roulette in Brooklyn on May 6, 2013 (Taborn, piano, not pictured). Photo by Claire Stefani.

Cleaver's refined merger of intellect and intuition, ear for color, pliable rhythmic pulse, and ability to steer a clear path through all manner of musical concepts have all earned him high status within free-jazz circles in New York. He's a favorite of exploratory musicians across a wide spectrum, recording with Roscoe Mitchell, Matthew Shipp, Craig Taborn, William Parker, Charles Lloyd, Miroslav Vitous, Michael Formanek, Tomasz Stanko, and Aruán Ortiz. The broader story is that Cleaver is a second-generation Detroit drummer. His father, John Cleaver Jr., played with many of the heroes from the city's golden age, and Gerald early on internalized the glories of Detroit's jazz tradition. The younger Cleaver's mainstream credentials, often overlooked, include Jeremy Pelt, Jacky Terrasson, and Rene Marie. He also played gigs around Detroit with bebop royalty Kenny Burrell, Tommy Flanagan, Barry Harris, and Marcus Belgrave.

Cleaver can play inside or outside, swing time or no time, standard forms or complete abstraction. Most rewarding is how he traverses the vast territory between the poles and how his experience in one idiom informs his choices in another. Strategies vary but shared truths connect the dots—feeling, gesture, structure, harmony, tension and release, dynamics, spontaneous dialogue, common roots, and mutual history.

In abstract settings like pianist Craig Taborn's celebrated *Chant* (ECM) from 2012, Cleaver creates a circular flow of rhythm. He seems untethered to steady metrical time yet still connected to a meta-groove with Taborn and bassist Thomas Morgan. On bassist Miroslav Vitous' *Remembering Weather Report* (ECM), Cleaver gives shape to amorphous structures and communal marriages of composition and improvisation. On the other hand, Cleaver states the basic time with a swinging cymbal beat on Jeremy Pelt's straight-ahead *Soul* (High Note) from 2011, but the drummer's malleable phrasing and textures echo his free playing. Cleaver illustrates the wide gulf between many left-of-center musicians who play *at* swing and those, like Cleaver, who *actually* swing.

"I think Gerald has an understanding, because of how solidly he owns his roots and how clearly he is able to see how all the roots connect to his own," said Taborn, who met Cleaver when they were students at the University of Michigan in Ann Arbor. "He has the sensitivity and solidity to be a great, supportive player. But as he has developed, and as we have both grown in the music, the aspect of challenge and creative risk have proven very important. These days I would say that Gerald is an unpredictable player in the best ways—always searching the moment for inspiration and not afraid to risk failures in seeking the greater rewards that come from such brave actions."

Cleaver's work as a bandleader and composer mirrors the breadth of his experience. He has had three primary outlets: Uncle June (his father's nickname) honors his family heritage and pursues an eclectic, inside-outside approach. Violet Hour, a more conventional sextet, references the hard-bop legacy of Detroit. Black Host, an avant-rock quintet, emerges from the pure-energy wing of free jazz. No matter what the setting, a conceptualist streak runs through Cleaver's music. Saxophonist Andrew Bishop, who teaches at the University of Michigan, recalled playing with Violet Hour at the Cornelia Street Café in New York. The band started a medium-tempo tune and Cleaver began playing quarter notes on his cymbal—ding, ding, ding, ding, ding, ding. He kept the minimalist pattern going for the entire number, never once playing a syncopated "da-ding." It was a crazy choice, yet Bishop said it created a hypnotically swinging groove. A friend told Bishop: "Gerald is the only drummer in New York with the courage to do that."

Born in Detroit on May 4, 1963, Cleaver grew up on the west side not far from the Blue Bird Inn, the site of so much modern jazz history. His childhood memories are of a city still streaked with homey grandeur. He could walk to a nearby bakery, and he bought his first watch at a nice jewelry shop in the neighborhood. His father made a living working for the city driving a truck but was on the scene as a professional drummer at night. His dad's work ethic and open mind remain inspirations. "He never stopped listening and never stopped buying stuff," said Cleaver. "I was fascinated with that because a lot of guys of my dad's generation did stop. Like I remember hanging out with my dad and he put on John Coltrane's *Cosmic Music*. I was like, 'What the hell is that?!' He was laughing at me, because it seemed so out. I put it on now and it doesn't seem out at all. He was a bebop baby checking out late Trane."

Cleaver's musical education was bifurcated. He sang in the school choir, took up the violin in elementary school, and switched to trumpet in junior high. At home, however, he played the drums from the age of five or six. He heard all the classic jazz records but also grew up with AM pop radio, Motown, James Brown, and the Beatles. Once when he was in elementary school his friends were talking about their favorite groups like the Jackson 5 and the Four Tops. Cleaver asked if they had ever heard of Yusef Lateef. (Sadly, no.) When he discovered the Beatles around age 11, his father bought him a gaggle of their records. Cleaver was particularly hooked by the quasi-Latin beat Ringo Starr plays on "I Feel Fine."

Cleaver was serious about the trumpet but technical difficulties and a predilection for the drums led to a switch as a senior at Cass Tech. Cleaver joined the jazz band and began going to jam sessions. His father's reputation helped pave his way into the scene, but all earnest newcomers were warmly embraced. "If you were trying, you were welcome, and people would help you," Cleaver said.

He went to Wayne State University, but this is where things went awry. He didn't click with the faculty or big-band-oriented jazz program. He lasted only a semester, contributing to a growing identity crisis. For five years he bounced around minimum-wage jobs and got married at 20. In 1987 he enrolled as a music education major at the University of Michigan, where fate brought him together with the Minneapolis-born Taborn, who had a vast record collection and introduced Cleaver to progressive voices like Oliver Lake, Muhal Richard Abrams, and others who played beyond formal conventions. Cleaver and Taborn formed a band that played weekly at Ann Arbor's Bird of Paradise, where they worked out ideas that remain part of their shared vocabulary.

"Gerald had a grounded approach and an inquisitive mind that melded nicely with my own sensibilities that were perhaps weighted in inverse proportion," Taborn said. "The path we were both on turns out to have been in many ways the same, but we met coming from slightly different places."

Cleaver began to assimilate the lessons of his favorite drummers—Tony Williams, Roy Haynes, Jack DeJohnette, Elvin Jones, Paul Motian, Philly Joe Jones, and Art Blakey, as well as Detroit stalwarts Roy Brooks, Lawrence Williams, George Goldsmith, Pistol Allen, and Cleaver's own father. He graduated from Michigan in 1992 and spent the next three years teaching at a middle school in Detroit. It was the hardest job he ever had, and Cleaver realized he was by temperament an artist, not a schoolteacher. Two major breaks rescued him in 1995: He was hired by the University of Michigan as a half-time jazz percussion professor, and he began an eight-year association with saxophonist and composer Roscoe Mitchell, a poet of sound and silence and an innovator and conceptualist of the first rank.

Mitchell—long associated with the Art Ensemble of Chicago and the Association for the Advancement of Creative Musicians—hired Cleaver on the recommendation of Detroit bassist Jaribu Shahid. Mitchell favors compositional detail, control, clarity, and whispered dynamics. He makes free jazz on speaking terms with contemporary classical music by Morton Feldman and John Cage. Cleaver estimated that 80% of the music he played with Mitchell was notated, with transparent lines between composition and improvisation.

Cleaver made four CDs with Mitchell, among them *Nine to Get Ready* (ECM) and *Song for My Sister* (Pi). Both feature nine-piece bands built around double rhythm sections with a Detroit flavor—Cleaver, Taborn, Shahid, and drummer Tani Tabbal on the ECM disc, with guitarist A. Spencer Barefield added on the Pi recording. The music ranges from the lushly scored ballad "For Lester B" to meticulous examinations of sound and color in which single notes are subject to subtle variation and gradation.

"It's the exact opposite of what people often think about free playing," said Cleaver. "Roscoe is a *composer*. It changed my life, the way he kept coming up with strategies. Big pieces, small pieces. He was always writing. He helped me understand how to play in a free context. I gained focus and stamina. I learned to pace myself and achieve the exact sounds I wanted, so nothing is random. One of the big lessons that Craig and I learned from Roscoe was how to be compositional in our improvisations—having a strong idea of how your input will impact the composition as a whole and direct it in a way that's clear, cogent and powerful. After a while you get to a place of incredible clarity. If you just opened the door on the concert you might not hear that, but if you allow yourself to surrender to it and accept it, then it becomes profound."

Cleaver relocated to New York in 2002 at age 39. By then he had split up with his first wife and had spent about a year touring with Jacky Terrasson, an Ahmad Jamal–influenced pianist with a flair for the dramatic. Cleaver taught elementary school for one semester in Brooklyn, and it took a couple of years before he earned a stable living from playing. Once the calls started coming, however, they never stopped. "He's just an all-around musician, someone with a deep understanding, who always brings a special quality to the music," said Mitchell.

Cleaver's flexibility made a memorable impression at the 2012 Detroit Jazz Festival, where he played three sets in 24 hours. He showed a command of flowing rhythm and texture with tenor saxophonist Ellery Eskelin's outward-bound organ trio, and he swung confidently with Detroit-bred tenor saxophonist Rick Margitza's mainstream quartet. Best of all was Cleaver's band Uncle June, a showcase for his chamber-like compositions and thematic ideas that encompass the Great Migration and his family's journey to Detroit. The core sextet was the same as on Cleaver's 2011 recording *Be It as I See It* (Fresh Sound)—top New York improvisers Tony Malaby on saxophones and bass clarinet, Drew Gress on bass, Mat Maneri on viola, and Taborn on keyboards, plus Ann Arbor multi-reedman Andrew Bishop. (There were also walk-on roles for guitar and vocals.)

Though many would classify the music as avant-garde, nothing Uncle June played at the festival was forbidding or hermetic. The music was pitched at listeners with open ears and a willingness to let the band take them on a trip. Cleaver's "Charles Street Quotidian" began with a long-breathed melody for flute and violin floating over rumbling piano, bass, and drums. A Malaby soprano saxophone solo of theatrical swirls emerged as the rhythm section locked into an ominous groove and viola and clarinet added color. A transition led to an alluring jazz waltz with attractive harmony. Elsewhere, Cleaver folded electronics, sampled text, rock rhythms, elementary harmony, and wild group improvisation into the music. Cleaver was driving the bus but also sharing the wheel.

Cleaver's brand of (mostly) swinging post-bop comes to the fore on Violet Hour's *Gerald Cleaver's Detroit* (Fresh Sound), a 2008 recording whose title and cover design—a map of his hometown—wink at *Yusef Lateef's Detroit* LP from 1969. The fresh marriage of solid grooves and freer passages inspires the players, including Detroit-born saxophonist JD Allen. Cleaver's Black Host is something else entirely: a plugged-in quintet specializing in frenetic collective improvisations, art-rock noise, and careening electric guitar and synthesizer textures. The intense fury sounds like the end of the world, except when Cleaver's serene melodies sound like world peace.

Back at the Manhattan coffee shop, Cleaver expressed frustration with the typecasting and divisions within the New York scene and the willful ignorance of "the other" among many within all camps. Detroit had it right all along, he argued, pointing to drummers Roy Brooks and Lawrence Williams. "You take somebody like Roy Brooks, who played with Horace Silver, but he would do all kinds of things," Cleaver said. "He was almost like a conceptual artist, because he'd set up these installations like having a guy dribbling a basketball, or he'd set up his monkey drummers—wind-up toys. Those things made an indelible mark on me. Lawrence too: He wrote *tons* of music. That was a huge inspiration."

I suggested that Detroit musicians like trumpeter Thad Jones and pianist Tommy Flanagan played with such rich personal expression and in-the-moment creativity that reductive ideas about style have little relevance. They might have been bebop musicians, but nobody played freer in terms of the flow of their improvisations and the sense of possibility.

"That's what I'm talking about with Lawrence and Roy," Cleaver responded. "They were free and decidedly in the tradition. People like Marcus Belgrave are so free *within* the harmony. That's what I grew up with. I didn't grow up with some fake, boxed-in version of jazz. I grew up with the real deal, and I'm fortunate. That's what I'm representing in the way I play. Detroit gave me the confidence to be myself."

Cleaver turned 62 in May 2025. He relocated to Graz, Austria in 2024.

Recommended Recordings

Miroslav Vitous, *Remembering Weather Report*
Gerald Cleaver, *Be It as I See It* (Fresh Sound)
Craig Taborn, *Chant* (ECM)

Robert Hurst

PLATONIC IDEAL

Bassist Robert Hurst was only 15 when he started playing gigs around Detroit with Marcus Belgrave. The teen got schooled every night but not just on the bandstand. It takes a village to raise a jazz musician, and one reason Detroit has produced so many front-rank players is that the villagers are as hip as they come. The cognoscenti always reminded Hurst that even though he wasn't old enough to drive, he was already part of a Detroit jazz bass tradition including Paul Chambers, Ron Carter, and Doug Watkins. "Everyone let me know this was a bass town," Hurst said in 2011. "They'd say to me over and over, 'Paul Chambers, Ron Carter and Doug Watkins.'" He repeated the names, slapping his right hand into his left on the beat. "Paul Chambers. Ron Carter. Doug Watkins. That's all I heard growing up. It was this Mount Rushmore of people you needed to know."

Roughly 45 years later Hurst has earned his own spot in the pantheon of great Detroit bassists. Hurst, who turned 60 in 2024, approaches the Platonic ideal of a contemporary bassist. Fluent across a range of styles, he marries a fearsomely swinging pulse, espresso-rich tone, lucid ideas, virtuoso technique, and sweeping authority in matters of rhythm, harmony, melody, and form. "The bass is hard to play with total clarity because of the nature of the instrument, but Bob is one of the very best," said bassist Christian McBride. "You can understand every note he plays, even at fast tempos. That clarity applies to his thinking too, which is on a high level. If you can't think it, you can't play it."

Hurst made a splash early. He was 21 when he joined Wynton Marsalis in 1985, cementing his reputation with Tony Williams and Branford Marsalis in the late '80s and early '90s. Since then he's worked with everyone from Charles Lloyd, Greg Osby, Ravi Coltrane, and David Virelles to Paul McCartney, Barbra Streisand, Diana Krall, and Willie Nelson. Still, his career path has kept him largely under the radar of the jazz press and fans. Hurst spent eight lucrative seasons on television with the *Tonight Show*

Bassist Robert Hurst performs with Wynton Marsalis, *left*, with Marcus Belgrave sitting in with Marsalis' quartet in Detroit c. 1986. Photo by Pam Grady.

band from 1992 to 1999, followed by a period of freelancing based in Los Angeles. He returned to metro Detroit in 2008 to become a professor at the University of Michigan in Ann Arbor.

During the last decade, he has balanced teaching with extensive touring as a sideman and occasional gigs as a leader in New York. But most of his road work has been with star vocalist Diana Krall—the kind of Cadillac gig that has rewarded his bank account more than critical standing. Had Hurst remained in New York all these years, he certainly would have a higher profile, at least on record. Tom Lord's *The Jazz Discography*, for example, cites 153 separate sessions with Hurst through 2024, compared to 515 by bassist Peter Washington, a contemporary who has spent his entire career in New York. Hurst has issued seven recordings under his own name, but they haven't gotten the attention the best of them deserve.

Now Hurst is pushing for more visibility. He has attracted significantly more attention since starting to tour and record in 2024 with the critically acclaimed trio led by progressive pianist Kris Davis. Hurst also leads a dynamic sextet comprised of mostly young Detroiters, including some of his former students. His 2018 release, *Black Current Jam* (Dot Time Records), is the most satisfying of his career as a bandleader and composer. The music casts a wide net. Anyone who thinks of Hurst as wedded solely to acoustic jazz will be surprised by this music, which contains African, Caribbean, and Brazilian rhythms, mixed meters, funky contemporary beats, R & B and hip-hop allusions, electronics, vocals, politically minded spoken word, and no-nonsense improvisation. *Black Current Jam* distills an encyclopedia's worth of black music without sounding like a generic potpourri. "I just need a few gigs," Hurst said, laughing, in 2017. "I have a great band. But it's hard to book bands with unrecognized talent, partly because people in the industry and clubs prefer booking groups with known artists or VIP lineups."

Black Current Jam is *band* music. The ensembles and compositions make a greater overall impact than fireworks by individual soloists—though the populist scrim doesn't squelch meaningful improvisation. The optimistic "Detroit Day" opens with an acoustic bass ostinato that immediately gets your head bobbing, even as the phrase groupings deceptively hide the bar lines. The melody has a catchy African vibe that morphs into something closer to Brazilian carnival on the bridge. Vocalist Brendan Asante joins tenor saxophonist Rafael Leafar (Statin) as a second "horn" on the front line and carries the anthem-like lyric—"*Hey / It's Detroit day / It takes a village to raise one / This is the village I'm from.*" Statin and pianist Ian Finkelstein solo creatively, and drummer Nate Winn and percussionist Pepe Espinosa sound at once rooted and in motion.

Hurst kicks off "Albert Collins" with another driving ostinato, this time on electric bass. The feel suggests calypso-funk. The meter shifts between 4/4 and 9/8 yet feels as natural as breathing. The samba "Bela Bunda" reveals Hurst's ability to write a seductive melody, its lyricism amplified by elastic phrases and sequential harmony. There aren't many extended bass solos on the recording. Hurst tells his students their primary job as bassists is to always ask what they can do to make the music swing harder. "Sometimes I have to step up, but usually I like to stay out of the way and just keep it feeling good," he said. "That's what pays the mortgage."

Hurst's expansive music surprised his younger bandmates, who knew him primarily through his work with Branford Marsalis. "Bob's versatility is one of those things that shocked me but in a good way," said Winn. "He swings harder than anyone, but that's not all he does." The players also see him as role model. “He’s managed to make a good living as a jazz musician, and his life is like what I would want mine to be,” said Finkelstein, a U-M graduate. “He’s so renowned for his musicianship that he’s working nonstop. He’ll go play with Diana Krall, come back and teach, and he has the resources to finance his own projects and raise a family. His reputation affords him the ability to do whatever he wants. And he’s laid back and humble.”

Hurst lives with his wife, Jill, in a palatial home with cathedral ceilings in an upscale subdivision near Plymouth, about 10 miles east of campus and 35 miles west of downtown Detroit. The couple’s daughter is an undergraduate at U-M. Natural light floods the house, and African masks line the living room. Jill, a trained architect, contributed the drawings that grace the dining room. Hurst spent most of the summer of 2017 on the road with Diana Krall, but he had two weeks off in July, and one day he sat in his living room and spoke about his life and career. He wore casual slacks, T-shirt and sneakers. He is six foot three, handsomely mustached, with a sturdy build and fleshy cheeks. Jill, who manages her husband’s business affairs, talks at least twice as fast as he does, and at times he seems barely able to get in a word. But he respectfully waits his turn and then has his say. After 35 years of marriage—and 42 years as a couple—they are a team in every respect.

“I did my first record right when I started *The Tonight Show*, and I think if had been able to tour and really work a band, I would have more opportunities today as a bandleader,” Hurst said. “With Diana Krall, it’s a wonderful gig executed at an extraordinarily high level that uplifts me, my craft, and my family on many fronts. I appreciate all of the opportunities I’ve received from musicians who have sought me out.”

Robert Leslie Hurst III was born into a well-to-do family on October 4, 1964. His father, Robert Hurst II, rose from sales manager to become president of Michigan Bell and then president of Ameritech Network Services. He was a trailblazer, the first African American head of a local company as prominent as Michigan Bell. He died of a heart attack at 51 in 1994. His work ethic and sense of personal responsibility left a big imprint on his son. All the men in the family set an example. “Every male figure in my family owned their house—my grandfathers and uncles,” Hurst said. They owned their homes, and their thing was getting a Cadillac. To see everybody do that meant something to me.” That’s why Hurst had an IRA at age 20 and why, when he was making serious money on *The Tonight Show*, he had no trouble sidestepping Hollywood temptations.

"Bob is a well-studied person," Christian McBride said. "A lot of musicians don't have that kind of sophistication, but he balances that with a lot of street cred. He can talk politics, business. But you sit at the bar and he starts to feel comfortable and the needle starts to shift."

Hurst grew up listening to his parents' jazz LPs by Miles Davis, Modern Jazz Quartet, and the like, and his father taught him jazz was a glory of black culture. He started guitar lessons at 7, switching to electric bass at 9. The family moved briefly to Grand Rapids, returning to metro Detroit when Hurst was 12 and settling in the upscale suburb of Rochester north of Detroit. He studied acoustic bass with Dan Pliskow, a seasoned Detroit jazz musician. One day Marcus Belgrave came to Rochester High School for a master class and concert. Hurst, a precocious sophomore, asked if he could play a duet with him, choosing the Charlie Parker standard "Confirmation." Belgrave was stunned when Hurst played the technically demanding melody on the bass.

Belgrave asked Hurst's parents for permission to work with their son, who was soon rehearsing at the trumpeter's home all day and joining him on gigs. Belgrave considered Hurst the most naturally gifted of all the kids he mentored, and he pushed Hurst hard at times. On one job, for example, Belgrave called "Quasimodo," a Charlie Parker song based on the harmony of Gershwin's "Embraceable You." At 15, Hurst didn't know it: "Marcus came back and grabbed the bass and started pounding out the roots to 'Embraceable You.' It was a small bandstand, and I couldn't leave. I just had to stand there and look stupid." Many years later, Belgrave told him: "That's because I trusted you. I knew if I played it once, you'd get it."

Hurst was barely into his first year at Indiana University in Bloomington when Wynton Marsalis offered him a spot in his band; Hurst said his parents would have killed him had he left school so quickly. He stayed at IU three years, studying jazz with David Baker, as well as classical music. At 20, Hurst won a spot in the band Out of the Blue (OTB), a group of up-and-comers organized by Blue Note Records that also included Kenny Garrett, another Belgrave pupil from Detroit. The group's debut recording, *OTB* (1985), features two Hurst compositions. By the end of 1985, Hurst was recording with Marsalis' new quartet including Marcus Roberts on piano and Jeff "Tain" Watts on drums. Regarded by many as Marsalis' best band, it was certainly his most aggressive and liberated group, deep into the rhythmic and harmonic abstractions of Miles Davis' 1960s quintet that included Ron Carter. You can hear how much Hurst was influenced by Carter's architectural thinking on a trio of Marsalis records made for Columbia within 12 months in 1985–86—*J Mood, Standard Time, Vol. 1*, and *Live at Blues Alley*.

The play of tension and release—of spontaneously disguising the beat, harmony, or form of a song and resolving the disruptions convincingly—ignites this brand of post-bop. "Bob was a key, because his mind would instantly recognize the grouping we were working with and create a new pattern on the spot," Watts said. "He knew in his mind, 'OK, we're now in 5, so I have to resolve to the next chord in the middle of my pattern. And now how can I elaborate on it?'"

The speed and enunciation of Hurst's first recorded solos were eye-openers. McBride points to the rapid-fire improvisation that Hurst plays on "Autumn Leaves" on *Standard Time, Vol. 1* as a landmark that set a new standard for younger bassists. Worth noting too is Watts' clever metric-modulation arrangement of "Autumn Leaves" in which every bar of the melody changes meter up to the bridge by adding a beat—thus giving the impression of a train speeding out of control, only to reverse course and slow down during the last eight bars when beats are taken away. Hurst and Watts deepened their rapport working with Branford Marsalis. The live 1991 recording *Bloomington* (Columbia) shows what a commotion this obstreperous trio raised in performance.

Hurst's first two CDs as a leader were recorded in 1992–93 for Japanese DIW/Columbia. *Robert Hurst Presents Robert Hurst* adds Belgrave to the core Marsalis quartet. *One for Namesake* ditches the horns for a trio with Kirkland and drummer Elvin Jones. It's particularly valuable as one of only two trio recordings made by Kirkland, among the best pianists of his generation, who died at 43 in 1998. *Bob: A Palindrome* (Bebob), recorded in 2001 but not issued until 2013, documents Hurst's growing maturity with Marsalis and Bennie Maupin on reeds, Belgrave, Watts, pianist Robert Glasper, and percussionist Adam Rudolph. Hurst's compositions are meaty, particularly the 21-minute "Middle Passage Suite," a cathartic work that traces the voyage of a slave ship. On the fast waltz "3 for Lawrence," Hurst picks up the bow and plays an exceptional arco improvisation rich with melodic development. "Bob is a great technical bass player, but his focus isn't virtuosity," said Branford Marsalis. "His solos are conceptual. He doesn't play a boilerplate style."

QUESTION: *What did you like best about The Tonight Show?*
HURST: "Thursday—that was payday." (*laughs*)

When Jay Leno replaced Johnny Carson, Branford Marsalis took over the studio band and offered Hurst a spot. Hurst enjoyed the job at first, less so after Marsalis left in 1995. Leno liked him, and he became the arbiter for whether jokes that touched on race were funny or offensive; Hurst got a workout during the O. J. Simpson trial. "When Bob first got there, he practiced eight hours a day," said Jill Hurst. "He was committed to making sure that if someone like Dolly Parton came on and he had to play country or whatever, he played authentically. The checks came, but not without Bob doing his due diligence."

Not long after leaving the show, Hurst crossed paths with Lionel Loueke, the brilliant West African guitarist born in Benin. Hurst invited Loueke over to his house one day to play with him and an African drummer. Loueke suggested the trio tackle John Coltrane's "Giant Steps."

"That was the moment when I put it altogether—how to reconcile the harmonic complexities of jazz with the rhythmic complexities of African music," Hurst said. He demonstrated by singing "Giant Steps" along with interlocking African rhythms. "The song has lots of moving key centers, and we played them combining the 'Giant Steps' changes with the building rhythmic propulsion from African music. All those rhythmic elements go together: the four against the six, the six against the two, and all the possible variations that can happen."

Hurst began to write music that reflected his new understanding. He first documented his evolving concept on *Bob Ya Head* (Bebob), issued in 2010, and the music on *Black Current Jam* takes the ideas to another level of invention. The pieces of a larger statement have all come together in recent years. "I've got the music, and I've got the band," he said "I think jazz musicians for the most part get better and better, and it feels like I've put in the work. I'm ready."

Recommended Recordings

Wynton Marsalis, *Live at Blues Alley* (Columbia)
Kris Davis, *Run the Gauntlet* (Pyroclastic)
Robert Hurst, *Black Current Jam* (Dot Time Records)

Rodney Whitaker

FAMILY MAN

The Detroit-born bassist Rodney Whitaker, head of jazz studies at Michigan State University, sat in his office in East Lansing on a spring day in 2013 talking to a gangly 19-year-old trumpeter. The student, recently engaged and considering a transfer to MSU, asked about balancing family and a music career. "I, uh, heard you have a bunch of kids," he said sheepishly. Whitaker laughed. "I do have a tribe," he said. "When you have as many kids as I do, you can go to sleep with three in the house and wake up with six!"

Whitaker, who turned 57 in 2025, has seven children with his wife, Cookey. Married at 18, a father at 19, and on the road at 20, Whitaker is best known as an inexhaustibly swinging bassist with a mammoth-sized sound and an infectious personality as radiant as his playing. Extended tenures with Wynton Marsalis, Terence Blanchard, and Roy Hargrove, appearances on some 150 recordings, and countless A-list tours attest to his blue-chip status. Since 2000, however, he has also run the jazz studies department at MSU, building the program from almost nothing into a breeding ground for talent and a signature success for the university. The first tenured black music professor at MSU, he was also promoted to Distinguished Professor in 2013 at age 45—the youngest in MSU's history. Whitake was inducted into the prestigious American Academy of Arts and Sciences in 2024.

Most notable is how the strands of Whitaker's life merge into a single quilt. His Detroit roots, playing career, and commitment to teaching, family, and community have seeped into the marrow of the jazz program at MSU. Whitaker moves through life with an easygoing intelligence and charm that wins friends and influences people. "He's always been mature beyond his years," said Marsalis. "He was married young, and he and Cookey are still together. He's got a great deal of integrity, and he's very direct in his communication. There's no b.s. He's got the kind of personality that makes him a leader—that people want to follow."

Bassist Rodney Whitaker, his wife Cookey Whitaker, and five of their seven children (*left to right*): Garrison, Jamerson, Langston, Sarah, and Essence, in 2013 at Michigan State University. Photo by Ryan Garza / Detroit Free Press.

Whitaker explained to the young trumpeter in his office that being a musician with a family was no different than anything else in life: "We did whatever we had to do," he said. "When I was going to college at Wayne State University, I was working at a gas station and my wife was working for the Detroit board of education. When you start out playing music, you might have to have another job. That's the reality. When I was almost 20, I made a thousand bucks playing music one month when the average gig was paying 50 bucks; that's a lot of gigs. I started teaching lessons and my income jumped to $1,400 or $1,500 a month. Then I started getting opportunities to go on the road. Those were things I created. I networked. We didn't have Facebook. One night I was driving to a gig and heard Terence Blanchard and Donald Harrison interviewed on the radio. I pulled over at a pay phone and called the station and invited them to my gig. Donald came and heard me, and I ended up joining their band."

Whitaker had a lot on his plate the day he met with the trumpet student: A morning concert by his MSU big band at a Lansing school, a midday meeting with officials from a local jazz festival, an afternoon lesson, and an evening concert on campus. He squeezed in 45 minutes of practicing (Bach) and phone calls to his wife, a former musician who works for the jazz department as an adviser, logistician, and den mother to some 70 majors. Whitaker is a barrel-chested man with a welcoming grin and close-cropped mustache and beard. He has a corner office where there's a desk, a couch, an upright piano, and a bookshelf filled with jazz titles and books on leadership. On the wall are photos of MSU jazz faculty, vintage pictures of Detroit bassists Ron Carter and Paul Chambers, and framed teaching awards.

At 2:00 p.m., Louie Leager, a tall 20-year-old sophomore from Portland, Oregon, with a scraggly beard, arrived carrying his bass. Leager had been assigned a transcription of Ron Carter's bass lines on "Hesitation" from Wynton Marsalis' 1981 debut LP. Whitaker cued up the tune. It's a brightly paced swinger with a stop-and-go theme and "I Got Rhythm" harmonies. With no piano in the mix and drummer Tony Williams using brushes, the bass is easy to hear. Playing from memory, Leager shadowed Carter note-for-note for five choruses. Carter's lines are Bach-like in their clarity and voice leading. Whitaker studied his student's hands like a cat eyeing a canary. He stopped the music and asked, "What did you learn from the transcription?"

"Well, a bunch of killin' lines," responded Leager.

"What about the lines?"

"He introduces ideas early in the chorus and kind of carries them out later."

"So, he really completes his ideas, right?" Whitaker said. "What else?"

"I also learned that his notes are pretty much all at the same volume, they're all even, they all have the same attack and same duration."

"Right," responded Whitaker. "Swing involved straighter eighth notes at that time. If you accented 2 and 4 it would clash with the way Tony Williams is playing. Ron is playing what people think of as the modern way of walking. If you're playing with somebody that plays more like Tony Williams, then if you play like this it'll be compatible."

MSU's program is entrenched in the jazz tradition. Students must swing, play the blues, and master the standard repertoire. The school's profile would be considered conservative in some quarters, but Whitaker is concerned with transmitting the fundamental values that have sustained the music throughout its history and that he grew up with in Detroit. Before the jazz education boom of the 1970s and '80s, young musicians learned the language primarily on the bandstand and through apprenticeships with established leaders. But with the collapse of the club scene and disappearance of working bands crisscrossing the country, opportunities dwindled, leaving universities to take up the slack. Codifying improvisation and bringing a blues-based oral art into the classroom has pitfalls. The Jazz Education Industrial Complex has often been cast as a villain for (take your pick) emphasizing technique and imitation over individualized expression, trumpeting history over innovation or, conversely, promoting a do-your-own-thing mentality in place of discipline and tradition. These are complex issues, but a blanket condemnation is unfair and reductive. *Bad* jazz education creates problems, but the best teachers and schools avoid the quagmire.

The MSU program feels like jazz, because, as Whitaker put it, "We remember that it *is* jazz." Swing, blues, ear training, intuition, and learning from recordings and on the bandstand retain primacy. Faculty have high-level professional experience and a commitment to teaching, and not all lessons arrive in classrooms. It's common to see Whitaker or drummer Randy Gelispie—who spent time on the road with Wes Montgomery, Sonny Stitt, and others—holding court surrounded by students.

"After rehearsal Rodney would sometimes just hang out with us for an hour or two telling stories," said bassist Ben Williams, a 2007 graduate who won the 2009 Thelonious Monk International Bass Competition and toured and recorded with Pat Metheny. "He'd talk about music but also politics, religion, lots of things. You saw he understood the bigger picture—that music is a reflection of life, and that music is about more than locking yourself in the practice room and more than the notes. It's about relationships and connecting with other people."

At MSU, it's also about Detroit. Whitaker has imported the Detroit model of tradition, mentorship, and community into the university. "Each one, teach one," Whitaker said, repeating a favorite saying by pianist Kenn Cox, one of many Detroit veterans who guided his education. Marcus Belgrave took the same approach, having older students coach younger students at workshops. Whitaker has older students mentor younger ones in groups that play for university functions. "What we're really doing is teaching leadership through jazz," Whitaker said. "Our goal is to raise 1,000 people, who are going to raise 1,000 people, who are going to raise 1,000 people who are all going to go out and change the world. To make them better performers, we have to educate the whole person."

Whitaker and his wife consider students family. "When are you coming home?" is an MSU jazz motto and recruiting pitch. Ben Williams' mother, Bennie Barnes, remembered when she brought her 17-year-old son from Washington, D.C., to audition. Shortly after the audition began, Whitaker stepped out of the room and told her that her son was special. "Where are you staying?" Whitaker asked.

"A hotel in Lansing," Barnes replied.

"Cancel the reservation. I want you to come and stay with me and my family in Detroit. I've got a gig and I want you to come."

Whitaker invited Williams to sit in that night at an east side restaurant. "This young man is thinking of coming to Michigan State," he told the audience. "Should he come?" The house erupted in cheers. Game over. "I fell in love meeting Rodney, Cookey, and the children," said Barnes. "They were so generous and went so far out of their way. We immediately wrote off everyone else."

Rodney T. Whitaker was born February 22, 1968. The son of an autoworker, he started on violin at 7 and switched to bass at 13. The first day he was carrying the instrument home from school an older neighbor spotted him and ran outside to give him two LPs: Miles Davis' *Seven Steps to Heaven* (with Ron Carter) and John Coltrane's *Soultrane* (with Paul Chambers). "Both of these cats are from Detroit!" the man told Whitaker excitedly. "Both went to Cass Tech. Maybe you can go there when you get older. You're part of the legacy now!" The records were Whitaker's introduction to jazz. He put on *Soultrane* and was stunned by Chambers' articulate solo on "Good Bait." The next morning, he told his parents that he wanted to be a jazz bassist. You can still hear Chambers' influence in the melody and momentum of Whitaker's bass lines and his snazzy bebop solos.

Growing up in Detroit in the 1980s had its challenges. One day at age 14 Whitaker was walking to a rehearsal carrying an electric bass. A group of thugs approached ready to jump him. "Man," Whitaker said with conviction. "Is that what you really want to do—take my bass?!"

"Is that what that is?" one responded. "Hey, do you know 'Super Freak'?"

Whitaker got his bass out and played the Rick James hit. That led to requests for other funk and R & B tunes. From then on, whenever those hoods saw Whitaker in their neighborhood he had to sit on a porch and play a few tunes to guarantee safe passage.

Whitaker was soon practicing or rehearsing up to 10 hours a day. Trumpeter Herbie Williams, a former Motown session player who gigged with Charlie Parker in Boston, was a resident artist at Martin Luther King High

School and taught Whitaker harmony. The bassist joined Donald Washington's youth ensemble, Bird-Trane-Sco-Now!, whose members included budding saxophonist James Carter and a flute player named Monzola Harrell—nicknamed Cookey. Whitaker took lessons from Detroit Symphony Orchestra principal bassist Robert Gladstone and assistant principal Stephen Molina, and he studied jazz bass with Ralphe Armstrong. Whitaker spent a year at Wayne State, before hitting the road with Harrison and Blanchard in 1988.

When the co-leaders broke up, Whitaker stayed with Blanchard until 1991, followed by four years with trumpeter Roy Hargrove and seven years with Marsalis' Jazz at Lincoln Center Orchestra from 1995 to 2002. Whitaker said working with Marsalis was like graduate school, especially in terms of studying Duke Ellington, but it was not always a smooth ride. Whitaker's penchant for speaking his mind sometimes clashed with Marsalis' strong-willed personality. Still, the pair remain close. "Rodney has such a powerful, warm, and deep feeling when he plays that you want to connect with it, because it's so *for real*," said Marsalis.

Whitaker's discography grew swiftly, including dates with Johnny Griffin, Dianne Reeves, Orrin Evans, Clarence Penn, and Kenny Garrett. Of Whitaker's recordings under his own name, *Get Ready* and *Work to Do* on Mack Avenue in 2007–8 document a band co-led with drummer Carl Allen in which the marriage of straight-ahead fundamentals with Motown, pop, and gospel covers suggests 21st-century soul-jazz. *Ballads and Blues* (Criss Cross) is a casual 1998 blowing session with New Yorkers. Whitaker's energetic first recordings as a leader, *Children of the Light* and *Hidden Kingdom* (1995–96), on the Japanese label DIW, focus on Detroit players and composers. They shed light on undervalued locals like Kenn Cox, Francisco Mora, and Cassius Richmond.

Back on campus, Whitaker arrived around seven for the concert at Demonstration Hall, an armory-like structure. White music stands with "Be-Bop Spartans" across the front in green letters set the stage. Whitaker's band delivered a rousing set. The playing wasn't as virtuosic as some college bands, but the ensemble was expressive and swinging and soloists told stories. Whitaker began teaching adjunct at MSU in 1995. Jim Forger, dean of the College of Music, recognized his potential and put him in charge of jazz studies in 2000. "He had a family and was on the road 230 days a year and wanted to change his life and make a commitment to education," Forger said. "He embraced the notion that he could shape the faculty and program in a vision rooted in the city he loves."

Whitaker's gregarious personality and ability to read others were assets, but he was unpolished in an academic setting. Forger paired him with a mentor, Ruth Hamilton, an African American sociologist. Hamilton, who died in 2003, was an invaluable guide to campus politics, and she offered tough love forged on the front lines of the civil rights movement. "You know," she would say when Whitaker complained about obstacles or slights, "Martin Luther King got shot so you could have this job."

Roughly 30% of the jazz majors at MSU are African American in most years. That's a high figure compared to most programs and a by-product of aggressive nationwide recruiting, scholarship dollars, and a jazz faculty that's predominantly black. "A lot of black kids don't want to go to school where there's no black jazz faculty," he said. "They're not comfortable. It speaks to that whole thing of what makes jazz authentic. A lot of black people have been told this is black music and white people can't play it. That's not true, but that's what they've been told. Then you've got some white faculty who are jaded, because they've had black students before who refused to learn from them. Who wants to deal with that for four years? I have to teach a lot of black kids not to distrust white people. And I have to educate white faculty not to treat the black kids poorly or overlook them. A lot of white faculty don't realize that some black kids are terrified of being in this environment."

Whitaker mentioned a black student from Mississippi who grew up in a segregated environment. "He comes here and says, 'Man, it's all white people!' I tell him, 'If you want to be a citizen of the world, there's white people all over. If you want to play jazz and not deal with white people, you're not going to have a career.' In his environment he was sold this myth that it's just black people's music. Man, it's *American music!* Music doesn't have any color. I tell kids if you can *play*, then somebody is going to want to play with you."

After the concert, Whitaker and Cookey unwound at a campus hangout with cognac (him) and soft drinks (her). Cookey is a round-faced, light-skinned African American with an animated presence and a degree from the Detroit Business Institute. Her father was a bluesman named Chicago Pete. When they met as kids Whitaker almost looked past her because his tastes ran to darker skin. "I liked brown sugars," he said. Cookey rolled her eyes.

Their large family appears preordained. He was the youngest of eight children in his family; she was the oldest of eight in hers. Marriages are often a casualty of the jazz life, but the Whitakers are at 39 years and counting. They did what they had to do. Cookey managed the chaos at home while her husband was on the road. He still travels weekends and summers to do clinics, camps, perform or record. The return flights, however, are sweeter than ever. He has two sets of kids waiting for him—one at home and one at school. "Outside of being a family man," Whitaker said, "teaching is the most important thing I've done in my life."

Whitaker was inducted into the American Academy of Arts and Sciences in 2024. He turned 57 in February 2025.

Recommended Recordings

Roy Hargrove, *Of Kindred Souls* (Novus)
Rodney Whitaker, *Children of the Light* (DIW)
Kenny Garrett, *Pursuance* (Warner Bros.)

James Carter

VOLCANO

The packed house at the Blue Note in New York certainly got its money's worth on a June night in 2012 when saxophonist James Carter's Organ Trio blew the roof off the club. But what else is new? JC was on the set. One of the most celebrated jazz prodigies of recent vintage, the Detroit-born Carter plays like a volcano erupting. His a cappella tenor opened one set with a trilling long note loud and resonant enough to carry from Greenwich Village to Harlem. The note ended in a violent squawk that Carter choreographed with a whiplash snap of his upper body. He barked. He brayed. He played the blues. He used circular breathing—taking air through the nose without stopping the sound. Finally, Detroiters Gerard Gibbs on organ and Leonard King on drums entered, and the trio roared into "Winter Meeting," a swinging soul-jazz tune from the '60s.

Carter built a swaggering solo that referenced a big chunk of saxophone history—from the gruff vibrato and vocalizations of old school tenors Ben Webster and Eddie "Lockjaw" Davis, to frenzied squeals associated with free-jazz firebrand Albert Ayler. If the bar had been closer to the stage, Carter might have leapt up and walked it like an R & B saxophonist of yore. Carter's more-is-more aesthetic is not for everyone. He can turn into a circus in the blink of an eye. But if you're willing to surrender to the charisma of his virtuosity, and if his taste antennae are fully engaged, the results can be exhilarating. There's nobody like him.

Carter turned 56 in 2025. Forty years have passed since his days as a precocious 16-year-old man-child in Detroit, and 32 years have gone by since he recorded his astonishing debut as a leader in 1993, *JC on the Set* (DIW/Columbia). Much was made initially that his first champions and employers came from opposing philosophical camps: traditionalist Wynton Marsalis and avant-gardists Lester Bowie and Julius Hemphill. The historical sweep of Carter's playing was rare in a musician so young, as was his freakish facility on every size saxophone (and clarinet). If he was prone to showboating, well, he was young, gifted, and electrifying.

James Carter performs at Orchestra Hall in Detroit in March 2013. Photo by John Osler.

Carter remains a gunslinger, the kind of aggressive virtuoso and benevolent assassin who mows down friends and foes alike. He's the Toughest Tenor of his generation, a stylist of larger-than-life proportion. He belongs to a line of burly toned tenors who brought the manly countenance and swing-to-bop rhythms of Don Byas and Lockjaw Davis into a contemporary idiom. Like Bennie Wallace (b. 1946) and David Murray (b. 1955), Carter connects the dots between historical eras and personalized "inside" and "outside" vocabularies. And more than anyone else today, Carter channels the anarchic fervor that Rahsaan Roland Kirk once brought to bear on mainstream material. "I think James was probably born too late in that what he would love to be doing is killing other saxophonists in Kansas City in 1939 or on stage with Jazz at the Philharmonic in the '40s and '50s, duking it out with other great saxophonists," said producer Michael Cuscuna. "He is so good at that; it's his essence."

The challenges facing prodigies and virtuosos in any idiom is finding ways to edit, to move beyond the excesses of youth, and home in on an individual voice. One additional hurdle for Carter has been generational: He came of age as the apprentice system in jazz was collapsing, offering fewer opportunities for young musicians to tour regularly with a working band led by a master. Powered by major-label recording contracts, a lot of hotshots during the young lion era were thrust into leading bands before they were fully formed. Carter signed with Atlantic at the end of 1994 and became a feature attraction by age 26.

A talent and personality as big as his were always destined for stardom, but had he been born a generation or two earlier, he would have almost certainly acquired additional seasoning before striking out on his own. Carter did work early on with Bowie, Hemphill, Frank Lowe, Mingus Big Band, and the Jazz at Lincoln Center Orchestra, but these were not the extended gigs of yesteryear. It's intriguing to consider how a Duke Ellington or Charles Mingus might have framed Carter's outsized personality and panhistorical flexibility.

Carter demurs when asked if he considers himself born out of time. "I think there's an easy way of saying yes, but I'd have to say no," he said. "If I say yes, then that puts my particular influences at a particular time and freeze-dries them, as opposed to saying no, which would mean that these same influences have a deeper impact and relevancy that reverberates to this day."

Fair enough. Carter's playing *has* matured. He hasn't exactly mellowed, but he's wiser, more experienced, and his own man. At the Blue Note, he played more compact solos than in the past and revealed a more cogent sense of structure in his improvisations. The ballads offered heartfelt expression, and even a wild ride like Ronald Shannon Jackson's down-home "Aged Pain" found Carter's pyrotechnics on alto anchored to a coherent emotional arc. He divided his time between soprano, alto, and tenor. Absent were two basement register horns that he often plays—baritone sax and bass clarinet. He's also recorded on F mezzo saxophone, contrabass clarinet, and bass flute. "There's more refinement and space in my playing now," Carter said. "I'm a bit more lyrical in my eccentricities, if you will. I listen to a whole lot more vocalists, and the more I listen, the more I incorporate certain phonetic devices they use to make the language of a nonvocal instrument more palatable—where you can hear the vowels, lyrics or an implied lyric. The stories I'm trying to tell are more informed, as opposed to looking at a song from just a theoretical standpoint."

On the afternoon of Carter's Blue Note gig, he walked into Sam Ash Music on 48th Street in Manhattan with a wide grin and a tenor saxophone case slung over his shoulder. Well over six feet tall, Carter is a physically imposing man with an imperial presence and a voluble manner of speaking. Dressed in a baby-blue track suit and custom straw cap, he was a peacock in the city. Married with two children, Carter divides his time between living in Detroit and New York. At Sam Ash, a landmark instrument dealer and repair shop, Carter greeted every worker by name, before heading up the stairs to the inner sanctum where the repair staff works its magic. "Sometimes we lock the store and forget he's still here," a clerk said with a laugh.

Carter owns a world-class collection of rare vintage saxophones and other reed instruments, including exotica like a 100-year-old contrabass sarrusophone, a kind of saxophone-bassoon hybrid. He danced around the question of how many horns he owns, allowing that it was at least 100. He's always buying, selling, repairing. He started taking saxophones apart soon after learning to play them, and if his performing career ever tanks he could make his living as a repairman. Donald Washington, Carter's saxophone teacher and main mentor growing up, is one of the rare people to have seen the collection. "He opened that door, and they were stacked to the ceiling," said Washington. "I didn't think he had that many. You could hardly get in the room."

Carter needed a new cork for the neck of the tenor he had brought with him, a Selmer Super Balanced Action made around 1951 that he paid $4,300 for in 2000. He also wanted to check on the cost of gold-plating the keys of a dinged-up vintage baritone sax and silver-plating the rest of the horn. Behind the counter, Josh made a phone call: "Their price on the silver with the gold keys is $2,600." Carter raised an eyebrow: "So, that's just the plating, not even the collision work?" He paused, dubious: "That's one to grow on."

Once the neck cork was replaced, Carter settled onto a stool in a practice room at the back of the store and talked about growing up in Detroit and his affection for the city and its musicians. As he spoke, he casually assembled his tenor, playing it once to illustrate a point but otherwise letting it rest on his knee like an infant. Carter has always carried the banner for Detroit by stocking his touring bands and recordings with Detroit musicians, even when pressured by record companies and promoters to use "name" sidemen. Carter's first working band in the '90s was built around a left-of-center rhythm section consisting of homeboys Jaribu Shahid on bass and Tani Tabbal on drums, with Minnesota-born Craig Taborn, a newly minted graduate of the University of Michigan, on piano. The organ trio heard at the Blue Note was together for more than a decade, before another Detroiter, Alex White, replaced Leonard King on drums.

"Behind the scenes I've had to fight tooth and nail," Carter said. "I don't look at that like it's a feather in my cap. I look at it more as a necessity. I'm coming from the D, and I needed folks around me from the D. Spiritually and professionally, there are people in Detroit who have basically given their lives to the arts and left an indelible mark not only on my life but the others they've touched musically. In a world that's seriously changing, it's important to try and hold onto as much of what made your formative years both sweet and hip. At the same time, you have to look forward, because life and music always call for that."

Carter was born into a musical family on January 3, 1969. His mother played piano and violin, a brother played guitar with Parliament Funkadelic, and another brother sang in a soul band. Carter took up the saxophone at 11, but the big bang came a year later when he began studying with Washington, a school band director. Carter calls him Pops. "Pops always emphasized sound," Carter said. "That's basically your calling card. That's the first thing that's going to permeate somebody's core. If you don't have a sound, your ideas aren't going to mean anything."

Washington, who moved to Minneapolis in 1987, said that Carter, whom he nicknamed Mash, had music "in his blood." Every Saturday Pops would give him a lesson, and Mash would have it perfect by the following week. Washington stressed long-tone exercises to develop a robust sound, and he introduced Carter to improvisation. Carter practiced for hours on end and devoured records the way other kids binged on burgers. He played along with the Basie, Ellington, and Billie Holiday records he discovered at home. He borrowed LPs from others that covered the modernist waterfront.

Carter joined Washington's legendary youth ensemble, Bird-Trane-Sco-Now! The name was a contraction of saxophonists Charlie "Bird" Parker, John Coltrane, and Roscoe Mitchell. It's not unusual for junior high and high school students to play Parker and Coltrane, building blocks of the mainstream. But it's virtually unheard of for students so young to tackle group improvisation and exploratory strategies associated with avant-gardists like Mitchell and Sun Ra. "I didn't tell them that any particular music was better than any other," Washington said. "They got the whole spectrum. Mash didn't leave anybody out."

It's hard to imagine Carter ever needed extra encouragement to strut his stuff, but Washington recalled an early gig when Carter retreated inside of himself, playing too softly, afraid to put it all on the line. Washington lit into him. "I said, 'James, you're sucking in, man! Don't be sucking in!'" Washington broke into big laugh. "From that day on, he's never sucked in."

Washington's lessons transcended music. He taught students to respect their elders and members of the opposite sex. He made sure young men understood it was their responsibility to provide for their families. He taught them that not everybody was going to like what they did but their responsibility was to be honest and serious about their art and themselves. "If it wasn't for Pops, I would probably be a beaker-head scientist right now," Carter said.

He started attending the Blue Lake Fine Arts Camp in western Michigan at 14 and two summers later in 1985 toured Europe as a member of the camp's faculty band led by Marcus Belgrave. Carter practiced constantly on tour. He was forever listening to tapes on his Walkman, trying to figure out what some saxophonist was doing. Some nights he'd stay at it until three in the morning. Sometimes his roommate would find Carter asleep in bed with his horn and would have to carefully extract the instrument and put it away. Wynton Marsalis met Carter on a school visit in Detroit and invited him to play a handful of gigs in Washington, D.C., and elsewhere when he was still 16. Carter sat in with trumpeter Lester Bowie at the Detroit Institute of Arts in 1988. That same year Carter met Taborn, a college freshman, on a restaurant gig in downtown Detroit.

"James took it way out—and I followed him," Taborn said. "I'll never forget this. People are trying to eat, and on my first gig I meet this guy named James Carter and he starts to do James Carter things, this crazy stuff. I thought, 'Oh, I know the appropriate response.' I was drawing from reference points like Don Pullen, and we went from there. It was a completely inappropriate move on his part. But I thank him for it to this day. These people were, like, eating spaghetti. That was so vivid. I remember food sort of dropping out of people's mouths. But you always have to follow the music."

Carter moved to New York at age 21 in 1990 and began appearing on recordings a year later. His discography as a leader covers a lot of bases. There's an homage to the nicotine-stained music of Gypsy guitarist Django Reinhardt, a lovely Billie Holiday tribute with strings, a major classical concerto written for him by Roberto Sierra and commissioned by the Detroit Symphony Orchestra, an avant-funk record, and a CD recorded live at Baker's Keyboard Lounge in Detroit. It has never been easy to capture Carter's gestalt on record, but two CDs on Emarcy produced by Michael Cuscuna found a sweet spot between the excitement of his live performances and the judicious planning and discipline required to elevate a studio date into a larger statement: *Present Tense* (2007) coalesces around savvy material from obscure corners of the repertoire, four Carter originals, and a well-chosen cast—Detroit-based trumpeter Dwight Adams, pianist D. D. Jackson, and the vigorous but poised team of James Genus on bass and Victor Lewis on drums. The funk-driven *Heaven on Earth* (Half Note), a 2009 club recording in New York, is a cut above too; a dialed-in Carter meshes with the exhilarating band including guitarist Adam Rogers, organist John Medeski, bassist Christian McBride, and drummer Joey Baron.

Back at the Blue Note, Carter's trio hit hard the entire night. The elemental power of the organ and its grits 'n' gravy lineage suit the saxophonist's gutbucket temperament. Still, the highlight was a little-known romantic ballad by Don Byas called "Gloria." Carter's opening cadenza sneaked up on the tune. Aside from a growling multi-phonic—where Carter played two notes at once in a kind of playful love bite—he addressed the melody with a tender caress and virile emotion. Leonard King swept his brushes across the snare drum in a walking tempo, and Gerard Gibbs tastefully outlined the warm harmony on organ.

Carter's passionate vibrato, wide and deep, picked up intensity. As the tension built, you could feel the audience leaning forward, bracing for an explosion. But it never came. This time Carter played it cool, and the music sailed higher for it. With JC on the set, you've got to be ready for anything.

Recommended Recordings

James Carter, *Gardenias for Lady Day* (Columbia)
James Carter, *Present Tense* (Emarcy)
James Carter, *Heaven on Earth* (Half Note)

Karriem Riggins

DUAL IDENTITY

Two of Karriem Riggins' primary employers have been the champagne-and-caviar jazz singer Diana Krall and the celebrity rapper Common—two artists without much in common besides a boatload of Grammy Awards, a high tax bracket, and a fondness for the same Detroit-born drummer. Riggins, who turned 50 in 2025, is the rare musician to have achieved equal stature at the highest levels of straight-ahead jazz and hip-hop. These idioms have been speaking to each other at least since the early '90s, but there are still few bilingual players who have forged separate-but-equal identities as distinct as Riggins.

His résumé includes performing and recording with such jazz luminaries as Ray Brown, Mulgrew Miller, Roy Hargrove, Ravi Coltrane, Orrin Evans, and fellow Detroiters Geri Allen and Robert Hurst. Meanwhile, he has worked as a producer for the Roots, Slum Village, Erkykah Badu, Kanye West, and J Dilla. Riggins counts a Beatle among his credits, appearing on Paul McCartney's *Kisses on the Bottom*, and Riggins draws on myriad idioms backing Esperanza Spalding's 2016 crossover project *Emily's D+Evolution*. More recently, Riggins, Common, and pianist-producer Robert Glasper—who also enjoys dual citizenship in jazz and hip-hop / R & B circles—came together as August Greene and issued an eponymous recording in early 2018. "Karriem is a creative artist with such a broad range that there's no limit to what he can do," said Common. "Any genre you want to take him to he can handle. You know when somebody is born to do what they're doing, and he is."

Despite his hip-hop cred, Riggins fell first and hardest for jazz, and he views his place within Detroit's jazz legacy as both an honor and a responsibility. "Jazz is my calling," he said one night at the Carr Center in downtown Detroit in 2012. "I love the other stuff too, but it's a sidelight. Jazz is what I live for. I'm honoring those who came before me from this city."

Riggins was playing this night with a quartet in which he and Hurst joined two heavyweights from the East Coast—vibraphonist Steve Nelson

Drummer Karriem Riggins in front of his record collection, including an autographed Elvin Jones LP, at his metro Detroit home in 2013. Photo by Jarrad Henderson / Detroit Free Press.

and pianist Mulgrew Miller. Riggins wore black slacks, a black shirt, and a gray cardigan. He is a small, wiry man, trim, with a freckled face, goatee, and inviting smile. Quiet and reserved off the bandstand, he comes alive behind the drums. He draws an animated snap-crackle from his cymbals and snare drum, and the focused intent of his accents suggests targeted airstrikes. He often turns his head sideways to the band as if trying to hear more completely into its core.

There was nothing fancy about the quartet's repertoire. Evergreens like Herbie Hancock's "Dolphin Dance," Thelonious Monk's "Round Midnight," and Milt Jackson's "Bags' Groove" were cast in frames too casual to be called arrangements. A cynic or trend-spotter might have called the music old-fashioned. Yet this was no paint-by-numbers bebop. The foursome melded into a band, and the offhanded mastery and depth—the swing, spontaneity, blues, eloquence, and passion—forged a deep connection to the folklore of jazz. But the music also breathed the air of the 21st century.

Nothing sounded like it was under glass with a museum label next to it that read: "Jazz Music, 1965."

One set ended with "You and the Night and the Music" at a racehorse tempo with a juiced-up Latin vamp framing choruses that swung with reckless abandon. Riggins' red-hot cymbal beat drove the music forward. He started his own solo in timekeeping mode, continuing to swing his cymbal beat at modest volume as if accompanying a phantom soloist. Then he moved to the rest of his drum kit, expanding his dynamic range and organizing his rhythms into larger shapes. Faint echoes hovered of his idols—Philly Joe Jones, Elvin Jones, Tony Williams, Jimmy Cobb, Roy Haynes—but Riggins' testimony was his alone.

"Karriem was always a quick study," said Miller, who hired Riggins at 19. "He's a great listener, which is one of the key factors to being a great musician. I pointed out some things to him, because I had played with Art Blakey and Tony Williams, and he took those things to heart. He had to learn how to play the bass drum softly, what drummers call feathering, and he used to stumble on the high hat. But from the get-go, he could really swing. What I liked most about him besides that was that he had a natural creative spark. He was always trying to get inside of the music."

Not long after the Carr Center performance, Riggins met to talk about his life and career. He was near the end of a three-and-a-half-year period in which he had returned his base of operations to Detroit after extended stays in Los Angeles and New York. He enjoyed the more relaxed pace of Detroit, but he moved back to Los Angeles in 2013 to be closer to his son. He's now based in Atlanta. Steady work with Common and Krall and royalties from hip-hop productions have earned Riggins a comfortable lifestyle. He's been careful with his money, starting an IRA in his mid-20s on advice from bassist Ray Brown, who was as much a life coach as a musical mentor. The condominium that Riggins had bought in the wealthy suburb of Bloomfield Hills north of Detroit was undergoing renovations, so we met at my home. He walked in wearing vintage, oversized Cazal sunglasses from 1985, a flashy marker of old-school hip-hop. The latest Roy Haynes CD was on the stereo, and Riggins, without being told what he was hearing, cocked his ear. Haynes, 85 at the time of the recording, threw himself into a daredevil break. Riggins shook his head and smiled: "Roy—whew!"

Born August 25, 1975, Riggins was weaned on jazz. His father, Emmanuel Riggins (1942–2015) was a pianist and organist best known for appearing on a handful of recordings by guitarist Grant Green in the early '70s. Riggins grew up in Southfield, an inner-ring suburb. His father wasn't around much, but Riggins was able to witness rehearsals from time to time and heard classic records at home by Miles Davis and John Coltrane. He started showing interest in the drums at age three. After a brief flirtation with the trumpet at seven, he returned to the drums for good. Like Louis Hayes and Roy Brooks, two young-gun drummers in Detroit in the 1950s, Riggins was a teenage prodigy whose natural gifts were matched by a formidable work ethic. At 15, Riggins began playing with Marcus Belgrave, who taught him musical form and how melody and rhythm intersect. Belgrave had Riggins scat-sing melodies, catching all the syncopation, and showed him how a drummer delineates the form of a song.

"Marcus taught me how to play melodies on the drums," said Riggins. "Having that in mind when you play—that's knowing the music and how to be melodic as a drummer. Marcus is one of the most melodic trumpeters I've ever heard. Hearing his sound on his instrument taught me to try to have a warm sound on the drums."

Riggins never studied privately, but he played in marching band and drum corps in school. He reads music, but it's not a strong suit. Otherwise, he learned by listening, playing along with recordings and absorbing the essence of Detroit drummer Lawrence Williams, who favored a loose, triplet feeling that floated over the beat in the manner of Elvin Jones. Riggins also gravitated to music favored by his peers: hip-hop. He started a rap group in middle school, and he listened to Run-DMC, Public Enemy, early UTFO, and the Fat Boys. His jazz tastes put him at odds with most of his friends, though other young jazz musicians of his generation in Detroit—pianist Carlos McKinney and drummer Ali Jackson—were also listening across genres. Riggins heard jazz and hip-hop as part of a continuum of black music rooted in rhythmic grooves, dance music and personal expression. "I think the spirit was the same," he said.

Riggins left high school early at age 18 to pursue his musical career. His friend, drummer Greg Hutchinson, who was five years older and already making a name for himself with trumpeter Roy Hargrove, recommended Riggins to the legendary Detroit-bred singer Betty Carter. (Hutchinson later recommended Riggins to both Hargrove and Ray Brown.) Riggins played with Carter for two nights in 1993 at a young talent showcase in Brooklyn and two more nights with her at the Apollo Theatre. His name got around fast, and he settled into New York. He roomed briefly with Orrin Evans, a pianist his age from Philadelphia.

"What I liked about Karriem as a person is what I liked about him musically," Evans said. "The support, the camaraderie. With those things you can't help but swing. It's always about the greater good with Karriem. If there was a bass player that wasn't happening, Karriem wasn't the one who'd complain. He'd say, 'How do I make this groove? How do I make the group sound good?' With Karriem it feels like everything's going to be all right."

Riggins went to a club one night to hear Mulgrew Miller, whose pedigree and versatility made him one of the most recorded musicians of his generation. Riggins introduced himself: "I'm Karriem. I'm a drummer from Detroit. I love your music, and I'd love to play with you." Miller set up a rehearsal, and Riggins soon joined Miller's trio. The relationship lasted on and off until the pianist's death in 2013 and yielded four satisfying recordings. Miller's *Getting to Know You* (RCA Novus) from 1995 with bassist Richie Goods and percussionists Big Black and Steve Kroon was Riggins' coming-out party on CD. He plays with exceptional maturity for a 19-year-old drummer, handling tricky rhythmic and tempo shifts on "Sweet Sioux" with an instinctual musicianship that you can't teach. "With Mulgrew I learned to be grounded," said Riggins. "He has such deep respect for the music. He goes into like a trance when he plays, and I learned that it's like musical meditation. That's when I really started to dig deep when I played."

In the mid-'90s Riggins started working with Hargrove's vigorous ensemble, but by 1998 he was with the Ray Brown Trio, which put him on the bandstand with one of the all-time great bassists. Brown played with a gargantuan sound that rode the front of the beat with such galvanic force that you either hopped on board or got run over. The arrangements were scripted like big-band charts. Riggins listened to the Count Basie Orchestra to prep for the gig, and for the next three years played countless press rolls and cymbal crashes. "Ray was the strongest bass player I ever played with in my life," Riggins said. "He would always bring his A-plus game. There was never a weak night. He would play golf all day and still come to the gig and be burning. And he was like 74."

One of Riggins' first gigs with Brown was a high-profile engagement at the Blue Note in New York in November 1998 that included Oscar Peterson on piano and Detroiter Milt Jackson on vibes. Riggins was about 50 years younger than everyone else. He plays with the confidence of a peer on the recordings issued from the engagement on Telarc, but inside his stomach was in knots on opening night. "I was so nervous I left my cymbals at the hotel," Riggins said. "I got to the gig, and I didn't have my cymbals. I'm getting to the drums like 10 minutes before the hit, and I'm looking on stage and I'm like, 'Aw, there's no cymbals.' I didn't tell anyone, because I didn't want Ray to freak. I called my sister at the hotel and said, 'Please just jump in a cab and rush these cymbals over here.' She made it about a minute before were supposed to go on stage and play. I said, 'I don't want to lose this gig; I just got *on* this gig!'"

Riggins' tenure with Brown is well-documented on *Live at Starbucks* (Telarc) from 1999 with Geoff Keezer on piano, but the party came to a somber end with Brown's death at age 75 in 2002. He died in his sleep at an Indianapolis hotel. "He played golf that day and he was going to meet us at the gig," Riggins said. "He was always early. We thought maybe he overslept, but finally we knew something was wrong. I went to the hotel and they had to break the door down. The pianist Larry Fuller and I were there. It was unreal. It was one of the saddest days of my life."

Even before Brown's death, Riggins had been spending more time in the hip-hop world. He met Common in Chicago around 1995, when the rapper, still something of an underground figure (and jazz fan), came to the Jazz Showcase to hear Hargrove's band. Riggins already knew who he was. "I was honored that he knew my music," Common said. They became friends and Riggins began playing drums with Common in 1996. Riggins soon bought his first drum machine-sampler and began creating his own beats—the musical accompaniment for hip-hop songs.

Riggins brings a sophisticated musical sensibility to the work, layering samples from an expansive universe of genres—jazz, funk, fusion, R & B, Brazilian—in ways that create sonic landscapes with unusual rhythmic displacements and meters that leave the scent of improvisation in the air. His approach grows out of J Dilla, the influential producer from Detroit and another hip-hop artist on speaking terms with jazz. It was Common who introduced Riggins to Dilla. The two grew so close that before Dilla's death from a rare blood disease at age 32 in 2006, he entrusted Riggins to finish production on what became the posthumously released album *The Shining*.

As in his jazz playing, Riggins can go in a lot of different directions as a producer, from the edgy bass-and-drums minimalism of "The Clapper" with Dilla (2001) to the smooth neo-soul of "Play Your Cards Right" with Common (2007). For Riggins it all boils down to the groove and finding the pocket. "People call it hip-hop, but it's really just funk music," he said, singling out James Brown and his drummer, Clyde Stubblefield. "It's all James Brown influenced. That's how I hear it. He's the godfather of soul and the godfather of hip-hop."

Riggins has experimented with melding the two sides of his personality into a single band, though his concepts remain a work in progress. He led a quintet at the 2009 Detroit Jazz Festival that included Geri Allen, Robert Hurst, vibraphonist Warren Wolf, and DJ Pete Rock on turntables. Some tunes were post-bop burners; others were pure hip-hop with rappers from Slum Village. The high quality of all the music softened the aesthetic whiplash but didn't eliminate it. However, when Riggins brought a new quintet to the 2013 festival with Orrin Evans and DJ Dummy, the electronics, improvisation, and disparate grooves melded into something more organic. An artist-in-residence at the 2023 Detroit Jazz Festival, Riggins' marriage of jazz and hip-hop continued to mature. The August Greene collaboration with Common and Glasper is hip-hop, but its rhythmic and improvisational subtleties would not exist without jazz in its DNA.

Riggins' albums as a leader compile his creative hip-hop beats; *To the Jungle* (2024) is a particularly kaleidoscopic example. His 2025 single, *Long Live J Dilla*, with rappers Westside Gunn and Busta Rhymes, honors his fallen friend with an alluring groove both breezy and beguiling. Riggins also produced most of Common's acclaimed *Black America Again* (2016). On the jazz front, Riggins highlights Orrin Evans' exceptional *The Evolution of Oneself* (2014), an adventurous post-bop date with Christian McBride on bass. The music is cinematic in its flow of diverse rhythm and walk-on spots for guitar and vocals. Japanese pianist Junko Onishi's arresting *Jatroit* (2019), reaches orbit on the Detroit-powered fuel of Robert Hurst's bass and Riggins' drums.

Riggins, who started working with Diana Krall in 2005, still plays with her occasionally and holds her musicianship in high regard. It may be a long way from Krall's *Turn Up the Quiet* to Common's *Black America Again* to Evans' *The Evolution of Oneself*, but Riggins, a 21st-century Detroiter, makes the journey seem as simple as walking from one room of a house into another.

Recommended Recordings

Mulgrew Miller, *The Sequel* (Max Jazz)
Orrin Evans, *The Evolution of Oneself* (Smoke Sessions)
August Greene, *August Greene* (August Greene)

PART SIX

Tradition and Transition in the 21st Century

Michael Malis and Marcus Elliot perform at the 2017 Detroit Jazz Festival on Labor Day weekend. Photo by John Osler.

Opening Chorus

In late 2017, saxophonist Marcus Elliot and pianist Michael Malis played a series of concerts in Detroit and environs to celebrate the release of their terrific duet recording *Balance* (Polyfold). In their late 20s at the time of the concerts, Elliot and Malis are among the most compelling Detroit jazz musicians of their generation. Their high level of artistry underscores the truism that Detroit's jazz legacy remains a *living* tradition.

At the duo's concert at the Kerrytown Concert House in Ann Arbor, their original material traversed the landscape of contemporary forms and strategies: meditative ballads, odd-meter romps, static modality, vamps, ostinatos, songful melody, free improvisation, multisection compositions, sophisticated harmony, and swing. Malis' "Serpent's Serpent" developed from an exotic piano scale, rising and falling like lapping waves. Elliot's incantatory "The Mediator" married a swirling 6/8 unison theme with a mischievous bridge that slipped into 7/8. The melody spun into improvised counterpoint and dialogue. Elliot's tone on tenor and soprano was warm, resonant, and round, and his solos were less concerned with showing off his knowledge of harmony than crafting melodies that communicated directly to listeners. Malis' supple technique and flexible attack was by turn sumptuous, splashy, or spikey. Both players projected a forward-leaning edge while honoring the markers of Detroit jazz since the 1950s—bebop roots, craftmanship, an intelligent and eloquent flow of melody and harmony, and an affinity for the blues. Their Detroit lineage manifested most clearly on "No. 3," a fast, invigorating waltz with a 4/4 bridge by the late Detroit drummer and composer Lawrence Williams. The song is a favorite among Detroiters, because Marcus Belgrave played it and Geri Allen recorded it. Elliot and Malis gave the piece a joyous, swinging ride.

Elliot and Malis grew up mentored by Belgrave protégés like Allen, Rodney Whitaker, and bassist Marion Hayden—but they also worked professionally with Belgrave in the last years of the trumpeter's life. If Allen, Whitaker, Hayden, Robert Hurst, Regina Carter, and so many others are Belgrave's children, then Elliot and Malis are his grandchildren.

Present and Future

RALPHE ARMSTRONG, MARION HAYDEN, MICHAEL MALIS, MARCUS ELLIOT

Jazz in Detroit in the early 21st century must be understood in the context of both the music's celebrated legacy in the city and Detroit's troubled history as a shrinking city over the last 60 years. Contraction of the auto industry, systemic racism, government and private disinvestment, blight, crime, failing schools, ineffectual political leadership, corruption, regional disunity, and the Great Recession all led to a population exodus of epic proportion. Tax revenues fell, city debt exploded. Census estimates put Detroit's population as of 2025 at 645,705—down 65% from its high point of 1.85 million residents in 1950. The good news, however, is that for the first time since the 1950s, Detroit's population is increasing, having inched up by nearly 12,500 since 2021. About 78% of city residents were black as of 2020, a complete reversal from 1950, when about 83% were white. Detroit remains one of the poorest and most segregated cities in the country..

Detroit hit financial rock bottom in 2013, becoming the largest American city to file for bankruptcy. It faced $18 billion in debt and unfunded pension and health-care liabilities. By the end of 2014, however, the city had exited bankruptcy court, having shed its debt. A nascent renaissance, which had been percolating for years, shifted into higher gear. Since 2008, several billion dollars in private capital and hundreds of millions in philanthropic dollars have poured into the city. The comeback so far has been largely limited to the central core of the city, but there's an optimism about Detroit's future that has long been absent in the city's consciousness.

Like Detroit itself, the city's jazz musicians took their share of punches over the last half century, but the bullish feelings about the city have also found expression amid the jazz scene. One sign is that while the city is still graduating musicians to New York and elsewhere, accomplished young players like Marcus Elliot and Michael Malis have doubled down on the Motor City. They've found opportunities to work, teach, and develop professional relationships across a range of idioms in a city where the cost of living is a fraction of New York and the jazz legacy has bred a true feeling of community.

"This city will take care of you, and people will take care of you," said Elliot.

There are still more quality jazz musicians in Detroit than you can count—veterans with international reputations, seasoned foot soldiers, and promising newcomers. The jazz audience in Detroit remains robust, passionate, and discerning. Standards remain high. Several nightspots offer jazz nearly every night of the week—Cliff Bell's, Dirty Dog Jazz Café, Baker's Keyboard Lounge—and there are other venues where jazz of all kinds is part of the mix, including Trinosophes, which welcomes the avant-garde. The annual Detroit Jazz Festival, held downtown each Labor Day weekend, celebrated its 46th anniversary in 2025 as one of the city's signature cultural events and the largest free jazz festival in the world. Festival artistic director Chris Collins, a tenor saxophonist and director of jazz studies at Wayne State University, keeps the core jazz tradition and Detroit's legacy at the center of the event.

Significant philanthropic funds also flow to jazz in the city, including several million dollars annually from the Detroit Jazz Festival Foundation created by Gretchen Valade, an heir to the Carhartt clothing fortune and for the last two decades the financial angel behind the festival. Valade, who died at age 97, in 2022, had also owned Mack Avenue Records and the Dirty Dog Jazz Café, a fine dining restaurant and full- time jazz club in tony Grosse Pointe Farms about 10 miles east of downtown Detroit. In 2024, the Gretchen C. Valade Jazz Center—a 325-seat performance space and 120-seat nightclub dubbed Dee Dee Bridgewater's after the Michigan-raised singer—opened on the Wayne State University campus. The local Fred A. and Barbara M. Erb Family Foundation has also been giving hundreds of thousands of dollars annually to jazz education initiatives in Detroit since 2009. (The foundation's late benefactor, Fred Erb, made his fortune in the lumber business and loved jazz.)

Not all is rosy. The supply of deserving musicians exceeds demand, and clubs offering decent wages are few. Ultimately, Detroit is a midsize pond. Opportunities to regularly hear and play with the leading figures in the field and challenge oneself against the stiffest competition are still largely reserved to the biggest cities, particularly New York. The disappearance of music programs from Detroit schools, which seeded so much jazz greatness since the 1940s, is an ominous issue.

Cuts to music education programs began in the late 1970s and '80s as

Detroit's tax revenues shrank. Some schools hung on, nurturing musical excellence through the turn of the century. But even these programs were decimated when Detroit's beleaguered school system was under the control of state emergency management from 2009 to 2016. The *Detroit Free Press* reported in November 2017 that only 27% of the district's schools offered instrumental or vocal music classes. In recent years, the Detroit public schools' administration and board have made restoring music (and art) classes a priority and budgets have been rising. But even if the restoration can be sustained, the process will take years.

Recognizing the threat to Detroit's storied jazz history, a gaggle of nonprofit cultural institutions, universities, and foundations have made perpetuating jazz a priority. With funding from the Erb Foundation, organizations including the Detroit Symphony Orchestra, Michigan State University, Carr Center, Music Hall Center for the Performing Arts, and the Detroit Jazz Festival are investing in jazz education in the city. The initiatives include private lessons, improvisation and theory instruction, ensemble training, jazz appreciation, school residencies by leading Detroit jazz musicians, and fellowship dollars for advanced students and emerging professionals.

Historically, for every Detroit jazz musician who moved away and got famous, another stayed behind who played almost as well—sometimes just as well. They may not have had the temperament for New York. They may have had families that precluded leaving. They may have lacked a necessary final degree of skill, polish, or confidence. Whatever the reason, to paraphrase Detroit jazz historian Jim Gallert, it's the musicians who remain in Detroit that define the scene from generation to generation. Here are four snapshots of musicians living and working in Detroit in 2018. They represent flame keepers from two generations—improvisers, composers, bandleaders, and teachers whose diverse personalities, styles, priorities, and versatility embody the present and future of jazz in the city. As always, the Detroit tradition is regenerating itself, and these four players are in the thick of it.

Ralphe Armstrong

I was sitting at my desk at the *Detroit Free Press* one afternoon in 1998 when a call came from a man who launched into an excited pitch without identifying himself: "You should write about Ralphe Armstrong!" he bellowed. "He's from Detroit, and he's one of the best bass players in the world. He's played with John McLaughlin and the Mahavishnu Orchestra, Frank Zap-

Ralphe Armstrong leads his own band in 2013 at the Dirty Dog Jazz Café in Grosse Pointe Forms just outside of Detroit. Photo by John Osler.

pa, Jean-Luc Ponty, Herbie Hancock, Eddie Harris, Carlos Santana, Milt Jackson, Geri Allen, Kenny Burrell, Aretha Franklin, B. B. King. He plays acoustic bass, electric bass, jazz, funk, fusion, R & B, soul . . ." I finally cut him off: "Who *is* this?"

"This is Ralphe!"

It ain't bragging if it's true. Born in Detroit in 1956, Armstrong really is one of the best and most versatile bass players around—a fleet-fingered virtuoso on the acoustic and electric basses who can groove in any idiom and has the resume to prove it. He's also a character of Falstaffian proportion whose rakish humor and charisma comes tethered to sharp business instincts and a commitment to nurturing young musicians. Twice a week he's at Cass Tech, working with young bassists through a residency program spearheaded by the Detroit Jazz Festival. He's donated instruments and amps to the school and even given basses directly to talented students in need. "Don't trash young people," Armstrong said. "Help 'em! Pass it on. Ron Carter, James Jamerson, Ray McKinney, Ali Jackson—they all passed it to me, and I'm passing it on to others."

The son of blues musician Howard Armstrong, Ralphe took up the bass at age 7. He progressed at warp speed, traveling to Washington, D.C., at 13 to perform with the Miracles (of Motown fame). He studied classical bass at Cass Tech, spent summers at the prestigious Interlochen arts camp in northern Michigan, and took lessons with Ron Carter whenever the former Detroiter was in town.

One day in 1973, a 16-year-old Armstrong stopped by bassist Michael Henderson's house after school. Henderson, then working with Miles Davis, told Armstrong that friends in Connecticut needed a bass player for a project. Armstrong auditioned over the phone for a group that included drummer Narada Michael Walden. A few days later, Armstrong was on a plane bound for Hartford. Guitarist John McLaughlin heard him at a rehearsal, and in early 1974 Armstrong joined the Mahavishnu Orchestra, a defining band of the fusion era. He was 17.

Armstrong has always remained based in Detroit because the low cost of living allows a lifestyle he couldn't afford on the East or West Coasts—he resides in a high-rise on the river—and he likes the energy of his hometown. "This city has a helluva pulse," Armstrong said.

He divides his time between high-profile tours with James Carter and others and leading his own eclectic group around Detroit and on the road. He also holds down the bass chair at the long-running Thursday night jam sessions at Bert's Marketplace. Armstrong is always working an angle—

securing endorsement deals for instruments, hosting regional cable and streaming TV shows, making friends in high places. He took an online finance class to sharpen his knowledge. Armstrong knows his rights. In the '90s, the best-selling rap group Massive Attack sampled without permission his 1975 composition "Planetary Citizen," recorded by the Mahavishnu Orchestra. Armstrong sued multiple parties and won settlements totaling several hundred thousand dollars. Whether he's teaching, performing. or holding court in front of an audience with a mic in his hands, Armstrong elevates the scene.

"Ralphe brings a prestige to the city," said drummer Gayelynn McKinney. "And he's determined to give back. He's a Detroit gem."

Marion Hayden

Born in 1956, Marion Hayden has been a top-call bassist in Detroit for decades, working with Nancy Wilson, Hank Jones, Geri Allen, Doug Hammond, Barry Harris, Lenny White, and others. She stayed partly for family reasons and partly because her mentors offered experience in everything from ragtime to hard bop to experimental directions. "Detroit was the best jazz college you could go to," Hayden said. "I considered myself a student until my mentors started to leave the planet."

Hayden started studying cello in school at 9 and took up the bass at 12. Her father, who worked for the city's parks and recreation department, had a huge jazz record collection that captivated her. Hayden quickly began copying by ear bass lines by Ray Brown, Paul Chambers, and Sam Jones. Later she dug into Ron Carter's work. She spent two years at Cass Tech, but transferred to Henry Ford High School after her parents, especially her mom, a high school chemistry teacher, decided Hayden needed to focus more on academics.

Hayden took bass lessons from jazz veterans Ray McKinney and Will Austin and later studied with Stephen Molina of the Detroit Symphony. She met Marcus Belgrave when he was an artist-in-residence at Cass Tech. "He wouldn't always introduce us to music with a piece of paper," Hayden said. "He'd just sing a bass line to me, so not only would I get the notes but the inflection of the line. That's a deep and organic way to get music from somebody."

Hayden majored in journalism at the University of Michigan and minored in natural sciences. She studied etymology in graduate school at

Marion Hayden performs at the Dirty Dog Jazz Café in Grosse Pointe Farms just outside of Detroit in November 2012. Photo by John Osler.

Michigan State University, before landing a job with the state agriculture department as a field inspector. Meanwhile, she continued her jazz apprenticeship, working nights with top Detroit musicians such as Belgrave, Kenn Cox, Wendell Harrison, Donald Walden, Roy Brooks, Charles Boles, Buddy Budson, and Ursula Walker. She backed up visiting stars like Art Farmer, Charles McPherson, and Hank Jones. Hayden finally quit her day job in the early '90s, after she found herself calling in sick from airports on tour with the all-female Detroit band Straight Ahead. A good place to hear Hayden is Blue Note's 2015 compilation *Detroit Jazz City*. Her strong pulse, flexibility, and ability to do whatever is necessary to swing the band elevates a house rhythm section behind a diverse cast of Detroiters, including Belgrave, James Carter, Sheila Jordan, and A. Spencer Barefield.

Hayden teaches everywhere—at the MSU Community Music School in Detroit, in a Detroit elementary school as resident artist under the banner of the Detroit Jazz Festival, and U-M and Oakland University as adjunct faculty. She brings young musicians into her groups, championing the Detroit style of mentorship that transcends musical training and speaks to life coaching and sustaining a community. The Detroit-based Kresge Foundation recognized the sweep of her contributions with the 2025 Eminent Artist Award, a $10,000 prize. "I try to be an extension of that tradition," Hayden said. You're going to come to my house. When we're finished rehearsing we're going to eat and talk. We're going to have that kind of relationship, because that's what I had with people."

Michael Malis and Marcus Elliot

Born a year apart, Michael Malis and Marcus Elliot were both raised in suburban Detroit. Both received key training as members of the student jazz ensemble sponsored by the Detroit Symphony Orchestra—the only major symphony in the country to maintain jazz bands among its student ensembles. Both studied with Marcus Belgrave protégés in college and later apprenticed with Belgrave. Both were among the cofounders of Polyfold, a loose collective of young Detroit area composers and improvisers that winks at Detroit's history of self-determination. Both completed master's degrees in 2018—Malis in composition at Wayne State University and Elliot in improvisation at U-M—while remaining active on the jazz scene. As of 2025, Malis was working toward a doctorate in composition at U-M.

Born in 1988, Malis grew up in Grosse Pointe Park. He started piano lessons at age 5 and began composing and improvising in an informal manner right away. By the time he was 10, he had written incidental music for a school play. A local piano teacher, Carrie Roach, introduced him to jazz at 13 and began feeding him the theory lessons she was studying at Wayne State. Roach sent him to study with Detroit jazz pianist Bess Bonnier at age 14. A year later he joined the DSO's Civic Jazz Band, directed by Belgrave. After a couple months, Belgrave gave Malis a Nat Cole CD and told him to transcribe two tunes by ear. This was new to Malis; until then he was learning voicings from a method book. "That put me on the path of what it means to study this music in a legitimate way," Malis said. The DSO opened new cultural vistas for Malis—a white suburban kid of Greek-American descent—bringing him into contact with a far more diverse circle of people, principally African Americans.

Malis studied with Geri Allen at the University of Michigan and, after graduating with degrees in music and English, relocated from Ann Arbor to Detroit. He's since worked with Detroit veterans like Belgrave, trumpeter John Douglas, and bassists Jaribu Shahid and Marion Hayden. Malis was a charter member of Elliot's quartet, and out of that group emerged the pianist's own trio with peers Ben Rolston on bass and Stephen Boegehold on drums.

Though he doesn't sound like Allen, Malis is in the mold of his teacher in that he's comfortable accompanying a singer, swinging a standard, surging into post-bop territory, or playing free. His 2015 debut recording, *Lifted from the No of All Nothing* (Polyfold), features his trio in an intuitive, spontaneous environment, alert to dynamics and texture while balancing formal details and disciplined freedom. Before Rolston and Boegehold relocated to New York, the group toured the Midwest and East Coast, and Malis performed in New York in 2016 with a large ensemble under the baton of noted experimental composer, conductor, and drummer Tyshawn Sorey.

"I've been able to engage in a wide variety of activities in Detroit," Malis said. "I've been able to work, I've been able to tour, I've been able to do bebop gigs with Marcus Belgrave and crazy, experimental gigs with friends. I feel like being here I haven't had to force myself into one box."

Born in 1989, Elliot grew up in Milford, a town of roughly 6,000 people, located 50 minutes northwest of Detroit. His father was one of the first black computer programmers at Ford; his mother was an auditor at the post office. Elliot sang in choirs at school and church. He got a little Casio keyboard at age 4 and started on tenor saxophone at 11. He was mostly into hip-hop, R & B, and pop music, but his father was a jazz fan, so Elliot heard the music around the house. A friend told the 13-year-old Elliot about the DSO's Civic Jazz Band. Elliot went to hear a concert, and it changed his life.

There were almost no other African Americans living in Milford, and Elliot's only black friends were his cousins. But at the DSO he met a gaggle of talented young black kids already into jazz—an affirmation of his cultural identity. Then he heard the band—by now Rodney Whitaker had succeeded Belgrave as director—and was literally moved to tears. "I knew that I wanted to dedicate my life to this music," Elliot said.

He joined the DSO group shortly thereafter and started taking saxophone lessons with Diego Rivera, who taught at Michigan State University. Elliot's father started taking his son to Detroit jazz clubs like Baker's Keyboard Lounge and Bert's Marketplace, and Elliot began playing gigs in Detroit on weekends. By his junior year at MSU, he had worked his way into Belgrave's orbit. By osmosis, the trumpeter schooled him in blues and swing. "I had to learn to play the blues," said Elliot—unknowingly repeating the same words that Belgrave used to describe a lesson absorbed from Ray Charles.

"I was missing a stylistic thing that I couldn't connect to unless I checked out the blues," Elliot said. "I'm also talking about how your concept of time has a huge role in how you play music. Marcus' concept of time—with him being more than 50 years older—was a *lot* different than mine. I felt as if I couldn't hook up with him for at least a couple years. But gradually, I was able to slow myself down and get into the nuances and details of what he was doing. Once I started to do that, then some magic started to happen."

Elliot worked with Belgrave for about five years and now sounds like an old soul. He avoids clichés, and there's patience in Elliot's phrasing that reveals itself whether he's playing a Charlie Parker song or an abstract, contemporary piece. When Belgrave's all-Detroit band played at Dizzy's Club in New York in 2014, *New York Times* jazz critic Ben Ratliff praised Elliot and pianist Ian Finkelstein (another young Detroiter) as "convincing and confident, evolved in touch and tone, the kind of musicians New York would be lucky to have."

Elliot has traveled the world, from South Africa to Indonesia and Egypt, with another peer from metro Detroit, trumpeter Anthony Stanco, whose quintet has undertaken two extensive tours under the umbrella of the U.S. State Department. Back home, Elliot's quartet held down a once-a-week gig for four years at Cliff Bell's and released a terrific album, *When the City Meets the Sky* (Polyfold), in 2015. In late 2018, Elliot and Finkelstein (as Ian Fink) toured five European capitals with the Detroit-based electronic music artist Shigeto (Zachary Saginaw). For a time, Elliot also assumed the title of director of the DSO's Civic Jazz Ensembles, inheriting the position once held by his own mentors. "It's still a little strange when students say how much they've been inspired by me," he said. "But you want to talk about a payoff? What a gift. That's what Marcus Belgrave was always talking about."

Since 2020, a gaggle of additional young Detroiters, several of whom fit the definition of Marcus Belgrave's grandchildren—musicians mentored not only by Belgrave protégés but by Belgrave himself late in his life—have come to national attention. Their rising careers reinforce the ongoing vitality of Detroit's jazz legacy.

Bassist Endea Owens has become a television mainstay in the studio band for *The Late Show with Stephen Colbert*. She also leads own band, The Cookout, and founded the Community Cookout, a non-profit organization that provides meals and music to underserved neighborhoods in New York City. By spring 2025, drummer Kayvon Gordon was gaining impressive traction in New York, working at the Village Vanguard with bands led by pianist Sullivan Fortner and tenor saxophonist Nicole Glover.

Tenor saxophonist De'Sean Jones and pianist Ian Finklestein remain based in Detroit but perform with important contemporary bandleaders across genres like jazz and techno. Jones has toured widely and recorded with drummer Makaya McCraven. Finklestein has worked with such musicians as drummers Terri Lyne Carrington and Kassa Overall.

Recommended Recordings

Ralphe Armstrong

Mahavishnu Orchestra, *Inner Worlds* (Columbia)
Eddie Harris, *Eddie Who?* (Timeless)
Ralphe Armstrong, *Detroit Rising* (Rack 'em Up Records)

Marion Hayden

Various artists, *Detroit Jazz City* (Blue Note)
Doug Hammond, *It's Born* (JPC/CDBY)
Marion Hayden, *Visions* (Equinox Mansion)

Marcus Elliot / Michael Malis

Marcus Elliot Quartet, *When the City Meets the Sky* (Polyfold)
Michael Malis Trio, *Lifted from the No of All Nothing* (Polyfold)
Marcus Elliot and Michael Malis, *Balance* (Polyfold)

Coda

One weeknight in January 2018 at the Carr Center in downtown Detroit, the Gathering Orchestra, comprised of 15 young professionals and students, worked through arrangements by Thad Jones. The region's major collegiate jazz programs were represented in the band, as were several of the scene's rising stars, among them Marcus Elliot, Ian Finkelstein, and Anthony Stanco. There was also a veteran Detroiter sitting in each section to coach the younger players. The musicians ranged from their late teens to late 20s. Most were African American, and there were two women. Rodney Whitaker directed the band.

The Gathering was Geri Allen's idea, hatched during her brief tenure as artistic director of the Carr Center. Her vision was to create a training orchestra to provide apprenticeship opportunities that mirror those she received growing up in Detroit. Funded by the Erb Foundation, the Gathering meets several times a year for weeklong residencies to rehearse and perform. The players each receive stipends of $1,500 per week—significant pay for students and those making the often-fraught transition into full-time life as a musician.

The band launched into "The Little Pixie," Jones' challenging piece that turns on prodigious call-and-response between brass and reeds. Whenever the band started to rush, Whitaker clapped calmly but deliberately on beats two and four, and the ensemble slipped back into the pocket. The Grammy and Tony Award–winning Dee Dee Bridgewater, who sang with the Thad Jones–Mel Lewis Jazz Orchestra in the 1970s, was also in the house. Bridgewater, dressed in chic black with her small white dog at her side, was one of two high-profile Allen friends who took over as co-artistic directors of the Carr Center after Allen's death in 2017.[1] She pushed the band to play with a greater range of louds and softs. "If you don't play with dynamics, it's hard for the audience to absorb the music," she said.

After another stab at the opening choruses, Vincent Chandler—a Wayne State professor and the trombone section mentor—told the group, "It's the accents that make the music speak, not the force with which you play." Chandler's words were like turning on a light switch. The band suddenly radiated swinging intensity and nuanced feeling. It sounded worthy of Detroit, and after the rehearsal Whitaker summed it all up: "That's what we do in Detroit. We make cars, and we make jazz musicians."

Note

1. Drummer Terri Lyne Carrington was co-artistic director with Bridgewater.

APPENDIX A

JAZZ MUSICIANS FROM DETROIT

Space limitations prevent the inclusion of every notable jazz musician from Detroit, but this list of more than 170 captures the breadth of the city's contributions. Not all were born in Detroit or environs, but all were nurtured by the city's scene or made contributions to it, even if their time in the city was brief.

Bandleaders

Jean Goldkette, b. Mar. 18, 1899, Valenciennes, France; d. Mar. 24, 1962, Santa Barbara, Calif.
Don Redman, b. July 29, 1900, Piedmont, W.Va.; d. Nov. 11, 1964, New York City

Trumpet

Howard McGhee, b. Mar. 3, 1918, Tulsa, Okla.; d. July 17, 1987, New York City
Gerald Wilson, b. Sept. 4, 1918, Shelby, Miss.; d. Sept. 8, 2014, Los Angeles
Wilbur Harden, b. Dec. 31, 1924, Birmingham, Ala.; d. June 10, 1969, New York City
Clarence "Gene" Shaw, b. June 16, 1926, Detroit; d. Aug. 17, 1973, Los Angeles
Thad Jones, b. Mar. 23, 1928, Pontiac, Mich.; d. Aug. 20, 1986, Copenhagen, Denmark
Louis Smith, b. May 20, 1931, Memphis, Tenn.; d. Aug. 20, 2016, Ann Arbor, Mich.
Donald Byrd, b. Dec. 9, 1932, Detroit; d. Feb. 4, 2013, Dover, Del.
Marcus Belgrave, b. Chester, Pa., June 12, 1936; d. May 24, 2015, Ann Arbor, Mich.
Tom Saunders, b. Apr. 21, 1938; d. Feb. 13, 2010, metro Detroit
Johnny Trudell, b. May 11, 1939, Detroit; d. May 29, 2021, location unknown
Lonnie Hillyer, b. Monroe, Ga., Mar. 25, 1940; d. July 1, 1985, New York City
Charles Moore, b. Oct. 6, 1940, Sheffield, Ala.; d. May 30, 2014, Los Angeles
Walt Szymanski, b. July 8, 1954, Detroit

Rayse Biggs, b. May 3, 1960, Detroit
Walter White, b. June 1, 1963, Detroit
Jon-Erik Kellso, b. May 8, 1964, Dearborn, Mich.
Dwight Adams, b. Sept. 7, 1964, Detroit
Kris Johnson, b. Oct. 22, 1983, Detroit
Anthony Stanco, b. Aug. 5, 1989, Grosse Pointe, Mich.

Trombone

Bobby Byrne, b. Oct. 10, 1918, Columbus, Ohio; d. Nov. 25, 2006, Irvine, Calif.
Jimmy Wilkins, b. May 26, 1921, St. Louis, Mo.; d. Aug. 25, 2018, Las Vegas
Frank Rosolino, b. Aug. 20, 1926, Detroit; d. Nov. 27, 1978, Los Angeles
Charles Greenlee (Harneefan Majeed), b. May 24, 1927; d. Jan. 22, 1993, Springfield, Mass.
Curtis Fuller, b. Dec. 15, 1932, Detroit; d. May 8, 2021, Detroit
George Bohanon, b. Aug. 7, 1937, Detroit; d. Nov. 8, 2024, Los Angeles
Phil Ranelin, b. May 25, 1939, Indianapolis, Ind.
Vincent Chandler, b. Nov. 5, 1970, Detroit

Euphonium

Kiane Zawadi (Bernard McKinney) (also trombone), b. Nov. 26, 1932, Detroit
Brad Felt (also tuba), b. May 6, 1956, Royal Oak, Mich.; d. Oct. 6, 2011, Pontiac, Mich.

Alto Saxophone

Charles "Lefty" Edwards (also tenor saxophone), b. Apr. 7, 1927, Hamtramck, Mich.; d. July 11, 1994, Wayne, Mich.
Sonny Red (Sylvester Kyner), b. Dec. 12, 1932, Detroit; d. Mar. 20, 1981, Detroit
Charles McPherson, b. Joplin, Mo., July 24, 1939
Larry Nozero, b. Aug. 11, 1943, Detroit; d. February 19, 2005, Southfield, Mich.
Larry Smith, b. Aug. 19, 1943 Aliquippa, Pa.; d. May 6, 2023, location unknown
Kenny Garett, b. Oct. 9, 1960, Detroit

Tenor Saxophone

Sam Donahue, b. Mar. 18, 1918; d. Mar. 22, 1974, Reno, Nev.
Yusef Lateef (William Huddleston aka Bill Evans), b. Oct. 9, 1920, Chattanooga, Tenn.; d. Dec. 23, 2013, Shutesbury, Mass.
Wardell Gray, b. Feb. 13, 1921, Oklahoma City, Okla.; d. May 25, 1955, Las Vegas

George "Big Nick" Nicholas, b. Aug. 2, 1922, Lansing, Mich.; d. Oct. 29, 1997, New York City
Eli "Lucky" Thompson, b. June 16, 1924, Columbia, S.C.; d. July 30, 2005, Seattle, Wash.
Theodore "Teddy" Edwards, b. Apr. 26, 1924, Jackson, Miss.; d. Apr. 20, 2003, Los Angeles
Billy Mitchell, b. Nov. 3, 1926, Kansas City, Mo.; d. Apr. 18, 2001, Rockville Centre, N.Y.
Frank Foster, b. Sept. 21, 1928, Cincinnati, Ohio; d. July 26, 2011, Chesapeake, Va.
Charlie Gabriel (also clarinet), b. July 11, 1932, New Orleans
Joe Henderson, b. Apr. 24, 1937, Lima, Ohio; d. June 30, 2001, San Francisco
Donald Walden, b. July 12, 1938, St. Louis, Mo.; d. Apr. 6, 2008, Detroit
Bennie Maupin, b. Aug. 29, 1940, Detroit
Faruq Z. Bey (Jesse Davis), b. Feb. 4, 1942, Detroit; d. June 1, 2012, Detroit
Wendell Harrison, b. Oct. 1, 1942, Detroit
Allan Barnes, b. Sept. 27, 1949, Detroit; d. July 25, 2016, Detroit
Ralph M. Jones, b. Oct. 17, 1949, Detroit
David McMurray, b. Feb. 20, 1955, Detroit
Tim Ries, b. Aug. 15, 1959, Tecumseh, Mich.
Rick Margitza, b. Oct. 24, 1961, Detroit
Chris Collins, b. Aug. 12, 1964, Detroit
James Carter, b. Jan. 3, 1969, Detroit
JD Allen, b. Dec. 11, 1972, Detroit
Marcus Elliot, b. Nov. 16, 1989, Southfield, Mich.
Rafael Leafar (Statin), b. Jan. 21, 1990, Detroit

Baritone Saxophone

Marvin "Doc" Holladay, b. Jan. 30, 1929, Chanute, Kan.; d. Nov. 25, 2024, Manta, Ecuador
Pepper Adams, b. Oct. 8, 1930, Highland Park, Mich.; d. Sept. 10, 1986, New York City
Tate Houston, b. Nov. 30, 1934, Detroit; d. Oct. 18, 1974, Los Angeles
Alex Harding, b. Apr. 5, 1967, Detroit

Clarinet

Dave Bennett, b. May 18, 1984, Pontiac, Mich.

French Horn

Julius Watkins, b. Oct. 10, 1921, Detroit; d. Apr. 4, 1977, Short Hills, N.J.

Violin

Gwen Laster, b. Nov. 11, 1957, Detroit
Regina Carter, b. Aug. 6, 1962, Detroit

Guitar

Kenny Burrell, b. July 31, 1931, Detroit
James "Blood" Ulmer, b. Feb, 8, 1940, St. Matthews, S.C.
Ron English, b. Jan. 3, 1941, Ft. Wayne, Ind.
A. Spencer Barefield, b. May 27, 1953, Detroit
Earl Klugh, b. Sept. 16, 1953, Detroit
Perry Hughes, b. Dec. 3, 1953, Memphis, Tenn.
Randy Napoleon, b. May 30, 1978, Brooklyn, N.Y.

Vibraphone

Milt Jackson, b. Jan. 1, 1923, Detroit; d. Oct. 9, 1999, New York City
Abe Woodley (Nasir Hafiz), b. December 13, 1925, Detroit; d. May 1980 (date and place unknown)
Jack Brokensha, b. Jan. 5, 1926, Adelaide, Australia; d. Oct. 28, 2010, Sarasota, Fla.

Harp

Dorothy Ashby, b. Aug. 6, 1930, Detroit; d. Apr. 13, 1986, Santa Monica, Calif.

Accordion

Julien Labro, b. Sept. 17, 1980, Rodez, France

Piano

Bob Zurke, b. Jan. 7, 1912, Hamtramck, Mich.; d. Feb. 16, 1944, Los Angeles
Johnny Allen, b. Sept. 20, 1917, Uchee, Ala.; d. Jan. 29, 2014, Detroit
Ivelee Patrick "Pat" Flowers, b. Oct. 6, 1917, Detroit; d. Oct. 6, 2000, Detroit
Hank Jones, b. July 31, 1918, Vicksburg, Miss.; d. May 16, 2010, New York City

Willie Anderson, b. Mar. 3, 1924, Detroit; d. Apr. 15, 1971, Detroit
Will Davis, b. Feb. 17, 1926, Chicago; d. Mar. 23, 1984, Detroit
Bess Bonnier, b. May 26, 1928, Detroit; d. Oct. 6, 2011, Grosse Pointe, Mich.
Harold McKinney, b. July 4, 1928; d. June 20, 2001, Detroit
Barry Harris, b. Dec. 15, 1929, Detroit; d. Dec. 8, 2021, North Bergen, N.J.
Tommy Flanagan, b. Mar. 16, 1930; d. Nov. 16, 2001, New York City
Terry Pollard (also vibes), b. Aug. 15, 1931, Detroit; d. Dec. 16, 2009, New York City
Roland Hanna, b. Feb. 10, 1932, Detroit; d. Nov. 13, 2002, Harris, N.Y.
Theodore "Teddy" Harris (also saxophone), b. Aug. 27, 1934; d. Aug. 22, 2005, Detroit
Hugh Lawson, b. Mar. 12, 1935, Detroit; d. Mar. 11, White Plains, N.Y.
Kirk Lightsey, b. Feb. 15, 1937, Detroit
Alice (McLeod) Coltrane (also harp), b. Aug. 27, 1939, Detroit; d. Jan. 12, 2007, Los Angeles
Kenn Cox, b. Nov. 8, 1940, Detroit; d. Dec. 19, 2008, Detroit
Stanley Cowell, b. May 5, 1941, Toledo, Ohio
Bob Neloms, b. Mar. 2, 1942, Detroit; d. July 28, 2020, Royal Oak, Mich.
Emmanuel Riggins, b. Sept. 17, 1942, Yazoo City, Miss.; d. May 28, 2015, Cleveland, Ohio
Robert "Buddy" Budson, b. Feb. 19, 1945, Detroit
Kevin Toney, b. Apr. 23, 1953, Detroit
Gary Schunk, b. Sept. 27, 1953, Detroit; d. April 2, 2021, Redford, Mich.
Rod Williams, b. Apr. 15, 1954, Detroit
David Janeway, b. June 4, 1955, Rochester, N.Y.
Kamau Kenyatta (also saxophone), June 27, 1955, Detroit
Johnny O'Neal, b. Oct. 10, 1956, Detroit
Geri Allen, b. June 12, 1957, Pontiac, Mich.; d. June 27, 2017, Philadelphia
Carlos McKinney, b. Jan. 10, 1978, Detroit
Mike Jellick, b. Aug. 31, 1980, New Delhi, India
Michael Malis, b. July 7, 1988, Grosse Pointe, Mich.
Ian Finkelstein, b. Mar. 29, 1990, Royal Oak, Mich.

Organ

Milt Buckner, b. July 10, 1915, St. Louis, Mo.; d. July 27, 1977, Chicago
Lyman Woodard, b. Mar. 3, 1942, Owosso, Mich.; d. March 3, 2009, Owasso, Mich.
Gerard Gibbs, b. Nov. 16, 1967, Detroit

Bass

Al McKibbon, b. Jan. 1, 1919, Chicago; d. July 29, 2005, Los Angeles
Major Holley, b. July 10, 1924, Detroit; d. Oct. 25, 1990, Maplewood, N.J.
Ernie Farrow, b. Nov. 13, 1928, Huntington W.Va.; d. July 14, 1969, Detroit
Gene Taylor, b. Mar. 19, 1929, Toledo, Ohio; d. Dec. 22, 2001, Sarasota, Fla.
Will Austin, b. Feb. 22, 1932, St. Louis, Mo.; d. April 28, 2020, location unknown

Ray McKinney, b. Mar. 28, 1931, Detroit; d. Aug. 3, 2004, Detroit
Ali Jackson Sr., b. Mar. 29, 1931, Detroit; d. 1987
Herman Wright b. June 20, 1932, Detroit; d. June 6, 25, 1997, New York
Doug Watkins (also cello), b. Mar. 2, 1934, Detroit; d. Feb. 5, 1962, Holbrook, Az.
Paul Chambers, b. Apr. 22, 1935, Pittsburgh; d. Jan. 4, 1969, New York
Cecil McBee, b. May 19, 1935, Tulsa, Okla.
Ron Brooks, b. Oct. 3, 1936, Chicago
Ron Carter, b. May 4, 1937, Ferndale, Mich.
John Dana, b. Sept. 20, 1941, Saginaw, Mich.; d. Oct 11, 2018, Detroit
Cameron Brown, b. Dec. 21, 1945, Detroit
Michael Henderson, b. July 7, 1951, Yazoo City, Miss.
Jaribu Shahid, b. Sept. 11, 1955, Detroit
Ralphe Armstrong, b. May 17, 1956, Detroit
Marion Hayden, b. Oct. 13, 1956, Detroit
Robert "Bob" Hurst, b. Oct. 4, 1964, Detroit
Rodney Whitaker, b. Feb. 22, 1968, Detroit
Tassili Bond, b. Feb. 26, 1970, Westland; d. Nov. 5, 2016, New York City
Noah Jackson, b. July 31, 1988, Detroit
Endea Owens, b. June 12, 1991, Detroit
Jonathon Muir-Cotton, b. Sept. 20, 1997, Ann Arbor, Mich.

Drums

J. C. Heard, b. Aug. 10, 1917; d. Sept. 27, 1988, Royal Oak, Mich.
Art Mardigan, b. Feb. 12, 1923, Detroit; d. June 6, 1977, Detroit
Frank Isola, b. Feb. 20, 1925, Detroit; d. Dec. 12, 2004, Detroit
Elvin Jones, b. Sept. 9, 1927, Pontiac, Mich.; d. May 18, 2004, Englewood, N.J.
Eddie Locke, b. Aug. 2, 1930; d. Sept. 7, 2009, Ramsey, N.J.
Frank Gant, b. May 26, 1931, Detroit; d. July 19, 2021, New York
Richard "Pistol" Allen, b. Aug. 8, 1932, Memphis, Tenn.; d. June 30, 2002, Detroit
Oliver Jackson, b. Apr. 28, 1933, Detroit; d. May 29, 1994, New York City
Otis "Candy" Finch, b. Sept. 5, 1933, Detroit; d. July 13, 1982, Seattle, Wash.
Paul Humphrey, b. Oct. 12, 1935, Detroit; d. Jan. 31, 2014, location unknown
Louis Hayes, b. May 31, 1937, Detroit
Roy Brooks, b. Mar. 9, 1938, Detroit; d. Nov. 15, 2005, Detroit
Jerry McKenzie, b. May 1, 1938, Cleveland, Ohio
Frederick "Freddie" Waits, b. Apr. 27, 1940, Jackson, Miss.; d. Nov. 18, 1989, New York City
Danny Spencer, b. Apr. 17, 1942, Ishpeming, Mich.
George Davidson, b. Aug. 1, 1942, Detroit; d. Oct. 30, 2022, Detroit
Doug Hammond, b. Dec. 26, 1942, Tampa, Fla.
Bobby Battle, b. Jan. 8, 1944, Detroit; Dec. 6, 2019, location unknown
Francisco Mora Catlett, b. Aug. 31, 1947, Washington, D.C.
Leonard King, b. Feb. 14, 1948, Detroit
Tani Tabal, b. Jan. 16, 1954, Chicago

Pheeroan akLaff, b. Jan. 27, 1955, Detroit
Gayelynn McKinney, b. July 14, 1962, Detroit
Gerald Cleaver, b. May 4, 1963, Detroit
Clarence Penn, b. Mar. 2, 1968, Detroit
Karriem Riggins, b. Aug. 25, 1975, Detroit
Sean Dobbins, Dec. 5, 1975, Ann Arbor, Mich.
Ali Jackson Jr., b. Apr. 3, 1976, Detroit
Nate Winn, b. May 5, 1985, Detroit
Alex White, b. Aug. 31, 1990, Detroit
Kayvon Gordon, b. April 23, 1995, Detroit

Vocals

Bulee "Slim" Gaillard (also guitar, piano). Details of Gaillard's birth remain unclear. Most sources say he born in Detroit or Cuba on Jan. 1 or 4, 1916, but recent scholarship points to June 1918, Clairborne, Ala.; d. Feb. 26, 1991, London, England
Kenny "Pancho" Hagood, b. Apr. 2, 1926; d. Nov. 9, 1989, Farmington Hills, Mich.
Sheila Jordan (Sheila Jeanette Dawson), b. Nov. 18, 1928, Detroit; d. Aug 11, 2025, New York
Betty Carter (Lillie Mae Jones), b. May 16, 1929, Flint, Mich.; d. Sept. 26, 1998, Brooklyn, N.Y.
Della Reese, b. July 6, 1931, Detroit; d. Nov. 19, 2017, Encino, Calif.
Teri Thornton, b. Sept. 1, 1934, Detroit; d. May 2, 2000, Englewood, N.J.
Jean DuShon (Anna Jean Harris), b. Aug. 16, 1935, Detroit; d. July 19, 2019, Stone Mountain, GA
Freda Payne, b. Sept. 19, 1942, Detroit
Dennis Rowland, b. Feb. 3, 1948, Detroit
Miche Braden, b. Nov. 14, 1953, Detroit
Kathy Kosins, b. Feb. 15, 1954, Highland Park, Mich.
Shahida Nurullah, b. Dec. 30, 1956, Detroit
Carla Cook, b. Jan. 19, 1962, Detroit

APPENDIX B

LIST OF INTERVIEWS

The following interviews by the author are quoted in the text:

Geri Allen
Ralphe Armstrong
A. Spencer Barefield
Bennie Barnes
Kenny Barron
Bob Belden
Joan Belgrave
Marcus Belgrave
David Berger
Andrew Bishop
Bess Bonnier
Bobby Broom
Kenny Burrell
Gary Burton
Donald Byrd III
Gary Carner
Grace Carter
James Carter
Regina Carter
Ron Carter
Bill Charlap
Gerald Cleaver
Scott Colley
Common
Kenn Cox
Michael Cuscuna
John Dana
Steve Davis
Jerry Dodgion
Marcus Elliot
Ron English
Peter Erskine

Orrin Evans
Ian Finkelstein
Tommy Flanagan
Jim Forger
Curtis Fuller
Jim Gallert
Kenny Garrett
Rick Germanson
Tim Hagans
Doug Hammond
Herbie Hancock
Michael Hanna
Barry Harris
Wendell Harrison
Marion Hayden
Louis Hayes
Nisha Hayes
Joe Henderson
Jill Hurst
Robert Hurst
Hank Jones
Sheila Jordan
Steve Kuhn
Ayesha Lateef
Yusef Lateef
Mike LeDonne
David Liebman
Kirk Lightsey
Joe Locke
Joe Lovano
Dennis Mackrel
Michael Malis
Branford Marsalis
Wynton Marsalis
Bennie Maupin
Christian McBride
Gayelynn McKinney
Jim McNeely
John McNeil
Charles McPherson
Pat Metheny
Mulgrew Miller
Roscoe Mitchell
Larry Mizell
Famoudou Don Moye
Jimmy Owens

Jeb Patton
Phil Ranelin
Karriem Riggins
Sonny Rollins
Marlene Rosenberg
Ellen Rowe
Adam Rudolph
Don Sickler
Kelly Sill
John Sinclair
Donald Sinta
Bill Sorin
Steve Swallow
Craig Taborn
Charles Tolliver
Kevin Toney
Rudy Tucich
McCoy Tyner
Jack Walrath
Cedar Walton
Donald Washington
Kenny Washington
Ernie Watts
Jeff Watts
David Weiss
Michael Weiss
Cookey Whitaker
Rodney Whitaker
Ben Williams
Anthony Wilson
Gerald Wilson
Steve Wilson
Nate Winn
Warren Wolf
Phil Woods

ACKNOWLEDGMENTS

This book was a long time in coming, and I owe thanks to many people who helped along the way, starting with Chris Hebert, my patient first editor at the University of Michigan Press. Chris green-lighted the project and then proceeded to publish two of his own novels—show-off—in the time it has taken me to finish one book of nonfiction. It has been a joy working with my second U-M editor, Mary Francis, who adopted me after Chris' departure, helped shape the final manuscript, and guided me to the finish line. I appreciate production editor Kevin Rennells' steady hand and professionalism and senior designer Paula Newcomb's beautiful cover design and elegant layout. Thanks to the *Detroit Free Press* for permission to reprint material first published in different form in its pages. A few key arts editors during my tenure at the paper—particularly Steve Byrne, but also Amy Culbertson and Christine Ledbetter—deserve my gratitude for editing early versions of some of the profiles in the book and for ensuring that jazz coverage remained an essential part of my responsibilities at the paper. I also want to acknowledge the late *Free Press* executive editor Bob McGruder, who loved the music and championed my work.

Michael Weiss and Ethan Iverson read portions of the manuscript and offered invaluable feedback, and informal talks with Rodney Whitaker sharpened my thinking on several key issues. The ongoing conversation about jazz and recordings that Ryan Shultz and I started 35 years ago in Urbana, Illinois, also finds reflection in the text, as do ideas gleaned from my longtime friend Andrew Agnew. I could not have written this book without the wisdom of three musical and scholarly mentors at the University of Illinois: conductor John Garvey, trumpeter and bandleader Ray Sasaki, and musicologist Larry Gushee.

Many others contributed in myriad ways, from providing hard-to-find recordings and photographs to clarifying points of jazz history and music theory. For these and other mitzvahs I thank Aaron Anderson, Dave Barber, David Berger, Lars Bjorn, Herb Boyd, Gary Carner, Barbara and Ken Cox, Michael Cuscuna, Donald Dietz, Ken Flaherty, Chris Flanagan, Jim

Gallert, Dan Gould, Pam Grady, Steve Griggs, Brad Hales, Jeff Helgesen, Fred Irby III, Sheila Jordan, Kathy Kieliszewski, the Kresge Foundation, Allen Lowe, Lissa Fleming May, Matt Merewitz, Pat Metheny, Frank Morelli Jr., the gang at Organissimo.org, the librarians at the University of Michigan Music Library, Skip Norris, John Osler, Ted Panken, Tina Pelikan, Lewis Porter, Sonny Rollins, Ellen Rowe, Emiliana Sandoval, Jim Sangrey, Mary Schroeder, Kelly Sill, RJ Spangler, Claire Stefani, Clyde Stringer, Michael Stryker, Rudy Tucich, Kenny Washington, Peter Washington, and David Weiss.

Hat tips go to two influential figures from my youth, David Miller at Schoolkids Records in Bloomington, Indiana, and Morgan Usadel at Record Service in Champaign, Illinois, who first turned me on to many of the Detroit musicians and LPs that appear in this book. I am blessed that metro Detroit is Used Record Store Heaven, and my research benefited enormously from the deep stock, knowledgeable staff, and warm camaraderie found at Peoples Records (Detroit), Hello Records (Detroit), Encore Records (Ann Arbor), Street Corner Music (Oak Park), Dearborn Music (Dearborn), and two gone-but-not-forgotten stores, Car City Records (St. Clair Shores) and The Record Collector (Ferndale).

My wife, Candace Stuart, offered an ideal balance of generous support and, when necessary, tough love. I benefited from encouragement along the way from my siblings Robin, Jeff, David, and Michael. My biggest regret is that my parents, Sheldon Stryker (1924–2016) and Alyce Stryker (1928–2009), did not live to see the publication of this book. I am grateful for their love and support, and I take heart that my father, whose passion for jazz helped spark my own, was able to read early versions of some chapters.

I've been consistently inspired by the Detroit jazz community since arriving in the city in 1995. I owe debts not only to the musicians who have trusted me to tell their stories but also to the most informed and passionate jazz audiences in the country for offering me unending encouragement. It's a privilege to write about jazz in Detroit. I don't take that for granted.

Finally, a shout-out to Bartok the Mutt and the late Burton the Beagle. Frankly, you guys were no help at all in writing this book, but I'm glad you were around anyway.

INDEX

NOTES: Page numbers in *italics* indicate photographs and in **boldface** indicate primary discussions.

Recording titles refer to LPs, CDs, or digital versions unless noted. Pre-LP era records that have not been reissued are also identified.

ABC Records, 195

Abrams, Muhal Richard, 165, 203, 239, 246

Adams, Dwight, 187, 270

Adams, Pepper: Blue Bird Inn House band and, 57; Byrd recording with, 82, 85; on Detroit jazz in the '50s, 14; Flanagan and, 67, 68; Fuller and, 104, 107; Barry Harris as mentor to, 56; on Harris as teacher, 53; Elvin Jones and, 171; McPherson and, 139; *Mean What You Say* (with Thad Jones), 164; *Motor City Scene*, 16, 16*n*4; *Pepper Adams' Joy Road: An Annotated Discography*, xiv*n*1; Thad Jones–Mel Lewis Orchestra and, 159; Workshop Jazz (Motown subsidiary label) and, 213

Adderley, Cannonball, 26, 32, 58, 103, 109, 110, 114, 116–17, 151, 119, 226

Adderley brothers, 147

African Americans: Islam and, 29. *See also* black musicians

Afrocentrism: Tribe LPs and, 201

Ahmadiyya Muslim Community, 29

Aladdin label, 22

Alessi, Joseph (the elder), 85

Alexander, Joe, 94

Alexander, Monty, Trio, 43

Alexander, Roland, 212

Ali, Rashied, 242

Allen, Carl, 261

Allen, Geri, **217–25**; Ralphe Armstrong and, 286; Belgrave and, 208, 209, 215; Blakey's band or graduate school, 220–21; Cass Tech's music program and, 14; O. Coleman and, 219; as contemporary influence, 217–18; death of, 224; early life and music education, 221–22; experimentalism and historicism and, 219–20; Gathering Orchestra and, 293; Hancock influence on, 219–20, 223–24; Hayden and, 287; Hurst and, 224–25, 225*n*1; at Kerrytown Concert House (2014), *214*; Malis' study with, 290; Riggins and, 224–25, 225*n*1, 272, 278; Shahid and Tabbal and, 204; sound of, 217–19

Allen, Geri, COMPOSITIONS: "A Celebration of All Life," 218; "Dolphy's Dance," 215, 223; "Feed the Fire," 223; "For John Malachi," 223; "Minor Complication," 222

Allen, Geri, OTHER PERFORMANCES: "Round Midnight," 222; "Tears of a Clown," 220; "That Girl," 220

Allen, Geri, RECORDINGS AS LEADER: *Flying Toward the Sound*, 220; *The Gathering*, 223–24; *Grand River Crossings*, 220; *Homegrown*, 217, 223; *Maroons*, 223; *The Nurturer*, 209, 223, 225; *Open on All Sides*, 217; *Perfection*, 224; *The Printmakers*, 217, 223, 225; *Twenty-One*, 219, 223; *Twylight*, 217; *Zodiac Suite: Revisited*, 224
Allen, Geri, RECORDINGS WITH OTHERS: *Bemsha Swing* (Shaw), 224; *Children of the Light* (Whitaker), 261; *Etudes* (Haden and Motian), 223, 225; *Feed the Fire* (Betty Carter), 223; *Gallery* (Oliver Lake), 224; *Hidden Man* (O. Coleman), 224; *Jumping the Creek* (Lloyd), 224; *Live at the Kerrytown Concert House* (Belgrave), 213, 215, 216; *Three Women* (O. Coleman), 224; *Triangular* (Ralph Peterson), 224; *Working Together* (Belgrave), 215, 216
Allen, JD, 208, 248
Allen, Pistol, 246
Allied Artists Association of America, 193
American Federation of Musicians, xii, 179–80
American Jazz Orchestra, 19
Andersen, Arild, 50–51
Anderson, Willie, 39, 65, 67, 68
Arabesque (label), 143
Arcadia Ballroom, 4
arghul (Middle Eastern instrument), Lateef and, 30
Argo (label), 31, 43*n*4
Argue, Darcy James, 165
Arista (label), 195
Arlen, Harold, 70
Armstrong, Howard, 286
Armstrong, Louis, 74, 150, 153, 159, 213
Armstrong, Ralphe: Belgrave and, 215; Cass Tech's music program and, 14; Detroit jazz and, 284, 286–87; *Detroit Rising*, 292; at Dirty Dog Jazz Café, 285; *Eddie Who?* (Eddie Harris), 292; *Inner Worlds* (Mahavishnu Orchestra), 292; Massive Attack, unauthorized sampling and, 287; "Planetary Citizen," 287; Whitaker's study with, 261
Art Ensemble of Chicago, 31, 183, 203, 246
Asante, Brendan, 251
Ashby, Dorothy, 14
Association for the Advancement of Creative Musicians (AACM), Chicago, xi, 179, 183, 246
Atco (label), 96
Atlantic (label), 15, 33, 42, 239, 266
August Greene (band), 272, 278
Austin, Will, 27, 30, 59, 195, 201, 287
auto industry: development of, 3; Great Migration and, 4; World War II Arsenal of Democracy and, 6
avant-garde: Geri Allen and, 219; Detroit Artists Workshop and, 181; Detroit Contemporary 4 (or 5) and, 183; Detroit free jazz and, 179; Focus Novii and, 186; Griot Galaxy and, 203; Joe Henderson's bebop with, 129, 132; Once Festival, Ann Arbor and, 189. *See also* free jazz
Ayler, Albert, 142, 264

Badu, Erykah, 272
Baker, David, 253
Baker's Keyboard Lounge, ix, xiii, 7, 224, 270, 283, 291
Banks, Billy, 187*n*1
Baraka, Amiri, 172, 180
Barefield, A. Spencer, 203, 204, 246, 289
Barnes, Allen, 88
Barnes, Robert, 84
Baron, Joey, 125, 270
Barretto, Ray, 72
Barron, Kenny, 32, 69, 151, 222, 234, 236, 237
Basie, Count: band, Thad Jones leading after death of, 165; as Burrell

influence, 76; Thad Jones and, 158, 161, 162; Orchestra, as Riggins influence, 276; Orchestra, Fuller touring with, 107, 108; Gerald Wilson and, 17, 22–23
Battle, Bobby, 180
Baylor, Marcus, 229, 233
BBE Music (label), 196*n*4
bebop: Belgrave as teacher of, 208; Detroit and, 132; Detroit musicians' roots in, xii; Detroit public school music programs and, 11–12; elements and development of, 6; first wave of Detroiters to pick up on, 6; Barry Harris and, 53, 56–57, 58, 61; Jackson's vibraphone and, 37, 38, 39–40; Hank Jones and, 154; Thad Jones and, 148; Lateef and, 26; McPherson on, 143; Gerald Wilson and, 21–22, 37
Before Motown: A History of Jazz in Detroit, 1920–60, xii, 7*n*2, 67, 77, 113
Begian, Harry, 12, *13*, 14, 122
Beiderbecke, Bix, 5, 153
Belgrave, Joan, 209
Belgrave, Kasan, 216
Belgrave, Marcus, 207–16; Geri Allen and, 217, 222; James Carter and, 269; Regina Carter and, 235, 239; Ray Charles and, 208, 211–12; Cleaver and, 243, 248; on craft and tradition, xii; DCMA and, 185; Detroit jazz and, xi, 206, 207–8, 213, *214*, 215–16; early gigs and recordings, 211–13; early life and music education, 210–11; Elliot and, 281, 291; as Garrett mentor, 228, 230, 231, 232; Hayden and, 287, 288, 289; health issues, 209; Hurst and, 249, 253; Jazz Development Workshop and, 203, 208, 215; at Kerrytown Concert House (2014), *214*; Malis and, 281, 289–90; with Wynton Marsalis and Hurst, 250; Metro Arts, Detroit and, 197; Charles Mingus and, 208, 213; Riggins and, 275; style and sound of, 211, 213; as teacher, 215–16; Tribe collective and, 198, *198*, 201
Belgrave, Marcus, COMPOSITIONS: "All My Love," 213
Belgrave, Marcus, OTHER PERFORMANCES: "Alexander's Ragtime Band," 211; "Blues Waltz," 211; "Chasin' the Bird," 210, 213; "Cool Eyes," 216; "Dolphy's Dance," 215; "Duke Ellington's Sound of Love," 212; "It's Good to Be Home Again," 215; "Lottie the Body's Mood," 207; "Mean What You Say," 213; "Sweet Loraine," 213, 215; "Willow Weep for Me," 211–12; "Zec," 213
Belgrave, Marcus, RECORDINGS AS LEADER: *Gemini II*, 201–2, 215, 216; *Live at the Kerrytown Concert House*, 213, 215, 216; *Working Together*, 215, 216
Belgrave, Marcus, RECORDINGS WITH OTHERS: *Changes One* and *Changes Two* (Mingus), 212; *Detroit Jazz City* (compilation), 207; *An Evening with the Devil* (Harrison), 201; *Fathead* (Newman), 211; *The Genius of Ray Charles*, 211; *Grand River Crossings* (Allen), 220; *Hidden Kingdom* (Whitaker), 261; *Message From the Tribe* (collective), 199, 200, 202*n*2; *Motor City Moments* (R. Carter), 239; *The Nurturer* (Allen), 209, 223, 225; *Pre-Bird* (Mingus), 212; *Ray Charles at Newport*, 211; *Robert Hurst Presents Robert Hurst*, 254; *The Soul of Jazz Percussion*, 212–13; *The Time Is Now!* (Ranelin), 201, 202; *Vibes from the Tribe* (Ranelin), 201; *Voices and Rhythms of the Creative Profile* (McKinney), 201–2
Benjamin, Benny, 94
Bennett, Tony, 64, 108
Benson, George, 75
Berger, David, 22, 25*n*3, 93, 97, 163, 164
Bernheimer, Martin, 24

Bert's Marketplace, 286, 291
Best, Denzil, 49
Bethlehem (label), 16, 16*n*4
Bey, Faruq Z. (born Jesse Davis), 203–4
Big Black, 276
Birdland (New York club), 105, 113, 160
Bird of Paradise (Ann Arbor club), 191, 246
Bird-Trane-Sco-Now!, 261, 269
Bishop, Andrew, 244–45, 247
Bishop, John, 204
Bistritzky, Michael, 12, 122
Bizerte (club), 7, 39
Black, Claude, 103
Black & White (label), 22
Black Artists' Group (BAG), St. Louis, 179
Black Arts Movement, 179
Black Bottom, 4, 72, 76, 177, 178
Blackbyrd Productions, 88–89
Blackbyrds, 83, 88–89
Black Messengers, 199
black musicians: bebop in Detroit and, 6; Detroit communities and, 11; students, lack of black jazz faculty and, 262; white musicians and, xii, 5, 20, 104, 179–80
Blade, Brian, 233
Blake, Betty, 212
Blake, John, 236, 239
Blakey, Art: Byrd and, 85; as Cleaver influence, 246; drums pushed forward by, 168; Garrett and, 228, 232; hard bop and, 15; Hayes as link between Williams' post-bop and, 111; Islam and, 29; and the Jazz Messengers, Geri Allen and, 220; and the Jazz Messengers, Byrd and, 81, 85, 89; and the Jazz Messengers, Fuller and, 106–7; as Elvin Jones influence, 170
Blanchard, Terence, 256, 257, 261
Bley, Carla, 50
Bley, Paul, 183
Blood, Sweat and Tears, 134
Blue Bird Inn: Miles Davis and, 161; Flanagan at, 68; Fuller and, 103–4; Barry Harris in house band at, 57; Joe Henderson and, *128*, 134; Elvin Jones in house band at, 170; Thad Jones in house band at, 160–61; legendary Detroit jazz and, 7
Blue Note (label): Geri Allen and, 223; Burrell and, 72, 74; Byrd and, 15, 85, 86; CJQ and, ix, 188, 190–91; Coltrane's *Blue Train* and, 105; Detroit musicians and, 15–16; Fuller and, 15, 100; Henderson and, 133–34; Milt Jackson with Monk on, 40; Elvin Jones and, 173; Thad Jones and, 15, 161; Jordan and, 49; Out of the Blue and, 231–32, 253; Was as president of, 207
Blue Note (New York club), 264, 266–67, 270, 276–77
Boegehold, Stephen, 290
Bohanon, George, 196*n*7, 213; *Beat* (Roy Brooks), 194; *Boss: Bossa Nova*, 194; and Ronnie Fields Quintet, 194–95
Boles, Charles, 288
Bond, Jimmy, 24
Bonnier, Bess, 66–67, 222, 289
Boulanger, Nadia, 83, 87, 94
Bowie, Lester, 183, 264, 266, 269
Bowles, Beans, 131
Bowl-O-Drome (club), 7
Boyd, Herb, 194, 199
Brazil, Joe, 132, 135*n*1
Brecker, Michael, 135
Brecker, Randy, 133
Bredshall, Edward, 94
Bridgewater, Dee Dee, 293
Broadside Press, 179
Broadway orchestras, playing for, 74, 78, 155–56, 163, 165, 231
Brookmeyer, Bob, 159, 163, 165
Brooks, Ron, 188–89, *189*, 191
Brooks, Roy: as Geri Allen mentor, 222; *Bemsha Swing* (Shaw), 224; as Cleaver influence, 246, 248; Barry

Harris as mentor to, 56; Hayden and, 288; Henderson and, 131, 132
Broom, Bobby, 75
Brown, Cameron, 51, 231
Brown, Clifford, 15, 81, 105, 210–11
Brown, James, 74, 185, 277
Brown, Ray, 40, 155, 287; Riggins and, 272, 274, 275, 276
Brown, Vernell, Jr., 233
Brubeck, Dave, 69
Bruner, Ronald, Jr., 233
Bryant, Ray, 38
Buckner, Milt, 28
Buckner, Ted, 28
Budson, Buddy, 288
Bunn, Jimmy, 22
Burrell, Billy, 76, 78
Burrell, Kenny, 72–80; Blue Note sessions and, 15; Cleaver and, 243; in Detroit (1980), 73; early life and music education, 12, 76–77; early recordings, 77–78; Flanagan and, 67, 68, 69, 70; Gillespie and, 74, 77; growth as musician, 78–79; hard bop and, 74–75; Hayes and, 113; Elvin Jones and, 171; Thad Jones and, 161; Jordan and, 47; Lateef and, 29; Harold McKinney and, 182; Metheny on, 74; New Music Society and, 78; Schlitz Malt Liquor radio commercial, 79; sound of, 72, 74; as teacher, 75, 79–80
Burrell, Kenny, COMPOSITIONS: "Chitlins Con Carne," 72; "I Goofed" (Turner, Ridall and Burrell), 77; "Kenny Sound," 78; "Soul Lament," 72
Burrell, Kenny, OTHER PERFORMANCES: "Birks' Works," 77; "But Not for Me," 74–75; "Gee Baby Ain't I Good to You," 72; "My Funny Valentine," 78; "Why Was I Born," 74–75
Burrell, Kenny, RECORDINGS AS LEADER: *Blues Bash!*, 79; *Blues: The Common Ground*, 79; *Bluesy Burrell*, 79; *God Bless the Child*, 79; *Guitar Forms*, 78–79, 80; *Have Yourself a Soulful Little Christmas*, 79; *Introducing Kenny Burrell*, 78; *Kenny Burrell & John Coltrane*, 78; *Kenny's Sound*, 78 rpm, not reissued, 77–78; *Midnight Blue*, 72, 74, 78, 79, 80; *My Funny Valentine*, 78 rpm, not reissued, 77–78; *A Night at the Vanguard*, 78, 80; *Sky Street*, 79; *Soul Call*, 79; *The Tender Gender*, 79; *Up the Street, 'Round the Corner, Down the Block*, 79; *Weaver of Dreams*, 77
Burrell, Kenny, RECORDINGS WITH OTHERS: *Bean Bags* (with Hawkins), 42; *Beyond the Blue Bird* (Flanagan), 70; *Birks' Works*, reissued on Dizzy Gillespie, *Odyssey 1945–52* (Savoy), 77; *Detroit–New York Junction* (T. Jones), 161–62; *I Goofed* (Turner) (78 rpm, never reissued), 77; *Milt Jackson Quintet & Sextet with Lucky Thompson: Complete Savoy and Atlantic Sessions*, 43; *Motor City Scene* (Adams), 16; *Soul Meeting* (Jackson and R. Charles), 42
Burton, Gary, 38, 133, 135*n*2
Butts, Hindal, 76, 77, 80
Byard, Jaki, 123
Byas, Don, 266, 270
Byrd, Donald, 81–89; Pepper Adams and, 82, 85; on Begian, 12, 14; Bell's palsy and, 86, 87, 89; Blackbyrds and, 83, 88–89; Blue Note (label) and, 15, 85, 86; Detroit Institute of Arts visits by, 84; early life, 81, 84; education, wealth, and success of, 83–84; Barry Harris and, 56, 58; Jazz Lab Quintet, 85; Elvin Jones and, 171; marriage and relationships, 84–85, 86–87; Mizell brothers and, 87–88; musical interests, 82–83, 87; musical voice and tone, 81–82, 85–86; teaching jazz, 87

Byrd, Donald, COMPOSITIONS: "French Spice," 86; "Hush," 86; "Omicron" (with Chambers), 85; "Royal Flush," 82; "Shangri-La," 86; "When Your Love Has Gone," 85–86
Byrd, Donald, OTHER PERFORMANCES: "Bobbin' at Barbee's," 84; "Cristo Redentor," 86; "Flight Time," 87; "Loungin'" (Guru video), 89; "Mr. Thomas," 87; "Walking in Rhythm," 88
Byrd, Donald, RECORDINGS AS LEADER: *At the Half Note Café* (vols. 1 and 2), 86; *Black Byrd*, 82–83, 87–88; *Byrd in Flight*, 86; *Byrd in Hand*, 86, 89; *Byrd Jazz*, 15; *Caricatures*, 88; *The Catwalk*, 86; *First Flight*, 16*n*3; *Free Form*, 86; *A New Perspective*, 86; *Off to the Races*, 85–86; *Places and Spaces*, 88; *Royal Flush*, 86, 89; *Stepping into Tomorrow*, 88; *Street Lady*, 88
Byrd, Donald, RECORDINGS WITH OTHERS: *Bobbin' at Barbee's* (Barnes), 78 rpm, not reissued, 84; *Davis Cup* (Walter Davis), 86; *The Jazz Messengers* (Blakey), 85, 89; *My Conception* (Sonny Clark), 86; *New Soil* (McLean), 86; *Six Pieces of Silver* (Silver), 85; *Whims of Chambers* (Chambers), 85
Byrd, Donaldson Toussaint L'Ouverture, III, 84, 86
Byrd, Lorraine Glover, 84, 86–87
Byrne, Bobby, 14
Byrne, Clarence, 20

Cabrera, Louis, 12, 28, 39, 77
Cadena, Ozzie, 31
Café Bohemia (New York), 105
Café Ziegfeld (New York), 156
Calandrelli, Jorge, 239–40
Callender, Red, 22
Candido (percussionist), 78
Carner, Gary, xiv*n*1, 16*n*4, 104, 213
Carr Center, 224, 272–74, 284, 293–94
Carrington, Terri Lyne, 224, 294*n*1
Carter, Benny, 24
Carter, Betty, 45, 219, 223, 275
Carter, Clarence "Chic," 17
Carter, Grace, 235–36, 237
Carter, James, **264–71**; Ralphe Armstrong and, 286; jazz apprentice system and, 266; Orchestra Hall, Detroit, 265; playing style, 264, 266–67; saxophone collection, 267–68; Shahid and Tabbal and, 204; Taborn and, 268, 269–70; use of musicians from Detroit by, 268; Whitaker and, 261
Carter, James, PERFORMANCES: "Aged Pain," 267; "Gloria," 270; "Winter Meeting," 264
Carter, James, RECORDINGS AS LEADER: *Blood on the Fields* (Marsalis), 236; *Chasin' the Gypsy*, 270; *Gardenias for Lady Day*, 270, 271; *Heaven on Earth*, 270, 271; *JC on the Set*, 264; *Live at Baker's Keyboard Lounge*, 270; *Motor City Moments* (Regina Carter), 239; *Present Tense*, 270, 271
Carter, James, RECORDINGS WITH OTHERS: *Children of the Light* (Whitaker), 261; *Hidden Kingdom* (Whitaker), 261
Carter, Janet, 121
Carter, Quintell Williams, 121
Carter, Regina, **234–41**; Belgrave as mentor to, 208; Cass Tech's music program and, 14; at Detroit Jazz Festival, 235; early life and music education, 237–39; Hammond and, 187; hospice work, 235–36, 240; on jazz community in Detroit, xi; researching family tree, 240; String Trio of New York and, 239; on touching people with music, 241; versatility of, 234–35
Carter, Regina, COMPOSITIONS: "Shades of Gray," 237
Carter, Regina, PERFORMANCES: "Shoo-Rye," 240; "Softly as in a Morning Sunrise," 237; "Squatty Roo," 237

Carter, Regina, RECORDINGS AS LEADER: *Accentuate the Positive*, 240; *Freefall* (with Kenny Barron), 237, 241; *Motor City Moments*, 239; *Paganini: After a Dream*, 239–40; *Reverse Thread*, 240; *Southern Comfort*, 240, 241

Carter, Regina, RECORDINGS WITH OTHERS: *Chasin' the Gypsy* (J. Carter), 270; *It's Born* (Hammond), 187; *Octagon* (String Trio of New York), 239, 241; *We People* (Hammond), 187

Carter, Ron, **118–26**; Geri Allen and, 219; as bass player, 118–20; Burrell recording with, 79; Cass Tech's music program and, 14; M. Davis Quintet and, 118, 124–25, 188; Detroit jazz and, 286; at the Dirty Dog Jazz Café, *119*; discography, 125–26; early life and music education, 122–23; Henderson and, 134; Hurst and, 249; as Hurst influence, 253–54; Milt Jackson and, 42; Hank Jones and, 151, 156; McBride on, 124; musical trademarks of, 121, 123–24; New York home of, 121–22; New York Jazz Quartet and, 98; as Whitaker influence, 260

Carter, Ron, COMPOSITIONS: "Einbahnstrasse," 124; "El Noche Sol," 124; "Little Waltz," 124; "Parade," 124; "Rufus," 124; "Third Plane," 124; "Tinderbox," 124; "12+12," 124

Carter, Ron, OTHER PERFORMANCES: "Hesitation," 258; "My Funny Valentine," 120; "No Blues," 125; "Stella by Starlight," 120

Carter, Ron, RECORDINGS AS LEADER: *All Alone*, 125; *All Blues*, 125; *Etudes*, 125; *The Golden Striker Trio*, 125; *The Great Jazz Trio at the Village Vanguard* (with H. Jones, T. Williams), 156; *Live at the Village West*, 126; *Orfeu*, 125; *Piccolo*, 125; *Third Plane*, 125; *Uptown Conversation*, 125, 126; *Where?* 123

Carter, Ron, RECORDINGS, OTHER: *The Big New Band of the '60s* (Wilkins), 123; *Blues: The Common Ground*, 79; *Complete Live at the Plugged Nickel* (M. Davis), 125; *Components* (Hutcherson), 125; *Contours* (Sam Rivers), 125, 126; *Down Home* (Baron), 125; *Empyrean Isles* (Hancock), 125; *ESP* (M. Davis), 125; *Far Cry* (Dolphy), 125; *Filles de Kilimanjaro*, 125; *God Bless the Child*, 79; *Guitar Forms* (Burrell), 78, 79, 80; *The In Sound* (E. Harris), 125; *Invitation* (Jackson), 42; *The Jazz Statesmen* (Persip), 123; *Live in Europe 1967: The Bootleg Series Vol. 1* (M. Davis), 125; *Maiden Voyage* (Hancock), 125; *Miles in the Sky* (M. Davis), 125; *Miles Smiles* (M. Davis), 125; *My Funny Valentine* (M. Davis), 120, 126; *Nefertiti* (M. Davis), 125; *Power to the People* (Henderson), 125; *The Real McCoy* (Tyner), 125, 134, 135, 172; *Red Clay* (Hubbard), 125; *Seven Steps to Heaven*, 260; *Sorcerer* (M. Davis), 125; *Speak No Evil* (Shorter), 125, 172; *The State of the Tenor (vols. 1 and 2*, Henderson), 134; *Stone Flower* (Jobim), 125; *Sunflower* (Jackson), 42, 43; *Trident* (Tyner), 125; *Twenty One* (Allen), 219, 223

Cass Technical High School: Geri Allen at, 222; Ralphe Armstrong teaching at, 286; Byrd at, 84; Regina Carter at, 237–38; Ron Carter at, 122; Cleaver at, 245; Cox and, 189; Hanna at, 94; Hayden at, 287; Jordan at, 47; music program at, 12, 13, 14; Gerald Wilson at, 20–21

Catlett, Buddy, 97

Catlett, Sid, 170

Challis, Bill, 5, 153

Chamber Music Society of Detroit, 42

Chambers, Joe, 193

Chambers, Paul: Burrell and, 77, 78; Ron Carter as heir to, 123; Cass Tech's music program and, 14, 122; Coltrane's *Blue Train* and, 100; "Good Bait," 260; Barry Harris as mentor to, 56; as Hayden influence, 287; Henderson and, 135; Hurst and, 249; Elvin Jones and, 171; Thad Jones recording with, 161; leading Blue Note sessions, 15; recording with Fuller, 104; *Whims of Chambers*, 85; as Whitaker influence, 260
Chambliss, Eddie, 113
Chandler, Vincent, 293–94
CHANGE (journal), 183
Charlap, Bill, 150
Charles, Ray, 17, 42, 151, 208, 211–12
Cherry, Don, 27, 86
Chic's Show Bar, 94
Childs, Billy, 234
Christensen, Jon, 50
Christian, Charlie, 75, 76
Chrysler, 3
civil rights movement, 179
CKLW, Windsor, Ontario, 39
Clark, Ralph, 57
Clark, Sonny, 86, 100
Clarke, Kenny: Burrell and, 78; Flanagan and, 69; as Hayes influence, 113; Islam and, 29; Milt Jackson and, 42; *Jazzmen: Detroit* (Savoy), 16; as Elvin Jones influence, 168, 170; Hank Jones and, 155; Modern Jazz Quartet and, 40
classical music: Ralphe Armstrong and, 286; black communities in Detroit and, 11; Burrell and, 77; Ron Carter and, 121, 122–23; contemporary, Roscoe Mitchell and, 246; Detroit public school music programs and, 12; Flanagan and, 67; Hanna and, 90–91, 92–93, 95–96; Barry Harris and, 55–56, 57; Hawkins and, 96; Henderson and, 130–31, 132; Hurst and, 253; Hank Jones and, 154; Lateef and, 29, 30, 33–34; Parker and, 48; Gerald Wilson and, 22, 23
Clayton, John, 43, 165
Clayton-Hamilton Jazz Orchestra, 43
Cleaver, Gerald, **242–48**; Belgrave as mentor to, 208; Black Host (band), 244, 248; Cass Tech's music program and, 14; Craig Taborn Trio and, 243; on Detroit influence, 248; early life and music education, 245–46; free jazz and, 242–44, 246–47; Roscoe Mitchell and, 246–47; playing style, 244–45; post-bop and, 247–48; reputation of, 242; Taborn and, 243, 244, 245–46; Uncle June (band), 244, 247; Violet Hour (band), 244, 247–48
Cleaver, Gerald, COMPOSITIONS: "Charles Street Quotidian," 247
Cleaver, Gerald, OTHER PERFORMANCES: "For Lester B," 246
Cleaver, Gerald, RECORDINGS AS LEADER: *Be It as I See It*, 247, 248; *Gerald Cleaver's Detroit*, 247–48
Cleaver, Gerald, RECORDINGS WITH OTHERS: *Chant* (Taborn), 244, 248; *Hidden Kingdom* (Whitaker), 261; *Nine to Get Ready* (R. Mitchell), 246; *Remembering Weather Report* (Vitous), 244, 248; *Song for My Sister* (R. Mitchell), 246; *Soul* (Pelt), 244
Clef (label), 154
Cliff Bell's (club), 283, 291
Club Congo Orchestra, 5–6, 7
Club El Sino, 7, 47–48
Club Juana, 77
Club Plantation, later Club Congo, 5, 21
Club Sudan (formerly Club Congo), 7, 47, 76
Club Tropicano, 113
Club Zombie, 7
Cobb, Jimmy, 135, 219, 274
Cobb's Corner, 231
Cobham, Billy, 42, 125

Cole, Nat, 65, 67, 151
Cole, Richie, 231
Coleman, George, 173, 231
Coleman, Ornette, 132, 142, 172, 179, 186, 193, 219, 224
Coleman, Steve, 186, 219, 221
Collective Black Artists, New York, 179
Collette, Buddy, 22, 24
Colley, Scott, 120
Collins, Chris, 283
Coltrane, Alice (McLeod), 14, 67, 201
Coltrane, John: Burrell and, 74, 77; Byrd and, 81; as James Carter influence, 269; Detroit avant-garde and, 183; Flanagan and, 70; Fuller and, 100, 104, 105; Fuller and Shorter and, 105–6; as Garrett influence, 226, 228; Barry Harris as mentor to, 56; Hayes and, 110; Joe Henderson and, 129, 132, 139*n*1; "India," Lateef and, 27; Milt Jackson and, 42; jazz avant-garde and, 179; Hank Jones and, 150; as Thad Jones influence, 158; Lateef compared with, 33; on Lateef's approach to Eastern music, 31; Miles Davis Quintet and, 15; post-bop and, 142; Quartet, Elvin Jones and, 147, 167, 168, 171–72; as Riggins influence, 275
Coltrane, John, COMPOSITIONS: "Blue Train," 100, 102; "Giant Steps," 69, 255; "Impressions," 183
Coltrane, John, OTHER PERFORMANCES: "Afro-Blue," 169; "Bye, Bye Blackbird," 172; "Chim Chim Cheree," 169; "Lover," 111; "My Favorite Things," 169; "Naima," 156; "Tunji," 169
Coltrane, John, RECORDINGS AS LEADER: *Bags and Trane* (with Jackson), 42; *Blue Train*, 100, 102, 105; *Coltrane Plays the Blues*, 172; *Coltrane's Sound*, 172; *Cosmic Music*, 245; *Crescent*, 172; *Giant Steps*, 69; *Impressions*, 168; *Kenny Burrell & John Coltrane*, 78; *Live at Birdland*, 168; *A Love Supreme*, 168, 172, 174; *My Favorite Things*, 172; *One Down, One Up*, 172; *Soultrane*, 260; *Transition*, 172
Coltrane, Ravi, 173, 249, 272
Common (hip-hop artist), 272, 274, 277, 278
Contemporary Jazz Quintet (CJQ): Blue Note (label) and, 188, 190–91; DCMA and, 185; formation and members of, 188–90, *189*; longevity of, 178; Strata and, 188, 191, 193. *See also* Brooks, Ron; Cox, Kenn; Henderson, Leon; Moore, Charles; Spencer, Danny
Contemporary Jazz Quintet (CJQ), RECORDINGS: *The Black Hole*, 195, 196*n*2; *Introducing Kenny Cox and the Contemporary Jazz Quintet*, 190, 195; *Location*, 191, 195; *Multidirection*, 190, 191, 195
Cook, Carla, 14, 237
Cook, Junior, 109, 115, 130
Corea, Chick, 173, 193, 228, 229–30
Corporation (Motown team), 87
Cortot, Alfred, 94
Coss, Bill, 161
Cotton Club (Harlem), 20
Cowell, Stanley, 181, 183, 188, 194, 196*n*6
Cox, Kenn: Bohanon–Fields Quintet and, 194–95; CJQ and, 188–89, *189*, 191; on Detroit jazz, ix–x, xiii; Hayden and, 288; Etta Jones and, 189; as mentor, 208; Strata Corporation and, 192; Whitaker and, 259, 261
Cox, Kenn, COMPOSITIONS: "Mystique," 190; "Spellbound," 190; "Trance Dance," 190
Cox, Kenn, RECORDINGS AS LEADER: *Clap Clap! The Joyful Noise*, 195. *See also* Contemporary Jazz Quintet

Cox, Kenn, RECORDINGS WITH OTHERS: *Alive 'n Well* (Myrick), 194–95; *Fish Feet* (English), 195; *Live at Baker's Keyboard Lounge* (J. Carter), 270; *Love Shout* (Etta Jones), 189; *Vibes from the Tribe* (Ranelin), 201
Craig, Carl, 202
Cranshaw, Bob, 43, 130
Crawford, Hank, 197, 211, 226
Creative Arts Collective (CAC), 203. *See also* Barefield, A. Spencer
Creeley, Robert, poetry by, 51
Crystal (club), 7
CTI (label), 42, 125
Cunningham, Bob, 32
Cuscuna, Michael, 266, 270

Dameron, Tadd, 22, 40, 50, 64, 65–66
Dana, John, 180, 183–84, 186, 187, 195, 201
Daney, Ike, 201
Danish Radio Big Band, 165
Dave, Chris, 233
Davidson, George, 201
Davis, Eddie "Lockjaw," 264, 266
Davis, Jesse, 25
Davis, Kris, 217, 251, 255
Davis, Miles: as Byrd influence, 82, 83; as CJQ influence, 188; Detroit avant-garde and, 183; Flanagan and, 68, 69; Fuller and, 105, 106; Garrett and, 228, 232; Henderson and, 134; Milt Jackson and Monk on Prestige with, 40; Elvin Jones and, 168, 171; Hank Jones and, 150, 151, 154; on Thad Jones and Hubbard, 161; living in Detroit, 161; as Moore influence, 185, 190; on Morgan's articulation style, 106; 1950s Quintet, 15; 1960s Quintet, Ron Carter and, 118, 120, 123, 124–25, 126; post-bop and, 142; Thad Jones–Mel Lewis Orchestra and, 164; Gerald Wilson and, 23, 40
Davis, Miles, COMPOSITIONS: "Donna Lee," 47; "Little Willie Leaps," 47; "So What," 183
Davis, Miles, OTHER PERFORMANCES: "Bitty Ditty," 161; "Walkin'," 56
Davis, Miles, RECORDINGS AS LEADER: *Bags' Groove*, 70; *Collectors' Items*, 69; *Complete Live at the Plugged Nickel*, 125; *ESP*, 125; *Filles de Kilimanjaro*, 125; *Live Around the World*, 233; *Live in Europe 1967: The Bootleg Series Vol. 1*, 125; *Miles in the Sky*, 125, 188; *Miles Smiles*, 125; *My Funny Valentine*, 120, 126; *Nefertiti*, 125, 188; *Seven Steps to Heaven*, 260; *Sorcerer*, 125, 188
Davis, Miles, RECORDINGS WITH OTHERS: *Somethin' Else* (Adderley), 155
Davis, Nathan, 222
Davis, Richard, 78, 97–98, 118, 164
Davis, Steve, 100
Davis, Ursula Broschke, 84
Davis, Walter, 86
Davis, Will, 57
Dawud, Talib, 29
Debut (label), 161
Dee Gee (label), 40, 43*n*4, 57, 77, 161, 170, 192
DeJohnette, Jack, 135, 246
de Konigswarter, Pannonica, 58–59
DeSilva, Yourna, 84–85
Detroit: LPs named for, 16; municipal bankruptcy, Detroit jazz and, xi, 282; race riots (1943), 6–7; racial tension in, 48–49, 68–69; Ranelin on black awareness in, 197; riots and violence (1967), 177–78, 189. *See also* public school music education programs; *specific institutions*
Detroit Artists Workshop: "Adolescence," 184; Detroit Contemporary 5 at, *182*; Detroit jazz history and, 178, 179; formation of, 181; jam sessions and concerts, 182–83; New Music Society as precursor to, 78; Sinclair and, 181–82; *The Work Box*, 184. *See also* Detroit Contemporary 4 (or 5)
Detroit Artists Workshop Press, 183

Detroit Community Music School, 237
Detroit Conservatory of Music, 28, 190
Detroit Contemporary 4 (or 5), *182*, 183, 184; "All Blues," 184; "The Coaster," 183; "Gazzelloni," 183; "Impressions," 183; "The Killers," 183; "Prayer for the Future," 184; "So What," 183, 184; "Stan," 183; "Twins," 183
Detroit Creative Musicians Association (DCMA), 178, 179, 184, 185–86
Detroit Free Jazz, 187*n*1
Detroit Free Press, xiii, 284
Detroit Institute of Arts, 39, 84, 198–99, 203
Detroit jazz: big bands and, 4–6; community of audiences and musicians, 14–15, 149, 283; Cox on, ix–x, xiii; culture of mentorship, x–xi, 137–39, 208–9, 233, 259, 289; defining stylistic characteristics, x–xii, 11, 123, 147; Flanagan on role models in, 67; impact and influence, ix–xi, 15–16, 204, 208; as multilayered story, x–xi, xii; from 1900–1950, 3–7; musicians in New York, 15–16; nonprofits and jazz education, xi, 202, 208–9, 224, 283, 284, 293–94; other coverage of, xiii, xiv*n*1; race relations between black and white musicians, xii, 5, 20, 104, 179–80. *See also specific musician profiles*
Detroit Jazz Center, 203
Detroit Jazz Festival: Geri Allen and, *218*; Ron Carter and Metheny at, 120; Cleaver and, 247; importance of, 283; Fuller and, 107; jazz education and, 284; Elvin Jones and, 174; Lateef and, 26, 34; Michael Malis and Marcus Elliot at, 280; Riggins and, 278; Gerald Wilson and, *18*, 19, 20, 25
Detroit Jazz Festival Foundation, 283
Detroit Jazz Musician Co-Op (label), 213
Detroit Repertory Theatre, 185
Detroit Symphony Orchestra: Belgrave and, 208; James Carter and, 270; Regina Carter and, 234; Cass Tech music teachers in, 12; Civic Jazz Band (students), 289–91; Fuller and, 103; Hanna and, 98; jazz education and, 284; Thad Jones with Ellington and, 162; Lateef and, 32
DeVeaux, Scott, 6
Dewberry, Cynthia, 239
Dial (label), 40, 154
Di Battista, Stefano, 233
Dillard, Gladys Wade, 57, 67
Dirty Dog Jazz Café, 283
DIW (label), 261
Dizzy's Club (New York), 291
DJ Dummy, 278
Dodds, Baby, 170
Dodds, Johnny and Baby, 147
Dodgion, Jerry, 23, 25*n*4, 90, 97, 159
Do It Yourself Handbook for Keyboard Playing, 92
Dolphy, Eric: Geri Allen and, 222; Belgrave and, 212; Ron Brooks and, 189; Ron Carter and, 119, 123, 125; Detroit avant-garde and, 183; "Gazzelloni," 183; Mingus and, 142
Dorham, Kenny, 106, 133, 212
Dorsey, Jimmy, 5
Dorsey, Tommy, 5, 103
Dotson, Hobart, 22
Douglas, Dave, 27, 204
Douglas, John, 290
Downbeat, 23, 31, 38, 42, 50, 53, 84, 88, 92, 148, 160, 161, 166*n*2, 182, 212
Drew, Kenny, 100, 114
Drummand, Ray, 143
Duke, George, 24
Dummy George's (club), 217
Durham, Eddie, 21
Durrah, David, 177; *Reflections in the Sea of Nurnen* (with Hammond), 187
Duvivier, George, 156

Eastman School of Music, 94, 121, 122
Eckstine, Billy, 67, 154

Eclipse (Thad Jones big band), 165
Edison, Sweets, 171
Edwards, Teddy, 24
Eichele, Robin, 181
Eldridge, Roy, 28, 57–58
Ellington, Duke: as Geri Allen influence, 222; Belgrave refuses tour with, 212; Burrell and, 74, 76, 79; *Great Paris Concert*, 23; as Hanna influence, 96; Hank Jones' introduction to jazz and, 153; Thad Jones and, 162–63, 166*n*3; "Lady Mac" (with Strayhorn), 209–10; "Night Creature" with Detroit Symphony, 162; Whitaker's study of, 261; Gerald Wilson and, 17, 20, 22, 23
Ellington Orchestra, Duke (led by Mercer Ellington), 228, 231, 232
Elliot, Marcus: *Balance* (with Malis), 281, 292; Detroit jazz and, 282–83, 289, 290–91; at Detroit Jazz Festival, 280; Gathering Orchestra and, 293–94; *Lifted from the No of All Nothing* (Malis Trio), 292; Malis and, 281; "The Mediator," 281; "No. 3," 281; *When the City Meets the Sky* (with Malis), 291, 292
Ellis, Don, 123
Ellis, Herb, 78
Emarcy (label), 270
Emery, James, 239
employment discrimination, 6
English, Bill, 72
English, Ron, 180, 183, 193, 195
Enrica (label), 123
Erb (Fred A. and Barbara M.) Family Foundation, 283, 284, 293
Erskine, Peter, 111–12
Eskelin, Ellery, 247
Espinosa, Pepe, 251
Eubanks, Charles, 201
Eubanks, Robin, 174
Evans, Bill, 50, 125, 151
Evans, Gil, 78–79, 171
Evans, John, 57
Evans, Orrin, 261, 272, 275–76, 278
Excelsior (label), 22

Farmer, Art, 104–5, 123, 125, 288
Farrell, Joe, 173
Farrow, Ernie, 30, 31, 96, 113, 131, 132
Fat Boys, 275
Fava, Joe, 77
Favors, Malachi, 183
Fears, Vivian (Vivian Glasby), 22
Fields, Ernie, 28
Fields, Ronnie, and George Bohanon Quintet, 194–95
Fillius Jazz Archive, Hamilton College, 95, 97
Finkelstein, Ian, 251, 252, 291, 293–94
Fitzgerald, Ella: *Ella in Hamburg*, 69; Flanagan and, 64, 69; Fuller and, 108; Hank Jones and, 150, 154; Gerald Wilson and, 17, 22
Flame Show Bar, 7, 68
Flanagan, Diana, 66–67, 71
Flanagan, Tommy, **63–71**; as band leader and sideman, 64–65, 70; on bebop in Detroit, 7; Burrell and, 69, 70, 76, 77, 78; Cleaver and, 243; as Cox influence, 189; Detroit and, 68–69, 248; early life and music education, 67–69; Hanna and, 90, 91, 94; Barry Harris compared with, 59; Hawkins and, 58; Elvin Jones and, 171; Hank Jones and, 151; Thad Jones and, 161; Jordan and, 47; music lessons with Dillard, 57; in New York, 64; piano style, 63–64, 65–66, 69, 70–71
Flanagan, Tommy, COMPOSITIONS: "Verdandi" ("Mean Streets"), 66
Flanagan, Tommy, OTHER PERFORMANCES: "A Blue Time," 65; "Bouncing with Bud," 68; "Giant Steps," 69; "Gone with the Wind," 63; "How High the Moon," 68; "How Long Has This Been Going On?" 70; "In Your Own Sweet Way," 69; "Lament," 66; "Last Night

When We Were Young," 70–71; "Raincheck," 66; "Where Are You?" 70; "Yesterdays," 68
Flanagan, Tommy, RECORDINGS AS LEADER: *Alone Too Long*, 70; *Beyond the Blue Bird*, 70; *Eclypso*, 65–66, 70; *Jazz Poet*, 66, 70, 71; *Let's*, 70; *Nights at the Vanguard*, 70; *Overseas*, 70, 71; *Sea Changes*, 70; *Solo Piano*, 70; *Sunset and the Mockingbird*, 70; *Super-Session*, 70; *Thelonica*, 70; *The Tommy Flanagan Trio*, 70
Flanagan, Tommy, RECORDINGS WITH OTHERS: *At Ease with Coleman Hawkins*, 64, 71; *Bean Bags* (with Hawkins), 42; *Bluesy Burrell*, 79; *Boss Tenor* (Ammons), 64; *The Cats* (collective), 70; *Collectors' Items* (M. Davis), 64, 69; *Detroit–New York Junction* (T. Jones), 161–62; *Ella in Hamburg* (Fitzgerald), 69; *Giant Steps* (Coltrane), 64, 69; *Good Old Broadway* (Hawkins), 69; *The Incredible Jazz Guitar of Wes Montgomery*, 64; *Introducing Kenny Burrell*, 78; *Invitation* (Jackson), 42; *Live at the Kerrytown Concert House* (Belgrave), 213, 215, 216; *Make Someone Happy* (Hawkins), 69; *Milt Jackson Quintet & Sextet with Lucky Thompson: Complete Savoy and Atlantic Sessions*, 43; *Motor City Scene* (Adams), 16; *Motor City Scene* (T. Jones), 16; private tape, 1950, Blue Bird Inn, Detroit, 68; *Saxophone Colossus* (Rollins), 64
Fletcher, Arthur, Jr., 187*n*1
Focus Novii, 186–87, 203; "Before and After the Fact (Hammond), 187; "Raw Groove" (Ulmer), 187; "Sneakin' and Peekin'" (Dana), 187; "Tangential Diorama," 186–87
Ford, Art, television show, 96
Ford, Henry, 3
Ford, Ricky, 33
Ford Motor Company, 3
Forest Club, 58
Forger, Jim, 261, 262
Formanek, Michael, 243
Fortune, Sonny, 173
Fortune Records, 67, 77, 84
Foster, Al, 134, 135
Foster, Frank, 15, 48–49, 51, 57, 68, 104, 148, 173, 231
Fountaine, Eli, 113
Four Sharps (Kenny Burrell group), 77
Four Sharps (Milt Jackson group), 39
Foxx, Redd, 24
Franklin, Aretha, 74, 78, 286
Franklin, C. L., 77–78
free jazz: Cleaver and, 242–44, 246–47; Detroit collectives of 1960s and 1970s and, 179; Detroit musicians and, xii; Lateef and, 26; McPherson and, 142–43. *See also* avant-garde
Freeman, Von, 33
Frisell, Bill, 125
Frishberg, Dave, 49
Frolic Show Bar, 7
Fuller, Curtis, 100–108; Adderley and, 103; Basie and, 107–8; Blakey and Jazz Messengers and, 106–7; as Blue Note leader, 15; "Blue Train" solo, 100, 102; Coltrane and, 100, 105–6; early life and music education, 102–4; Barry Harris as mentor to, 56; on Hayes, 112; J. J. Johnson as influence, 56, 102, 103, 104, 105; paying dues, earning dividends, 107–8; Rosolino and, 103; Sinatra and, 108; at Van Gelder Studio, *101*; on what makes a good solo, 106; Yusef Lateef Quintet and, 30, 31
Fuller, Curtis, COMPOSITIONS: "A La Mode," 106; "Buhaina's Delight," 107; "Suite Kathy," 107
Fuller, Curtis, OTHER PERFORMANCES: "Blue Train," 100, 102; "In the Wee Small Hours of the Morning," 108; "It's All Right with Me," 105; "Just You, Just Me," 104; "Moment's Notice," 105; "Three Blind Mice" (Fuller arrangement), 106–7

Fuller, Curtis, RECORDINGS AS LEADER: *The Curtis Fuller Jazztet with Benny Golson*, 104; *Fire and Filigree*, 107; *Four on the Outside*, 107, 108; *Imagination*, 104; *Jazz in Transition* (with Pepper Adams), 104; *The Opener*, 104, 108
Fuller, Curtis, RECORDINGS WITH OTHERS: *Blue Train* (Coltrane), 100, 102, 105; *Caravan* (Blakey), 106; *Before Dawn* (Lateef), 31; *Free for All* (Blakey), 106; *Groovin' with Golson*, 104; *Indestructible* (Blakey), 106; *Jazz for Thinkers* (Lateef), 31; *Jazz Mood* (Lateef), 31; *Meet the Jazztet* (Golson and Farmer), 105; *Mosaic* (Blakey), 106, 108
Fuller, Larry, 277

Galbraith, Barry, 49
Gallert, Jim, 284
Gant, Frank, 15, 27, 30, 59
Garbarek, Jan, 50
Gardner, Harold, 193
Garner, Erroll, 92, 96
Garnett, Alvester, 237
Garrett, Kenny, **226–33**; Adderley and, 226; as band leader and mentor, 232–33; Belgrave as mentor to, 208; curiosity as fundamental to, 229–30; M. Davis and, 228, 232; at Detroit Jazz Festival, 227; early gigs, 231–32; early life and music education, 230–31; foreign languages studied by, 229; Hurst and, 253; McBride on, 229–30; sound and style of, 226, 228–29; Whitaker and, 261
Garrett, Kenny, COMPOSITIONS: "Boogety, Boogety," 233; "J-Mac," 229
Garrett, Kenny, OTHER PERFORMANCES: "Billie's Bounce," 231; "Have You Met Miss Jones," 232
Garrett, Kenny, RECORDINGS AS LEADER: *Introducing Kenny Garrett*, 232; *Prisoner of Love*, 232; *Pursuance: The Music of John Coltrane*, 233; *Seeds from the Underground*, 232–33; *Songbook*, 233; *Triology*, 233
Garrett, Kenny, RECORDINGS WITH OTHERS: *Inside Track* (Out of the Blue), 231; *Live Around the World* (M. Davis), 233; *Live at Mt. Fuji* (Out of the Blue), 231; *The Nurturer* (Allen), 223; *One Night at Cobb's*, YouTube audio (1978), 231; *OTB* (Out of the Blue), 231, 253; *Three or Four Shades of Dannie Richmond Quintet*, 231
Garrett, Sayydah, 230
Garrison, Jimmy, 118, 168, 172, 173
Gathering Orchestra, at the Carr Center, 293–94
Gaye, Marvin, 116, 195
Gelispie, Randy, 259
Geller, Herb, 148–49
General Motors, 3
Genus, James, 270
Germanson, Rick, 112
Getz, Stan, 105, 131, 150–51, 154
Gibbs, Gerard, 264, 270
Gibson, Rob, 93
Giddins, Gary, 58, 160
Gillespie, Dizzy: as Belgrave influence, 210; Burrell and, 74, 77; Dee Gee (label) and, 40; Milt Jackson and, 39, 40; Thad Jones and, 158, 159–60, 161; Lateef and, 26, 29; "Shaw 'Nuff," 160; Gerald Wilson and, 17, 21–22, 23
Gladstone, Robert, 261
Glasper, Robert, 233, 254, 272, 278
Gleason, Ralph J., 38
Glenn, Tyree, 171
Glover, Millard, 39
Goldkette, Jean, 5
Goldsmith, George, 213, 246
Golson, Benny, 104, 105, 106
Gonsalves, Paul, 25*n*4
Gonzales, Benito, 233
Goodman, Benny, 67, 76, 90, 95–96, 150, 171
Goods, Richie, 276

Gordon, Dexter, 29, 68, 78, 151
Gordon, Max, 156, 158
Gordy, Berry, 57, 178
Goren, Itay, 54
Granz, Norman, 42–43, 154, 155
Grappelli, Stephane, 236, 237–38
Gray, Wardell, 14, 28, 67, 104
Graystone Ballroom, 4, 5; Basie and Kenton battle at, 163, 166*n4*
Great Migration, x, 3–4, 76, 147–48, 247
Green, Bill, 23, 25*n4*
Green, Grant, 75, 114, 134, 172, 274
Greene, Shecky, 108
Greenleaf Music (label), 204
Greer, Sonny, 170
Gress, Drew, 247
Griffin, Farah Jasmin, 219
Griffin, Johnny, 261
Griot Galaxy: "After Death," 204; Bey and, 203; *Live at the DIA*, 204; "The Z Series," 204
Grossman, Steve, 173
Gruntz, George, 215; Concert Big Band, Jordan and, 50
Gryce, Gigi, 85
Guinness World Records, 118
Guinyard, Freddie, 94

Haden, Charlie, 118, 134, 156, 219, 223
Hagans, Bill, 187*n1*
Hagans, Tim, 161
Hajdu, David, 21
Hall, Jim, 75, 126
Hamilton, Chico, 123, 194
Hamilton, Jimmy, 25*n3*, 162–63
Hamilton, Lamont, 228
Hammer, Jan, 173
Hammond, Doug: "Before and After the Fact," 187; DCMA and, 184; Detroit Artists Workshop and, 181; Focus Novii and, 186–87, 187*n2*; Hayden and, 287; *It's Born*, 187; *Reflections in the Sea of Nurnen* (with Durrah), 187; with a *sanza*, 185; *We People*, 187
Hampton, Lionel, 38, 39, 84, 231
Hancock, Herbie: Ralphe Armstrong and, 286; Byrd and, 84, 86; Ron Carter and, 119, 125; as Cox influence, 189; M. Davis Quintet and, 118, 124–25, 126, 188; Henderson and, 129, 134; Milt Jackson and, 42; Mwandishi sextet, CJQ compared to, 191; Sextet, at Strata Concert Gallery, 193, 196*n4*; Sextet, Henderson and, 134
Hanna, Michael, 95
Hanna, Ramona Woodard, 95
Hanna, Roland, 90–99; Ron Carter and, 90, 92; Cass Tech's music program and, 14; as "A Child is Born" composer, 97–98, 164; classical music and artistic identity of, 90–91, 92–93, 95–96; as composer and leader, 91–92; early life and music education, 93–94; Flanagan's influence on, 91, 94; Erroll Garner's influence on, 92, 96; Barry Harris compared with, 59; Hawkins and, 58, 96–97; Hank Jones' influence on, 151; Juilliard studies, 90, 93–94, 95–96; physical appearance and personality, 93; studio session with Hawkins and, 96–97; Thad Jones–Mel Lewis Orchestra and, 90, *91*, 97, 159
Hanna, Roland, COMPOSITIONS: "After Paris," 92; *Asphalt Girl* (film score), 96; "A Child Is Born," 97–98, 164; "Free Spirit—Free Style," 92; "I Love You" (Porter), 97; "Lover Come Back to Me" (with Mingus), 96; "My Name Is Jasmine but They Call Me Jazz" (ballet score), 98; "Oasis," 98; Sonata for Chamber Trio and Jazz Piano, 98; "Swing Me No Waltzes," 92; "24 Preludes, Book 1 and 2," 98
Hanna, Roland, OTHER PERFORMANCES: "Body and Soul," 90; "I Love You," 97; "Lover Come Back to Me," 96; "Rhapsody in Blue," 98

Hanna, Roland, RECORDINGS AS LEADER: *Bird Tracks*, 98; *Child of Gemini*, 98; *Destry Rides Again*, 96; *Easy to Love*, 96; *A Gift from the Magi*, 98; *Jazz Sonatas (includes* Sonata for Chamber Trio and Jazz Piano), 96; *Mingus Dynasty*, 96; *Perugia*, 98, 99; *Sir Elf*, 93, 98; *Sir Elf Plus One*, 98; Sonata for Chamber Trio and Jazz Piano, 98; *Swing Me No Waltzes*, 92, 98, 99; *This Must Be Love*, 98; *Tributaries: Reflections on Tommy Flanagan*, 98; *24 Preludes, Book 1 and 2*, 98; Unissued session, c. 1968, 96–97

Hanna, Roland, RECORDINGS WITH OTHERS: *All Blues* (Carter), 125; *Art Ford's Jazz Party* (with Hawkins), television show, 96; *Central Park North* (Jones-Lewis), 164; *Consummation* (Jones-Lewis), 164; *Live at the Village Vanguard* (Jones-Lewis), 164; *Monday Night* (Jones-Lewis), 164; *Monday Night / Central Park North* (Jones-Lewis compilation), 166; *Muses for Richard Davis*, 97–98; *Plays the Music of Alec Wilder*, 98, 99; *Pre-Bird* (Mingus), 96, 212; *Presenting / Live at the Village Vanguard / The Big Band Sound* (Jones-Lewis compilation), 166; *Presenting Thad Jones–Mel Lewis & the Jazz Orchestra*, 164

Harburg, Yip, 71

hard bop: as alliance of bebop and bluesy roots, 15; Burrell and, 74; Byrd and, 81; Detroit jazz and, x; Hayes's drumming and, 109; Jazz Messengers and, 106; Elvin Jones and, 148; Thad Jones and, 161; Lateef and, 26, 31; Gerald Wilson and, 23

Harden, Wilbur, 30

Hargrove, Roy, 256, 261, 263, 272, 275, 276

Harris, Barry, **53–62**; Adderley and, 58; as band leader and sideman, 57–58, 59–60; bebop and, 53, 56–57, 58, 61; with BeBop Boys in Ypsilanti, Mich., 137; Byrd and, 84; Cleaver and, 243; as Cox influence, 189; on craft and tradition, xii; Detroit jazz and, x–xi, 14, 53; early life and music education, 57, 67; Fuller's studies with, 103, 104; Hanna compared with, 90; Hawkins and, 55, 58; Hayden and, 287; Hayes and, 113, 114; as Henderson mentor, 131; Hank Jones and, 151; Thad Jones and, 161; Jordan and, 47; with Jordan and Watkins, 45; Lateef and, 30, 31, 32; as McPherson mentor, 136, 137–39; Monk and, 58, 59; Lee Morgan and, 53, 61; racial harassment and, 48; teaching jazz, 11, 53–55, 54, 56–57, 60–62; theory fundamentals, 56

Harris, Barry, COMPOSITIONS: "Burgundy," 138; "Hopper Topper" (with Porter Roberts), 57; "Lolita," 59; "Stay Right with It," 59

Harris, Barry, OTHER PERFORMANCES: "Del Sasser," 58; "Is You Is or Is You Ain't My Baby," 59; "My Ideal," 59; "The Sidewinder," 61; "Symphonic Blues Suite," 61; "Take Me Out to the Ballgame," 57

Harris, Barry, RECORDINGS AS LEADER: *At the Jazz Workshop*, 59, 62; *The Bird of Red and Gold*, 60; *Breakin' It Up*, 59; *Bull's Eye*, 59, 62; *Chasin' the Bird*, 59; *Hopper Topper*, 78 rpm, not reissued, 57; *Luminescence!*, 59; *Magnificent!*, 59; *Solo*, 60; *Vicissitudes*, 59, 62

Harris, Barry, RECORDINGS WITH OTHERS: *Byrd Jazz*, 15; *Into Something* (Lateef), 31; *Louis Hayes*, 115; *McPherson's Mood*, 144; *Motor City Moments* (Carter), 239; *The Sidewinder* (Morgan), 61; *Siku Ya Bibi* (McPherson), 144; *Suite 16*

(Lateef), 32; *Take Me Out to the Ballgame* (Rosolino), 57; *Today's Man* (McPherson), 144
Harris, Eddie, 119, 125, 286
Harris, Joe, 38
Harris, Teddy, Jr., 208, 217
Harrison, Donald, 257, 261
Harrison, Patricia, 198
Harrison, Wendell: "Angry Young Man," 201; "An Evening with the Devil" (Tribe), 202*n*2; *An Evening with the Devil* (Tribe), 201, 202, 202*n*2; "Farewell to the Welfare," 199; Hammond and, 187; Hayden and, 288; "Mary Had an Abortion," 201; Ranelin and, 197–98; Rebirth (nonprofit) and, 202; "Tons and Tons of Bull Shit," 199; Tribe collective and, 178, 197–99, *198*, 201; *Tribe* magazine and, 199, 200; "Where Am I?" 201
Hart, Antonio, 233
Hart, Billy, 224
Hawkins, Coleman: Willie Anderson and, 67; Burrell and, 74; Flanagan and, 69; Hanna and, 67, 96–97; Barry Harris and, 55, 58; Milt Jackson and, 39, 40, 42; Hank Jones and, 150, 154, 155
Hawkins, Coleman, RECORDINGS AS LEADER: *At Ease with Coleman Hawkins*, 69, 71; *Bean Bags* (with Jackson), 42; *Good Old Broadway*, 69; *Make Someone Happy*, 69
Hawkins, Coleman, RECORDINGS WITH OTHERS: Unissued Roland Hanna session, c. 1968, 96–97
Hayden, Marion: Belgrave's quintet and, 207; Ron Carter and, 287; Detroit jazz and, 287–89; *Detroit Jazz City*, 289, 292; at Dirty Dog Jazz Café, 288; Elliot and, 281; *It's Born* (Hammond), 292; Malis and, 281, 290; in Straight Ahead, 239; *Visions*, 292
Hayes, Louis, 109–17; Adderley's Quintet and, 58, 109, 114–15; Atlantic City gig, 109, 116–17; Cannonball Adderley Legacy Band and, 110, 116–17; cymbal beat of, 111, 113, 115; early life and music education, 112–13; Erskine on, 111–12; Flanagan recording with, 70; Barry Harris and, 59; Papa Jo Jones and, 113–14; Lateef and, 32; as link between Williams' post-bop and Blakey, 111; Louis Hayes–Woody Shaw Quintet, 115–16; in New York, 112, 113; as sideman, 109–10; Silver and, *110*; Walton's quartet and, 115; Yusef Lateef Quintet and, 30, 31
Hayes, Louis, OTHER PERFORMANCES: "Dance with Me," 116; "Easy to Love," 114; "Fiddler on the Roof," 115; "For B.P.," 115; "In Case You Haven't Heard," 115; "Invitation," 116; "Lover," 111; "Moon Rays," 114; "The Moontrane," 115; "Morning," 30; "The Outlaw," 114; "Pyramid," 114; "Spacetrack," 115; "Stardust," 116; "Tetragon," 115; "This Here," 114; "What's Goin' On," 116; "Work Song," 114
Hayes, Louis, RECORDINGS AS LEADER: *Breath of Life*, 115; *Ichi-Ban* (with Shaw), 115–16; *Louis Hayes*, Lateef and, 115; *The Real Thing* (with Shaw), 115–16; *Serenade for Horace*, 110; *Variety Is the Spice*, 116, 117
Hayes, Louis, RECORDINGS WITH OTHERS: *At the Jazz Workshop* (Harris), 59, 62; *Before Dawn* (Lateef), 31; *Blowin' the Blues Away* (Silver), 114; *Cannonball in Europe* (Adderley), 114, 117; *Finger Poppin'* (Silver), 114; *Further Explorations* (Silver), 114, 117; *Jazz for Thinkers* (Lateef), 31; *Jazz Mood* (Lateef), 31; *Motor City Scene* (Adams), 16; *Nippon Soul* (Adderley), 114; *Six Pieces of Silver*, 85, *110*, 114; *The Stylings of Silver*, 114

Hayes, Nisha, 109, 112
Haynes, Roy, 70, 78, 112, 168, 170, 189, 228, 246, 274
Head Hunters, 220
Heard, J. C., 16, 40, 208
Heath, Albert "Tootie," 32, 96
Heath, Percy, 40
Heath brothers, 147
Hemphill, Julius, 264, 266
Hence, Henry, 185
Henderson, Joe, 127–35; becomes a star, 127; at Blue Bird Inn, *128*; Blue Note LPs, 133–34; Ron Carter and, 119, 125; on Detroit jazz audiences, 14; early life and music education, 131–32, 135*n*1; Fuller and, 103; Barry Harris as mentor to, 56; on his career, 128–29; style and sound, 128–131; Jazz Communicators and, 109; Elvin Jones and, 172; McPherson on bebop and, 143; Milestone LPs, 134; mouthpiece and sound of, 132; as odd duck, 132–33, 135*n*2; saxophonists influenced by, 135, 226; Sextet, at Strata Concert Gallery, 193; Thad Jones–Mel Lewis Orchestra and, 164; Verve recordings, 127, 134–35
Henderson, Joe, COMPOSITIONS: "Inner Urge," 130, 133; "Isotope," 133; "Recorda-Me," 131, 133; "Serenity," 133; "Shade of Jade," 133; "Tetragon," 115
Henderson, Joe, OTHER PERFORMANCES: "Lush Life," 135; "Song for My Father," 130; "Straight Ahead," 133
Henderson, Joe, RECORDINGS AS LEADER: *Double Rainbow* (Jobim tribute), 127; *An Evening with Joe Henderson*, 134; *Forces of Nature*, 135; *Four!*, 134–35; *Inner Urge*, 130, 133, 135, 172; *In 'N' Out*, 133; *Joe Henderson in Japan*, 134; *Lush Life: The Music of Billy Strayhorn*, 127; *Mode for Joe*, 133; *Our Thing*, 133; *Page One*, 133; *Power to the People*, 134, 135; *So Near, So Far (Musings for Miles)*, 127; *The State of the Tenor (vols. 1 and 2)*, 134
Henderson, Joe, RECORDINGS WITH OTHERS: *All Blues* (Carter), 125; *Black Fire* (Andrew Hill), 134; *Cape Verdean Blues* (Silver), 134; *Idle Moments* (Grant Green), 134; *The Montreal Tapes* (Haden), 134; Private tape, 1958, Joe Brazil's house, Detroit, 132, 135*n*1; *The Real McCoy* (Tyner), 125, 134, 135, 172; *Red Clay* (Hubbard), 125; *Song for My Father* (Silver), 134; *Una Mas* (Dorham), 133; *Unity* (Young), 134, 172
Henderson, Leon, 131, 188, 189, *189*, 190, 191
Henderson, Michael, 286
Hendrix, Jimi, 75
Henry Ford High School, 287
Hentoff, Nat, 191
Herman, Woody, 40
Herring, Vincent, 117
Hersch, Fred, 238
Hibbler, Al, 17, 96
High Note (label), 116
High School of Commerce, Detroit, 47
Hill, Andrew, 129, 134, 172, 183, 219
Hillyer, Lonnie, 56, 137, *137*
Hines, Earl, 153
Hines, Rosetta, 185
Hino, Terumasa, 174
Hirschfeld, Al, 66
Hobby Bar, 7
Hodges, Johnny, 110
Holiday, Billie: Burrell and, 74; as James Carter influence, 270; Elvin Jones compared with, 168; Hank Jones and, 150; on solo as dialogue, 106; with Teddy Wilson, Flanagan and, 67; Gerald Wilson and, 17
Holladay, Marvin (Doc), 159, 208, 238–39
Holland, Dave, 98, 187
Holland, Tony, 203, 204
Holley, Major, 14, 69, 72, 94

Holt, Corcoran, 233
Hooker, John Lee, 77
Horowitz, Vladimir, 153
Houston, Tate, 16
Howard University, 87, 222
Hubbard, Freddie: Burrell and, 79; Byrd and, 86; M. Davis comparing Thad Jones with, 161; "For B.P.," 115; Garrett and, 228–29, 232; Milt Jackson and, 42; Jazz Communicators and, 109; Jazz Messengers and, 106; Elvin Jones and, 172; McPherson on bebop and, 143; *Ready for Freddie*, 172; *Red Clay*, 125; "Spacetrack," 115
Humair, Daniel, 98
Hurst, Jill, 252
Hurst, Robert, **249–55**; on Geri Allen, 222–23; Belgrave as mentor to, 208, 209, 215, 216, 249, 253; on Ron Carter, 125, 126; early life and music education, 252–53; Elvin Jones and, 174; at Kerrytown Concert House (2014), *214*; Lionel Loueke and, 255; Branford Marsalis and, 254; Wynton Marsalis and, 250, 253–54; McBride on, 249, 253, 254; Out of the Blue and, 231–32; Riggins and, 272–74, 278; *Tonight Show* and, 254–55
Hurst, Robert, COMPOSITIONS: "Albert Collins," 251; "Bela Bunda," 251; "Detroit Day," 251; "Middle Passage Suite," 254
Hurst, Robert, OTHER PERFORMANCES: "Autumn Leaves," 254; "Confirmation," 253; "Giant Steps," 254; "Quasimodo," 253; "3 for Lawrence," 254
Hurst, Robert, RECORDINGS AS LEADER: *Black Current Jam*, 251, 255; *Bob: A Palindrome*, 254; *Bob Ya Head*, 254; *One for Namesake*, 254; *Robert Hurst Presents Robert Hurst*, 254
Hurst, Robert, RECORDINGS WITH OTHERS: *Bemsha Swing* (Shaw), 224; *Bloomington* (B. Marsalis), 254; *J Mood* (W. Marsalis), 254; *Jumping the Creek* (Lloyd), 224; *Live at Blues Alley* (W. Marsalis), 254, 255; *The Nurturer* (Allen), 209, 223, 225; *OTB* (Out of the Blue), 253; *Standard Time, Vol. 1* (W. Marsalis), 254
Hutcherson, Bobby, 24, 37–38, 119, 125, 129, 228
Hutchins Intermediate School, 84
Hutchinson, Greg, 275

Improvisation (film), 155
Impulse Records, 32, 155, 172
Indiana University, 253
Iverson, Ethan, 131, 224
Iyer, Vijay, 27, 217, 218, 224

Jackson, Ali, 94, 208, 275, 286
Jackson, Alvin, 15, 39, 68, 77
Jackson, D. D., 270
Jackson, Ira, *137*
Jackson, Javon, 135
Jackson, Milt, **35–43**; as band leader, 41, 42; bebop in New York and, 15, 39–40; as blues musician, 35, 38; Burrell and, 74, 77; Burton on, 36–37, 38; early life and music education, 12, 38–39; as Flanagan role model, 67; Hawkins and, 39, 40, 42; with Jimmy Wilkins Big Band, 36; Hank Jones and, 150; Modern Jazz Quartet and, 36, 40–42; musical development, 39–40; as naturally swinging and soulful jazz musician, 35; as vibraphonist, 35–39. *See also* Modern Jazz Quartet
Jackson, Milt, COMPOSITIONS: "Bags' Groove," 40, 43; "True Blues," 37
Jackson, Milt, OTHER PERFORMANCES: "Birks' Works," 77; "The Comedy," 41; "Delaunay's Dilemma," 41; "Django," 41; "Epistrophy," 40; "Evidence," 40; "I Got Rhythm," 41; "I Mean You," 40; "I Should Care," 37, 42; "Jazz Ostinato," 41; "Misterioso," 40; "Nature Boy," 43; "Night Music," 40; "Round Midnight," 39; "Time on My Hands," 40; "Vendome," 41

Jackson, Milt, RECORDINGS AS LEADER: *Bags and Trane* (with Coltrane), 42; *Bags Meets Wes*, 42; *The Ballad Artistry of Milt Jackson*, 42; *Bean Bags* (with Hawkins), 42; *Explosion*, 43; *Invitation*, 42; *Jackson's-Ville*, 42; *The Jazz Skyline*, 42; *Live at the Village Gate*, 42; *Milt Jackson Quartet*, 42; *Milt Jackson Quintet & Sextet with Lucky Thompson: Complete Savoy and Atlantic Sessions*, 43; *Milt Jackson Sings*, 40; *Sa Va Bella*, 43; *Soul Believer*, 40; *Soul Fusion*, 43; *Soul Meeting* (with R. Charles), 42; *Sunflower*, 42, 43; *True Blues, reissued on Early Modern* (Savoy), 36; *The Very Tall Band* (with Peterson and Brown), 43

Jackson, Milt, RECORDINGS WITH OTHERS: *Bags' Groove* (M. Davis), 40; *Birks' Works*, reissued on Dizzy Gillespie, *Odyssey 1945–52* (Savoy), 77; *Dorothy*, reissued on *Howard McGhee On Dial—The Complete Sessions 1945–47* (Spotlight), 154; *European Concert* (MJQ), 41; *The Last Concert* (MJQ), 41; *Night Music*, same reissue as *Dorothy*40, 154; Sensation label recordings (1948) reissued on *Roots Of Modern Jazz: 1948 Sensation Sessions* (Ace), 40; *Time on My Hands*, same reissue as *Birks' Works*, 40

Jackson, Oliver, 30, 94

Jackson, Ronald Shannon, 267

Jacquet, Illinois, 103

Jamal, Ahmad, 29

Jamboree (label), 67

Jamerson, James, 56, 286

James, Bob, 189

James, Etta, 189

James, Rick, 260

James, Stafford, 115

Jammin' the Blues (film), 155

Janes, Elmer, 103

Jarman, Joseph, 183, 219

Jarrett, Keith, 193

Jarvis, Clifford, 59

Jasper, Bobby, 171

jazz: black communities in Detroit and, 11; regional styles, geography and, xi–xii. *See also* Detroit jazz

Jazz at Lincoln Center Orchestra, 93, 210, 261, 266

Jazz Communicators, Hayes and, 109, 110

Jazz Cultural Theatre, 60, 61

Jazz Development Workshop, Belgrave and, 203, 208, 215

The Jazz Discography (Tom Lord), 250

Jazz Factory (label), 25*n*2

Jazz Journalists Association, 153

Jazz Moon (label), 25*n*2

Jazz Showcase, 136

J Dilla, 272, 277

Jefferson, Eddie, 231

Jellick, Mike, 207

Jobim, Antonio Carlos, 125, 127

Joe's Record Shop, 77–78

Johnson, Candy, 140

Johnson, J. J., 24, 56, 63, 66, 70, 102, 103, 104, 105, 114, 123, 154, 171

Johnson, Lyndon, 177

Johnson, Ronnie, 181, 183

Jones, Carmell, 24

Jones, Eddie, 148

Jones, Elvin, **167–74**; as bandleader, 173–74; Blue Bird Inn House band and, 57, 160–61; brothers and, *146*, 156–57; as Cleaver influence, 246; Coltrane and, 171–72; drumming technique, 168–69, 170; early life and music education, 147–48, 169–70; Flanagan and, 65, 67, 68, 70; Hayes compared with, 112; Joe Henderson and, 130; Hurst and, 254; influence of, 167; on jazz as humanist calling, 167–68; Elvin Jones Jazz Machine, 174; Thad Jones recording with, 161; Lateef and, 31; Liebman on, 167, 169, 173; lifestyle choices, 170–71; as Riggins influence, 274;

Strata Concert Gallery and, 193; on World Stage audiences, 15. *See also* Jones brothers

Jones, Elvin, COMPOSITIONS: "Keiko's Birthday March," 173

Jones, Elvin, OTHER PERFORMANCES: "Afro-Blue," 169; "Alone Together," 161; "Blue Room," 161; "Bye, Bye Blackbird," 172; "Chim Chim Cheree," 169; "Compulsory," 161, 170; "Gingerbread Boy, 173; "I'm a Fool to Want You," 173; "Impressions," 168; "My Favorite Things," 169; "Old Devil Moon," 171; "One Down, One Up," 168; "Sonnymoon for Two," 171; "Striver's Row," 171; "Transition," 172; "Tunji," 169; "Water Pistol," 31; "Zec," 161, 170

Jones, Elvin, RECORDINGS AS LEADER: *Earth Jones*, 174; *Elvin!*, 148; *Elvin Jones Is on the Mountain*, 173–74; *Live at the Lighthouse*, 173; *Merry-Go-Round*, 173, 174; *Momentum Space* (with Redman and Taylor), 174; *Puttin' It Together*, 173

Jones, Elvin, RECORDINGS WITH OTHERS: *Coltrane Plays the Blues*, 172; *Coltrane's Sound*, 172; *Crescent* (Coltrane), 172; *Eclypso* (Flanagan), 65–66, 70; *Guitar Forms* (Burrell), 78, 79, 80; *Gypsy* (Geller), 148–49; *Hank Jones Piano Solo*, 155; *Have You Met Hank Jones* (reissued as "Hank Jones Piano Solo"), 155, 157; *Impressions* (Coltrane), 168; *Inner Urge* (Henderson), 130, 133, 135, 172; *Into Something* (Lateef), 31–32; *Judgment* (Shorter), 172; *Juju* (Shorter), 172, 174; *Keepin' Up with the Joneses* (with H. Jones and T. Jones), 148; *Kenny's Sound* (Burrell), 78; *Live at Birdland* (Coltrane), 168; *A Love Supreme* (Coltrane), 168, 172, 174; *Motion* (Konitz), 172; *Motor City Scene* (T. Jones), 16; *My Favorite Things* (Coltrane), 172; *New Sounds in Modern Music* (Mitchell), 7-inch 45 rpm, reissued on *Swing . . . Not Spring!* (Savoy), 161, 170; *New York Is Now!* (Coleman), 172; *A Night at the Village Vanguard* (Rollins), 171; *One Down, One Up* (with Coltrane), 172; *Overseas* (Flanagan), 70, 71; *Ready for Freddie* (Hubbard), 172; *The Real McCoy* (Tyner), 125, 134, 135, 172; *Speak No Evil* (Shorter), 125, 172; *Street of Dreams* (Green), 172; *Super-Session* (Flanagan), 70; *Thelonica* (Flanagan), 70; *Transition* (Coltrane), 172; *Unity* (Young), 172

Jones, Etta, 43

Jones, Hank, **150–57**; *Ain't Misbehavin'* and, 155–56; brothers and, 146, 156–57; colleagues recording with, 150–51; dignity of, 152–53; early 1940s, 10; early life and music education, 147–48, 153–54; as Flanagan influence, 65; Hanna compared with, 90; Barry Harris compared with, 59; Hawkins and, 58; Hayden and, 287, 288; influences on, 151; Milt Jackson and, 40, 42; *Jammin' the Blues* (film) and, 154–55; in New York, 154–56; preparation by, 152; as professional musician, 155; style, 151; Art Tatum influence on, 151, 153–54, 155; Thad Jones–Mel Lewis Orchestra and, 159. *See also* Jones brothers

Jones, Hank, OTHER PERFORMANCES: "Big 'D' Blues," 154; "The Bird," 154; "Dorothy," 154; "Happy Birthday," 155; "How About You?" 155; "Laird Bird," 154; "Moose the Mooche," 156; "Naima," 156; "The Night We Called It a Day," 154; "Thanks for the Memories," 155

Jones, Hank, RECORDINGS AS LEADER: *Bop Redux*, 156; *The Great Jazz Trio at the Village Vanguard*, 156, 157; *Have You Met Hank Jones*, 155, 157; *Satin Doll*, 156; *The Trio*, 155, 157; *Upon Reflection*, 156; *Urbanity*, 154

Jones, Hank, RECORDINGS WITH OTHERS: *And Then Again* (E. Jones), 149; *Big 'D' Blues,* reissued on *Hot Lips Page/Rubberlegs Williams* (Cool Note), 154; *The Bird,* reissued on *Bird: Original Recordings of Charlie Parker* (Verve), 154; *Dorothy* (McGhee), reissued on *Howard McGhee On Dial—The Complete Sessions 1945–47* (Spotlight), 154; *Elvin!*, 148; *Gypsy* (Geller), 148–49; *I Just Stopped by to Say Hello* (Hartman), 155; *Jackson's-Ville* (Jackson), 42; *The Jazz Skyline* (Jackson), 42; *Keepin' Up with the Joneses* (with T. Jones and E. Jones), 148; *Laird Bird* (Parker), same reissue as *The Bird,* 154; *Milt Jackson Quintet & Sextet with Lucky Thompson: Complete Savoy and Atlantic Sessions*, 43; *Night Music* (McGhee), same reissue as *Dorothy* (Spotlight), 40; *Somethin' Else* (Adderley), 155; *Steal Away* (with Haden), 156

Jones, Isham, 148

Jones, Jimmy, 42

Jones, Jo, 170

Jones, Keiko, 172, 173

Jones, Papa Jo, 113–14

Jones, Philly Joe, 100, 111, 113, 130, 168, 170, 246, 274

Jones, Quincy, 24, 42

Jones, Rodney, 75

Jones, Sam, 59, 114, 115, 287

Jones, Shirley DeFranco, 172

Jones, Thad, **158–66**; as Belgrave influence, 213; Blue Bird Inn House band and, 160–61; brothers and, 146, 156–57; on Byrd's crossover success, 88; Danish Radio Big Band and, 165; Detroit influence on, 248; early life and music education, 147–48, 159–60; Flanagan and, 64, 68, 69; as Fuller influence, 103; Max Gordon and, 158; Hanna and, 90, 94–95, 97–98; Barry Harris and, 58; as improviser, 161–62; on individualism in jazz, 165–66; influence, 158, 165; innovations as arranger, 158, 163–64; Jonesisms, 161, 162, 163–64; leading Blue Note sessions, 15; Lewis and, 158–59, 163, 166*n*4; *Motor City Scene* (United Artists), 16, 16*n*4; personality and temperament, 160, 164. *See also* Jones, Thad–Mel Lewis Jazz Orchestra; Jones brothers

Jones, Thad, COMPOSITIONS: "All My Yesterdays," 164; "Backbone," 163; "Big Dipper," 163; "Bitty Ditty," 161; "Central Park North," 163; "Cherry Juice," 164; "A Child Is Born" (*see* Hanna, Roland, COMPOSITIONS); "H.R.H.," 162; "Kids Are Pretty People," 164; "The Little Pixie," 159, 166*n*1, 293; "Little Rascal on a Rock," 164; "Mean What You Say," 163, 213; "Quietude," 164; "Scratch," 161–62; "The Second Race," 163; "Speaking of Sounds," 162; "Three and One," 164; "Tow-Away Zone," 163; "To You" (Basie), 162; "Yours and Mine," 164; "Zec," 161, 170, 213

Jones, Thad, OTHER PERFORMANCES: "Alone Together," 161; "Blue Room," 161; "Body and Soul," 162; "Compulsory," 161

Jones, Thad, RECORDINGS AS LEADER: *Detroit–New York Junction*, 16, 161–62, 166; *Mean What You Say* (with Adams), 164; *Motor City Scene* (United Artists), 16; *Thad Jones–Mel Lewis Quartet*, 164

Jones, Thad, RECORDINGS WITH OTHERS: *And Then Again* (E. Jones), 149; *Elvin!*, 148; *Five by Monk by Five* (Monk), 162; *Gypsy* (Geller), 148–49; *Imagination* (Fuller), 104; *Keepin' Up with the Joneses* (with H. Jones and E. Jones), 148; *New Sounds in Modern Music* (Mitchell), 7-inch 45 rpm,

reissued on *Swing . . . Not Spring!* (Savoy), 161, 170
Jones, Thad–Mel Lewis Jazz Orchestra: as counterpart to Wilson's band, 17; Hanna and, 90, *91*, 97; Henderson and, 134; Hank Jones and, 153; at Village Vanguard, 162. *See also* Jones, Thad; Lewis, Mel
Jones, Thad–Mel Lewis Jazz Orchestra, RECORDINGS: *All My Yesterdays*, 158–59; *Central Park North*, 164; *Consummation*, 164; *Live at the Village Vanguard*, 164, 166; *Monday Night*, 164; *Monday Night / Central Park North* (compilation), 166; *New Life*, 164; *Presenting / Live at the Village Vanguard / The Big Band Sound* (compilation), 166; *Presenting Thad Jones–Mel Lewis & the Jazz Orchestra*, 164
Jones brothers: at Carnegie Hall, *146*; family and, 147–48; recordings together, 148–49
Jordan, Clifford, 115
Jordan, Duke, 46, 49
Jordan, Sheila, **44–52**; early life and music education, 46–48; first recordings and musical growth, 49–50; Hayden and, 289; improvisation by, 45–46; later life touring, 51–52; racial tension (1940s) and, 48–49; sound and style of, 44–45; with Watkins and Harris, 45
Jordan, Sheila, COMPOSITIONS: "The Crossing," 51
Jordan, Sheila, OTHER PERFORMANCES: "Falling in Love with Love," 49–50; "If You Could See Me Now," 50; "I'm a Fool to Want You," 46; on Norwegian TV, 50; "You Are My Sunshine," 50
Jordan, Sheila, RECORDINGS AS LEADER: *Comes Love*, 52n1; *The Crossing*, 51; *Old Time Feeling*, 51; *Portrait Now*, 51; *Portrait of Sheila*, 49–50, 52; *Sheila* (Andersen), 50–51, 52
Jordan, Sheila, RECORDINGS WITH OTHERS: *Detroit Jazz City* (compilation), 207; *Home* (Swallow), 51; *Last Year's Waltz* (Kuhn), 51, 52; *The Outer View* (Russell), 50
Juilliard School, 90, 93–94, 95, 96
J-V-B (label), 77

Kahn, Albert, 3
Kay, Connie, 40
Keepnews, Orrin, 134
Keezer, Geoff, 277
Kelly, Wynton, 135
Kenton, Stan, 21, 163
Kern, Jerome, 68
Kerouac, Jack, 70
Kerrytown Concert House, Ann Arbor, *214*, 281
King, B. B., 17, 75, 286
King, Leonard, 264, 268, 270
Kirchner, Bill, 158
Kirk, Rahsaan Roland, 266
Kirkland, Kenny, 174, 222–23, 254
Klein, George, 30
Klein's Show Bar, 7, 27, 30, 113
Knight, Gladys, 230
Konitz, Lee, 57–58, 172
Kottler, Mischa, 94
Krall, Diana, 249, 250, 252, 272, 274, 278
Kroon, Steve, 276
Krupa, Gene, 170
Kuhn, Steve, 51

LaBarbera, Pat, 173
Lacy, Steve, 171
LaFaro, Scott, 118
Lake, Oliver, 219, 224, 246
Land, Harold, 24
Landmark Records, 89
Lanier, Patrick, 186–87
Laredo, Ruth Meckler, 94
Lateef, Ayesha, 29
Lateef, Sadie Harper, 28, 29
Lateef, Saeeda, 29
Lateef, Tahira (Simpson), 29

Lateef, Yusef, **26–34**; Adderley and, 26, 32, 114; artistic range, 26–27; Burrell and, 78; Cabrera at Miller High and, 12; classical music and, 29, 30, 33–34; as Detroit jazz role model, 14; early life and music education, 11, 28–30; as Flanagan role model, 67; Fuller and, 100, 104; Garrett and, 228; Barry Harris as mentor to, 56; Islam and, 28, 29, 30; at Klein's Show Bar, 27, 30; McPherson and Hillyer and, 141; moral code, 32–33; musical explorations, 33–34; Nigerian fellowship, 33; non-Western elements in music of, 27, 30, 33; Rollins on, 28; Teal and, 132
Lateef, Yusef, COMPOSITIONS: "Arjuna," 31; "Love and Humor," 31; "Morning," 30, 31; "Robot Man," 33; "Sounds of Nature," 30, 31; String Quartet No. 3, 34; "Symphonic Blues Suite," 32, 61; "Water Pistol," 31
Lateef, Yusef, OTHER PERFORMANCES: "Hey Pete! Let's Eat Mo' Meat," 29; "Jump Did-Le Ba," 29; "Prayer for Passive Resistance," 31; "St. Louis Blues," 29
Lateef, Yusef, RECORDINGS AS LEADER: *Autophysiopsychic*, 33; *The Centaur and the Phoenix*, 31; *Before Dawn*, 31; *The Dreamer*, 31; *Eastern Sounds*, 31; *Hey Pete, Let's Eat 'Mo Meat*, reissued on Dizzy Gillespie, *Complete RCA Victor Recordings* (RCA Bluebird), 29; *Into Something*, 31, 34; *Jazz for Thinkers*, 31; *Jazz Mood*, 31; *Jump Did-Le Ba* (Gillespie), same reissue as *Hey Pete*, 29; *Live at Pep's*, 32, 34; *St. Louis Blues* (Gillespie), same reissue as *Hey Pete*, 29; *Suite 16*, 32; *10 Years Hence*, 33; *The World at Peace* (with Rudolph), 33, 34; *Yusef*, 16*n*3; *Yusef Lateef's Detroit*, 33; *Yusef Lateef's Little Symphony*, 33
Lateef, Yusef, RECORDINGS WITH OTHERS: *Byrd Jazz*, 15, 16*n*3; *Cannonball in Europe* (Adderley), 114, 117; *Louis Hayes*, 115; *Nippon Soul* (Adderley), 114; *Pre-Bird* (Mingus), 96
Lauper, Cyndi, 232
Lawrence, Elliot, 78
Lawson, Hugh, 14, 30, 31, 132
Leager, Louie, 258
Learning to Listen (Burton), 38, 133
Leary, Timothy, 133
LeDonne, Mike, 38, 43, 224
Lee, Cecil, Orchestra, 5, 21
Lee, George E., 39
Lee, Jeamel, Tribe and, 202*n*2
Leno, Jay, 255
Lewis, John, 37, 40, 41
Lewis, Mel, 24, 158–59, 163, 164, 166*n*4, 231. *See also* Jones, Thad–Mel Lewis Jazz Orchestra
Lewis, Victor, 143, 270
Liebman, Dave, 135, 167, 169, 173, 174
Lightsey, Kirk, 14, 67, 131, 177, 213, 215
Lindberg, John, 239
Lion, Alfred, 72, 105, 133, 190. *See also* Blue Note
Liston, Melba, 22
Little, Booker, 86, 213
Little, Wilbur, 70
Lloyd, Charles, 183, 219, 224, 243, 249
Locke, Eddie, 69, 95, 96–97
Locke, Joe, 38
Long, Barbara, 148
Los Angeles Philharmonic, 17–18, 24
Los Angeles Times, 24
Loueke, Lionel, 75, 255
L'Ouverture, Toussaint, 81
Lovano, Joe, 129, 135, 150, 152
Love, Josephine, 93
Loving, Al, 121
Lowe, Frank, 266
Lunceford, Jimmie, 14, 17, 20, 21

Mabern, Harold, 116
MacArthur Foundation Fellowship, 234

Mack Avenue Records, 19, 261, 283
MacKenzie High School, 230
Mackrel, Dennis, 151
Madison Ballroom, Detroit, 140–41
Mahanthappa, Rudresh, 27
Mahavishnu Orchestra, 284, 286, 287, 292. *See also* McLaughlin, John
Mainstream (label), 143
Malaby, Tony, 247
Malachi, John, 222
Malcolm X, 24
Malis, Michael: *Balance* (with Elliot), 281, 292; Detroit jazz and, 282–83, 289–90; at Detroit Jazz Festival, 280; Elliot and, 281; *Lifted from the No of All Nothing*, 290, 292; "No. 3," 281; "Serpent's Serpent," 281; *When the City Meets the Sky* (Elliot Quartet), 292
Malone, Russell, 75, 125
Maneri, Mat, 247
Manhattan School of Music, 32, 85, 86, 122
Mardigan, Art, 10, 39, 68, 170
Margitza, Rick, 247
Marie, Rene, 243
Marsalis, Branford, 135, 249, 251, 254–55
Marsalis, Wynton: Belgrave and, 208, 209–10, 215; *Blood on the Fields*, 236; James Carter and, 264, 269; Hurst and, 249, 250, 253; Whitaker and, 256, 261. *See also* Jazz at Lincoln Center Orchestra
Marsalis family, 147
Marsh, Warne, 130
Marshall, Wendell, 42, 155
Martin Luther King High School, 260–61
Massive Attack, 287
Matthews, Ronnie, 115
Maupin, Bennie, 133, 135, 213, 254
M-Base collective, 219
McBee, Cecil, 116, 174, 213
McBride, Christian, 124, 229–30, 249, 253, 254, 270, 278
McCartney, Paul, 249, 272
McGhee, Howard, 14, 15, 40, 154
McHugh, Jimmy, 70
McKibbon, Al, 14
McKinney, Bernard (Kiane Zawadi), 15, 30, 147
McKinney, Carlos, 147, 174, 275
McKinney, Gayelynn, 147, 207, 239, 287
McKinney, Harold: Burrell and, 77; DCMA and, 185; Detroit Artists Workshop and, 181, 182; Detroit jazz and, 147; as mentor, 208; Metro Arts, Detroit and, 197; Tribe and, 198, 201; *Voices and Rhythms of the Creative Profile* (Tribe), 201–2
McKinney, Ray, 57, 94, 147, 286, 287
McKinney family, 147
McKinney's Cotton Pickers, 4–5
McLaughlin, John and Mahavishnu Orchestra, 284, 286, 287
McLean, Jackie, 81, 86, 100, 183, 229
McLean, Rene, 33, 115
McMurray, David, 203, 204
McNeely, Jim, 131, 158, 162, 165
McNeil, John, 160, 162
McPherson, Charles, **136–44**; with BeBop Boys in Ypsilanti, Mich., 137; early life and music education, 138–39; Barry Harris as mentor to, 56, 136, 137, 139; on his musical approach, 142–44; with Mingus, 141–42; on Parker's influence, 139–41
McPherson, Charles, COMPOSITIONS: "Fire Dance," 143
McPherson, Charles, OTHER PERFORMANCES: "Burgundy," 138; "The Chill of Death," 141; "Spring Is Here," 144
McPherson, Charles, RECORDINGS AS LEADER: *Beautiful!*, 144; *But Beautiful*, 144; *Horizons*, 144; *Jazz Dance Suites*, 136; *Manhattan Nocturne*, 144; *McPherson's Mood*, 144; *New Horizons*, 144; *Reverence*, 136; *Siku Ya Bibi*, 144; *Spring Is Here*, 144; *Today's Man*, 144

McPherson, Charles, RECORDINGS WITH OTHERS: *Let My Children Hear Music* (Mingus), 141; *Mingus at Monterey*, 141; *Newer than New* (Harris), 137–38
McRae, Carmen, 96
Meadow Brook Music Festival, 32
Medeski, John, 270
Mehta, Zubin, 24
Mercury Records, 22
Metheny, Pat, 74, 75, 120, 233, 259
Metro Arts, Detroit, 197, 215
Michaels, Matt, 208
Michigan National Guard, 177
Michigan State Fair, 166*n*3
Michigan State University: jazz education in Detroit and, 284; Whitaker teaching at, 256, 258, 259, 261–62
Michigan Theater, Ann Arbor, 135
Miles, Charles, 184
Miles, Reid, 72
Milestone (label), 125, 134
Mili, Gjon, 155
Millan, Bruce, 185
Miller, Marcus, 228
Miller, Mulgrew, 125, 143, 222–23, 231, 232, 272–74, 276
Miller, Ron, 187*n*1
Miller High School, 12, 28, 39, 76–77
Millinder, Lucky, 28
Mills, Charles, 31
Minerve, Harold, 231
Mingus, Charles: Belgrave and, 208; "The Chill of Death," 141; Hanna and, 90, 96; Hillyer and, 141–43; on Thad Jones, 161–162; Elvin Jones and, 171; Lateef and, 26, 31; McPherson and, 136, 141–43; "Prayer for Passive Resistance," 31; Strata Concert Gallery and, 193, 196*n*4
Mingus, Charles, RECORDINGS AS LEADER: *Changes One* and *Changes Two*, 212; *Let My Children Hear Music*, 141; *Mingus at Monterey*, 141; *Mingus Dynasty*, 96; *Mingus: Jazz in Detroit/ Strata Concert Gallery/46 Selden*, 196*n*4; *Pre-Bird*, 96, 212
Minor Key (club), 7
Minor Music (label), 223
Mintzer, Bob, 165
Mitchell, Billy, 14, 68, 103, 160–61
Mitchell, Leroy, 47
Mitchell, Matt, 217
Mitchell, Roscoe: as James Carter influence, 269; Cleaver and, 243, 246, 247; Creative Arts Collective and, 203; Detroit Contemporary 4 and, 183; Shahid and Tabbal and, 204
Mizell, Larry and Alphonso (Fonce), 83, 87
Mobley, Hank, 58
Modern Jazz Quartet: "The Comedy," 41; "Delaunay's Dilemma," 41; "Django," 41; *European Concert*, 41; as Hurst influence, 253; Milt Jackson and, 37, 40–42; "Jazz Ostinato," 41; *The Last Concert*, 41; "Vendome," 41
Molina, Stephen, 261, 287
Momenta Quartet, 34
Moncur, Grachan, III, 183
Monk, Thelonious: as Geri Allen influence, 219, 222; Byrd recording with, 81; de Konigswarter and, 58, 59; *Five by Monk by Five*, 162; as Flanagan influence, 64, 68; Barry Harris and, 58, 59; Milt Jackson and, 39, 40; Thad Jones and, 162; Gerald Wilson and, 40
Monroe, Marilyn, 155
Montgomery, Wes, 42, 75, 114, 150, 189, 259
Montgomery brothers, 147
Moodsville (label), 69
Moor, Alina (Eileen Orr), 239
Moore, Charles: "Adolescence," 184; CJQ and, 188, *189*, 190, 191, 196n2; Detroit Artists Workshop and, 181; Detroit Contemporary 4 and, 183; *An Evening with the Devil* (Tribe) and, 201; as Moye mentor, 183–84;

Strata Corporation and, 192; teaching at Oberlin, 194
Moore, Charles, COMPOSITIONS: "Number Four," 190; "Snuck In," 190
Moore, Charles, OTHER PERFORMANCES: "The Killers," 183; "Mystique," 190; "Spellbound," 190; "Trance Dance," 190
Moore, Charles, RECORDINGS: *The World at Peace* (Lateef and Rudolph), 33, 34. *See also* Contemporary Jazz Quintet
Moore, Oscar, 76, 77
Mora, Francisco, 261
Moran, Jason, 217, 219–20, 224
Morelli, Frank, 27, 30
Morgan, Lee, 61, 100, 105, 106
Morgan, Thomas, 243, 244
Morton, Jelly Roll, 20
Mosaic (label), 19
Motian, Paul, 219, 223, 246
Moye, Don, 183–84, 187*n*1
MPS (label), 59
Mraz, George, 65, 66, 98, 135, 156, 174
Mulligan, Gerry, Concert Jazz Band, 163
Murray, Albert, 35
Murray, David, 215, 224, 266
Myrick, Bert: *Live 'n Well*, 194–95

Nance, Ray, 236
Nash, Lewis, 213
National Symphony Orchestra, 98
Nation of Islam, 29
Navarro, Fats, 40, 57, 81
Neloms, Bob, 231
Nelson, Steve, 272–74
Nelson, Willie, 249
Nesbitt, John, 5
Newborn, Phineas, 114
New England Conservatory, 165, 238
New Jersey Performing Arts Center All-Female Residency, 224, 240
Newman, David "Fathead," 211, 215
New Music Society, 15, 78, 178
Newport Jazz Festival, 58
New Song (label), 57
New World Stage, Detroit, 203
New York Jazz Quartet, 98
Nichols, Herbie, 219
North Carolina Central University, 87
Northeastern High School, 12, 57
Northern High School, 12, 68, 94
Northwestern High School, 12
Norvo, Red, 38
Norwood Hotel, 5
Nozero, Larry, 183, 193, 195, 202
Nuccilli, Ed, 195
Nururdin, Maulawi, 195

Oakland University (Michigan), 208, 238–39
Oberlin Conservatory, Ohio, 87, 192, 193–94, 210
Oliver, King, 20
Oliver, Sy, 21
Once Festival of avant-garde music, Ann Arbor, 189
180 Proof (label), 194, 196*n*4
Onishi, Junko, 215, 278
Origin Records, 204
Ortega, Anthony, 24
Ortiz, Aruán, 243
Osby, Greg, 249
Ouellette, Dan, 122
Out of the Blue (OTB), 231–32, 253
Owens, Jimmy, 83, 133

Pablo (label), 42–43, 172
Pacific Jazz (label), 19, 23–24
Page, Hot Lips, 28, 153, 154
Page Three (New York gay bar), 46, 49
Paradise Theatre, 7, 103
Paradise Valley (black entertainment district): Burrell and, 76; destruction of, 177, 178; growth of, 4; jazz clubs in, 5–6, 7; Lateef and, 28
Paris without Regret (Davis), 84, 86–87

Parker, Charlie "Bird": bebop and, 37, 132; Burrell and, 74; as Flanagan influence, 68; as Fuller influence, 105; as Garrett influence, 226; in Gillespie's sextet with Jackson, 39; Barry Harris and, 58, 61; as Hayes influence, 113; as Joe Henderson influence, 131; Hank Jones and, 150, 151, 154–55; as Thad Jones influence, 160; as Jordan influence, 44–45, 47–48, 51; as McPherson influence, 136, 138, 139–41, 142; Blue Bird Inn house band and, 161; as Gerald Wilson influence, 36, 39

Parker, Charlie "Bird," COMPOSITIONS: "Billie's Bounce," 231; "The Bird," 154; "Chasin' the Bird," 210, 213; "Confirmation," 47, 154, 253; "Kim," 140; "Laird Bird," 154; "Moose the Mooche," 156; "Now's the Time," 47; "Ornithology," 47; "Out of Nowhere," 131; "Quasimodo," 253; "Scrapple from the Apple," 155; "Shaw 'Nuff" (with Gillespie), 160

Parker, Charlie "Bird," OTHER PERFORMANCES: "Cherokee," 131; "Indiana," 131; "Now's The Time," 47; "Round Midnight," 39; "Tico Tico," 138; "Willis," 139–40

Parker, Charlie "Bird," RECORDINGS: *The Washington Concerts*, 139–40

Parker, Leo, 154

Parker, Maceo, 226, 230

Parker, William, 243

Pass, Joe, 24

Patton, Jeb, 92

Payne, Cecil, 123, 210, 215

Pearson, Duke, 83, 86, 190, 191

Pelt, Jeremy, 117, 243, 244

Peluso, Jim, 195

Penn, Clarence, 261

Pepper, Art, 174, 197

Perla, Gene, 173, 174

Perry, Rich, 135

Persip, Charli, 123, 212, 231

Person, Houston, 125, 126

Peterson, Oscar, 78, 109, 115, 276–77

Peterson, Ralph, Jr., 224

Pettiford, Oscar, 69

Phelan, Ellen, 181

Phillips, Flip, 57–58

Pierson, Jack, 208

Pliskow, Dan, 253

Plugged Nickel, Chicago, 125

Pointer, Noel, 238

Pollard, Terry, 27, 30, 31, 160–61

Polyfold (label), 289

Pontiac Central High School, 170

Ponty, Jean-Luc, 238, 286

Poole, Valter, 98

Porcino, Al, 24

Possibilities (Hancock), 86

Potter, Tommy, 70

Powell, Bud, 57, 65, 68, 90, 100, 151

Powell, Seldon, 95

Pratt, Richard, 98

Prestige (label), 15, 31, 40, 59, 74, 100, 143

Prince, 232

Public Enemy, 275

public school music education programs: bebop and, 11–12; Belgrave hiring students from, 208–9, 215; funding cuts and, 283–84; historical information about, 16*n*1; instruction and high standards in, 11–12, 14; integrated, xii, 12, 20, 180. *See also* Cass Technical High School

Qwest (label), 43

rabab (rubab or rabat), Lateef's compositions using, 30, 31, 34*n*4

racial discrimination or harassment: Ron Carter and, 122, 123; Fuller and, 103; Hanna and, 95; Milt Jackson on, 42; Jordan and, 48–49; Lateef and, 30; Modern Jazz Quartet and, 41; riots (1943) and, 6–7; riots (1967) and, 177. *See also* segregation

Randall, Dudley, 179

Ranelin, Phil: Harrison and, 197–98;

on race and Detroit musicians, 180; *The Time Is Now!* (Tribe), 199, 201, 202; Tribe collective and, 178, 198–99, *198*, 201; *Vibes from the Tribe*, 201, 203; "What's Now?" 202*n*2
Ransom Olds, in Detroit, 3
Ratliff, Ben, 291
Rebirth (Harrison's nonprofit), 202, 203
Red, Sonny, 15, 84, 115
Redman, Dewey, 174
Redman, Don, 4–5, 72
Reedus, Tony, 232
Reeves, Dianne, 261
Reeves, Nat, 232
Reinhardt, Django, 76, 270
Rich, Buddy, 155, 170
Richardson, James "Beans," 57, 68, 160–61
Richardson, Jerome, 90, 159
Richmond, Cassius, 261
Richmond, Dannie, 231
Riggins, Emmanuel, 274
Riggins, Karriem, **272–78**; Geri Allen and, 224; Belgrave as mentor to, 208; *Black America Again* production and, 278; at Blue Note with Ray Brown, Oscar Peterson, and Milt Jackson, 276–77; Common and, 272, 274, 277, 278; early life and music education, 274–75; hip-hop and, 272, 274, 275, 277, 278; at Kerrytown Concert House (2014), *214*; and Mulgrew Miller, 272–74, 276; in New York, 275–76; and record collection of, 273
Riggins, Karriem, AS PRODUCER: "Black America Again" (Common), 278; "The Clapper" (J Dilla), 277; "Play Your Cards Right" (Common), 277
Riggins, Karriem, OTHER PERFORMANCES: "Bags' Groove," 273; "Dolphin Dance," 273; "Round Midnight," 273; "Sweet Sioux," 276; "You and the Night and the Music," 274
Riggins, Karriem, RECORDINGS AS LEADER: *August Greene* (with Glasper and Common), 278; *Headnod Suite*, 278; *To the Jungle*, 278
Riggins, Karriem, RECORDINGS WITH OTHERS: *Black America Again* (Common), 278; *Children of the Light* (Whitaker), 261; *Emily's D+Evolution* (Spalding), 272; *The Evolution of Oneself* (O. Evans), 278; *Getting to Know You* (Miller), 276; *Hidden Kingdom* (Whitaker), 261; *Jatroit* (with Onishi), 278; *Kisses on the Bottom* (P. McCartney), 272; *Live at Starbucks* (R. Brown), 277; *The Sequel* (M. Miller), 278; *The Shining* (J Dilla), 277; *Turn Up the Quiet* (Krall), 278; *The Very Tall Band* (Brown), 276
Riley, Ben, 98, 156
Riser, Paul, 213
Rivera, Diego (saxophonist), 291
Rivers, Sam, 119, 125, 126, 193
Riverside (label), 15, 31, 42, 59, 114
Roach, Carrie, 289
Roach, Max, 15, 58, 85, 111, 154, 168, 170, 208, 212
Roberts, Marcus, 253
Rochester High School (Michigan), 253
Rochester Philharmonic Orchestra (New York), 123
Rock, Pete, 278
Rodca, Jean Carla, 242
Rodgers, Ernie, 208
Rogers, Adam, 270
Roker, Mickey, 43
Rollins, Sonny: Burrell and, 74; Byrd and, 81; Flanagan and, 69; Foster and, 68; as Garrett influence, 226; Barry Harris as mentor to, 56; as Joe Henderson influence, 129, 130; Elvin Jones and, 171; on Lateef, 28; Lateef compared with, 31–32
Rolston, Ben, 290
Romney, George W., 177
Roney, Antoine, 174
Roney, Wallace, 219, 221

Roots (band), 272
Rosenberg, Marlene, 133
Rosolino, Frank, 12, 39, 57, 103
Rouge Lounge, 7, 57–58
Rowe, Ellen, 221
Rowles, Jimmy, 66
Rubinstein, Arthur, 91
Rucker, Mathew, 28
Rudd, Roswell, 50
Rudolph, Adam, 33, 34, 254
Run DMC, 275
Russ, Eddie (as Gaff Dunsun), 202
Russell, George, 49, 50, 51

Sanabria, Bobby, 143
Sanders, Pharoah, 201
Sanders, Sam, 195
Santana, Carlos, 286
Sauer, Emil von, 94
Savoy (label), 15, 31, 42, 85, 100, 155
Schiff, David, 234
Schillinger, Joseph, 192
Schlitten, Don, 59
school system. *See* public school music education programs
Schunk, Gary, 213
Scott, Cyril, 23
Sebesky, Don, 42, 79
segregation: Christian churches and, 29; in Detroit, xii, 12; Graystone Ballroom and, 5; housing, in Detroit, 4; Southern, Hank Jones and, 153; Southern, Thad Jones and, 160; Gerald Wilson and, 20. *See also* racial discrimination or harassment
Semark, Jim, 181
Sensation (label), 40
7th Avenue South (New York club), 133
Shahid, Jaribu, 203, 246, 268, 290
Shank, Bud, 24
Shaw, Woody: *Bemsha Swing*, 224; Garrett and, 228, 231, 232; Hayes and, 109; "In Case You Haven't Heard," 115; "The Moontrane," 115; Quintet, Hayes and, 115–16
Shearing, George, 151
Shepp, Archie, 33, 183, 193
Shigeto (Zachary Saginaw), 291
Shihab, Sahib, 29
Shipp, Matthew, 243
Shorter, Wayne: Ron Carter and, 119; as CJQ influence, 188; Coltrane and, 106; cueing system of, 188; M. Davis Quintet and, 124, 188; Joe Henderson and, 129, 134; as Leon Henderson influence, 190; Jazz Messengers and, 106; Elvin Jones and, 172, 174
Showplace (club), 142
Sickler, Don, 83
Sidran, Ben, 14
Sierra, Roberto, 270
Sill, Kelly, 124
Silver, Horace: Belgrave refuses tour with, 212; *Blowin' the Blues Away*, 114; Byrd and, 81, 85; Cape Verdean Blues, 134; *Finger Poppin'*, 114; *Further Explorations*, 117; hard bop and, 15; Barry Harris as precursor to, 57; Hayes and, *110*, 113, 117; Henderson and, 134; Quintet, Hayes and, 109; *Six Pieces of Silver*, 85, *110*, 114; *The Stylings of Silver*, 114; "Song for My Father," 130; *Song for My Father*, 134
Sinatra, Frank, 108
Sinclair, John: "Adolescence" (scenario), 184; on *The Black Hole*, 196*n*2; Detroit Artists Workshop and, 181–82; Detroit Jazz Center and, 203; "Songs of Praise for John Coltrane," 183
Sinclair, Leni, 181, 183
Sinta, Donald, 132
Skeeter, Mitch, and Jean (trio), 47
Sklar, Bob, 187*n*1
Slatkin, Leonard, 98
Slay, Emmett, 39
Slim Jenkins (Oakland club), 23
Slum Village, 272, 278
Smith, Allen, 23

Smith, Jimmy, 74, 79, 100
Smith, Leonard B., 84
Smith, Stuff, 236
Smith, Wadada Leo, 239
Smith, Walter, III, 135
Smith, Willie, 21
Sorey, Tyshawn, 290
Sorin, Bill, 96–97
Spalding, Esperanza, 272
Spencer, Danny, 181, *182*, 183, 188, *189*, 190, 191
Sphere, *Inside Ourselves*, 195
Spight, Skeeter, 47
Spirits of Swing (Rucker's band), 28
Springer, Jack, 190
Stamps, Clarence, 112–13
Stanco, Anthony, 291, 293–94
Stanko, Tomasz, 243
Stanley, Gordon, 95
Statin, Rafael, 251
Stenson, Bobo, 50
Stewart, Bill, *137*
Stewart, Rex, 159–60
Stitt, Sonny, 40, 57, 151, 161, 226, 259
Stokowski, Leopold, 123
Stones Throw (label), 278
Straight Ahead (all-female band), 239, 289
Strata Concert Gallery, 193
Strata Corporation: accomplishments, 192–94; charter of, 192; CJQ and, 188, 191; Cox and, ix; financial and operational details, 196*n*3; New Music Society as precursor to, 78; self-determination in Detroit and, 178, 179, 203; Sinclair and, 182; Strata-East and, 194
Strata Corporation, RECORDINGS: *Alive 'n Well* (Fields and Bohanon), 194–95; *Clap Clap! The Joyful Noise* (Cox), 195; *Fish Feet* (English), 195; *Inside Ourselves* (Sphere), 195, 196*n*8; *Location* (CJQ), 194, 195; *Maulawi* (Nururdin), 195; *Mirror Mirror* (Sanders), 195; *The Saturday Night Special* (Woodard), 195; *Time* (Nozero), 195
Strata-East Records, 193, 194
Strayhorn, Billy, 21, 22, 64, 66, 127, 209–10
Streisand, Barbra, 249
String Trio of New York, 239
Strozier, Frank, 116
Stryker, Dave, 75
Stubblefield, Clyde, 277
Studio Museum in Harlem, 121
Sulieman, Idrees, 70
Sun Ra, 28–29, 197, 203, 269
Swallow, Steve, 45–46, 49, 51
Swartz, Harvie, 51
Sweet Basil (club), 66
Synanon (drug rehab facility), 197, 202*n*1
Szglaggi, Paul, *10*

Tabbal, Tani, 203, 204, 246, 268
Taborn, Craig, 217, 243, 244, 245–46, 268, 269–70
Tamburini, James, 84
Tapscott, Horace, 215
Tate, Grady, 98
Tatum, Art, 65, 67, 91, 95, 151, 153–54, 155
Taylor, Cecil, 66, 142, 174, 179, 220
Taylor, Creed, 42
Taylor, Gene, 113, 114
TCB (label), 116
Teal, Larry, 30, 130–31, 132, 230
Terrasson, Jacky, 243, 247
Terry, Clark, 25*n*3, 25*n*4, 209–10
Terry, Mike, *137*
Thelonious Monk Institute, Los Angeles, 255
Thomas, Leon, 116
Thompson, Charles, 22
Thompson, Lucky, 14, 15, 28 40, 42, 43, 67, 68, 154
Timeless All-Stars, 107
Timmons, Bobby, 106, 123
Tini, Dennis, 195
Tin Palace, 231
Tolliver, Charles, 24, 194

Toney, Kevin, 14, 88–89
The Tonight Show, 127, 249–50, 252, 254–55
Transition (label), 85, 104
Tribe: aesthetic of, 201; as business venture, 179, 199; disbanding of, 202; formation and members of, 197–98, *198*; LP production by, 187, 199, 201–2; New Music Society as precursor to, 78; self-determination in Detroit and, 178, 203; Strata Concert Gallery and, 193; Strata Corporation and, 193; *Tribe* magazine, 199, 200; *Wait Broke the Wagon Down* (play), 199
Tribe, RECORDINGS: *An Evening with the Devil* (Harrison), 201, 202; *Gemini II* (Belgrave), 201–2, 216; *Message from the Tribe* (collective), 199, 202, 202*n*2; *Mixed Bag's First Album*, 202; *The Time is Now!* (Ranelin), 201, 202; *Vibes from the Tribe* (Ranelin), 201; *Voices and Rhythms of the Creative Profile* (McKinney), 201–2
Tristano, Lennie, 49, 130
Tucich, Rudy, *137*, 170
Tucker, Mickey, 215
Turner, Billy, 201
Turner, Bu Bu, 77, 186
Turner, Mark, 135
Turner, Richard Brent, 29
Turrentine, Stanley, 72, 74, 226, 230, 232
Twenty Grand (club), 7
ii-V-I Orchestra, 231
Tyner, McCoy: Geri Allen and, 220; Belgrave and, 215; Ron Carter and, 119; Coltrane Quintet and, 168; Hayes and, 110; Henderson and, 130, 135; on Hank Jones, 150; Elvin Jones and, 172, 174; "Passion Dance," 61; *The Real McCoy*, 125, 134, 135, 172; Strata Concert Gallery and, 193
Tysh, George, 181

Ulmer, James "Blood," 184, 186, 187
Union of God's Musicians and Artists Ascension, Los Angeles, 179
United Artists, Gerald Wilson and, 22
Universal Music Group: Motown's Workshop Jazz tapes and, 213; *Motown Unreleased 1962: Jazz, Vol. 1*, 196*n*7
University of Massachusetts, Lateef and, 32, 33
University of Michigan, 245–46, 250, 289
University of North Texas, Byrd and jazz education at, 87
urban renewal (1950s and 1960s), 4, 178
Usher, Dave, 40, 43*n*4
UTFO, 275

Vacchiano, William, 85
Valade, Gretchen, 283
Van Battle, Joe, 77–78
Van Gelder, Rudy, recording studio, 72, *101*, 191
Vanguard Jazz Orchestra, 158
Vaughan, Sarah, 17, 90, 96
Venuti, Joe, 236
Verve, 31, 127, 134–35
Village Vanguard, 63, 70, 156, 158–59, 164, 165
Violet Hour, 244, 247–48
Virelles, David, 249
Vitous, Miroslav, 243, 244
Vreeland, Keith, 195, 201

Walden, Donald, 203, 208, 288
Walden, Narada Michael, 286
Walker, Ursula, 288
Wallace, Benny, 174, 266
Waller, Fats, 65, 153
Walrath, Jack, 212, 231
Walton, Cedar, 38, 106, 115, 150, 152
Walton, Earl, 5
Ware, Wilbur, 171
Was, Don, 207
Washington, Dinah, 22, 40
Washington, Donald, 208, 261, 267, 268–69
Washington, Kenny, 66, 111
Washington, Peter, 213, 250

Washington Junior High School, Detroit, 170
Watkins, Doug, 14, 16, 45, 56, 70, 113, 123, 249
Watkins, Julius, 14, 15
Watts, Ernie, 19, 24
Watts, Jeff "Tain," 253, 254
Wayne University / Wayne State University: Burrell attends, 77, 79; Byrd attends, 84, 85; Cleaver attends, 245; Detroit Artists Workshop and, 181–83, 184; Fuller attends, 103; Joe Henderson attends, 130–31, 132; Lateef attends, 29; Malis attends, 289; Spencer attends, 190; Whitaker attends, 257, 261
WDET-FM, Strata concerts on, 193
Weather Report, 191, 193
Webb, Chick, 170
Webster, Ben, 57–58, 264
Webster, Beveridge, 95
Weems, Carrie Mae, 219
Weiss, David, 188
Weiss, Michael, 55, 56–57, 65
Weist, Fred, 170
Wess, Frank, 98, 148
West, Kanye, 272
West End Hotel jam sessions, 7, 131, 163
Weston, Randy, 123, 171, 219
Wetzel, Ray, 21
Whitaker, Cookey, 256, 257, 260, 261, 262–63
Whitaker, Rodney, **256–63**; Belgrave and, 208, 209, 215; Civic Jazz Band and, 290–91; Cox and, 259; Detroit tradition of mentorship and, 259–60; early life and music education, 260–61; family and, 256–57, 257, 260, 262–63; Garrett and, 233; Gathering Orchestra and, 293–94; MSU jazz program and philosophy and, 261–62; MSU jazz program and race and, 262
Whitaker, Rodney, RECORDINGS AS LEADER: *Ballads and Blues*, 261; *Children of the Light*, 261, 263; *Get Ready* (with Carl Allen), 261; *Hidden Kingdom*, 261; *Work to Do* (with Carl Allen), 261
Whitaker, Rodney, RECORDINGS WITH OTHERS, 216; *Of Kindred Souls* (Hargrove), 263; *Pursuance* (Garrett), 263; *Working Together* (Belgrave), 215, 216
White, Alex, 268
White, Lenny, 215, 287
White, Michael, 236
Wiggins, Bill, 186, 208, 230
Wilborn, Dave, 5
Wilcox, Eddie, 21
Wilder, Alec, 70–71, 97
Wilkins, Ernie, 123
Wilkins, Jimmy, Big Band, 36
William Patterson University, New Jersey, Thad Jones teaching at, 165
Williams, Ben, 259
Williams, Buster, 224
Williams, Cootie, 231
Williams, David, 215
Williams, Herbie, 260–61
Williams, Joe, 17
Williams, Lawrence, 215, 246, 248, 275, 281
Williams, Mary Lou, 219, 224
Williams, Tony: Geri Allen and, 219; *At the Village Vanguard*, 156; Ron Carter and, 125; as CJQ influence, 188; as Cleaver influence, 246; M. Davis Quintet and, 118, 124–25, 188; Hayes and, 111, 112, 114; Henderson and, 129; Hurst and, 249; Hank Jones and, 151, 156; as Riggins influence, 274
Wilson, Anthony, 19, 24, 278
Wilson, Gerald, **17–25**; Basie and, 22–23; bebop in New York and, 15; Cass Tech's music program and, 14; as composer, arranger, and leader, 17–19, 21–25; at Detroit Jazz Festival, *18*, 20; early life and music education, 20–21; Gillespie and, 21–22; in Los Angeles, 17, 21, 22, 23–24; Lunceford's band and, 17, 21; Pacific Jazz label and, 23–24; in San Francisco, 23

Wilson, Gerald, COMPOSITIONS OR ARRANGEMENTS: "Algerian Fantasy," 23; "The Black Rose," 22; "Blues for Yna Yna," 24; "Bull Fighter," 23; "Debut: 52172," 24; "Dissonance in Blues," 22; "Dizzier and Dizzier" (or "Katy"), 23; "El Viti," 23; "Et-Ta," 22; "Groovin' High," 22; "Guarachi Guaro," 23; "Hi Spook, 21; "Imagine My Frustration," 23; "Lotus Land" (Scott), 23; "Lunceford Special," 21; "Moment of Truth," 19; "The Moors," 22; "Nancy Jo," 24; "Pensive Melody," 22; "Perdido," 23; "Romance," 23; "The Royal Suite," 23; "Viva Tirado," 18, 24; "Yard Dog Mazurka," 21; "You Gotta Crawl Before You Walk," 23; "You're Just an Old Antidisestablishmentarianismist," 23
Wilson, Gerald, OTHER PERFORMANCES: "Lunceford Special," 21
Wilson, Gerald, RECORDINGS AS LEADER: *Big Band Modern*, 23, 25*n*2, 25*n*4; *Chronological Classics: Gerald Wilson and His Orchestra 1946–1954*, 25, 25*n*2; *Chronological Classics: The Very Best of Gerald Wilson 1946–54*, 25*n*2; *Detroit*, 25; *The Golden Sword*, 24; *In My Time*, 25; *Lomelin*, 24; *Moment of Truth*, 23–24, 25; *New York New Sound*, 25; *Portraits*, 24, 25; *Progressive Sounds*, 25*n*4; *Theme for Monterey*, 24–25; *The Very Best of Gerald Wilson 1946–54*, 25*n*2; *You Better Believe It*, 23
Wilson, Gerald, RECORDINGS WITH OTHERS: *Dizzier and Dizzier* (or *Katy*), reissued on Dizzy Gillespie, *Complete RCA Victor Recordings* (RCA Bluebird), 23; *Guarachi Guaro* (Gillespie), same reissue as *Dizzier and Dizzier*, 23; *Hi Spook*, reissued on *The Jimmie Lunceford Collection 1930–47* (Fabulous), 21; *Yard Dog Mazurka*, same reissue as *Hi Spook*, 21
Wilson, Jack, 24
Wilson, Mary, 221
Wilson, Nancy, 17, 287
Wilson, Phillip, 183
Wilson, Steve, 226, 233
Wilson, Teddy, 65, 67, 96, 151
Wilson, Tom, 104. *See also* Transition
Winn, Nate, 251–52
WJR national radio broadcasts, 5
Wolf, Warren, 35, 278
Wolff, Francis (Frank), 82, *101*, *110*, 133, 191
women: Detroit musicians mentoring, 222, 224, 240; in Gerald Wilson's band, 22
Woodard, Lyman, 184, 193, 195, 230, 239
Woodley, Abe (later Nasir Hafiz), 78
Woodman, Britt, 162
Woods, Phil, 69, 88
Woodward Avenue, Detroit, 4, 7, 7*n*5
Workman, Reggie, 106
Workshop Jazz (Motown label), 194, 213
World Stage, 15, 78, 113
Wright, Eugene, 28–29, 34*n*1
Wright, Herman, 31
Wrubel, Allie, 63
Wylie, Harold, 25*n*4

Xanadu (label), 59–60, 143

YAL (Lateef's label), 33
Young, Larry, 172
Young, Lester, 29, 57–58, 131, 150, 155
Young, Snooky, 22, 159

Zappa, Frank, 284, 286
Zawadi, Kiane (Bernard McKinney), 15, 30, 147
Zawinul, Joe, 32, 114
Zayde, Jascha, 154
Zimmerman, Oscar, 122